CICERO

A Political Biography

CICERO

From a bust in the Vatican, Rome

CICERO

A Political Biography

BY

DAVID STOCKTON

FELLOW AND TUTOR OF BRASENOSE COLLEGE, OXFORD

OXFORD UNIVERSITY PRESS

Oxford University Press, Walton Street, Oxford OX2 6DP

Oxford New York Toronto
Delhi Bombay Calcutta Madras Karachi
Kuala Lumpur Singapore Hong Kong Tokyo
Nairobi Dar es Salaam Cape Town
Melbourne Auckland

and associated companies in
Beirut Berlin Ibadan Nicosia

ISBN 0-19-872033-5

© Oxford University Press 1971

First published 1971
Reprinted 1978, 1982, 1986

Printed in Great Britain by
Antony Rowe Ltd,
Chippenham

A. L. S.

PARENTI · OPTIME · MERITO

PREFACE

I HAVE set out to write an account of the political life and activities of Cicero, not a full-scale study which would include a detailed examination and assessment of his literary achievement as well. An assessment of Cicero as a literary figure would not lend itself readily to a biographical treatment, and the public man can be studied separately from the literary giant, so long as we do not ignore the obvious truth that his literary reputation in his own day contributed to his influence in the political field. For Cicero himself, at any rate, his literary activities were always secondary to his political interests and ambitions, and were pursued only in the *subsiciva* of an incredibly busy life or fallen back on in periods of enforced withdrawal from the political centre-stage.

The years of Cicero's maturity are better known to us than any other period of ancient history, and not least because of the great good fortune that has preserved not far short of a thousand letters from and to Cicero for us to read. These letters give to a period otherwise well-supplied with source material a richness of texture unequalled either before or after; and if, together with the many speeches and treatises of Cicero's which have survived, they put us in danger of seeing events and issues too much through his eyes, that is a risk which we have to accept gladly and try to minimize. It has been said that we might understand the history of the late Republic better if none of Cicero's writings had survived; but whether we should enjoy studying it half so much or gain as much profit from the study is quite another matter. Thanks to his writings, and above all to the letters, the chief *dramatis personae* come back to life again and take on flesh and bones and colour—and of none of them is this more true than of Cicero himself.

This book is intended primarily for the student of Roman

history, and most particularly the undergraduate student; but I have tried not to neglect the interests of students of other periods of history or the general educated reader. In these days, it would be fallacious to assume in the latter, or even in the undergraduate classicist who is not a specialist in Roman history, any close familiarity with the background of Cicero's life and times. The study of classical literature and history is far less widespread and thoroughgoing than it was in the schools of fifty years ago; and many schoolbooks and handbooks are out of date and take little account of the considerable advances made by scholarship during this period. Yet interest in the civilization of Greece and Rome is in many ways more widespread among the educated public than it has ever been, if only because that public is so much more numerous now. Unconsciously perhaps, people have come to appreciate the truth that Matthew Arnold pointed out long ago, that the history and literature of classical Greece and Rome are in almost all respects far more 'modern' and relevant to us than much that is chronologically far more recent. Such readers will need a fairly generous allowance of background information if they are not unconsciously to be misled by false or half-true assumptions or analogies which are essentially anachronistic. This information I have done my best to supply within the limits available to me.

Since this book is meant to be a life of Cicero, and not a potted history of the late Republic with particular reference to Cicero, I have not argued or justified every controversial point in the general history of the period. I make no apology for this. The professional scholar will have his own views, and know the evidence and the arguments. But I have taken care to be generous in providing references to the original evidence of Cicero himself. The bibliography at the end of this book will enable any reader who so wishes to pursue particular topics in greater detail.[1]

---

[1] Although I have included M. Gelzer's book, *Cicero, Ein biographischer Versuch* (Wiesbaden, 1969) in my bibliography, it came into my hands only when I was completing the correction of my final typescript. I have therefore not been able to make use of it.

I should like to express my very sincere thanks to Dr. J. P. V. D. Balsdon. As an undergraduate I attended his scholarly, elegant, and exciting lectures on Cicero; and it was he who encouraged me to write this book, subsequently generously reading my first draft and drawing my attention to numerous errors, obscurities, and extravagances of style. The Revd. L. M. Styler did likewise, and Mr. L. D. Reynolds was kind enough to perform the same service for my final draft. None of them, of course, can be held to blame for any shortcomings that remain. Nor ought I to forget to thank my eldest daughter, Sally, who restrained my too frequent exuberances of expression with a stern discipline worthy of a Somerville scholar in English. But my heaviest debt is owed to my sometime tutor in Roman history, Mr. C. E. Stevens of Magdalen College. This is not the book he would have written—it is far too conventional and unadventurous; but, there is more of him in it than perhaps even he will recognize.

Oxford, January 1970   DAVID STOCKTON

CONTENTS

SELECT LIST OF ABBREVIATIONS

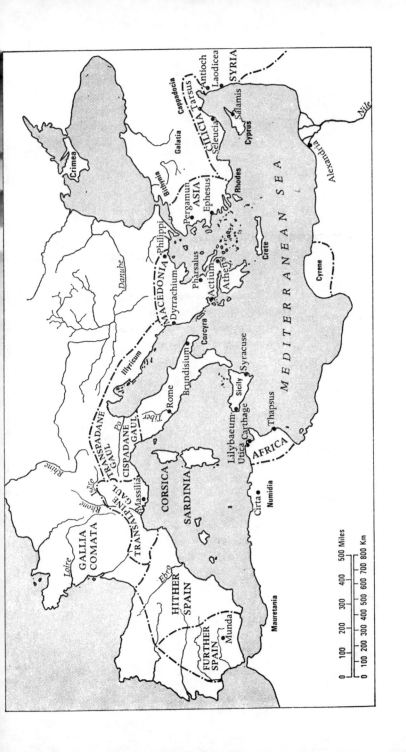

Ille se profecisse sciat, cui Cicero valde placebit.

Quintilian, *Inst. Or.* 10.1.112.

Of all the many changing things
In dreary dancing past us whirled,
To the cracked tune that Chronos sings,
Words alone are certain good.

W. B. YEATS

I

THE YOUNG MAN FROM ARPINUM

THE SOCIETY into which Marcus Tullius Cicero was born at the end of the second century* would have appeared familiar enough to an English eye a few generations ago. Italy was very much a land of country towns, each dominated by a handful of local families who together made up what might be called 'the gentry' or 'the quality'. These families ran the towns and the adjacent countryside, quarrelled over the ordering of local affairs, married off their sons to each other's daughters. Below them in the social scale were craftsmen and shopkeepers, small farmers, labourers, and peasants, whose activity in local politics was normally confined to casting their votes at election times for one or other of the leading families' candidates for municipal office. Even then, many of them had to vote as they were told: long after Rome went over to the written and supposedly secret ballot, Cicero's home town continued to employ the oral vote. Cicero's grandfather all his life strenuously resisted the attempts of his wife's brother, Marcus Gratidius, to introduce the written ballot into Arpinum.[1]

Above and beyond the local gentry of the country towns towered the august families of the aristocracy of the capital, who supplied Rome with her consuls and praetors, her provincial governors and the commanders of her armies and fleets. Themselves endowed with considerable landed estates, they maintained close relations with the local ruling classes, defending their interests and in return expecting their support. It was a society at once rigid and flexible: while

* All dates are B.C. unless otherwise indicated.
[1] *de legg.* 3.36.

distinctions of caste were clear-cut, movement from one class to another was always possible and on occasions encouraged. Earlier in the second century a substantial farmer from the Sabine region had caught the eye of a powerful Roman noble who had an estate in the same district: encouraged and assisted by the patrician Valerius Flaccus, Cato the Elder had scaled the pinnacles of office and power. More recently, a man from Arpinum itself had also made the breakthrough. Gaius Marius, born into a family of only local consequence, had by the year of Cicero's birth attained the consulship and the command in North Africa against Jugurtha. Soon to be recalled to lead Rome's armies against the invading German tribes, he was to win undying fame and an unprecedented total of seven consulships. Granted that Cato and Marius were too extraordinary to be typical, they were essentially only outstanding examples of a process that was repeated often enough in less spectacular fashion. And Marius' success and his connections with the leading families of Arpinum were not without consequence for the early career of Marcus Cicero.[2]

Arpinum, where Cicero was born on 3 January 106, lay in the Volscian highlands near the river Liris something under seventy miles south-east of Rome, and north of the *via Latina*, one of the great trunkroads which Rome early drove through Italy to knit together her expanding dominion. Towards the end of the fourth century the town had become a *civitas sine suffragio*: thus, while retaining its local autonomy and control of domestic affairs, its foreign and military policy became subservient to Rome's, while its citizens enjoyed such private rights of the Roman citizenship as the right to inter-marry with Romans, to hold real property in Roman territory, to enter into valid contracts with Romans, and so on. One hundred and fifty years later, in 188, Arpinum was granted the full Roman franchise, so that by the time of Cicero's birth three generations later his native town had become well and truly Roman. Cicero never thought of himself or re-ferred to himself as a Volscian; and despite his affection for

[2] E. Badian, 'Marius and the Nobles', *Durham Univ. Journ.*, 56 (1964), 141 ff.

the town of his birth, he remained always in his own eyes a Roman. Rome was to be his natural habitat. For all his expressed delight in the countryside, and although Catiline might taunt him with being a 'naturalized immigrant',[3] he was a creature of the Forum and the *via Sacra*, and at home there.

Calumniators alleged that Cicero's extraction was common, his father the son of a fuller and himself brought up in that trade.[4] Such denigrations were a commonplace of Roman invective (Cicero himself had recourse to the same sneering tactics often enough): there was a strong streak of snobbishness in the Roman character. Cicero's family may have had tradesman antecedents, there may have been an interest in a fulling concern. But the family was clearly of settled respectability and local importance by the time of Cicero's grandfather at latest. That gentleman's marriage connection with the Gratidii, and his prominence in local politics, we have already observed; and on the occasion of his opposition to the ballot proposal he was congratulated by the great Aemilius Scaurus, who expressed the wish that the elder Cicero might have elected to exercise his talents on the larger stage of the capital. The name 'Cicero' derives from the Latin for 'chick-pea' (*cicer*), and may suggest an ancestor who specialized in or significantly improved the cultivation of that vegetable; if so, the nickname could argue an agricultural (and hence for the Romans very respectable) ancestry.[5] There was also a story that the Tullii Cicerones went back to Attius Tullus, the Volscian chieftain who four centuries earlier had given refuge and aid to the renegade Roman Coriolanus.[6] But such ancient pedigrees, human nature being what it is and granted the cheerfully slipshod Roman approach to these matters, are to be mentioned only to be discounted. Cicero's own picture of himself is the true one: a man born of respectable upper-class local stock, the salt of Italy as he so often declared them to be.

[3] Sallust *Cat.* 31 : *inquilinus civis urbis Romae.*
[4] Plutarch *Cicero.* 1.
[5] Pliny *NH* 18.10. But Plutarch (loc. cit.) suggests a different explanation.
[6] Plutarch, loc. cit.

Cicero's early years were spent partly at Arpinum and partly at Rome. Plutarch tells us that he was a child prodigy, and that the fathers of the other boys came to school specially to observe his talents and admire them.[7] As a boy and a youth he took to writing poetry, and he clearly fancied himself in this line. But it is for his oratory and his prose writings that Cicero was and is remembered. His poems soon fell into oblivion, and only scattered fragments survive—not as bad as is often alleged, but pedestrian enough. It was part of Cicero's misfortune to be remembered as a writer of indifferent verse, and laughed at for it. Yet Julius Caesar and Marcus Brutus 'also wrote poetry and presented their poems to libraries; they were not any better poets than Cicero, only luckier in that fewer people are aware that they wrote poetry'.[8]

One of the early influences on Cicero was the Greek poet and scholar Archias, who came to Rome from Antioch at the very end of the second century. When he defended Archias in 62, he paid a generous tribute to his old teacher.[9] Throughout his life Cicero was at home in the whole field of Greek literature and thought, the widest open to the educated Roman of his day. Other Greeks with whom he came into contact in these years were the teacher of rhetoric, Molo of Rhodes, and the philosopher Philo, an adherent of the Athenian Academy. Later the Stoic philosopher Diodotus became not only a teacher but a close friend, and it was in Cicero's house that he died in 59, leaving him his heir.[10] It was to these scholarly Greeks and others like them that Cicero, in common with other Romans of his class and generation, owed his formal education in the liberal arts and his close acquaintance with Greek thought and theory. Such men constituted the academic, professorial class of his day.

Cicero's promise and his own and his father's ambitions

[7] Ibid. 2.
[8] Tacitus *Dialogus* 21. Cf. Juvenal *Sat.* 10.122–6.
[9] *pro Archia* 12 ff; below, p. 153.
[10] *ad Att.* II.20.6.

must very early have suggested that he aim at a career in politics. The right contacts were not lacking. The brother of Cicero's now enormously influential fellow-townsman Marius had adopted a Gratidius, henceforth known as Marius Gratidianus, later to be praetor twice, in 85 and 84. The adoption makes it as good as certain that a connection already existed between the two families. This Gratidianus was the son of Cicero's grandfather's opponent and brother-in-law and hence first cousin to Cicero's father.[11] When Cicero went off to Rome to complete his education, he was taken under the wing of the noble and distinguished Mucii Scaevolae, first Scaevola the Augur and then, after his death, his cousin Scaevola the Pontiff, who were related by marriage to Marius. At Rome Cicero also sat at the feet of the two leading forensic and political orators of their generation, Lucius Crassus and Marcus Antonius. Crassus was related to the Scaevolae and, like them, had marriage ties with the family of Marius; Antonius was often found mixing with Marius' circle and from time to time associated with him politically. When Antonius went out to Cilicia to command operations against the Levantine pirates in 102–100, he was accompanied by Cicero's uncle, Lucius Cicero, and by a Marcus Gratidius who served as one of his subordinate commanders and was killed in action. Cicero's mother's sister was the wife of Gaius Aculeio, a very intimate friend of Crassus; his sons were studying at Rome along with Cicero and his younger brother Quintus.[12]

This aspect of Cicero's education was typically Roman: empirical, practical, unschematized. It was a little like the experience of preparing for the English Bar by studying under an experienced lawyer in chambers. But there was a lot more to it than that. Cicero accompanied his mentors as they went about their daily business. They might be discussing the problems of their *clientes* (as the Romans termed dependents of various kinds), or speaking in the

[11] *de legg.* 3. 36; Asconius 84C.
[12] *de orat.* 2.2; *Brutus* 168; cf. Badian, art. cit. Cicero's mother was a Helvia; two Helvii held praetorships early in the second century.

Senate, or pleading in court. He would take note of what was said, of the nature of the various problems encountered, of the procedures followed. He might ask questions, or they might turn to him to put a question or elucidate a point. Above all, he was a privileged observer of the natural intercourse of these great men of affairs and of their conversations and arguments. He had been introduced by his father to Scaevola the Augur with the injunction that 'as far as I could and he would allow, I should never leave the old man's side'. This he tells us in the opening lines of his dialogue *On Friendship* (*de Amicitia*), setting the stage for a discussion based on the recollections of old Scaevola as he sits with a few of his friends and the young Cicero in a garden. The second book of the *de Oratore* opens with a picture of Crassus and Antonius, leading into a dialogue set in Crassus' house and beginning with Antonius strolling into the portico with Cotta, followed shortly by Quintus Catulus and Gaius Julius Caesar Strabo. Of course these introductory scenes are pastiches and not accurate reporting; but they convey the flavour of the sort of informal and shrewd and sometimes penetrating conversations of which the youthful Cicero was a privileged and discreet witness. How much he learned from men like these, how much he drew on their experience and reminiscence and judgement, is clear not only from the genuine warmth with which he speaks of them but also from all sides of his own speeches and writings. They were not only fine speakers and skilled lawyers, they were the leading statesmen of Rome and her empire, consuls and censors, governors and generals, the senior members of the Senate always among the first to catch the eye of the presiding consul, men of weight, of gravity, men above all endowed in rich measure with those two great Roman political qualities, *dignitas* and *auctoritas*. During these years of his mid- and late-teens, Cicero's aim now more than ever was directed towards the sort of career which these men had crowned with so much distinction and honour. Where they had trodden, he meant to follow.

Into the midst of this adolescent apprenticeship exploded

war. Late in 91, a number of Rome's Italian allies, goaded by the frustrations of a generation of agitation for political equality and economic security, took up arms to secure what political action had failed to win. In 89 Cicero, now aged seventeen, served under Pompeius Strabo, commander on the northern front. Here he surely made the acquaintance of Pompeius' son, known to history as Pompey the Great, Pompeius Magnus. Pompey, born in the same year as Cicero, was to shoot far ahead of him in public life. Precocious military genius and political audacity and versatility found him an army commander before he was twenty-five, and consul at the age of thirty-six, seven years before the legal age and without having held any of the preliminary offices of state. For much of his public life Cicero was to be an admirer of Pompey, often a collaborator, casting himself in the role of *fidus Achates* to Pompey's *Aeneas*. That Cicero got to know him now is likely enough; to judge by his reference to his service with Pompeius Strabo, he was serving in a capacity which gave him access to or close propinquity with the army commander, as one might expect of a young gentleman of his age, background, and connections.[13] Later in the war, probably in 88, Cicero also served for a time with Sulla, on the southern front.[14]

The chance survival of an inscription dating from 89 reveals an intriguing possibility.[15] The inscription lists some of the members of the staff of Pompeius Strabo as witnesses to an act of enfranchisement; it includes the name of a Lucius Sergius, almost certainly Lucius Sergius Catilina. That Cicero now met and got to know something of his future opponent is very likely, and may help to account for their friendly relationship in 65.

In 87, the Social War merged into the conflict between the factions of Cinna and Sulla. But, although these years are labelled as a period of civil war, despite the comparatively narrow basis of the government's support life at Rome went on in many ways as usual.[16] It was not until the death of

---

[13] *Phil.* 12.27.
[15] *ILS* 8888 = *ILLRP* 515.

[14] *de div.* 1. 72.
[16] Badian, *JRS* 52 (1962), 47–61.

Cinna and the return of the intransigent Sulla from Asia Minor that war broke out again in earnest in 83, bringing in the train of Sulla's victory the horrors of massacre and proscription.

During these years Cicero stayed at Rome, completing his training and taking his first steps in the profession of advocate. Antonius and Crassus had died, and Hortensius was the leading light of the Roman forensic world. Of Cicero's earliest ventures we know nothing, but in 81 the *pro Quinctio*, his earliest extant speech, finds him confronted by Hortensius himself leading for the other side. Of the decision in this case, a civil cause involving a complicated partnership dispute, we are ignorant. Cicero speaks with deference of Hortensius, and stresses his diffidence in taking a brief against him, skilfully deploying his own inexperience to set off by contrast the great strength of the case he is pleading.[17] He was beginning to make his mark, and the next year was to see the breakthrough. It came with his speech in 80 in defence of Roscius of Ameria (*pro Roscio Amerino*). Although Cicero was later to refer to it depreciatingly as a work full of youthful imperfections, it made his reputation. Henceforth his services were to be sought after.[18]

The background to the case was sordid enough, and typical of the period. With Sulla's victory had begun the reign of terror of the proscriptions. Men were outlawed, their property confiscated and often sold cheaply to those with political influence. Once unleashed, this violence and rapine and semi-legalized murder were not readily controllable. Many unsavoury but useful people took with both hands the chances to enrich themselves or pay off old scores. It was a dreadful time, and no one who lived through it ever forgot the brutality and the precariousness. Sulla was a determined, cruel, and remorseless man; granted he could not know and did not necessarily condone the many small uglinesses which his regime spawned, he did not exert himself conspicuously to uncover and repress them.

Sextus Roscius, a well-to-do citizen of Ameria, said by

[17] *pro Quinct.* 1 ff.   [18] *Orator* 108; *Brutus* 312.

Cicero to have been a partisan of Sulla's cause, was waylaid in the streets of Rome one night and done to death. The murderers were in fact neighbours and kinsmen of their victim who had a grudge against him.[19] A powerful figure now enters the story, Chrysogonus, a freedman and an influential assistant and confidant of the dictator Sulla. He arranged to have the dead man's name fraudulently inserted into the list of those outlawed by proscription, although the lists had officially been closed. This *ex post facto* action also meant that Roscius' goods were forfeit to the state. His considerable property was knocked down cheaply to Chrysogonus at public auction. The murderers got their share from Chrysogonus.[20]

This tidy arrangement was upset by the vigorous reaction of Roscius' fellow-townsmen at Ameria, who took exception to the violent extirpation of Roscius' son from the paternal estates. The town council sent a deputation to put the case before Sulla himself, but they failed to see him and were fobbed off with a promise from Chrysogonus to have Roscius senior's name removed from the list of proscribed and his son restored to his own.[21] Uneasy now, the conspirators first tried to have young Roscius murdered, then hit on the idea of prosecuting him for the murder of his own father. They hired some witnesses, and went ahead. They placed their faith in the influence of Chrysogonus and the general fear of his master Sulla, and no doubt too in the widespread confusion of the times. Such was the case which saw the young Cicero briefed to lead for the defence.[22]

The French historian, Jérôme Carcopino, has seen the defence of Roscius as a crucial move in a struggle by the nobility to unseat Sulla from power. Unwilling to attack him openly, they joyfully accepted the chance of a flank attack on his henchman Chrysogonus. Carcopino parades an impressive list of names on the side of young Roscius: and Cicero certainly does refer to friendly connections which had existed between Roscius senior and a number of

---

[19] *pro Rosc. Am.* 17–18.
[21] Ibid. 24 ff.
[20] Ibid. 19–21, 107–8.
[22] Ibid. 28.

noble families like the Metelli, Servilii, and Scipiones.[23] But it does not seem that they were very active for the son, and Cicero may well have exaggerated the closeness of their ties with the father. Later in his speech he says that the conspirators had reckoned that no one would dare to undertake Roscius' defence, and that they had been right: *patronos huic defuturos putaverunt; desunt.* Only the tough and ambitious young Cicero ventured to take it on.[24]

Carcopino's theories about the *pro Roscio Amerino*, and in general about the reasons leading up to Sulla's abdication of power, have not commanded general support.[25] His thesis compels him to date the speech to the year before that reliably attested by ancient authority. For the rest he is reduced to a search for nuances. Of course, there are nuances in all Cicero's speeches, and they can tell us more than direct statements. The trouble is that in looking for these nuances Carcopino assumes already proved what the nuances themselves are supposed to prove. If we decline to accept his premiss, we can refrain from drawing his conclusion: where Cicero is deferential to Sulla, Carcopino sees sarcasm and irony, others see deference. Cicero insists that Chrysogonus was at great pains not to let Sulla know what he was about, and Sulla made no serious attempt to intervene on his freedman's behalf. If Cicero stressed Roscius senior's connections with the nobility, it was no doubt in order to stress the respectability of the dead man. On any unbiased reading, Cicero takes great care in this speech to be tactful to Sulla and to dissociate him personally from the criminal excesses of Chrysogonus, thereby leaving him free to disown his subordinate.[26]

But the most powerful argument against Carcopino is the silence of Cicero himself. To Cicero Carcopino assigns a central role in this intrigue against Sulla. Yet Cicero, who

[23] Carcopino, *Sylla*, 155.

[24] *pro Rosc. Am.* 15 and 30.

[25] Munro, *JRS* 22 (1932), 239 ff. Stockton, 'Sylla, ou le monarque malgrè lui', in *Problems in Ancient History* (ed. Kagan, N.Y. 1966), II.259 ff.

[26] *pro Rosc. Am.* 21, 25, etc. Cf. Treggiari, *Roman Freedmen during the Late Republic*, 183–4.

never felt any love for Sulla, whose early connections were on the Marian and the *popularis* side, and who would have been delighted to have for use such a fine example of a tyrant's downfall, never uses it. Even his warmest admirers cannot deny that Cicero was nothing if not vain. He never hesitated to trumpet his own achievements, real or imagined. We recall Seneca's verdict on his consulship, *non sine causa sed sine fine laudatus*.[27] Yet so far from a shout of triumph over the downfall of Sulla, we strain our ears in vain for a whisper.

For all that, to undertake the case was a courageous act for a young advocate of Marian connections in the face of the power and influence of Chrysogonus; and it called for great delicacy to indict his crimes and those of his associates and to set them against the tawdry background of the whole situation in Rome and Italy without impugning the restoration of senatorial power before a court composed entirely of members of the Senate, and without arraigning the cruelty and enormities of Sulla himself. For all Cicero's later depreciation of it as a somewhat immature performance, it was a strong, effective, and subtle speech, in which the sincerity of Cicero's denunciation of the insecurity of the times and the illegality of much of what had been done in the name of the restoration of senatorial government is readily apparent; and his plea for the security of the rights of property and person, for a return to peace and order, strikes a consistent note in his own character.

To an impressionable young man of peaceful temper, literary tastes, and political ambition, the contrast between the comparatively placid years of the nineties and the awful decade of the Social and Civil Wars which followed must have been traumatic. In the civil wars themselves Cicero took no part, pursuing instead his studies in oratory and the law. He learned none the less to detest alike civil war and dictatorship, whether it was the autocracy of Cinna and the Marians or of Sulla and the Optimates. Sulla's 'peace', with its proscriptions in which hundreds of Cicero's own equestrian class suffered, was no less detestable than the

[27] *de brev. vit.* 5.

horrors of civil war itself. The Roscius case is above all interesting as illustrating the attendant circumstances of dictatorship, such as made it hateful to all decent men. The picture of the racket, the frame-up, is tellingly set forth.[28]

Whether from motives of prudence or not, Cicero left Rome the following year, 79, to travel abroad for two years. But not before he had again spoken out against another injustice of the Sullan regime. Before the decemviral court he argued successfully against the distinguished pleader Gaius Aurelius Cotta (and this while Sulla was still alive), on behalf of a lady from Arretium, that Sulla's action in disfranchising whole communities was a constitutional impossibility. After some initial hesitation the court decided in his favour—a good example of one important effect of judicial decisions, namely to nullify previous legislation by holding it to have been *ultra vires* or similarly vitiated.[29]

During the two years of his travel abroad Cicero spent six months studying at Athens along with his brother and his cousin and a friend whose importance in Cicero's life can hardly be exaggerated. Titus Pomponius Atticus had been at school in Rome along with Cicero and the young son of Gaius Marius. He came of an old and comfortably-off Roman family of the equestrian class. His father died while he was quite young, and Atticus, who was somewhat concerned for his personal safety in view of a family connection with the anti-Sullan tribune of 88, Sulpicius, left Rome for Athens, making his home there more or less permanently for the next twenty years or so. With a characteristic and easy smoothness which was never to desert him throughout life, he kept in with everybody. Three years older than Cicero, he was throughout their long friendship a steadying influence and an unfailing resource, not least in financial matters. His sister married Cicero's brother Quintus, an alliance which was less than ideally happy for Quintus but served further to cement the ties of the two brothers-in-law. For us the richest fruit of their long amity are the letters which Cicero addressed to Atticus on a variety of subjects, private

[28] *pro Cluentio* 21–5 paints a similar picture.   [29] *pro Caec.* 97.

and public. Beginning in 68 and continuing down to the end
of 44, a year before Cicero's death, they form a priceless
store of information. To Atticus, Cicero unburdened himself
of his hopes and fears with delightful frankness (only to his
own brother Quintus did he reveal so much of himself);
and Atticus' long absences from Rome meant that there
were many occasions for correspondence between the two
friends. But throughout his life Atticus remained studiedly
uncommitted to one side or the other in Roman politics,
maintaining good relations with one and all, lending his
money and expertise to anyone who might be useful. Who is
to blame him? He could look back at the end of a long life in a
violent epoch and declare, '*J'ai survécu*'. Indeed, he did better
than survive. He lived to see his daughter married to
Octavian's friend and chief marshal, Agrippa. The marriage
broker for this match was Mark Antony; and in this one
episode are united the great enemies Octavian and Antony,
themselves the men who had signed the warrant for the
execution of Atticus' old friend Cicero. Atticus predictably
died old.[30]

Altogether 575 letters survive from Cicero to Atticus (but
none at all from Atticus to Cicero). To and from his brother
Quintus we have 27. There are also 27 letters in the correspondence with Marcus Brutus, dating from the last
months of Cicero's life. Finally there is the vast correspondence 'with his friends' (*ad familiares*), who covered a very
wide range of Roman political society. The total of all the
letters together is well over nine hundred, constituting an
incomparable treasury of information about Cicero's life
and times, ranging from bread-and-butter letters of com-
mendation to formal despatches to the Senate, from brief
invitations to dinner to discussions of high policy, from
domestic details about house-decoration and family tiffs to
justifications of past politics and analyses of future prospects.
As Cornelius Nepos said of the letters to Atticus, to read

---

[30] On Atticus, see Nepos *Vita Attici*; Shackleton-Bailey, *Cicero's Letters to
Atticus*, I.3–59.

them is virtually to have a formal history of the period.[31] One cannot improve on the assessment of Carcopino: 'Now as vivid and clear as Voltaire's, now as lively and picturesque as Mme de Sévigné's, now as enigmatic and tantalizing as Mérimée's, as bitter and corrosive as Saint-Simon's ... a masterpiece which is a perfect blend of every quality and every style: narrative and portrait, argument and anecdote, maxim and metaphor, invective and irony, seductive coquetry and stinging sarcasm.'[32]

In 77, now in his thirtieth year, Cicero came back to Rome and won election as one of the twenty quaestors for the year 76. So began his career as a senator, since under the Sullan arrangements a quaestor automatically became a member of the Senate, a position held for life barring expulsion for certain crimes or for gross moral delinquency. Of the various quaestorian duties the one that fell to him by lot was the quaestorship at Lilybaeum in western Sicily (the modern Marsala), virtually a deputy-governorship of the province of Sicily whose governor, assisted by another quaestor, had his residence at Syracuse on the east coast. The job was a responsible one, and Cicero was well pleased with himself over the way he handled it. But after his return to Rome in 74 he never of his own choice left Italy again, for reasons which he gives in a light-hearted passage of his speech *pro Plancio.*

To tell the truth, I really believed at the time that people at Rome were talking about nothing else but my quaestorship. At a time of great scarcity I had sent home an enormous quantity of corn; I had shown myself courteous to the men of business, equitable to the traders, generous to the tax-agents, honest to the provincials, and everyone said that I had been most conscientious in every department of my office. The Sicilians had paid me unheard of honours. So I left Sicily expecting that the Roman people would rush to lay the world at my feet. While I was on my journey home I happened to call in at Puteoli at the height of the season when it was crowded with all the best people. Gentlemen, you could have knocked me down with a feather when someone came up to me and asked what day I had left Rome and what was the latest news from

---

[31] *Vita Attici* 16.
[32] *Les Secrets de la Corréspondance de Cicéron*, introd. 9–10.

Town. I told him that I was on my way back from my province. 'Good heavens, yes,' he said, 'from Africa, isn't it?' I was now pretty fairly annoyed. 'Not Africa, *Sicily*', I said. Then some know-it-all broke in, 'What, don't you know that our friend here has been quaestor at Syracuse?' I gave up and swallowed my annoyance and turned myself into an ordinary holidaymaker. But, gentlemen, I am not sure that that incident did not do me more good than if everyone had come up and congratulated me. After I realized that the Roman People were hard of hearing, but that their eyes were keen and sharp, I stopped worrying about what people might hear about me and took care that they should see me in the flesh every day. I lived in their sight, I was never out of the Forum.[33]

The half-dozen years between Cicero's departure for Greece in 79 and his return from Sicily in 74 were not happy ones for Rome. In Spain the old Cinnan supporter Sertorius held out against Metellus Pius and Pompey, who made headway against him only with great difficulty. There was trouble in the Balkans. The pirates were everywhere a nuisance. Servilius, consul in 79, had won the *cognomen* Isauricus for carrying out operations against them in the region of Isauria on the south coast of what is now Turkey; others had not done so well, and it was not until Pompey's lightning campaign in 67 that the nagging and erosive problem of piracy was properly solved. Finally, by 75 it had become clear that war was likely to break out again with King Mithridates of Pontus, and men began to jockey for this plum appointment. At home the consul Lepidus in 78 led an armed rising against the government. The movement was crushed by Lepidus' fellow-consul Catulus, with the valuable assistance of Pompey. But the rising was significant for all that it was short-lived. Lepidus, father of the triumviral colleague of Antony and Octavian, and a man of the bluest blood, presented himself as the leader of the reaction against the Sullan constitution, claiming the support of the disaffected throughout Italy. In the south, Sulla had made a clean sweep of the Samnites, his bitterest enemies. But Etruria, many of its towns deprived by Sulla of their recently acquired citizenship and with wide areas of its land confiscated as a punishment for resistance to him, offered Lepidus

[33] *pro Planc.* 64–6.

strong support. He signalled his return to the reforming cause by proposing to resume distributions of cheap corn, by promising to recall exiles and restore them to their estates. Lepidus was beaten, but nothing had been cured. Etruria was to provide the main strength of Catiline's following in 63, and the discontents of Rome and Italy were to prove highly combustible fuel for the fires that subsequent rogue politicians were to light under the blundering feet of the ruling oligarchy.

After the failure of Lepidus, no one dared to aim a violent revolution in Italy until Catiline was driven to it in 63. (We need not take the Spartacus revolt into account here, since this was a slave uprising.) But we do find fierce tribunician agitation against the Sullan constitution by men like Sicinius and Quinctius and Macer (tribunes in 76, 74, and 73 respectively).[34] They produced little or nothing in the way of constructive results. Sulla had deprived the tribunes of their independent legislative initiative; and so long as his law barring holders of the tribunate from higher office remained in force, the office was restricted to the unambitious and the compliant, the obscure, fanatical, or optimistic. However, in 75 the consul Gaius Aurelius Cotta carried a law abrogating the bar on the election of ex-tribunes to higher magistracies, once more opening this vital office to men of weight and ambition.[35] (In 70 his brother Lucius was to carry the law which broke the senatorial monopoly of the criminal courts, restored to them by Sulla.)

When Cicero got back to Rome from Sicily in 74 the reactionaries were still very much in control, but they had begun to give ground in face of the pressure of popular and equestrian opposition. Tribunician agitation continued. In 74 Lucius Quinctius was the chief agitator, and we can catch an echo of his powerful speeches in Cicero's *pro Cluentio*, delivered in 66.[36] Quinctius had defended a certain Oppianicus on a charge of murder. Oppianicus was condemned, and

---

[34] *pro Cluentio* 110–12; Sallust *Hist.* 3.48.
[35] Asconius 66C.
[36] *pro Cluentio* 77 ff.

Quinctius made a great to-do about the verdict, contending that it had been secured by scandalous bribery by Oppianicus' nephew, Cluentius. His political point was that senatorial juries were corrupt and venal, and should be done away with. It was a *cause célèbre*, and it was as such that Cicero referred to it more than once in his speeches against Verres in 70.[37] But here we may notice the differing tone of Cicero's references to it in his *pro Cluentio* delivered in 66 and in the *Verrines* of four years earlier. In his speech in 70 the condemnation of Oppianicus was for Cicero 'a disgraceful outrage', *turpissimum facinus*;[38] in 66 he asserts that the subsequent condemnation of the president of the Oppianicus court at the hands of Quinctius was 'on the most trivial and slightest grounds, which ought never to have been brought before a court at all'.[39] In 70 the condemnation of one of the jurors in the Oppianicus case for accepting a bribe to bring in a verdict of guilty is cited as one of many examples of the corruption of senatorial juries; in 66 the trial of the corrupt juror is said not to have been a proper trial at all.[40]

Perhaps the most amusing product of this change of tack came when Attius, the prosecutor in the Cluentius trial, threw a quotation in Cicero's face from his own speech against Verres.[41] Cicero, who spoke so often and published so much, was particularly vulnerable to this kind of move, whenever changing circumstances or conditions had led him to shift his ground. His handling of the awkward situation here is masterly. 'Attius has read out from some speech or other which he says is one of mine'—so he begins: *recitavit ex oratione nescio qua Attius quam meam esse dicebat*. Cicero refers, of course, to the *Verrines*, the *chef d'oeuvre* which had taken him at one bound to the primacy of the Roman bar. The court must have been dissolved into laughter at this point. Cicero went blandly on—he was not just a great orator but a great wit and a great actor as well—to jolly the court along

---

[37] *Verr.* I.29, 38–9; II.i.157, ii.78. [38] *Verr.* I.29.
[39] *pro Cluentio* 91. [40] Ibid. 115.
[41] Ibid. 138.

with half-outrageous, half-commonsensical references to the need of a pleader to change his ground to suit his case: 'the great orator Antonius always said that it was for this reason that he would never have any of his speeches published, so that if ever it were necessary for him not to have made a particular statement he could deny having ever made it.' He then moves into a more serious vein, and before one is aware of it he has slipped out of the trap and is off and away, leaving the court happily if vaguely conscious that the point has been answered whereas on careful reading one can see that it has simply been evaded. It is difficult for the unprofessional or humourless reader to appreciate the elegance and wit and skill of Cicero at such junctures, and to call to the imagination the impact of the physical delivery of the actual words.

The years from 74 to 70 were chiefly remarkable in Italian eyes for the series of drubbings handed out to senatorial commanders by Spartacus. Almost equally damaging to the prestige of the governing oligarchy was the scarcity and dearness of corn, largely because of the depredations of the pirates. (We saw how proud Cicero was of his contribution to the corn needs of Rome while quaestor at Lilybaeum.) The fragments of Sallust's *Histories* include speeches by Licinius Macer, tribune in 73 and himself a historian, who later committed suicide, faced with disgrace when accused of extortion in 66 before a court presided over by the praetor Cicero. These speeches included, besides a denunciation of Rabirius, the alleged murderer of the radical tribune Saturninus (a theme resumed by Caesar and Labienus in 63), comments on the corn situation and on the urgent need to restore full tribunician power.[42]

In these reformist agitations the young Julius Caesar, whose age and patrician birth rendered him ineligible for the tribunate, played some part. Just how active Cicero was on the same side we do not know, but he was at this time in sympathy with the cause of reform. It is likely enough that in these years he and Caesar, who was six years younger,

[42] Sallust *Oratio Macri* = *Hist.* 3.48; *pro Rab. perd.* 7.

saw a good deal of each other. Caesar's aunt, Julia, was the widow of Marius; and Cicero was a great friend of the Cotta brothers, whose sister Aurelia was Caesar's mother. That the two men came now on to terms of friendship would help to account for the intimate and familiar note that is always observable in their intercourse.[43] Against this background one may better comprehend Cicero's hopes in 60 of influencing the future consul Caesar for the better;[44] and Caesar one suspects had personal as well as political reasons for wanting Cicero on his side in 60 and 59 and for trying to shield him from the tender mercies of Publius Clodius.

From these years one speech of Cicero's survives, the *pro Tullio*, delivered in 71. Like the *pro Roscio Amerino*, its main interest lies in the invaluable glimpse it gives us of an otherwise little-known scene. It takes us into the wild hill-country of Lucania in southern Italy, the very region most disturbed by Spartacus. It is all very reminiscent of the American West: we find cattle-barons and their hired hands, armed slaves that is, raiding and plundering each other's herds and homesteads. In Italy, as in America, much of the trouble resulted from the absence of an efficient police force or civil gendarmerie: it was left to Augustus to give Rome a metropolitan police force (the *cohortes urbanae*) and Italy a gendarmerie (the praetorian cohorts), since under the Republic the oligarchy dared not entrust any individual with such forces—*quis custodiet ipsos custodes*? Of course, Cicero's client Tullius was relatively inoffensive and innocent—but Cicero says this of all his clients. Tullius had had some of his slave-herdsmen killed, and Cicero had to admit that there had previously been some question of their trespassing on a neighbouring ranch (for what purpose he neglects to say).[45]

This same year saw the return of Pompey from Spain and the success of Crassus against Spartacus. Cicero was soon to undertake the prosecution of Verres and align himself firmly in support of the forces of change; to begin his long

[43] See, for example, *ad QF* II.14.1 (June 54): *recordatio veteris amoris*.
[44] *ad Att.* II.1.6.
[45] *pro Tull.* 19–20, 48, 53.

unchallenged reign as leader of the Roman forensic world; to move steadily ahead to praetorship and consulship. He was now a mature and experienced man in his mid-thirties. But before we follow him any further, we must examine and try to understand the constitutional system and political practices and machinery which formed the backdrop against which his public life was to be played.

II

S.P.Q.R.

THE HISTORY of the tumultuous and exciting last century
of the Republic of Rome centres around the fight of the great
families of the senatorial ruling nobility to hold their controlling position against the assaults of their opponents. The
attack was launched with verve and skill by the brothers
Tiberius and Gaius Gracchus. The questions they raised,
the issues they fought, the proposals they championed were
to remain central to Roman politics for the next century:
agrarian reform, social justice, the rights of Rome's Italian
allies and partners in conquest, the food supply, the administration of justice, the curbing of the arbitrary power of
consuls and senate. They rested their position on the un-
compromising basis of the sovereignty of the *populus Romanus*.
They failed themselves to storm the citadel, but it was along
the line of advance they had mapped out that later assaults
were pressed home. At the end of the second century Saturninus renewed the attack. Cicero was nearly seven years old
when, like the Gracchi before him, Saturninus went down
in face of the force deployed by the ruling oligarchy, who
when it came to the point of decision were prepared to fight
rather than be legislated out of power. Cicero was already a
youth and studying at Rome when the murder of Livius
Drusus the Younger sparked off the Social War. In 88
Sulpicius Rufus assumed the mantle of Drusus, and from 87
Cinna and Carbo seized and held power. But first in 88 and
then again in 82 Sulla led his armies against Rome to overthrow his opponents. The arrangements which he made
during his later period of dominance ruthlessly restored the
senatorial position and left the nobility in tight control of

Rome. But the forces of reform were too deeply seated in the widespread and serious social and economic grievances of large sections of the populace to be long repressed. In 70, the year of the prosecution of Verres, the tribunate recovered its full Gracchan strength, ready to be deployed for new attacks.

Rome, like England, lacked a written constitution. In states so ordered the constitution consists of a jumble of elements which may be roughly sorted into three groups. First, statute law, the body of rules and regulations passed by the legislature and open to repeal by the legislature. Such law may be interpreted by the courts, and on occasion so interpreted as to alter or hamstring the original intention of the legislature. Next comes the common law (as we term it), the corpus of law which has grown up bit by bit, often over a long period of time, through the acceptance of certain principles by the courts which they have embodied in their decisions and judgements. Such law may be altered by the legislature by means of a statute, or affected by new interpretations and distinctions on the part of the courts themselves. Both common law and statute law are of course enforceable in the courts.

Thirdly we have custom and precedent. These comprise a large body of material and practices which, although observed, are not enforceable at law. Mostly, and most importantly, they belong to the constitutional sphere. For example, in the United Kingdom we can point to the rule that members of the Cabinet should also be members of one or other House of Parliament; or to the rule that generally the sovereign can exercise the royal prerogatives only on the advice of ministers of the Crown. It has long been accepted *de facto* that the Prime Minister must be a member of the Commons and not of the Lords; more recently the notion that all senior ministers should be members of the Commons has hardened into a firm rule. None of these rules is laid down by law. They rest on constitutional conventions, what the Romans called *mos maiorum*, ancestral practice, or *disciplina maiorum*.

All the same, such precedents and practices must not be written off as of inferior status. They are very powerful factors indeed. It was not for nothing that the Romans knew of only one term for 'revolution': *res novae*, literally 'new things'. And we have only to imagine the sort of rumpus that would ensue if a British sovereign were to try to dissolve Parliament against the advice of a Prime Minister, or if a Prime Minister or Chancellor of the Exchequer were to be appointed from among the members of the Upper House, to remind ourselves of the crucial importance of this element in a constitution.

In countries with this sort of constitution, sovereignty resides entirely in the legislative body, which can legislate about anything it chooses without formal restraint. There is no Supreme Court, no written charter, to say it nay. Hence change is easier, but change is also likely to be opportunistic and unsystematic. One piece of the constitution is excised, another is left standing long after it has fallen into desuetude and neglect. New bits are added piecemeal, as they are needed. The result, perfectly intelligible to those who live with and work the system, is full of pitfalls and surprises to the outsider, especially one nurtured in an altogether different constitutional tradition.

Again, the passage of the years and changes in accepted practice can leave the letter of the constitution unaltered while profoundly affecting its spirit and interpretation. Men and institutions retain powers on paper which it is understood they will not in fact deploy, but which in strict law they may deploy. In a disturbed period, with great issues at stake, such powers may be deliberately resumed. Thus, Tiberius Gracchus revived the obsolete character and powers of the tribunate of the plebs, and the sovereign right of the popular assemblies at Rome, to override or bypass the Senate and direct the policy of the state. Similarly, just before the Great War, the House of Lords threatened to revive its right to reject a Finance Bill approved by the Commons. On each occasion, predictably, a constitutional and political crisis of the first magnitude resulted.

Finally, change could be delayed or baulked by a system
of checks and balances. The Roman constitution gave the
Roman People the right to ratify any law they chose. But
the people had no right either themselves to propose a law or
to amend laws presented to them. These rights were reserved
to the magistrates, the officers of state. The people could
only vote Yes or No to the bills presented to them. Thus for
long periods, through the machinations of an executive
monopolized by the ruling class, the powers of the people
could be rendered largely illusory; as magistrates and Senate
came gradually to arrogate to themselves the authority to
decide, the people often did not even have the chance of
voting Yes or No.

It was largely by such haphazard means, above all by the
gradual establishment of custom and precedent, that the
Roman constitution had been moulded into the form which
it presented in the last century of the Republic. The magistrates, originally powerful and often independent, had by
the end of the second century been harnessed by the Senate.
De jure their powers were still immense, particularly the
imperium of the two consuls; but they had come generally
to exercise these powers at the discretion of the Senate.
This is not surprising. The magistracies of Rome were annual
offices, and re-election was rare. Continuity of policy could
be achieved only, if at all, by the Senate. It is worth stressing
the fact that the chief officers of the Roman State, the consuls, were very often men in their early or mid-forties. The
Senate on the other hand numbered in its ranks all the ex-
consuls (*consulares*), along with those men who would themselves be holding the consulship before very long. Their
experience and prestige were alike formidable, and a magistrate who set himself against the will of the Senate was
giving many hostages to fortune. He did well to remember
that his power and immunity would last only twelve months,
after which he would revert to private status.

The Senate in its turn was dominated by the *factiones*, the
groups of powerful nobles who thanks to their numerous
dependents (*clientes*) and their great prestige (*auctoritas*), to

their vast wealth and patronage and their nexuses of family alliances, controlled the assemblies and through them the elections, especially to the consulship. It was immensely difficult for an outsider to break into the charmed circle of hereditary influence, the aristocracy of office, around which the nobles strove to maintain a *cordon sanitaire* to ward off infection by undesirables.[1]

This state of affairs being largely *de facto* and not *de jure*, the oligarchs had always to guard against the danger that the legal rights of the people and their elected representatives might be re-asserted. When in 133 Tiberius Gracchus emerged from their own ranks as the first of the line of men who from various motives sought to deprive them of their monopoly of government, the *nobiles* closed their ranks fast and for a century fought tenaciously to repel the onslaught. On one front they were victorious: they beat off all direct attacks from hostile magistrates. But the attacks began to come in from another quarter, and the *nobiles* who had successfully harnessed the magistracy were in their turn bridled by the pro-magistracy. In the end it was no popular tribune or even a consul, but a pro-consul at the head of an army, an army achieved by the application of Gracchan methods, who broke the nobility and with them the Republic.

Rome had begun life as a town on the Tiber. Her institutions were those of the *polis*, the city-state, the political unit that dominates classical Greek history. The inhabitants of the town concerned and of the adjacent countryside constituted a sovereign state; as well as running their internal affairs they also ordered their external relations with other independent states. The precise political rights and obligations of the different categories and classes of inhabitants varied widely from one *polis* to another and from one time to another, the systems ranging from narrow oligarchies to egalitarian democracies; and the amount of genuine independence in external affairs enjoyed by individual cities

[1] Sallust *Jug.* 63.

ranged over a very broad spectrum, with some powerful enough to build up wide spheres of influence and even empire while others were too small and weak ever to be free from the domination of stronger neighbours. But, essentially, the scale of politics remains small. The citizens exercise their rights directly and in person. They live sufficiently near the administrative centre to go along and vote for or against laws, cast their votes at elections, serve on juries, be cajoled or harangued or swayed by arguments. As they look about them, they can see the strength of their own numbers. It is this smallness of scale and this immediacy which impart to much of Greco-Roman history its breathless pace, so that in some states we see political developments, which on the vaster scale of later European history occupy centuries, running their course within the space of generations.

To begin with, Rome followed a normal enough pattern of development. The kings were driven out; the kindred towns of Latium came first to be dominated, and finally to be absorbed, by their most powerful member. The rule of the patrician aristocracy which had succeeded the kings began to be challenged. The publication of laws was enforced, men of ambition from the ranks of the plebeians thrust forward with demands to be admitted to the offices of state alongside the patrician families. The mass of the people began to stand up for their rights, to extort concessions, to win recognition for their own assemblies and their own elected officers, to curb abuses of power and privilege.

However, Rome was not Athens. Athens was a great maritime, industrial, and commercial city, with a large urban population open to the manifold and disturbing influences which such cities breed like rabbits, and with time to spare for political arguments in barbers' shops and taverns and attendance at public meetings. Rome was not a great commercial or industrial centre, nor a great port open to the shipping of the world. Her population was more rural in its activities and interests; the backbone of Rome's power was her legions, the backbone of her legions the small peasant proprietor. The demands of the land were miserly of time to spare to trudge into the city. Its settled routines fostered a certain conservatism of outlook. The lack of wide horizons and new experiences, the pull of tried ancestral ways and traditional observances, the unvarying calendar of seed-time and harvest-time, have always made the peasant the despair of the radical reformer.

So Rome was content to leave far wider discretion in the hands of her executive than some of the more radically minded cities of the ancient world. The essential safeguards of popular influence on the government lay in the fact that the officers of state were elected by the people, and that on great matters such as war and peace the sovereign *populus* could and did make its voice heard. Further, if pushed to the limit, the people could and did take action on major social and economic issues. In some respects, if one is careful not to push the analogy too hard, Rome of the middle republican period came near to the modern concept of delegated, representative government. The executive and the council of state were armed with wide powers and ample discretion. They were also, directly or indirectly, responsive to the interests of the people by whom they were elected and who formed the armies on which the security and ex-pansion of Rome depended, her citizen-levies. Rome's astonishing success in her career of expansion in the fourth and third centuries is itself sufficient witness to the efficiency of her political organization. And we must remember that the ordinary Roman did not ask or expect very much.

Rome's very success was the seed of her future troubles. As she extended her hold over Italy, the *populus Romanus* spread further and further afield, moving out to people the new settlements sited along the strategic trunk-roads that were driven through the peninsula, or to farm individual plots of conquered Italian land. And with the great overseas expansion of the second century came an influx into Rome of unemployed or under-employed proletarians driven from the land in the economic upheaval, together with vast numbers of foreign slaves, the profits of conquest. Many of these slaves gained their freedom, and with it citizenship.

By the end of the first century A.D. the satirist Juvenal was to complain that the Syrian Orontes had long mingled its flood with the Tiber: *Iam pridem Syrus in Tiberim defluxit Orontes*.[2] But already in the second century B.C. Scipio Aemilianus could turn on a hostile assembly and label them 'step-children of Italy';[3] and Cicero can refer to the inhabitants of the imperial capital as a 'wretched, half-starved apology for a *plebs*' (*misera et ieiuna plebecula*), or 'the dregs of Romulus' (*faex Romuli*).[4]

This diaspora of the citizens of Rome, together with the increasing rootlessness and pauperization of the city proletariat, combined to break down the old *polis* machine. More and more, Rome's citizens or ex-citizens were prevented by sheer distance from attending the central assemblies in the city. More and more were the actual city-dwellers manipulable by the bribery and intimidation and seigneural influence of the rich aristocratic houses. The exigencies of the long struggle against Hannibal had strengthened the hand, as their own stubborn persistence and eventual victory had raised the prestige, of the Senate and its magistrate generals. The vast fields of war and expansion which subsequently opened up during the second century exaggerated the trouble. Those *nobiles* able and adaptable enough to accommodate themselves to the new pattern of things and profit by it won the prize of great riches from booty and slaves, and deployable influence and patronage in the new transmarine provinces or in the fresh spheres of indirect Roman influence.

Meanwhile the citizen-soldiery of Rome and her Italian allies, still clinging to its outmoded militia basis, was being broken on the wheel of protracted and distant campaigns far beyond the borders of Italy: in Spain, in the Balkans, in North Africa and Asia Minor. Individual soldiers and centurions might make a rich killing in booty, but in general the peasant farmers of Italy found themselves called from home

---

[2] Juvenal *Sat.* 3.62.
[3] Vell. Pat. 2.4.4: *quorum noverca est Italia*.
[4] *ad Att.* I.16.11; II.1.8.

and fields for long periods of foreign service; and in their absence their families often found it impossible to carry on, and gave up or sold out or were forced out by powerful men anxious to invest and exploit their new wealth.[5]

The damage had been done by the time that Marius, in Cicero's childhood, abandoned the old system and threw legionary recruitment open to volunteers without regard to their property qualification. The old system was never formally abolished, but the Marian practice held for the rest of the life of the Republic. But by now the basis on which the old *polis* had rested had quite crumbled away. Nothing had been put in its place to bear the weight of the structure. The result had been the growth of a ruling oligarchy of birth and wealth, inheriting wide resources of influence and patronage, manipulating the urban populace, and increasingly less responsible and responsive to the sovereign people by whom they were nominally elected and to whom they were nominally answerable, working the constitution to maintain and extend the vested interests of themselves and fellow-members of their class.

It is a commonplace that Marius' decision to open the ranks of the Roman legions to all classes of citizens transformed the army from a militia of yeoman farmers into a professional body of men mainly without property. Like other generalizations this one does not tell the whole truth, but it tells enough of the truth for our purposes.[6] The neglect of the state to provide fixed conditions of service, and pensions or discharge-bounties, left each general after a great war with the alternatives of leaving his men to starve or of forcing a reluctant senate and people to provide them with land— and since there was no good vacant land readily available, this meant the expropriation of existing owners or occupiers. Since much of the land in Italy was in the hands of large landowners, often senators, the conservatives and men of property were sure on each occasion to oppose such legislation.

---

[5] Appian *BC* 1.7 ff and 27.
[6] See, for a fuller treatment, R. E. Smith, *Service in the Post-Marian Army*; P. A. Brunt, *JRS* 52 (1962), 69 ff.

Even the distribution of land in the form of colonies overseas ran into the teeth of senatorial opposition: it is not
easy to see why, but perhaps the mere habit of opposition
to such measures played a part, and a general suspicion of
what were thought of as electoral bribes, coupled with an
instinctive reluctance to see the people taking too direct an
interest in the potential material profits of empire and
thereby sharpening their appetite for interference in the
control of foreign affairs. The plain fact is that politically,
socially, and economically the poorer people of Italy from
whom the legions were mainly recruited in Cicero's day
had no reason to feel loyalty, gratitude, or respect for a
governing class which exploited them and resolutely declined to grapple with their major grievances and consis-
tently beat down anyone who tried. The legionaries shared
the hopes and fears, the grievances and aspirations, of the
people from whom they sprang. The wonder is, not that
Roman armies could be got to march on Rome, but that
they did so so very seldom.

By its exclusiveness and selfishness the ruling oligarchy of
Rome forced into opposition able men of ambition or largeness of view or generosity of mind who were not members of
the enchanted circle of dominant families or who could not
be constricted within it. By its neglect of the deep-seated
and widespread social and economic grievances of Italy it
provided such men with a potential following and a programme, which in the right hands could be used to break the
traditional hold of the oligarchy over the assemblies, and to
secure for their champions office and high command. The
power and patronage so won could then be deployed to
strengthen a following and to resist attack or press ahead
with further changes. And Marius' innovation (although
there is no reason to suppose that he made it with this in
mind) served to provide later anti-oligarchic politicians
with a means of preventing themselves from following the
dead bodies of the Gracchi into the Tiber.

Italy since the eighties had been united in possession of the
full Roman citizenship as far north as the line of the Po.

Revolution was no longer likely to be fomented simply by claims to the franchise. But the franchise was not everything. Full political equality was not to come until the principate of Augustus, when at last the grip of the old Republican nobility was gently but firmly prised away from the higher magistracies and a new Italian aristocracy of office born. Thus throughout Cicero's lifetime a strong current of opposition to the ruling oligarchy continued to run in Italy, not merely among the masses but significantly in the ranks of the Italian upper classes who stood to gain most by a genuine equality of political opportunity. The communities north of the Po, the 'Transpadanes', lacked even the full citizenship in most cases, and formed a potential source of political pressure. Other elements of insecurity were provided by communities (in Etruria especially) disfranchised by Sulla and deprived of their lands to make way for Sulla's veterans. As we saw, Cicero was early active in the case of the lady from Arretium to secure recognition of the principle that no community could as such be legally disfranchised, and he himself says that this disfranchisement did not outlast Sulla.[7] But the confiscations were a different matter, and not so easily to be reversed. In general, inequality of property and harsh debt-laws and injustice and the continued existence of vast slave-run estates meant that all over Italy there was a large mass of wretched people living on the borderline of subsistence with little to lose and a lot to gain by revolution. Many of Sulla's own veterans became impoverished, and could add a valuable stiffening to a general rising. There were certainly very many people in Italy who would (and, when the time came, did) favour social revolution. Conversely, such factors led the well-to-do throughout Italy to draw together in face of the threat of a really radical social upheaval. The prosperous classes might and sometimes did support constitutional movements of reform, but the oligarchy could count on their aid to foil any attempt at redistribution of property.

[7] *de domo* 79.

In her overseas provinces misgovernment, which comprised partly lack of government and partly a failure to enforce rules which were in themselves sound, made Rome unpopular in many areas. Striking examples of this hostility are seen in the support given to Mithridates of Pontus in Greece and Greek Asia, and in the successes of the rebel Roman general Sertorius in Spain. But Pompey's victories in these areas in the seventies and sixties, and still more his fine and liberal reorganization in Spain and the East, did much to reduce this discontent. In any case, provincial discontent needed strong military support to make it really dangerous, and Roman reformers did not seek to exploit it for their own ends. This does not mean that areas of loyal support (*clientelae*) were not of vital importance for leading Roman statesmen; they were, especially if it were to come to open civil war. The strength of Pompey's *clientelae* in Spain and Asia Minor, for example, was a major factor when war broke out in 49. But discontent *could* be dangerous. For example, when Cicero in 51 as governor of Cilicia was faced with the threat of a Parthian invasion, he could not rely on the local levies since 'thanks to the harshness and injustice of our rule they are either too weak to give us much help or so alienated that we cannot expect anything from them or entrust anything to them'.[8]

The subject communities had generally been given conservative constitutions, and the dependence of their ruling classes on Roman support and protection for the continuance of their control often kept them in line. But the major role played by the provinces in Cicero's time was the opportunity they afforded of acquiring and exploiting important *clientelae* and, of course, of securing foreign commands which might bring wealth, glory, patronage, and military power. From this point of view they had a vital importance.

Nowadays, we are accustomed to a fairly tight party organization for electoral and legislative purposes. We take it for granted that each party has a durable and acknowledged

[8] *ad famm.* XV.1.5.

leadership and hierarchy; that normally it will vote as one unit in Parliament; that it will never seek to affect the verdict of the law-courts. These are fundamental assumptions for us, and it is not easy to adjust our thinking to a different system. But none of these assumptions holds for the Rome of Cicero's lifetime. There were something like organized parties, but in a far less rigid and disciplined form. Politics tended to be much more personal, and family groupings and dynastic marriages had a large part to play. Broadly speaking, among Roman politicians there was a group of conservatives, usually styled the *optimates* or the *boni* ('the good men'), interested in maintaining the status quo and the material advantages they derived from it. There were also the reformers, whose motives might range over a whole spectrum from a desire to exploit popular grievances for narrow and immediate personal advantages to an honest distaste for corruption and inefficiency. They were usually known as *populares*, not so much from the content of their programmes (although this needed to be popular to gain the support of the *populus*) as from their methods, which were in general to bypass the senate and appeal directly to the assemblies of the people. But we must be careful not to identify *popularis* with 'democratic': there were no democrats, as we understand the term, among the leading politicians of Cicero's time.

Between the powerful families of the nobility and the mass of the people we need also to take note of a large and rather inchoate middle group, which centred around the great financial interests but contained also a good many of the well-to-do in the country towns of Italy. Cicero himself was born into this class, and normally he identified himself publicly with its interests and hoped to direct its voting power at elections and at trials. It might attach itself either to optimate or to *popularis* politicians, when one or other failed to give due attention to its interests or when concrete proposals for its advantage were forthcoming. Its support was of the first importance, for generally it could tilt the balance one way or the other—in politics that is; open war was another matter.

4—c.

These men are usually known by the collective name of *equites* ('knights') or *ordo equester*. But the class was not so homogeneous as the name may suggest. Traditionally, the *equites equo publico* had served as the cavalry of the Roman army, and were recruited from the richer citizens of the highest census class. By the late Republic Rome's cavalry was provided by allies or mercenaries, but the eighteen centuries of 'public horse' remained a constituent part of the centuriate assembly. In Cicero's day, the *ordo equester* generally embraced all citizens of free birth who were registered as owning property worth at least 400,000 sesterces: precisely how many of these were actually enrolled in the eighteen centuries is arguable, and in any case censuses were irregular in their incidence and even then sometimes not completed. For practical purposes, we can break the *ordo* down into three categories: young *nobiles* not yet members of the Senate; rich financiers and entrepreneurs; and the propertied classes of the municipalities of Italy.[9]

The young *nobiles* were clearly not very cohesive with the other two categories. The interests and influence of the second category are evident, and they had a marked class-consciousness and unity of aim: very much a product of Roman imperialism, they undertook the multifarious state-contracts, whence their name of *publicani*. Apart from contracts to collect the various taxes due to the state, they also contracted for victualling the army and navy, for public works, for operating state-owned mines and quarries, and so on. There was, too, an enormous field for private financial and commercial activities in the territories that were brought under Roman political control or influence. Rich and influential, sometimes associated in joint stock companies (*societates*), and with their own *clientelae*, they were no small force in public affairs, and indispensable to the working of the machinery of empire.

The third category comprised the men who dominated the municipalities of Italy and who derived their wealth and local consequence from land or house-property or manu-

[9] Henderson, *JRS* 53 (1963), 61 ff.

facture. These *domi nobiles*, as they are sometimes termed, shared some interests with the financiers and entrepreneurs, but their objects and aims were not identical. Broadly, they favoured policies of social stability and respect for the rights of property. Their indirect influence was obviously considerable, and they exercised direct influence in the election of praetors and consuls in the *comitia centuriata*. This assembly was so constituted as to give a heavy bias to the votes of the richest citizens; and the comfortably-off country Italians could afford to travel to Rome to cast their votes at election-time, and so were an important factor in politics. But clearly they would not spend much time in Rome. Even if qualified to serve as *iudices*, it is extremely unlikely that those who lived any distance from Rome normally did so. They had far less interest in the provinces than the *publicani* and *negotiatores*, and far less ready money available for political use.

In accordance with Cicero's own practice, the terms *equites* and *equester ordo* and 'knights' will in this book be used to denote the second and third of the categories just described. The context will generally make it clear whether both are involved, or principally or solely the second category.

Roughly speaking, from 70 onwards the *equites* were in opposition to the optimates and in support of Pompey and of reform. By 63, the year of Cicero's consulship, they had been frightened off and could be welded into union with the *boni*. But the alliance was short-lived. It broke down over the trial of Clodius and a squabble over the revision of the Asian tax-contract. The split did a great deal to let in Caesar in 59.

The relation between the courts and legislation is indissoluble. Laws need teeth if they are to bite, and the teeth are provided by courts which are prepared to bring in verdicts against transgressors. All the criminal and constitutional statutes in the world are so much waste paper if the courts cannot be relied on to return a true verdict. Failing elaborate precautions,[10] bribery was an ever-present factor in

[10] cf. Asconius 38C ff for the precautions taken at Milo's trial in 52.

Roman trials. No less important was political bias. Many charges were brought from political motives, and the character of the court and its composition often affected the verdict and in so doing reflected the jury's prejudices. From Cotta's law of 70 onwards, the *iudices* who decided the verdicts in criminal trials, often politically inspired, were drawn in equal proportions from senators, *equites*, and *tribuni aerarii*. Since the last-named were in fact a specific section of the *ordo equester*, *equites* effectively outnumbered senatorial *iudices* by two to one.[11] Here the political influence of those *equites* who lived in and near Rome and could easily serve in the courts is readily apparent.

Magistrates themselves could sometimes flout public opinion to an amazing extent. Even in the Senate, granted the widest licence in debate and all sorts of opportunities for obstruction, a positive vote leading to effective action could be taken only on a measure approved by the competent authorities; while even so the veto of a single one of the ten tribunes could nullify the Senate's decision. Cicero's own consulship in 63 is an excellent example of the immense potential of the consular power and authority in the hands of an able and determined consul. We have only to reflect on what could have happened if Antonius had shared the consulship of 63 with Catiline, or even if the far tougher Catiline had pipped Antonius at the post to share the consulship with Cicero (as he nearly did), to understand why the struggle around the elections to the consulship was often so vital and desperate.

We need to bear in mind that the political groups or 'parties' of Cicero's Rome had no permanent and responsible leaders—this being itself partly a consequence of the system of annual magistracies. Normally there was no such position as 'party-leader'. Everything depended on the wealth, patronage, influence, power, and not least personal magnetism of each leader, on his capacity for organizing his supporters and effecting those compromises which are an irremovable part of politics in any country at any time. Such

[11] Henderson, art. cit. 63.

influential men were not always consuls or ex-consuls. The
rigid ladder of office, the *cursus honorum*, meant that no man,
however able, could move on to higher offices until he had
attained the minimum legal age. Pompey was the great
exception: Caesar, for example, could not legally be consul
until the year 59, however much more important he was
than some of the second-raters who held the office in the
later sixties. And Clodius and Milo in the early fifties should
not be dismissed simply as instruments in the hands of this or
that consul or consular, just because they had climbed only
the lower rungs of office. They were political powers of the
first order in their own right, at least from 58 onwards if not
earlier. Nor was actual tenure of office necessary: Crassus
(apart from his truncated censorship in 65) held no office
or commission of formal consequence between his first
consulship in 70 and his second in 55; his importance cannot
however be questioned. Crassus had a long purse, and was a
great backer of promising men. But this cuts both ways; he
did not stake men unless they were important, or potentially
important, in their own right. Caesar and Clodius might
take his money, they did not thereby become his employees.
Caesar was the great figure on the *popularis* side in the late
sixties and fifties, but it would be wrong to imagine that all
those who worked with him then were prepared to follow
him gladly in establishing an autocracy. Labienus, his
second-in-command in Gaul, went over to Pompey and the
optimates when Caesar took up arms against the state. Why,
we cannot say; there was an old loyalty to Pompey, but the
reason he chose to revert to it could have been disapproval
of the course Caesar was taking—or seemed likely to take.[12]
Cicero's able and likeable friend Caelius Rufus took Caesar's
side in the Civil War, but before long he died leading a
movement against Caesar's measures. And the assassins of
Caesar the Dictator numbered many of his own officers and
lieutenants in their ranks.

Cicero frequently claimed to speak for the *ordo equester*, the
financial interests and the propertied classes of Italy, for men

[12] Syme, *JRS* 28 (1938), 113 ff. (But see Last, *Gnomon* 22 (1950), 361–2).

of moderation in general. They respected him, but he had no sort of reliable control over their votes. The optimates had something approaching a leader as long as Catulus was alive, but when he died in the critical year of 60 no other man came forward to command a comparable influence. Cato, for all his youth and sometimes insufferable stuffiness, could on occasion stampede the optimates (usually, so Cicero sadly thought, in quite the wrong direction), but that was all. The optimates, as a group, were seriously handicapped in the fifties by this lack of central control and co-ordination. It may be that the coalition of Pompey, Crassus, and Caesar that we call the 'First Triumvirate' was unbeatable (though one may doubt it); even so, they could at least have been given a stiffer fight if only their opponents had shown more cohesion and purpose. But they were riven by intestinal feuds and suspicions; Cicero wrote ruefully to his friend Spinther in July 56, referring to the 'Triumvirate': 'Their strength lies in their resources, their armies, their sheer power. Yet it seems to me that the stupidity and vacillation of their opponents have presented them with superiority in *auctoritas* as well.'[13] Unlike their optimate opponents, Pompey, Crassus, Caesar, and their associates were well organized; they adapted themselves readily to changes of circumstances; they knew where they were going.

Finally, a brief word about legislation. Strictly speaking, senatorial decrees were generally confined to the executive sphere, and constituted directions to the competent magistrates or pro-magistrates which the latter put into effect. A *senatus consultum* could not override, and could itself be overridden by, a law of the people. In the last century of the Republic, the people were often encouraged to make this ultimate control effective, but inevitably routine administration was left to senate and magistrates. If vetoed by a tribune, a *senatus consultum* could still be recorded as an *auctoritas*, lacking binding force but an authoritative declar-

[13] *ad famm.* 1.7.10.

ation of the Senate's opinion. Normally legislation was carried in the tribal assemblies, either of the *populus Romanus* or of the *plebs Romana*. The *plebs* was simply the *populus* minus its patrician members; in Cicero's time there was only a handful of patricians left, so that for all practical purposes the people who attended the tribal assembly of the *populus*, *comitia tributa*, were the same as those who attended the tribal assembly of the *plebs*, *concilium plebis*. (In non-technical language *plebs* usually denoted the poorer citizens of the capital.) The important difference between the two assemblies was that the presiding officers of the former were the consuls and praetors, and of the latter the tribunes of the plebs. Hence the plebeian assembly (which elected the *tribuni plebis*) tended to be the assembly where reform legislation was introduced and carried, since it was easier to find aspiring politicians at the early tribunician stage of the *cursus honorum* ready to act in this way than to expect such an initiative from settled and established and noble-dominated praetors and consuls. The tribunes were, of course, also very important in that they had the power of veto (*intercessio*) over all legislative proposals, nearly all *senatus consulta*, and many executive actions; their obstructive power was therefore of great use to more powerful and senior politicians. Consuls and praetors themselves were elected by the centuriate assembly, with its heavy weighting in favour of the richest citizens; obviously the sort of man who might find favour with the more egalitarian plebeian assembly was not necessarily the sort of man who would win the suffrage of the wealthier, more conservative, less dissatisfied voters who dominated the *comitia centuriata*.[14] And we must never forget

---

[14] For a full treatment, see L. R. Taylor, *Roman Voting Assemblies*. The centuriate assembly was a survival from the earlier military organization of Rome, and so constituted that the number of centuries assigned to the wealthiest citizens was out of all proportion to their numbers. The 'tribes' were effectively geographical divisions. Four of them were urban, the remaining thirty-one rural, and a rural tribe might be represented in a number of scattered districts. The tribe voted as one unit; hence the mass of the proletarian inhabitants of the capital, confined to the four urban tribes, could by their votes carry very little weight among the assembly of thirty-five tribes. Much energy was from time to

that, although from the eighties onwards all freeborn inhabitants of the peninsular south of the Po were Roman
citizens, most of them were effectively disfranchised because
they could not attend the assemblies which met in the capital;
they had neither the time nor the money for the journey,
unless they were shipped to Rome by wealthy patrons to
vote in their interests. In some respects, the rural proletarians
gained representation only as professional soldiers in the
legions which came increasingly to hold the key to the political situation. And not merely the proletarians, for many
ambitious young Italians might see in service as officers under
men like Caesar and Pompey their best hope of political
advancement in face of the entrenched interest of the
'establishment'.

time expended by radical politicians in trying to get their supporters registered
in a rural tribe, where an individual vote carried more weight because for
obvious reasons fewer of the country inhabitants were present at assemblies
than those who lived in or near Rome.

III

'DISERTISSIME ROMULI NEPOTUM'

> Disertissime Romuli nepotum,
> Quot sunt quotque fuere, Marce Tulli,
> Quotque post aliis erunt in annis

CATULLUS' compliment[1] was graceful, but not startling. Cicero's primacy in the spoken word had been firmly established and acknowledged for many years before Catullus wrote his little poem, ever since the delivery and publication of the speeches against Verres.

In 71, the return of Pompey from Spain and the success of Crassus against Spartacus ushered in the penultimate act of the Republic's history. The armies of the two generals were anything but devoted to the Sullan establishment. The commanders themselves were flexible and ambitious. They could have been prevented from dominating the political situation only by mutual disagreement; but, despite their deep personal antipathy, the two men were prepared to co-operate. Their joint consulship in 70 found them presiding over the dismantling of the Sullan fortress of the oligarchs. The widest breach was made when the tribunes regained their unfettered right to initiate legislation. The reform of the courts was left to the praetor Cotta. These two reforms were all that was needed to cripple the Sullan establishment—the rest of Sulla's arrangements were essentially trimmings. Sulla had reinforced and restored to the Senate, and to the nobles who dominated it, that control of legislation and of judicial processes which it

---

[1] Catullus *Carmen* 49. Some see irony here, but I do not. (See Fordyce's note, ad loc.)

had enjoyed in the years before the Gracchi. Now, scarcely ten years later, it was all gone again.[2]

After his victory in 82, Sulla had handed over the courts, now organized by him into a comprehensive system, to *judices* drawn from the Senate. Cotta's law produced the compromise which lasted for the rest of the life of the Republic under which the Senate provided one third of the *judices*, the *equites* a second third, the remainder being drawn from the *tribuni aerarii*. (We do not know just what was the point of introducing this third element, but for all practical purposes we can identify it with the equestrian interest.[3]) How far Pompey and Crassus were personally responsible for this law cannot be ascertained with precision. They themselves carried the law to restore legislative freedom to tribunes, and Pompey was to reap a rich harvest from it in the shape of the two tribunician laws which gave him first the pirate command in 67 and then the charge of the Mithridatic War in 66. Neither of these appointments could he have got from the Senate, and both of them were supported by the equestrian interest as well as by the people at large. Pompey was ambitious, and also immensely capable; he did not mean that his unquestionably great abilities should be held back from being exercised by the jealousy and suspicion of a clique of old-fashioned oligarchs. Whether or not he foresaw the development of the extreme tribunician techniques is neither here nor there; we do not know, and in any case as a practical politician he must have directed his gaze to the needs of the moment and the close future. He hoped and expected to be accepted as the leader of the reformist elements and to profit therefrom. As consul-designate in 71 he had publicly committed himself to work for judicial reform.[4] That both he and Crassus were pleased to see the *equites* accommodated by Cotta's bill goes without saying. Their support and goodwill must have been invaluable.

[2] I cannot accept Sherwin-White's thesis (*JRS* 46 (1956), 5–8) that the military forces under Pompey's command were not an important factor, or that the damage to the Sullan arrangements was not vital.

[3] See chapter II, p. 36, note 11.

[4] *Verr.* I.45.

Certainly Cicero played a large part in the affair. It is there for all to read. That few do so, at any rate *in toto*, is not surprising. The *Orationes in Verrem* occupy almost all of the very fat third volume of the Oxford Text of his speeches. The *Verrines* (to give them their convenient short title) were a political manifesto on a gigantic scale. The variety and importance of the material they contain, the range of subjects they touch on, are dazzling. The speeches themselves were a historical event. They boosted Cicero into the foremost place among the advocates of his day, both at the bar and in politics. For the *Verrines* were more than speeches composed for the prosecution of a corrupt provincial governor; in attacking Verres Cicero put in the dock alongside him the whole system of government which had made possible the complex and far-spreading evils for which Verres had been responsible, and for which he had counted on not being made answerable. By the publication of the whole set of speeches, including those parts which were not delivered to the court, he produced a detailed and overwhelming justification for the cause of moderate administrative and constitutional reform.

The dominant motif of the whole prosecution appears already prominently in the *actio prima*, the first part of the process and the only part actually delivered: 'In this trial you, the *judices*, will be sitting in judgement on the accused; but you yourselves will be on trial before the Roman People.'[5] Sulla's judiciary law still stood, the court was manned by members of the Senate. If Verres is acquitted, it will stand as another scandalous example of senatorial corruption, and public opinion will cry out for the abolition of senatorial *judices*, and with them of all senatorial influence in judicial matters.

The *Verrines* themselves, with the help of some ancient commentators on Cicero, make it possible for us to establish the order of events with confidence:[6]

5 Verr. I.47.
6 For the dates and facts which follow, see *Verr*. I.30–31; II.i.16; II.v.177 ff., and the scholiasts in Stangl's edition pp. 185–6, 205–7, 212, 223.

End of 71: Verres returns to Rome from Sicily, and is accused by the Sicilians of extortion. Hortensius, Rome's leading advocate and a candidate for the consulship of 69, is retained to lead for the defence.

Early 70: Cicero, a candidate for the aedileship, accepts the invitation of the Sicilians to lead for the prosecution. Quintus Caecilius Niger, a former quaestor under Verres, also applies to be recognized as prosecutor, undoubtedly in order to collude with the defence. Cicero addresses the court to establish his claim (the *divinatio in Q. Caecilium*), and the presiding praetor, Manius Acilius Glabrio, son of an old colleague of Gaius Gracchus, decides in Cicero's favour and recognizes him as prosecutor.

There followed Cicero's fifty-day trip to Sicily to collect evidence. He had asked for 110 days, but he was in a hurry, because he wanted to get the trial over before 16 August, when a series of festivals began and marked the start of what was virtually a judicial vacation term.

27 July 70: Hortensius elected consul for 69 with a sweeping majority. The other consulship falls to Quintus Metellus, ally and backer of Verres. Curio, catching sight of Verres in the crowd, and taking the result of the elections as tantamount to acquittal for Verres, rushes up to him, flings his arms around him, and tells him to cast away all care. 'Here are to-day's election results: Verres acquitted'—*Renuntio tibi te hodiernis comitiis esse absolutum.*[7]

Soon after: *Illis ipsis diebus*, Marcus Metellus, praetor-elect for 69, is assigned by lot the presidency of the extortion court for 69. Verres was so overjoyed that he sent his sons straight home to tell his wife the news.[8]

5 August 70: The trial begins, and Cicero delivers the *actio prima*. Verres abandons his defence, and leaves Rome.

14 August 70: Verres condemned by default.

September 70: Cotta's jury-law passed.

[7] *Verr.* I.19.   [8] *Verr.* I.21. One is bound to suspect manipulation of the lot.

On examination, it can be seen that Cicero was working to a desperately tight schedule. Even when he had halved the time allotted to him to gather his evidence and witnesses, he had just ten days in which to get Verres condemned. Had this not been done by 16 August, the close-season would have been on him and the case must have dragged on into the next year, 69. Delaying moves were not lacking, and a man of Hortensius' vast experience knew well how to use them. In 69, the Verres group would have been in a formidably strong position: Hortensius, armed with the immense prestige, influence, and patronage of a consul, leading for the defence; Verres' patron Quintus Metellus his colleague as consul; Quintus' brother Marcus president of the court; and yet another brother, Lucius, governor of Sicily.

All through the *divinatio in Caecilium* and the *Verrines* Cicero harps on the consequences if Verres is acquitted. In the earlier speech, alongside a mention of those 'who want the courts to remain in the Senate's hands', Cicero attests an increasing demand to remove the senators and replace them by 'another order'.[9] It was the senatorial courts themselves by their corruption and irresponsibility who were to blame for the agitation for the restoration of tribunician power: the staunch optimate Quintus Catulus had admitted as much in the Senate.[10] The *judices* are adjured that if they do not conduct themselves correctly 'people will no longer be thinking of looking for other men better qualified from the Senate but for another class of men altogether to man their courts.'[11] And, at the very end of the Verrines, Cicero returns to the same theme in his peroration (not actually delivered to the court):

Now the Roman people are casting about for a new breed of men, a new class of men, to serve in the courts. A law has just been promulgated to provide new courts and new *judices* for the courts. This law has not been promulgated by the man in whose name it stands when you see it posted up. It is Verres who has promulgated it—it is Verres who by the hopes he reposes in you and the confidence he places in you has been responsible for the drafting and publishing of this law.[12]

9 *div. in Q. Caec.* 9. 11 *Verr.* I.49.
10 *Verr.* I.44 12 *Verr.* II.v.177.

When it had looked as if the elections might result in Verres' salvation, a bill was announced to hand over the courts to the *equites* lock, stock and barrel. The final version of Cotta's law was less extreme. But by then Verres had conceded defeat. No doubt his backers had urged him to, in order to salvage something from the wreck: to try to save Verres now could mean political bankruptcy.

Cicero's success owed much to his remarkable speed and flexibility. Failing to get their collusive prosecutor accepted by the court, Verres and his friends initiated a prosecution on the same charge of extortion against a former governor of Achaea[13]. They meant to bring their own prosecution on more quickly and without detailed preparation; they were not concerned to secure a conviction, only to occupy the ground before Cicero was ready to open against Verres. The Verres case would thus be pushed lower down the court calendar, in effect into the year 69. This move Cicero defeated by halving the time allotted to him to prepare his case, assemble his witnesses, and collect and digest his evidence—a superhuman feat of application and resource when one reflects on the distances involved and the mass of material he was dealing with, even allowing good measure to the experience and goodwill he had accumulated while serving as quaestor at Lilybaeum a few years earlier. The upshot was that he took the defence off balance, and was ready to go into court long before they had counted on his being able to and before they were ready with their own delaying prosecution.

Flexibility was also displayed in the presentation of the case. The normal practice was for the prosecution to open with a long formal address, which was answered at length by the defence; then witnesses were called, questioned, cross-questioned; finally each side again addressed the court before the verdict was finally delivered. For all his speed, this would simply have taken too long for Cicero to hope to get the case over in time to avoid the recess period. So with the permission of the court (and it is highly unlikely that this permission would have been forthcoming if Metellus had

[13] *Verr.* I.6; Stangl, p. 207.

been presiding in place of the more sympathetic Glabrio) instead of delivering the customary formal opening address and then giving way to Hortensius, Cicero moved straight from a comparatively short introduction to summon his witnesses and elicit and comment on their evidence. Hortensius was forced willy-nilly to follow along in this examination, so that from the very beginning Cicero pounded away with a devastating weight of evidence and witness, pitilessly shattering the weakness of the defence without allowing Hortensius the chance to filibuster time away. Once the witnesses had been examined Verres stood unarguably guilty as charged. The idea of wasting time by delaying tactics was futile. Public opinion would never tolerate an acquittal now. But, had the evidence and witnesses not been produced so early, they would have had to wait over into the next year, with Hortensius now consul and able to use his authority to obstruct or intimidate; with a (to the defence) complaisant president of the court; and with all sorts of obstruction and intimidation and influence at work in the witnesses' native home of Sicily.

Speed and flexibility: these were not sufficient causes, only necessary causes. More was needed if Cicero was to win; and that more was forthcoming. Relentless industry in preparing the case, superb clarity of exposition, complete mastery of a bewildering maze of detail, and all crowned by all the arts of public persuasion—cajolery, irony, sarcasm, the sly hint, the rolling thunder of justified reprobation, the neat joke neatly inserted, sad gravity and grave horror, often just the sheer music of the spoken word: these too were needed, and were called into service in a wealth which dazzled contemporary Rome. Boredom could easily set in with so long a catalogue of crimes to tell. It was kept at bay by a subtle variation of pace and superb narrative skill. To give examples could occupy pages. Let one stand for all. Cicero has just run through a list of the art treasures which Verres had looted, piling them up remorselessly item by item, keeping tedium at bay by a disingenuous but well-acted pretence of being himself an ordinary man in the street none too well versed in such aesthetic matters. Then, to lower the temperature and raise a chuckle: 'And what about the poor guides who used to make a living by showing people round the sights of Syracuse?'— We expect to hear that they are out of a job, but no: 'They have had to change their *modus operandi*. Once they showed people where all the art treasures were; now they show them where everything used to be before Verres made off with it.' The expected ripple of laughter—and the swift return to sobriety: 'But seriously, gentlemen, these are not joking matters. Holy shrines have been pillaged . . .', and so away again on a new note. It is all so deftly done, no cobbled stitch protrudes to mar the smooth fabric of the whole cloth.[14]

The verbal examination of the witnesses has not been preserved. It was too ragged and bitty for Cicero to regard it as worth publishing. It must have been first-class value, to judge by the examples of Cicero's wit and speed in repartee which have survived. But such things are very fragile and ephemeral. Quick retorts and *bon mots* depend on atmosphere and mood, on mien, delivery, and timing; cold print can lame them cruelly. A good deal of the witness examination is, however, obviously imbedded in discursive form in the five long sections of the *actio secunda*. Here Cicero maintains the fiction that Verres is still in the dock: he was not going to be cheated of the reward of his immense labours just because the defence had thrown up the case. The speeches were published and Cicero's reputation made, both as Rome's leading public speaker and as a forceful and fearless opponent of corruption.

His primacy was made all the more incontestable by the eclipse of Hortensius, whose consulship in 69 seems to have represented for him the crown of his achievement. According to Cicero, seeing that none of the consulars were in his own class as orators and pleaders, and tending to look down on speakers of lower rank, he began to ease up. 'It was like the fading of the colour from an old picture, so gradual that people did not notice it, only the expert and discriminating

[14] *Verr*. II.iv.132. This section was not, of course, actually delivered to the court.

ritic could spot it. But as time went on the deterioration got
verywhere worse; above all he began to stumble and lose
is pace and his smooth flow. He seemed to grow less and less
ke his old self every day.' Then with Cicero's consulship
n 63 he pulled himself together again. Cicero was now his
qual in rank; he was not going to have him his superior as
n orator. 'So for the next twelve years we found ourselves
ngaged in all the biggest cases, always on the friendliest
f terms. I always held him my master, he held me his.'[15]
Hortensius died in 50, at the age of sixty-three, having been
n court only a few days before. So he missed the death of the
Republic as he and Cicero knew it. Cicero was not to be so
ucky. Nor was the other chief party to the case: in 43, Verres
imself was proscribed and killed—Antony was said to have
coveted the works of art he had stolen in Sicily and carried
off with him into exile.

In the year after his Verrine triumph Cicero was engaged
n another *repetundae* trial—this time for the defence. His
handling of this case (the *pro Fonteio*) presents an interesting
and unhappy contrast. Fonteius had been governor of the
province of Gallia Transalpina (Provence) in the mid-
seventies. At his trial he was supported by all the Roman
businessmen operating in the province. Verres had made the
mistake of plundering Romans and provincials alike: not so
Fonteius. Cicero was able to brush the accusers aside with
scorn as mere natives, and ask for an acquittal almost on that
ground alone:[16]

If we will just look at the individuals concerned—and that surely ought
to count most in weighing up a witness—can any Gaul however respectable be compared, I will not say with the leading men of our own
country, but even with the humblest citizen of Rome? Does Indutio-
marus really *know* what it is to give evidence? When he stands before this
court, does that same awe which touches each one of us touch him?

It is consistent hitting below the belt, and not pretty to
watch. But the new judicial arrangements of 70 left plenty of
room for honour among thieves. A governor who did well by
the Roman men of business in his province, riding them with

---

[15] *Brutus* 320, 323-4.   [16] *pro Font.* 21 ff.

5—C.

a loose rein and closing a prudent eye to their misdemeanours
had little to fear. The equestrian order would look on
him with favour, and their representatives with their two
thirds majority on the courts would mirror this goodwill in
their verdicts; life was certainly made easier for governors
who preferred personal gain or a quiet life to the honourable
and conscientious discharge of their duties, and correspond
ingly difficult for governors who tried to protect the pro
vincials from the rapacity of Roman financiers and tax
farmers. In the *pro Fonteio* Cicero is assisting that sinister
aspect of the *concordia ordinum* which he so strongly favoured
throughout his political career. His letters to his brother
Quintus[17] when Quintus was governor of the province of
Asia (a fine governor from the natives' point of view, but
he got into bad odour with the Roman business interests
there) and his violent attacks in the mid-fifties on Gabinius
administration of Syria[18] make it clear that he perfectly
understood (regardless of whether he *approved* of it) the real
nature of the bargain between the two orders. As we shall
see, there was much about equestrian activities that pained
him. But Cicero was a practical politician, and he was
convinced that unless the *equites* stood by the Senate it would
be the end of constitutional government: given his premisses
he would not shrink from the consequences that followed.
Equestrian support could only be secured on a *quid pro quo*
basis. Of a *concordia ordinum* they would always ask, What is
in it for us?—and the answer would have to hold out
positive material advantage. Cato for his part, and a number
of reformers on the *popularis* side for theirs, thought otherwise
And they were not the only ones. In 60, an amendment was
voted to a senatorial decree specially to safeguard the interests of certain provincial communities against Roman financiers like Cicero's friend Atticus. Atticus and his friends were
not happy. What were they getting out of this *concordia
ordinum* if the Senate was to pass decrees insisting on the rights

[17] *ad QF* I.1, I.2.
[18] *de prov. cons.* 10 ff. For a favourable view of Gabinius as governor, Syme,
RR, 66–7.

of petty states like Sicyon in central Greece, who had borrowed money and then declined to pay it back and were disputing the right of Roman proconsuls to interfere in matters which they claimed through antique treaties and charters to come within their own jurisdiction? The offending amendment was proposed late in the discussion by young Publius Servilius Vatia Isauricus, later to be a consul in 48 and governor of Achaea under Caesar—evidently a good choice, if he had not changed. Atticus called him a 'copy-cat Cato' (*aemulator Catonis*) and blamed Cato as well. But the amendment was enthusiastically supported by many 'back-bench' senators (*summa pedariorum voluntate*). Cicero is emphatic in dissociating himself and his fellows, ex-consuls and distinguished *boni* in general, from this amendment: *nullius nostrum auctoritate factum*.[19]

In his other extant speech of 69 Cicero is seen in a better light. As a decade earlier in the case of the lady from Arretium, so now in the case of the gentleman of Volaterrae (the *pro Caecina*), he insists on the principle that Roman citizenship once duly given to a community cannot be revoked. Caecina's was an important test case. It was not until after 70 that he had ventured to insist on his rights to the extent of bringing an action at law to secure his succession to certain property under the will of another Volaterran. His anxiety about the view a Roman court might take of his status had caused the delay. Cicero rightly regards it as of paramount importance that the thousands of people, especially in Etruria, who were in the same position as Caecina should be reassured by the court's decision that Sulla's legislation disfranchising their communities was unconstitutional and hence invalid.[20] He had indeed won his case in 79, but evidently not all the magistrates in the intervening period had adopted his view and that of the court in the Arretium case.

This case may serve as a reminder of the differences of opinion among the Romans themselves about the interpretation of their constitution. Standard text-books may lead

---

[19] *ad Att.* I.19.9; II.1.10.   [20] *pro Caec.* 18, 101-4.

the reader to assume that there was at Rome a systematic body of constitutional law, and that our business is simply to discover what it was. But the history of the late Republic teems with disputes between the holders of rival views on fundamental issues. Could tribunes lawfully be deposed? Or re-elected? Did the *imperium* of a consul entitle him in a crisis, and after the passing of the *senatusconsultum ultimum*, to execute men without trial? Who was to decide in any given case whether the acts constituting rebellion had or had not occurred? On such matters, and many others, there was no one accepted answer. Thus the views of Sulla and Cicero on the citizenship were irreconcilable. Of course, under the Republic all men believed in the constitution (or claimed that they did); but they did not all always believe in the same constitution. In the age of Cicero's maturity we can discern two contrasting views of the constitution in active and violent co-existence. Cicero is found in his early years subscribing to the *popularis* view. In his consulship and later he did much to justify the optimate view. It says much for his powers of persuasion, and the greater volume of his later literary production that has survived, that the text-books give so much prominence to the optimate view and lay so little stress on the coherent and often respectable constitutional theory that lay behind the legislative activities of tribunes like Cornelius and Gabinius in 67 or Clodius in 58.

The two years following the reforms of 70 were fairly quiet at Rome. In Asia Lucullus was making steady headway against Mithridates, but manoeuvres were being begun to edge him out. In 69 Caesar became a quaestor and so entered the Senate, and it was probably in 68 that Quintus Cicero attained the same dignity. Marcus Cicero himself had his eyes fixed on the next rung of his ladder, the praetorship, for which he would be eligible in 66. Our knowledge of Roman politics becomes increasingly richer. Not only do we have Cicero's speeches, and the earliest letters in his extant correspondence; there are also later historians like Dio and Appian and biographers like Plutarch and Suetonius, who were able to draw on the very full sources available for this period, and the invaluable if fragmentary commentaries of Asconius on five of Cicero's speeches, compiled in Nero's reign. The now free tribunate was once more a vital factor, and in 67 the *populares* could count on two active and tough tribunes in Gaius Cornelius and Aulus Gabinius. The party-machine organized by Catulus and his friends went to unprecedented lengths in developing a system of bribery and influence which recalls the heyday of the old Tammany Hall in New York. The task of covering the electorate was a colossal one, and its agents, known as *divisores*, were legion. (The *Commentariolum Petitionis* of Quintus Cicero,[21] a sort of electoral vade-mecum which he addressed to his brother early in 64, gives a very good idea of the complexity of it all.) In 67 one of the chief aims of the reformers was understandably to diminish the optimate power of bribery. But bribery is a game which any number can play; and Crassus, with his immense wealth, played it with immense verve both in the courts and at elections, backing promising politicians like Catiline and Caesar and Clodius, none of them at all acceptable to the *boni*.

Beyond the electoral struggles, however, there was always the chance that the whole balance could be thrown out of true by the grant to one prominent man of special powers to meet an emergency (or what was alleged to be one), or by the setting up of special commissions on the pattern of the Gracchan agrarian commission, entrusting a board of men with wide powers and discretion in important spheres for a period of years. One of the major reasons for the intensity of the electoral struggles was the optimate fear that if ever the *populares* won a monopoly of the tribunate with two friendly consuls, they would probably carry legislation so

---

[21] The authenticity of the *Commentariolum* is disputed. For the most recent contributions to an old controversy, see (against) Henderson, *JRS* 40 (1950), 8 ff. and Nisbet, *JRS* 51 (1961), 84 ff; (for) Balsdon, *CQ* 57 (1963), 242 ff. I incline to follow Balsdon in accepting the work as genuine. However, it is generally agreed that, even if not genuine, its author was excellently informed about the political machinery and practices of the period; hence the *Commentariolum* can be used as a reliable source for these purposes.

far-reaching in either or both of these directions that the old governing machine would be sidetracked.

It was in 67 that Pompey secured his Mediterranean-wide command to exterminate piracy. Pompey's incredibly swift success was not only astounding in itself but all the more an advertisement for centralized control and extraordinary commands in its contrast with the helplessness and inefficiency of the government in the preceding years. Pompey's merciful and sensible arrangements for the settlement of the pirates as peaceful citizens was not the least admirable part of the business. His settlement of Spain earlier, and later of the East, were similar triumphs of good sense, patient attention to detail, and humanity. The Pompey of these great works of constructive statesmanship was a very different Pompey from the *adulescentulus carnufex*,[22] the 'young butcher' who had ruthlessly killed his Marian prisoners, and Marcus Brutus too, after promising them their lives. The East remained devoted to Pompey's cause not only in the Civil War with Caesar but later too in the struggle of Brutus and Cassius against Antony and Octavian. And Caesar himself admitted that his own victories during eight years in Gaul had done little to shake the loyalty of the neighbouring Spaniards to Pompey.[23]

Pompey won his command against the pirates as the candidate of what were still substantially the same forces as had provided the opposition in the post-Sullan decade and seen the triumph of reform in 70. Crassus, Pompey's most serious rival in the sixties, did not openly oppose Gabinius' bill; but he was notoriously jealous of Pompey's success, and we may suspect his influence behind the gesture of the tribune Lucius Roscius Otho who raised two fingers when the shouts of the crowd made his speech against the bill inaudible by way of indicating that Pompey should be given a colleague.[24] Another tribune, Lucius Trebellius, insisted on interposing his veto; only over his dead body should the command go to Pompey. Without hesitating, Gabinius invoked the full Gracchan rigour of the doctrine that the people was sover-

---

[22] Val. Max. 6.2.8.   [23] Caesar *BC* 2.18.7.   [24] Plutarch *Pompey* 25.

eign, adopting the tactic of Tiberius Gracchus against his obstructive colleague Octavius in 133. He put it to the assembly that Trebellius be deposed from his office. Seventeen of the thirty-five tribes having voted Yes to the motion, with only one more needed to make it effective, Trebellius withdrew his veto.[25] Beside the consul Piso and the tribune Trebellius, Catulus and Hortensius were the most serious avowed opponents of Pompey's appointment. Gabinius is said at one time even to have thought of passing a bill to depose Piso, but was restrained by Pompey himself. One way and another, we have here the highwater mark of Greek democratic theory in Roman politics.

Important though it was, Gabinius' Pirate Law does not exhaust the political interest of this year. Gabinius' other legislation, together with that of his fellow-tribune Cornelius, deserves close attention.[26] Another measure due to Gabinius forbade the courts at Rome to take cognizance of loans made to provincials at Rome.[27] The exact scope of the law is uncertain, but probably its main aim was to prevent bribery of senators by agents from the provinces by making it hard for the latter to put their hands on ready money; it seems naturally to be connected with another *lex Gabinia* which bound the Senate to turn its attention to provincial embassies during the second month of the year.

Gabinius' attachment to Pompey was so close that we must see something of Pompey in all this. It looks as if from 70 down to his return from the East in 62 Pompey wanted to be regarded as the champion of the party of reform. He was away from Rome from his appointment against the Pirates until the end of 62, so we must beware of attributing to him any detailed control or supervision of affairs at Rome, communications being what they were—and as we shall see this absence was to cost him dear when other men began to play the *popularis* game for themselves. But of his general position there can be no doubt.

[25] Asconius 72C.
[26] Asconius 57–81C. For a detailed study, Macdonald, *CQ* 23 (1929), 196 ff.
[27] Below, p. 240.

Nor can there by much doubt about the position of Gabinius' colleague Gaius Cornelius. Here we can only indicate the scope of his legislation, and emphasize its great interest. Above all we should be aware of the theory implied in it, a strictly constitutional theory but with a non-optimate point of view—the same theory as that on which Caesar based his objections in 63 to Cicero's proposal to execute the arrested conspirators, the same theory as that which lay behind Labienus' demonstration in the Rabirius case in the same year and behind the legislation of Clodius as tribune in 58.

One of Cornelius' four known proposals—it was blocked by the Senate—was complementary to Gabinius' law about lending money to provincials. Its object was 'that no one should provide funds for the embassies of foreign nations'. And the other three proposals were all designed to insist not on changing existing institutions but on their proper working. One (*de jurisdictione*) required praetors (probably not merely those at Rome but provincial governors as well) not to vary the terms of their initially published edicts in giving justice. Another (*de ambitu*) insisted on an extreme penalty for persons convicted of electoral bribery—they were to be prohibited permanently from standing for office, not just for a period of ten years as under Sulla's ordinance. It was in this form, and after a severe struggle, that the proposal was steered through by the consul Piso. Cornelius' original bill had included the infliction of penalties on the *divisores* (the bribery agents) also; but this had been successfully resisted by Piso and the *boni*, so that, while individual candidates might suffer, the bribery machine itself was left intact. Thirdly, there was a law (*de privilegiis*) whereby private bills exempting individuals from the laws could be passed by the Senate only at meetings attended by a quorum of 200. All these measures have their character stamped clearly on their faces.

Besides these legislative initiatives, we catch sight in 67 of a political manoeuvre which provides a foretaste of the part to be played by Publius Clodius in the next dozen or so years. Lucullus' command in Asia was sabotaged to clear the way for Pompey. His successor had indeed been appointed the previous year by the Senate itself, apparently on the intelligence that Lucullus had overstretched himself by trying to conquer Armenia while holding on to Pontus with only 6,000 men under his legate Triarius. The task of sapping the loyalty of Lucullus' troops was also begun in 68—and by his own brother-in-law Clodius, who was serving on his staff. Amongst Lucullus' soldiers were two war-weary legions originally recruited by Valerius Flaccus back in 87. They had been in the East ever since, under Fimbria, under Sulla, under Sulla's successors. Their Marian origins and their long service made them the natural focus of discontent in the army; and Clodius' work on the spot was aided and abetted in 67 by Gabinius at Rome, who passed a bill insisting on the right of these veteran legions to discharge after their twenty years of service.

These activities need to be noticed here because it is against this backdrop that we must place Cicero at this time. In 70 he had ranged himself publicly on the side of the forces of reform. In 65 he undertook the defence of Cornelius when he was charged with offences in connection with his tribunate, with men like Catulus, Hortensius, Metellus Pius, and Lucullus giving evidence against him. During his speech Cicero referred to Gabinius' move to depose his obstructive colleague Trebellius, and he made perfectly plain his approval and support of this extreme action: 'with the safety of the people of Rome at stake and the happiness and freedom of the whole world, Gabinius had rightly refused to allow the voice of a lone tribune to drown the demands of his country.'[28] This was *popularis* talk with a vengeance, the sort of thing which (as Quintus emphasized in the *Commentariolum*) won him backing from a wide section of the electorate— his support and advocacy for Pompey, his promised help for the Pompeian tribune Manilius, his defence of Cornelius.[29] But it was what one might call 'responsible' *popularis* talk, the talk of reformers and not of revolutionaries. Behind the activity and oratory of the reforming tribunes of these years and their supporters and sympathizers like Cicero lay

[28] Asconius 72C.   [29] *Commentariolum* 51.

the notion of a cleaned-up refurbished Republic, its grosser abuses checked, the machinery of administration improved, the tight grip of entrenched privilege loosened. But of any major moves to remedy the social and economic ills of Italy we hear nothing. The ideas are Gracchan; the practice is not.

In this same year Cicero grasped the penultimate rung of the ladder of office. He stood for the praetorship, and with gratifying success. He was a new man, without weighty family influence. As aedile in 69 he had given the normal public games, but on no lavish scale.[30] Yet he was returned at the top of the poll for the praetorship of 66. As it happened, the elections in 67 had twice to be abandoned, but not before on each occasion Cicero had been returned at the head of the list by all the centuries. So he was able to boast that he had been three times unanimously elected in first place.[31] It was a remarkable achievement. It had been earned by his skill at the bar, which had won him influential friends and a great reputation as an orator; by his identification of himself with the interests of the powerful equestrian order; by his support for the reforming movement of the early sixties. His speeches had so far been confined to the law-courts. Although the courts were not *horti conclusi* far removed from the passions and prejudices of politics, still it was true that Cicero had not yet—and he was coming up to forty—addressed the people or the Senate directly on a great political issue. To that extent he had avoided public commitment. At bottom he was a man of moderation, of compromise. He had not closed the door on support from members of the ruling oligarchy. They would be prepared to excuse much in Cicero's actions that could be seen to be necessary to a new man who had to make his own way and cull support wherever he could find it. Cicero would not be the first Roman politician to flirt with the *aura popularis* in his early years only to discard her later for a more staid and respectable partner. Conservatives might sense that as praetor or consul he was not the man to threaten the foundations of state and society.

[30] *pro Murena* 40; *de off.* 2.59.　　[31] *pro lege Man.* 2.

At last, as praetor in 66, at the age of forty, Cicero mounted the public platform where he was to achieve a supremacy as undoubted as that which he had won as an advocate, and clinch his claim to be the most effective moulder of public opinion at Rome. In the East, Lucullus had been superseded by Acilius Glabrio, but Glabrio was very slow in assuming his new command. Lucullus' troops were restive and re-calcitrant towards their old commander. Triarius and his men had been isolated and overwhelmed. Much of his kingdom of Pontus was back in Mithridates' hands, and he was once again on the offensive. Glabrio and Marcius Rex, on whom the safety of Asia Minor and the conduct of opera-tions must fall now that Lucullus was going, clearly lacked the prestige, the military virtues, and the special powers that were needed to finish the wily and indestructible Mithridates. Everything cried out for an extraordinary command to be created and given to a general and administrator of the highest quality—and who could that possibly be but Pompey, whose extraordinary command against the pirates the pre-vious year had been attended by a success so swift and so complete that it could scarcely be credited? It would be ingenuous to suppose that this sequence of events was accidental; the ground had been well prepared. The tribune Manilius promulgated the necessary bill, and Cicero stepped forward to lend the measure the full support of his oratorical genius.

Cicero was urged to deliver this speech, the *pro lege Manilia*, amongst other things by a direct appeal to him from the great financial interests with whose affairs he had for some time identified himself.[32] Indeed his main theme was the necessity to make Asia Minor safe for Roman finance and Roman businessmen. Other provinces might pay their way; Asia was rich enough to add jam to Rome's bread-and-butter. And 'where taxes are concerned, it is not simply the arrival of disaster, but the mere threat of disaster that can itself bring ruin. When hostile armies are not far off, flocks are abandoned, fields deserted, seaborne trade dies, even if no

32 Ibid. 4.

invasion actually takes place. So nothing can be recouped from customs dues or tithes or grazing taxes. So it happens that often a whole year's profit can be lost because of just one rumour of danger, one alarm of war.'[33] The interests of the financiers are the interests of Rome; taxes are the sinews of the state. 'So common humanity bids you save a great number of your fellow-countrymen from ruin, and common-sense tells you that the ruin of many citizens cannot but affect the whole state.'[34] Everyone could remember what had happened when Mithridates had first erupted into Roman Asia. The losses there had caused the collapse of the Roman credit market: 'Believe me—you know it yourselves—the Roman money-market, the Roman credit-market, are inextricably interlocked with those Asiatic funds. If they collapse they cannot but bring the Roman market down in the same ruin.'[35]

There was certainly much truth in this. Asia was the richest of Rome's provinces, the importance of the area could not be denied even by opponents of Manilius' bill. And who else but Pompey could be thought of to undertake the task of liberating and securing it? Pompey was the flower of generals all.

Italy is witness to it, Italy, which the conquering Sulla himself conceded owed her liberation to this man's courageous help. Sicily is witness, Sicily, which he rescued from an encircling sea of dangers not by the terrors of war but by the rapidity of his strategy. Africa is witness, steeped in the blood of the multitude of enemies who had overborne her. Gaul is witness, through which he cut a road to Spain for our legions over the bodies of the Gauls. Yet again Italy is our witness, Italy, which hard-pressed by the foul perils of the slave war called him home to her aid, and the very news of his coming brought a respite and a relaxation, and his coming itself an end and a death to the war. And now every coast is witness, all lands, all peoples, all nations, every sea and every gulf and every harbour in the world.[36]

What sort of 'general' allows centurions' commissions to be bought and sold in his army? Everybody knows the gentle-men who take public money voted them for war and put it

33 Ibid. 15.   34 Ibid. 17–18.
35 Ibid. 19.   36 Ibid. 30–1.

to their personal uses. The excesses committed in recent years by Roman generals in Italy make it easy to conjecture what happens abroad: more allied cities have been destroyed by Roman armies in winter quarters than enemy cities by Roman attacks. But Pompey's army is disciplined; public money does not stick to his fingers; his clemency is a byword even among Rome's enemies. As for his administrative powers—the very day he was appointed to the command against the pirates, his name and the confidence it inspired brought the price of corn abruptly down from extreme scarcity levels to a cheapness which could scarcely have been achieved in a bumper season at a time of settled peace.[37]

Cicero's other chief speech of this year of his praetorship was the *pro Cluentio*. Reference has already been made to this speech, one of his forensic masterpieces, in connection with the scandals about judicial corruption in the late seventies.[38] The prosecution now alleged that Cluentius had bribed the court in 74 to bring in a verdict of guilty against his uncle Oppianicus on a charge of murder. This allegation was not the formal charge on which Cluentius stood arraigned in 66 —indeed to the formal charge against his client Cicero devotes only one twentieth of his speech.[39] But the prosecution had a weak case, and chose to stir up the eight-year-old scandal to create prejudice against Cluentius. Cicero now took quite a different line from that which he had followed in the Verrines when he had used the Oppianicus affair to discredit senatorial juries. There are also some interesting remarks in disparagement of the powers of the censors, who had been called back to life by the reformers of 70. Such reflections go a long way towards justifying Clodius' legislation as tribune in 58, whereby the censors were prohibited from (for example) removing members from the senate-roll without due formality of trial.[40] Here at least we can see that Clodius was in tune with the spirit of such

[37] Ibid. 36–44.
[38] Above, p. 17. Cicero later boasted (Quintilian *Inst. Or.* 2.17.1) that he had succeeded at the Cluentius trial in 'pulling the wool over the eyes of the court'.
[39] *pro Cluentio* 160 ff.
[40] Ibid. 117 ff. For Clodius in 58, see Asconius 8C.

constitutional reformers as Cornelius and Gabinius in 67.
In the *pro Cluentio* Cicero is addressing a court composed of
men of property. He is praetor, he has ambitions for the
consulship. Just as in the *pro lege Manilia* he is careful while
opposing the arguments of Hortensius and Catulus to speak
of them with respect,[41] so now he designedly separates himself from those same reformers with whom he had been down
to 70 in open sympathy. Thus although in 66 Cicero still
appears as the champion of the knights and their interests
and a supporter of Pompey, it is as a moderate rather than
an out-and-out *popularis*.

Quite in harmony with such an attitude, we find Cicero
as praetor in his own court *de repetundis* taking a firm line in
the trial of Licinius Macer, the radical tribune of 73. Macer
was now an ex-praetor, and he was relying on the support
of Crassus to win acquittal on a charge of extortion as a
provincial governor (of which province we do not know).
When he found that Crassus' influence with the jury was not
as strong as he had hoped, he committed suicide before the
praetor passed sentence so as to die unconvicted and leave
his property to his son, the poet and orator Licinius Calvus,
who was later to make his mark as the accuser of one of
Cicero's *bêtes noires*, Vatinius. This case marks a stage in the
hostility between Crassus and Cicero which is a constant
feature of the relationship of the two men.[42]

Cicero then was showing himself to be no extreme *popularis*,
but there is still no doubt of his general position as a supporter of moderate reform and of Pompey personally. The
passage of the Manilian bill had been a foregone conclusion.
Pompey now plunged for nearly five years into the huge
job of not only once and for all dealing with Mithridates but
also carrying through a thorough re-organization of the
Roman East. During his absence Cicero was to represent
himself as the spokesman of Pompey and Pompeian supporters and causes at Rome, and thus mine very profitably
this rich vein of political support and influence. In 65, as we

[41] *pro lege Man.* 52–63.
[42] Plutarch *Cicero* 9; Val. Max. 9.12.7; *ad Att.* I.4.2.

saw, he defended Cornelius, the reforming tribune of 67.
The speech itself has not survived, though we have fragments
of it and of Asconius' commentary. It won an accolade from
the critic Quintilian which is worth quoting for its evidence
of the effect of Cicero's oratory on the Romans of his day—
something very difficult for us nowadays to comprehend
amidst the decay of public oratory on the grand scale and the
proliferation of media of communication.

Had Cicero in his defence of Cornelius been content simply to put the
facts before the court in clear unvarnished Latin, would he ever have
succeeded in getting the Roman people to show their admiration not
merely by their cries of acclamation but by actually bursting into applause? Of course not. It was the sublimity and magnificence of his
eloquence, its brilliance and authority, that wrung that thunderous
reception from his listeners. No more would his speech have won such
unprecedented acclaim if it had been of the ordinary everyday kind of
utterance. It is my belief that the audience were unaware of what they
were doing, that their applause was not a matter of deliberate decision
or judgement but that they were spellbound and quite unconscious of
where they were and broke into a spontaneous transport of delight.[43]

Cicero now stood poised for the final run forward to the
consulship. And on the domestic front too life was treating
him kindly. He had married Terentia soon after returning
from his trip to the East in 77. She was not the most self-
effacing of wives nor the softest-tongued, and the marriage
fell a good way short of being idyllic. But she had given
Cicero a daughter, Tullia, on whom he doted; and in 67 he
betrothed her while still a child (as was normal) to Gaius
Calpurnius Piso Frugi, descendant of a distinguished noble
house. In the summer of 65 Terentia gave birth to a son,
called Marcus like his father, to carry on his name and to
inherit the nobility which the consulship would bring. The
boy was born on the very day of the announcement of the
result of the consular elections for 64.[44] Next year it would
be Cicero's name that would be read out by the presiding
magistrate, and Cicero was already immersed in planning
his own candidature.

[43] Quintilian *Inst. Or.* 8.3.3.   [44] *ad Att.* I.2.1.

IV

CONSUL DESIGNATUS

ABOUT the middle of July 65, Cicero sat down to write to Atticus about the consular elections twelve months away:[1]

The position about my candidature is as follows, as far as one can foresee at the moment. Publius Galba is the only one who is actively canvassing. He is getting plain, old-fashioned, unvarnished Noes. The general opinion is that this over-hasty canvass of his has done my own chances no harm, for usually the refusals take the form of saying that there is a commitment to me. So I hope to get some advantage from this when it gets about that my friends are being found to be very numerous. I am thinking of beginning my own canvass just at the time when Cincius tells me your boy will be leaving with this letter, that is at the tribunician elections in the Campus on 17 July. As for my competitors, the certain starters seem to be Galba and Antonius and Quintus Cornificius. I imagine that this will make you either laugh or weep. To make you really clap your hands to your head, there are some who think that Caesonius will be standing too! Aquilius I surmise will not. He has said that he won't and moreover he has pleaded ill-health and urged that monarchy of his which he enjoys in the courts as an excuse for not standing. Catiline will certainly be a competitor, so long as the jury decides that it is night-time at noon. I don't suppose that you will be waiting to hear from me about Aufidius and Palicanus.

Of this year's candidates [Lucius] Caesar is reckoned to be a certainty. The other consulship is judged to lie between Thermus and Silanus. But they are so hard up for friends and reputation that it seems to me not impossible that Turius may slip in. But no one else thinks so, only me. It looks as if it would suit my chances best if Thermus got in with Caesar. None of the other candidates this year looks like being as strong a competitor if he falls over into my year, especially as he is Curator of the Flaminian Road, which will certainly easily be completed by then. I should be pleased to see him tacked on to Caesar as consul now. This, then, is my so far rather vague thinking about my fellow-candidates.

[1] *ad Att.* I.1.

For my part I shall work with might and main to do everything a candidate should do. And since [Cisalpine] Gaul seems likely to weigh heavily in the voting, I may perhaps run along to take up a post on Piso's staff in September, when we get a breather from the courts here in Rome, planning to come back in January. When I have got a clear idea of what the nobles incline to do, I shall write to you again. The rest I hope will be straightforward enough, at any rate so far as the local contestants are concerned. You are not far away so you must answer to me for that other crew, I mean our friend Pompey's. Tell him I shan't be angry with him if he doesn't turn up specially for my election!

Well, there you are, then. But there is something I must ask you to forgive me for. Your uncle, Caecilius, seeing himself defrauded of a large sum of money by Publius Varius, has instituted proceedings against Caninius Satyrus, Varius' cousin, for some property which your uncle alleges has been fraudulently conveyed to him by Varius. All the other creditors are joint plaintiffs, including Lucullus and Publius Scipio and the man they think is likely to be appointed receiver if Satyrus is sold up, Lucius Pontius—but this receiver business is nonsense. Anyway, this is the point: Caecilius has asked me to take the case against Satyrus. Hardly a day goes by without this fellow Satyrus calling on me at my house. Lucius Domitius [Ahenobarbus] is the man he pays most court to, but I come second. Satyrus has been very useful to me and my brother Quintus in our election campaigns. I was very put out because of my friendship not only with Satyrus himself but also with Domitius, on whom above all others my hopes of success rest. I pointed all this out to Caecilius, and at the same time I made it plain that if he were the only party involved in the suit with Satyrus I would have done as he asked; but as things are, in a case which involves all the creditors together, and very influential men into the bargain, men who could easily sustain their common cause without the help of anyone Caecilius might bring in on his own account, it would be reasonable for him (I said) to have a thought for my own commitment and my present delicate position. He seemed to me to take this rather more ungraciously than I might wish or than a gentleman should, and subsequently he quite abandoned the friendly intercourse with me that had begun only a few days earlier.

The letter is worth quoting at some length, because it brings out several interesting points: the relaxed, intimate tone characteristic of Cicero's letters to Atticus; the retailing of current talk and opinion at Rome, and Cicero's own ideas about how things stand and what is likely to happen; the 'band-wagon' feature of Roman elections, the desire of people to join the winning side as news spreads about the likely balance of support a candidate may enjoy; Thermus'

appointment as Curator of the Via Flaminia, an important
trunk-road, and the political advantage this is likely to
bring him—in the way of patronage and influence exerted
in favour of interested parties; the emphasis on the
importance of personal relationships, the need to win friends
and avoid making enemies; the awkwardness that may crop
up if a candidate's obligations pull him in opposite directions
the expectation of Pompey's support and the likelihood of
Catiline joining the starters. Three key-words in the
Roman political dictionary stand out: *amicitia*, *gratia*
officium.

Let us take a closer look at these innocent words, for an
understanding of them is crucial to an understanding of late
Republican politics. *Amicus* and *amicitia* ought to mean
'friend' and 'friendship'; and of course this *is* the meaning
they are designed to convey, to suggest that the important
persons linked by this relationship are bound by genuine
affection and common sentiment and mutual respect untarnished by gross considerations of material gain or political
horse-trading. But '*amicitia* was a weapon of politics, not a
sentiment based on congeniality'.[2] There was a less deceptive
word available, a word used by the spiteful or by those
without illusions: *factio*. We must understand *amicus* to be
equivalent to 'political ally', and *amicitia* to 'political alliance'.

How did a man enter into *amicitia* with others? It would be
wrong to suppose that other than immediately personal
considerations of material profit never entered into it. There
were from time to time great issues on which men might
make up their minds for what were, at any rate consciously,
objective reasons. Had Cicero himself thought only in terms
of immediate personal gain and advantage he would have
accepted with alacrity the tempting bait held out to him by
Caesar in 60 and 59.[3] But Rome was not continuously pre-

[2] Syme, *RR*, 12. The whole of the second chapter of this book is essential
reading. See, too, L. R. Taylor, *Party Politics*, chapters I–III; and Brunt
'Amicitia in the late Roman Republic', *Proc. Camb. Philol. Soc.* 191 (1965), 1–20.
[3] Below, pp. 167 ff.

occupied with great issues. It is difficult to be constantly
reminding ourselves of the narrow limits within which government operated in the ancient world: today hardly any department of life fails to find a paragraph in a party manifesto.
But we have only to go back a hundred years to appreciate
that this was not always so,[4] and that most of history even
under absolute rulers has seen wide tracts of human life and
activity left free for private grazing. Party politics, as practised in Europe and America today, are conspicuous in Rome
largely by their absence. Usually we are spectators of a
scene where ambitious men struggle fiercely for office and
for the fruits of office rather than for the chance to implement particular policies as we understand them. Hence
political alliances were more flexible and fluid than we are
accustomed to. The most obvious sign and guarantee of
amicitia was a marriage arranged between two families, giving
evidence of shared political interests and promise of continuing co-operation: money, influence, and patronage
would be pooled to common advantage. Sulla's marriage
to a Metella, Pompey's to Caesar's daughter Julia, publish
and proclaim the cementing of a new alignment. *Amicitiae*
between one family and another might well be hereditary;
and the converse of *amicitiae*, *inimicitiae*, could also be handed
down from one generation to the next.

Manus manum lavat covered a lot of politics: 'Each hand
washes the other.' And here terms like *gratia* and *officium*
come in. If you appeared for someone in the law-courts, for
instance, that would put him under an obligation to you
(*officium*), give you an account on which you could draw
when need arose, for a loan, for the delivered vote of a tribe
or a century, for a public demonstration of support. Cicero's
exceptional gifts and successes as an advocate were his chief
weapons in the acquiring of *amici* and *gratia*. But *gratia*
(loosely, 'influence' or 'pull') could be gained in any number of ways: by a loan to cover election expenses, or the cost

---

[4] Cf. what G. M. Young wrote of early Victorian England: 'the intermediate
sphere of administration did not exist, because there were hardly any laws to
administer.'

of bribing a court or providing public shows and games or even acquiring a suitably grand house; by delivering support at elections; by 'arranging' a particular vote in the Senate. A provincial governor had the gift of posts on his staff which could offer a young man the chance of profit and experience —Cicero wrote many letters asking for such appointments for friends or acquaintances of his which, if granted, won *gratia* for the governor with Cicero and the young men and their families, while Cicero too acquired *gratia* with the latter. Thus Piso put Cicero under an obligation by making available a post on his staff in Cisalpine Gaul in the latter part of 65 which would help Cicero to consolidate electoral support in that area. Other letters of Cicero's are addressed to provincial governors commending to their good offices certain men of business with interests in their part of the world.

Enough has been said to indicate the general working of these conventions. Imagination will easily supply other examples. The grantor of the favour or service won *gratia* with the beneficiary, who acquired an obligation to reciprocate if occasion arose; he owed an *officium* to his benefactor. The richer a man was, the more votes he could deliver, the weightier his influence with Senate or People or business interests, the greater his official power and prerogatives, the wider his circle of friends and relations, then the more potent was the *gratia* he could exercise, the deeper the reserve of undischarged obligations he could draw on.

But the more intricate the network, the more chances of its getting into a tangle. *Officia* owed to different people might pull a man in different directions. We see how Cicero had to make an unhappy choice between his obligation to Atticus' uncle and the rival and conflicting claims of Satyrus and Domitius Ahenobarbus. Another example of this sort of embarrassment occurred during Cicero's consulship. In the elections held in 63 for the consulships of 62 Lucius Licinius Murena was successful but Cicero's old friend Servius Sulpicius Rufus was not. Sulpicius lost no time in bringing a well-merited charge of electoral corruption against Murena, hoping to unseat him and win for himself the vacant place.

But Cicero had ties with Murena as well. Lucullus was behind Murena, and Hortensius also appeared for the defence along with Cicero. Cicero owed a lot to the *boni* in winning his election, and Hortensius and Lucullus were leading *boni*. To the defence of Murena Cicero brought not only his brilliance as an advocate but the authority of a consul. Understandably, Sulpicius was upset, and in his turn Cicero was put out by the blunt accusation that he was not behaving towards his old friend Sulpicius as a Roman gentleman should.[5]

In his campaign Cicero was anxious 'not merely to keep old supporters but to win new ones as well'. In achieving this object he would be helped 'if it gets about that my friends are being found to be very numerous'. People usually like to be on the winning side. At Roman elections to the consulship in the centuriate assembly one of the centuries of the first property class was chosen by lot to cast its vote first. This *centuria praerogativa* exercised a momentous influence on the subsequent voting. (At Rome each tribe or century cast its vote as a unit, and the vote was announced forthwith. Similarly, in Great Britain up to the beginning of the twentieth century different parts of the country voted at different times, so that the declaration of the poll in the earlier constituencies could influence the voting in the later.) In 54 two of the consular candidates let it be known in advance that they would pay the huge sum of ten million sesterces for the vote of the prerogative century, a price justifiable only by an informed conviction of the influence it would exert.[6]

But before it came actually to the Campus and the voting, much else could be done. Friends and supporters accompanied the candidate from his home to the Forum or the Senate, thereby publicly demonstrating their favour for him. It was good tactics for a candidate to be seen attended by leading politicians and by throngs of lesser supporters; it

[5] *pro Murena* 7–8. On the trial, see below, pp. 121 ff.
[6] *ad QF* II.14.4. On the importance of the prerogative century see also *pro Murena* 38.

might encourage 'floating voters' to swing to him. Me
who delivered their tribes or their centuries in support of
winning candidate would have a future claim on his goo
offices. Hence a tendency to tumble onto a band-wagon as i
became more and more apparent that it was heading for victory

Cicero had no inherited political influence to compare fo
one moment with that which could be deployed by the to
two or three dozen families of the ruling nobility. He had t
cull support wherever he could. Apart from such inherite
connections as we have noticed and the reasonable but no
enormous wealth of his own family, he had acquired a grea
deal of influence with the *equites*, whose wealth and *clientela*
and voting-power were of crucial importance. Partly he ha
done so by regularly championing their interests in the politi
cal field, and so representing himself as the sort of magistrat
of whom they could approve as reliable and right-thinking
In addition he had been very active in the courts in equest
rian cases. The speeches that have come down to us are, o
course, chiefly the big ones. But in the seventies he had mad
frequent routine appearances on behalf of men of financ
and business: in the *Verrines*[7] he points out that he has spen
perhaps the greatest part of his life in cases involving *publicani*
and this did not cease in 70. Strictly, advocates were for
bidden by law to accept fees; but ways could be found to ge
round this. A fat legacy in the will of a grateful client, a loar
that is interest-free and never called in, opportunities to
participate in prospectively lucrative enterprises—all these
were known. But not least valuable to Cicero was the
expectation that his services would be reciprocated in the
shape of electoral support. For example, his successful defence of the *eques* Cluentius in 66 won him not only the support of that rich client but also the goodwill of the numerous
and influential equestrian friends of Cluentius in a number of
important regions of Italy,—Ferentinum, the Marrucini,
Apulian Teanum, Luceria, Bovianum, and Larinum.[8]

The backing of Pompey and the Pompeian interests was
of the first importance. Cicero came out openly in praise of

[7] *Verr.* II.ii.181.   [8] *pro Cluentio* 197; cf. *pro Murena* 24.

Gabinius' forthright action in sweeping aside all obstacles to Pompey's pirate command. His support of the Manilian law giving Pompey the Eastern command missed no opportunity of highlighting the great man's virtues. Later he defended the tribune Cornelius and undertook to defend Manilius (but that case never came to trial). Quintus Cicero wrote late in 65:[9]

You have already won over the urban populace and the enthusiasm of those who dominate the public meetings by your glorification of Pompey, your acceptance of the brief for Manilius, your defence of Cornelius. It remains to bring it about that everyone should know how great is Pompey's goodwill towards you and how splendidly it would suit his plans for you to gain the office which you seek.

He then goes on to urge his brother to miss no opportunity of throwing mud at his fellow-candidates in the shape of allegations of criminal or licentious or corrupt behaviour 'as best fits their respective characters'. But he concludes on a cautionary note: 'Avoid any specific discussion of public policy either in the Senate or at public meetings. Try rather to hold on to the positions you have already won. Let the Senate see you from your past behaviour as a man who will champion its authority. Let the *equites* and all sound men of substance judge you on your past record as a man who is enthusiastic for peace and stability. Let the mass of the people go by the evidence of your speeches in which you have followed a *popularis* line, and look to you as a man who will not be hostile to their interests.'

Cicero's success was not merely remarkable, it was unique. He was not only the first *novus homo*, the first candidate without consular forebears, to win election to the consulship for many years, but, more than that, he was the first *novus homo* in Roman history to win election *suo anno*, i.e. at the earliest date allowed by law.[10] In this more was due to luck than he liked to allow: his competitors were not of the strongest. Above all, he owed an enormous amount to the 'backlash' of support in his favour as it became apparent that his rivals Catiline and Antonius threatened a radical

[9] *Commentariolum* 51–3.   [10] *de leg. agr.* II.3.

attack on the settled pattern of social and economic life. The *boni* and the well-to-do in general rallied behind a candidate they felt they could trust to resist revolutionary schemes of reform, and in the later stages of his campaign he came out publicly more and more strongly as the defender of the established order against the frightening threat of Catiline. But already in July 65, well before any of these developments had begun, he was counting heavily on the support of the *nobilis* Lucius Ahenobarbus, 'on whom above all others my hopes of success rest'.

Ahenobarbus was not merely the head of one of the greatest noble families in Rome, he was immensely rich. Crassus once declared that no man could be accounted really rich unless he could maintain a legion out of his own annual revenues.[11] Ahenobarbus demonstrated his ability to do so in practice. Early in 49, while in charge of the defence of Corfinium, he promised his soldiers grants of land from his own personal estates, just under three acres apiece to each private soldier and proportionately higher amounts for more senior men.[12] The precise number of men involved is disputed, but it was certainly not less than 10,000. Not long afterwards at the siege of Marseilles we find him demanding a flotilla of ships from the Massiliots and filling them with his tenants and agricultural workers whom he had brought along with him in large numbers.[13] Later Cicero was to describe Ahenobarbus as destined for the consulship since the day he was born.[14] He was to prove one of Caesar's bitterest opponents in the fifties. At this time he was in his early thirties, and married to Cato's sister, thus connected with another important power group among the *boni*. His vast wealth, his family connections, and his widespread political influence made his support of incalculable value to Cicero,

[11] Pliny, *NH* 33. 134; *de off.* 1.25; Plutarch *Crassus* 2.

[12] Caesar *BC* 1.17. The reading in the text is uncertain. It could have been as high as ten acres, but this is an improbable figure and the lower is therefore preferable.

[13] Ibid. 1.56.

[14] *ad Att.* IV.8B.2. In 49 Ahenobarbus boasted of his popularity at Rome (*urbana gratia*): Caesar *BC* 3.83.

not to be endangered even by the risk of a coolness with Atticus' uncle.

Atticus himself was summoned home to Rome to lend his immediate aid. He was back by the beginning of 64. When Cicero wrote to him in July 65 he was still far from confident of widespread optimate support. 'I need you here as early as possible. There is a firmly and widely held view about that the noble gentlemen who are your friends are going to oppose my election. I can see that you will be quite invaluable to me in winning them over.'[15] Atticus' talent for keeping in with everybody has already been remarked. His smooth skill would help to reassure doubters of Cicero's essential political soundness. He would also carry great weight with the non-senatorial rich of his own class.[16] That Atticus did his job well we need not doubt. Unfortunately for us, his return to Italy meant that for three years we have no letters from Cicero to him, and so we are deprived of confidential information that would have been of inestimable value.

At this time, July 65, Cicero was considering looking for support in another direction. A little earlier he had displayed a charming unconcern about the outcome of Catiline's impending trial for extortion and the chances of his emerging as a rival candidate: 'Catiline will certainly be a competitor, so long as the jury decides that it is night-time at noon.'[17] He now tells Atticus: 'Just now I am contemplating undertaking the defence of my fellow-candidate Catiline. We have got just the jury we wanted, the prosecution is co-operating splendidly. I hope, if he is acquitted, that he will collaborate with me in the campaign.'[18] There is nothing here to suggest the unspeakable villain of the speeches of 64 to 62. What made the wind shift?

In the elections held in 66 for the consulships of 65 the two men returned were Publius Cornelius Sulla, nephew of

---

[15] *ad Att.* I.2.2.

[16] Many of these were the superiors of senators in wealth; cf. the comment of Lucullus in *de legg.* 3.30.

[17] *ad Att.* I.1.1.

[18] Ibid. I.2.1.

the dictator, and Autronius Paetus. They were promptly charged with electoral corruption, convicted, unseated, and replaced by the previously defeated candidates, Lucius Aurelius Cotta (author of the judiciary law of 70) and Lucius Manlius Torquatus. Catiline himself, back from his praetorian governorship in Africa, tried to be a candidate at the elections (probably at the second set after the disqualification of Sulla and Autronius); but he was held disqualified to stand by the presiding consul, Lucius Volcacius Tullus, either because he was threatened with prosecution for misgovernment in Africa or on the grounds that his application was too late.[19]

The conventional account of what happened next is as follows.[20] Late in 66 a plot was hatched by Sulla, Autronius, Catiline, and a young and impoverished noble called Gnaeus Calpurnius Piso. Its aim was to murder the new consuls when they assumed office on 1 January 65, seize the *fasces*, and hand them over to Autronius and Sulla or (on another version) Autronius and Catiline. Behind this move rumour descried the shadowy figures of Crassus and Caesar. The plot miscarried because the preceding day Catiline was spotted in the Forum carrying a weapon, thus giving the game away. The consuls were given a bodyguard. All discussion of the incident was vetoed by a tribune. Oddly enough, part of the plot had envisaged sending young Piso to take over in Spain, and in due course Piso was sent there—by the Senate.

This is in outline the traditional version of the affair, as we read of it in Sallust and Cicero—though Sallust also notes a second equally abortive *coup* planned for February 65.[21] It

---

[19] The evidence of Asconius (89C) and Sallust (*Cat.* 18) is not consistent. Sallust's account is preferred here, that Catiline was a prospective candidate for the second round of elections but was ruled out because his application was too late. Probably it was a nice legal point; the presiding officer, the consul Volcacius, took advice on the matter. Perhaps it was held that not having given due notice of candidature for the first election Catiline could not now be admitted to the second, and that he was only hoping to seize an unexpected chance to secure immunity from his impending prosecution for *repetundae*.

[20] See, for example, Rice Holmes, *The Roman Republic*, I.233–5.

[21] Sallust *Cat.* 18.6.

cannot be accepted. It involves numerous difficulties which cannot be surmounted.

Far and away the most serious difficulty is this. If in 65 Catiline was widely suspected of (let alone credited with) intimate involvement in an abortive plot aimed at the murder of two consuls and a number of leading senators, how could Cicero for one moment have contemplated not merely defending Catiline in court but also publicly associating with him as a running-mate for the consulship of 63? Yet we know that he did so from his letter of July 65 to Atticus— and this at a time when Cicero was conscious of the need to tread warily, offend nobody, and secure the as yet doubtful support of a number of important *nobiles*. In fact this letter makes it certain that in the middle of 65 no such allegations were widely or seriously entertained about Catiline's part in such a plot.

But that is not all. Catiline was alleged to have plotted to murder the consul Torquatus. Yet when his extortion trial came on in 65, he was supported by Torquatus. That is odd enough in itself. And did Torquatus at the trial make any mention of the alleged plot? It is often said that he did, on the strength of a passage in Cicero's *pro Sulla* delivered in 62.[22] But that passage needs to be read with no less care than went into its composition. 'When Torquatus appeared for Catiline's defence after he had been given information of the conspiracy, *indicavit se audisse aliquid, non credidisse*, he indicated that he had heard something, but had not believed it.' Cicero did not say '*dixit*'—though Torquatus is usually reported to have 'said' that he had heard something—but '*indicavit*'. The use of the vaguer word means that there can be no certainty that Torquatus, or anyone else, did at Catiline's trial refer explicitly to any such allegation.

In any case, why should Torquatus defend his would-be assassin? Cicero can only suggest, lamely, that Torquatus may later have learned the truth of which as consul he had been unaware, or alternatively ascribe his action to '*humanitas*'. But it is far easier to suppose that in the summer of 65

[22] *pro Sulla* 81.

Torquatus knew no more of such allegations than Cicero did.

Surprising, too, is Quintus Cicero's failure to refer to the alleged conspiracy in the *Commentariolum*.[23] He lists the crimes of which Catiline has been guilty: lawlessness, incest with his sister, murderous activities under Sulla, a disgustingly promiscuous private life, association with the dregs of Italy, misgovernment of Africa, an acquittal on the extortion charge as the result of shameless bribery—'he left the courtroom as hard-up as some of the jurors had been when they entered it'. But there is no suggestion that he had recently planned to kill two consuls and carry out a general massacre of leading *boni*.

Two final points. Despite the failure of the alleged plot, Piso none the less was sent to govern Hither Spain. It was an extraordinary appointment in the strict sense of that epithet, since he was only a quaestor and yet was appointed acting-praetor for the purpose, and appointed by the Senate.[24] And the Senate made no inquiry into the supposed plot.

What are we to make of it all? It is easier to say that this or that cannot be true than to set one's finger unerringly on the one correct answer. By their very nature conspiracies are terrible things to unravel. Conspiracies are secret and devious undertakings. If they succeed, we have to rely on the version put out by the winners; if detected and punished,

---

[23] *Commentariolum* 9 ff. As noted earlier (above, p. 53), the authenticity of this work is disputed. Personally I should agree with Rice Holmes (op. cit., I. 451), citing Strachan-Davidson, that this passage is the strongest single argument for authenticity: 'a forger of later times, when detailing a list of Catiline's enormities, would never have omitted the so-called First Conspiracy of 66 B.C. If the the treatise were really written, as it professes to be, at the end of 65 B.C., or quite early in the next year, the omission may easily be explained by the supposition that at that time the myth had not taken shape.'

[24] Sallust *Cat.* 19, confirmed by *ILS* 875. Balsdon has argued (*JRS* 52 (1962), 134–5) that the appointment was not really extraordinary. But none of the scant parallels he cites is cogent. The inscription records that Piso was sent to Spain *ex s(enatus) s(ententia)*, which implies a specific decision by the Senate. Cato's later appointment as *pro quaestore pro praetore* in Crete was unarguably extraordinary. Cyrene, to which Marcellinus was sent as quaestor in 75 or 74, was like Crete relatively unimportant: neither could compare in importance with Hither Spain.

there is always the suspicion of a distortion of evidence. How much worse with a conspiracy that was abandoned before it came to anything; where there was no official enquiry; where none of the alleged ringleaders was examined or cross-questioned! Rome was alive with rumours. Nobody who knew the truth would tell it, but there was any amount of scope for speculation and subsequent vituperation. Suetonius in his biography of Caesar, drawing on named and anti-Caesarian sources, tells a story of the 66/65 conspiracy as a bid by Crassus and Caesar to seize power, a bid which failed because Crassus lost his nerve at the last minute. Suetonius does not so much as mention Catiline.[25] Cicero, for his own purposes in 64/63, made capital out of the affair as part of his crusade against his rival candidate Catiline. It was a free fight; anyone could join in.

Whatever else was true about the affair, we can rely on it that Catiline either was not involved or that, if he was, it was a very different affair from the 'slaughter of optimates' Cicero described. We have already seen some reasons for this. There is also the likelihood that up to summer 65 Catiline was in some sense in sympathy with Pompey. This would not be surprising. Pompey was at the peak of his power and influence, worth courting by an ambitious politician. Cicero, a self-proclaimed Pompeian, certainly seriously contemplated running in joint harness with Catiline for the consulship of 63—this in July 65, the time to which probably he was referring in a passage in the *pro Caelio* when he declares: 'Even I myself, even I was once almost taken in by him [Catiline], at a time when I thought him a loyal citizen, an enthusiastic and firm and reliable friend of all good men; his crimes I never believed until I saw them with my own eyes, never suspected until I ordered his arrest.'[26] As we saw, Cicero contemplated undertaking Catiline's defence in 65— 'we have got just the jury we wanted, the prosecution is co-operating splendidly'. The reliably collusive prosecutor was none other than young Publius Clodius[27]—in a speech ten years later Cicero actually threw the charge *Catilinae*

[25] Suetonius *DJ* 9.   [26] *pro Caelio* 14.   [27] Asconius 9C.

praevaricator in his face,[28] but he was cheerful enough about the prospect at the time. Clodius had not long before taken a leading part in the machinations which led to the replacement of his own brother-in-law Lucullus in the Asian command by Pompey.[29] At the height of the crisis of 63 he served as a volunteer member of Cicero's personal bodyguard.[30] Torquatus himself was married to a wife from Asculum in Picenum, the heart of the Pompeian 'barony' in Central Italy.[31] A Manlius Torquatus, either this same man or a close relative, served as *legatus* to Pompey in the Pirate War in 67.[32] Finally, Catiline was almost certainly a member of the *consilium* of Pompey's father Strabo in 89.[33] Taken together, these pieces of evidence, not individually conclusive, add up to a quite formidable sum. In this group of men in July 65, Catiline, Clodius, Torquatus and Cicero, we may perhaps not rashly discern a 'cell' of politicians of Pompeian connections and sympathies.[34]

The so-called First Catilinarian Conspiracy serves to illustrate that constant aspect of Cicero's writings which confronts the reader with a contrast between the public and published speeches, with their frequent distortion or suppression of unpalatable facts, and the private letters which can so often reveal the unvarnished truth. Whether the contrast justifies the moral opprobrium which it sometimes excites is another matter.

The jury did in the end decide that 'it was night-time at noon', for Catiline was acquitted on the extortion charge. But he did not draw closer to Cicero in a joint canvass. Apart from these two, there were five others competing for the two consulships of 63. Publius Sulpicius Galba was like Catiline

[28] *in Pis.* 23; cf. Asconius 9C.
[29] Evidence cited by Rice Holmes op. cit., I.198.
[30] Plutarch *Cicero* 29.   [31] *pro Sulla* 25.
[32] Broughton, *MRR*, II.151, note 16.

[33] *ILS* 8888 = *ILLRP* 515. We may also note here that Catiline's first wife was a Gratidia—hence another link with Cicero: Sallust *Hist.* 1.45; Syme, *Sallust*, 86.

[34] Add the facts that Piso was known as a bitter personal enemy of Pompey, and that his murder in Spain was alleged to have been the work of Pompeian partisans: Sallust *Cat.* 19; Asconius 92C.

a patrician as well as a *nobilis*. Gaius Antonius (son of the great orator and uncle of Mark Antony) and Lucius Cassius Longinus were also *nobiles*; while the remaining two, Quintus Cornificius and Gaius Licinius Sacerdos, were of very respectable ancestry. Cicero alone came from a non-senatorial family. After giving us these facts, Asconius goes on to say something about the general position:[35]

The rest of Cicero's fellow-candidates comported themselves in an unassuming way. Quintus Cornificius and Galba were regarded as decent and honest men. Sacerdos was perfectly respectable. At the time Cassius was thought to be slow and stupid rather than a villain, although a few months later it came to light that he was involved in the conspiracy of Catiline and had been responsible for the most bloodthirsty suggestions. These four, then, were not strong contenders. But Catiline and Antonius, for all that they had far and away the most disgraceful personal reputations, were nevertheless very powerful. For they had formed a combination to keep Cicero out of a consulship, and were most staunchly assisted in this by Marcus Crassus and Gaius Caesar.

That Crassus was by the latter part of 65 behind Catiline seems certain. Catiline is said to have owed his acquittal in 65 to lavish bribery. He would not have been the first nor the last promising man that Crassus staked. Caesar was already in his debt, and a few years later Publius Clodius was assisted to an acquittal by Crassus' cheque book.[36] Apart from Cicero and Antonius, none of the other candidates for 63 amounted to much. Crassus was very active at this time and associated with sweeping projects for legislation and reform. He needed to work hard to keep in the race with Pompey, who had for some time been making all the running. Crassus' interest in sympathetic consuls is evident. There was a great deal of money being laid out in behalf of the candidature of Catiline and Antonius. It was against this background that shortly before the elections in 64 Cicero delivered his speech *in toga candida*, fragments of which are preserved by Asconius together with his commentary. Following the sentences just quoted, Asconius continues:

So this speech was directed solely against Catiline and Antonius. The reason why Cicero delivered a speech of this nature in the Senate was

[35] Asconius 82–3C.   [36] *Commentariolum* 9 ff; and, for Clodius, see below, p. 160.

that, with unrestrained bribery reaching new heights every day because of the astonishing audacity of these two, the Senate had voted that a new bribery law be effected with severer penalties. This recommendation had been vetoed by the tribune Quintus Mucius Orestinus. It was at this juncture, with the Senate full of indignation at the veto, that Cicero got to his feet and launched an attack on the electoral combination of Catiline and Antonius only a few days before the poll.

Julius Caesar is not so easy to pin down as Crassus. The towering figure of the later giant has cast a long and broad shadow back over the earlier years, and invested the younger man with an importance and solidity and a fixedness of plan and purpose which, despite his unquestioned brilliance and promise, simply cannot be accepted. In 66 Caesar had like Cicero spoken up in support of Pompey's appointment under the *lex Manilia*. In 62 as praetor he was to commit himself to a public line which was, ostensibly, pro-Pompeian. It was Caesar who as consul-designate in 60 set out to reconcile Pompey with Crassus. In these years of the middle and late sixties his association with Crassus did not mean that he could have nothing to do with Pompey. If Caesar's activities were undoubtedly *popularis* in colour, there was much of the *popularis* about Pompey, too. All in all, it is wisest to see the Caesar of these years as a gifted and determined man moving inexorably towards the top, but not irrevocably committed to any particular allegiance. His political tone is indeed reliable and consistent, but there was room for flexibility at a tactical level. Furthermore, we need to remember that Catiline himself, able, determined, unscrupulous, daring, and magnetic, eligible for a consulship in 63 four years before Caesar could reach the same eminence, with a formidable package of reforms waiting for a tough consul to shelter and succour their passage into law, was a man who in 65 and 64 promised quicker returns to a backer. It was by no means to Caesar's long-term disadvantage that Catiline's eclipse and the wreck of the reform programme of 63 left him a clear field in 59.[37]

[37] On Caesar's early career see H. Strasburger, *Caesars Eintritt in die Geschichte*; L. R. Taylor, *Class. Phil.* 36 (1941), 113–32, and *Greece & Rome* 26 (1957), 10–18; Syme, *JRS* 34 (1944), 92–8.

If we are to believe Sallust, Catiline already a few weeks before the elections in 64 took the first definite steps along the road to violent revolution—summoning men to his house, expatiating on the glittering rewards of success, promising abolition of debts, talking of 'weapons' and of 'war'.[38] But Sallust is clearly wrong. Catiline was very much in the hunt for a consulship in 64: in fact he only just missed getting in. Then he was a candidate again in the 63 elections, enjoying powerful support until quite late in the day; until Cicero neutralized him, his colleague Antonius could be expected to help Catiline in the 63 attempt. It was only after two successive defeats at the polls that Catiline, discredited and baffled, abandoned by a backer who saw no further reason to throw good money after bad, and encouraged by the growing social and economic unrest in Rome and Italy, as men saw bright hopes dashed to nothing, moved to 'the inferior and desperate sort of revolution'.[39]

Cicero was committed to a head-on fight with Catiline and Antonius with no holds barred. He launched with great verve into a shamelessly scurrilous attack, on Catiline in particular, in the *in toga candida*, where alongside the small change of scabrous abuse he came out with the flat accusation that Catiline had been involved in a murderous plot in 66/65: 'I pass over that wicked attempt of yours, that day so nearly a day of bitterness and grief for our country, when with your accomplice Gnaeus Piso (to name no other names) you planned to carry out a massacre of the optimates.'[40] It is evident that Cicero has sensed that he is nearly home and dry. The fact that the Senate had voted to take strong action against electoral bribery with particular reference to the activities of Catiline and Antonius indicates the temper of its feeling. It is impossible not to detect a note of confidence in the passages cited from Cicero's speech by Asconius. In particular, his downright reference to the 66/65 affair, before

---

[38] Sallust *Cat*. 17 ff.
[39] For an examination of Sallust's anachronisms, see Syme, *Sallust*, 75–81— whence the phrase in inverted commas is borrowed.
[40] Asconius 92C.

the one body best placed to know just how tenuous the evidence for such a charge must have been, shows that he knew he could carry his audience with him.

We shall soon see just how big a programme of reform was scheduled for the year 63. It presupposes an enormous effort of organization, preparation, and rehearsal in the preceding months, in the discussion and drafting of statutes, arrangements about time-tabling, and the election of suitable men to put it through. As consul-designate, Cicero learned that the tribunes-designate were engaged on drafting an agrarian law; and he implies that all ten were involved. When its proponent, the tribune Rullus, entered office on 10 December 64, the bill was already in its final form and was immediately promulgated.[41] Cicero was certainly not the only man to get wind of all this; and the solidarity of the newly elected board of tribunes makes it reasonable to suppose that there were at the very least strong suspicions that something was brewing before the elections in the middle of 64. This tribunician solidarity was remarkable: with ten tribunes elected each year, the various powerful factions in the state could usually all count on finding supporters among their number. Apart from 63, no other year in the late Republic finds all ten tribunes solidly behind a programme of reform with the exception of 123, when there is no record of any tribunician opposition to Gaius Gracchus. In 133, Tiberius Gracchus' fellow-tribune Octavius stood out against him and had to be deposed as the only way to get round his obstinate veto. And by 122 the opponents of Gaius had sufficiently recovered to confront him in his second tribunate with an able and determined adversary in Livius Drusus. In 67, the year of Gabinius and Cornelius, Roscius Otho and Lucius Trebellius were active in the opposition interest. Thus to have secured what, at any rate to begin with, was apparently a solid board of ten was a remarkable achievement, and no doubt a very costly one as well.[42]

[41] *de leg. agr.* II.11 and 13.

[42] The Law of the Ten Tribunes of 52 was a special case; it was not a reform measure, and Pompey applied strong pressure.

On the first day of 63, when the new consul Cicero summoned the Senate to meet on the Capitol and announced his
opposition to the agrarian bill, the solid front cracked. The
tribune Lucius Caecilius Rufus now announced that he
would use his veto against the bill.[43] Rufus had previously
promulgated a bill to restore the civil rights of condemned
men—including Sulla and Autronius—which Cicero castigated.[44] (He was the half-brother by the same mother of
Publius Sulla, the unseated consul-elect of 66.) But Rufus'
defection was still in the future in mid-64, and many leading
boni must have been gravely exercised over the prospects for
the coming year, especially if Catiline and Antonius should
be elected consuls and cast their protective shield over the
reformers. No doubt Atticus had been performing his
appointed task of bringing the nobles round with his habitual
adroitness. Cicero's past record, his Pompeian connections,
his wooing of the *equites*, all bore their fruit. The actions of
his rivals gave him a superb chopping-block on which to
wield the keen edge of his oratory—in the *in toga candida* he
put aside the rapier in favour of the hatchet. Conservative
opinion swung decisively behind the man who promised
unflinching and unresting opposition to any serious attack
on the *status quo*. Antonius edged Catiline out of a consulship
and into third place. But Cicero was triumphantly declared
elected at the head of the poll, *consul prior* and *suo anno*.

In a speech in 66 Cicero had listed the glittering prizes
that lay at the peak of a successful senatorial career: position,
authority, magnificence at home, reputation and influence
abroad, the bordered toga, the curule chair of office, the
outward pageant, the rods, armies, commands, provinces—
*locus, auctoritas, domi splendor, apud exteras nationes nomen et
gratia, toga praetexta, sella curulis, insignia, fasces, exercitus, imperia, provinciae.*[45] Now all they lay in his lap.

---

[43] *pro Sulla* 65.   [44] Ibid. 62; *de leg. agr.* II.10.   [45] *pro Cluentio* 154.

V

CONSUL

ON 1 JANUARY 63 Cicero inaugurated his consulship with
an attack in the Senate on Rullus' agrarian bill, an attack
pursued in his first public address to the people.[1] He was all
for the people, a true *popularis*, a champion of peace and
order, a watch-dog of the Roman commons who would not
stand by and see unscrupulous politicians lead them up the
garden path and quietly rob them of all they possessed. When
accused by Rullus of defending his own interests and those of
his friends, he snapped back in a sparkling speech accusing
Rullus of being more Sullan than Sulla himself, of conferring
on Sullan land-allottees a security of tenure and legal title
beyond their dreams, of doing his own father-in-law a very
good turn indeed. He plays with Rullus like a terrier with a
rat:[2]

Rullus' exemption clause reads as follows: 'Whatsoever after the year
of the consuls Gaius Marius and Gnaeus Papirius . . .' Notice how
deeply he allays any suspicion by taking care to name those very consuls
who were Sulla's bitterest enemies. He judged that it would be too
plain and invidious to have mentioned Sulla the dictator by name. But
which of you did he imagine would be so slow-witted that he could not
recall that in the year after those consuls Sulla was dictator? What then
does our 'Marian' tribune say, this stirrer-up of ill-will against us
'Sullans'? 'Whatsoever after the year of the consuls Marius and Carbo,
whether lands, buildings, lakes, pools, territories or possessions'—he left
out the sky and the sea, but he got everything else in—'have been

---

[1] We have three speeches by Cicero on this bill. Of the first, delivered to the
Senate, only the last twenty-seven sections survive. The second and third,
delivered to the people, are intact. The second, over 100 sections long, is the
most important. The third is a short speech of sixteen sections in reply to a
personal attack on Cicero by the tribunes.

[2] *de leg. agr.* III.6–8.

publicly granted assigned sold or conceded'—by whom, Rullus? After
the consulship of Marius and Carbo who made assignments, who made
grants, who made concessions except Sulla? —'all these aforesaid are
to be held with the same legal title'—legal title? Evidently he is going to
upset legal titles in some way or other. Our supremely keen, supremely
energetic tribune is rescinding some Sullan decisions—'with the same
legal title as those private possessions held on the best freehold title'.
What, with a better title than those which come down to us by inheritance from our fathers? Yes, with a better! ... You, Rullus, what are
you asking? That your father-in-law should hóld his estate in the
Hirpine district, or rather the Hirpine district itself (he owns it all),
with a better legal title than I have to my family estate at Arpinum?
For that is what your law provides.

In his earlier speech he told the people that he would
speak frankly. (To a sceptical ear his words sound less frank
than disingenuous.)[3]

To speak frankly, I am not the man to abuse the whole idea of agrarian
legislation. My thoughts turn to those two great and brilliant men,
those truest friends of the Roman commons, Tiberius and Gaius Gracchus, who settled the commons on state-owned lands, lands previously
in the hands of private individuals. I am not the sort of consul who,
like most, would think it scandalous to praise the Gracchi; for I appreciate that thanks to their policies, their sound sense, and the laws they
carried, many departments of our country's administration were set on a
sound footing. So it was that, when at the very beginning while I was
consul-elect I was told that the tribunes-elect were jointly drafting an
agrarian bill, I was eager to discover what they had in mind ... But
when I tried to introduce myself into their discussions in a friendly way
and offer my services, I was shut out, I was rebuffed. When I made it
clear that, should I judge the law helpful to the commons, I should be a
proponent and a helpmate, they still spurned my generosity. I could
never, they said, be induced to approve any kind of distribution. So I
stopped putting myself forward in case my persistence should appear ill-
intentioned or rude.

But, for all his declared lack of hostility to agrarian legislation as such, Cicero could not bring himself to look with
any favour on this particular bill. In his speech to the Senate
he dismissed it as enshrining 'the dreams of drunkards, the
hopes of madmen'—*vinolentorum somnia, optata furiosorum.*[4]
Like some other professed moderate or 'Fabian' reformers,
Cicero always encountered difficulty in favouring specific

[3] Ibid. II.10–12.   [4] Ibid. I.1.

proposals to do something in fields where in theory he recognized that something needed to be done. He did not care for the Flavian land bill of 60; the Caesarian proposals in 59 made him quite ill. He liked his omelettes, but only if they could be made without breaking any eggs.

Rullus' bill, and the controversies it engendered, receive scant attention from ancient writers. Our main source of information remains Cicero. This renders the task of disinterring the corpse from under the heap of half-truths and distortions in which he sought to bury it more than usually difficult. But, thanks to the careful and perceptive work of E. G. Hardy, it can be done with reasonable confidence.[5] The bill proposed to establish a board of ten commissioners, *decemviri*, to administer the scheme. They were to be elected by only seventeen of the thirty-five tribes, chosen at random: thus only nine tribes would be needed to give a majority. (Cicero predictably sees this as designed to make manipulation easier by tampering with the lot. More plausibly it was to neutralize bribery by the rich since no one would know in advance which tribes were going to be picked to vote.) The commissioners were to supervise a widespread scheme of land-settlement throughout Italy. Since practically no public land remained for distribution apart from the Campanian Land, a fund was to be established for the purchase of additional land. The commissioners were to hold office for five years and enjoy wide judicial and administrative authority. They were to get their fund partly by selling off certain categories of public property in the provinces; partly by laying a special tax on certain provincial lands; partly by reclaiming the outstanding balance of any booty acquired by Roman generals in the recent past which they had kept to themselves, and laying a similar charge on all current and future generals (with the exception of Pompey) for the next five years; and partly by earmarking any income arising from new sources

---

[5] E. G. Hardy, *Some Problems in Roman History*, chapter 3. I do not accept all his assumptions or conclusions, but his detailed analysis, illuminated by his wide knowledge of constitutional and legal matters, is masterly and indispensable.

of revenue in and after 63 (the most obvious was, of course, Asia Minor, now being reorganized by Pompey).

Provided that there was an urgent and widespread need for some measure of land distribution to alleviate poverty in Rome and Italy, it was right than an attempt should be made to satisfy it. That the need existed cannot be doubted. It had been recognized since the time of the Gracchi, and even before that. The Agrarian Law of 111, the legislation of Saturninus and Livius Drusus in the period before the Social War, testify to its recognition and to the enthusiasm which could be aroused. The desperation of many of Catiline's supporters in 63 finds much of its explanation in a deep hunger for land. And, apart from the Campanian Land (to the distribution of which Cicero was also opposed), virtually no suitable land remained in Italy in public ownership; no other avenue was available but that of purchase, short of violent expropriation. This was accepted in Caesar's law of 59 and later by Caesar as dictator and by Augustus. The money must come from public sources, by sales of public property or revenues, by charges on state income, by (reasonably enough) compelling Rome's commanders or their heirs to disgorge any profits made in the state's service and with the state's resources.

Cicero made great play with the enormity of the idea that Rullus' bill would give Sullan gangsters and profiteers a firm and unequivocal title to their lands. A less prejudiced eye may see things differently. All Sulla's measures, including the confiscation, sale, or distribution of municipal and private lands in Italy, depended ultimately on the validity of the *lex Valeria*, which had ratified all his acts as dictator in advance of his appointment. On a number of grounds it was possible to argue that the *lex Valeria* was fundamentally unsound, and hence that the tenure of the land granted, bought, or simply appropriated or occupied by default, was precarious. But by 63 it could reasonably be urged that the time had come to forget the past: to unravel the whole tangled skein thread by thread would have been a daunting, probably an impossible, task. To try now to restore estates to their original owners or

to claim them for the state would be madness and folly—
as Cicero must himself have recognized; he was no man to
disturb a well-established *status quo*.[6]

The speeches against the Rullan bill must rank amongst
Cicero's most skilful efforts of public indoctrination. They
are masterpieces of misrepresentation. In addressing the
Senate he was, in the main, preaching to the converted. In
instructing the Roman *plebs* on the content and import and
objectives of the bill he was speaking to an ill-educated and
semi-literate audience incapable of reading and digesting the
technical legal terminology of a complicated and lengthy
document. It was not the sort of opportunity that Cicero
missed or mishandled. He draws his vivid pictures of Sullan
thugs being lapped about in an undeserved security; of tribal
votes shamelessly manipulated for personal ends; of the
birthright of the Roman people being sold up by ten 'kings'
(so he terms the *decemviri*) for their own selfish gain; of the
provinces of the Roman Empire exposed to their autocratic
manipulation; of the threat and affront to Pompey, the true
friend of the poor Roman; of corrupt sales of worthless land
at fancy prices; of cities like Capua turned into armed camps
under the guise of agrarian colonies to house violent and
armed men ready to hold Rome to ransom in the service of
their masters; of a treasury drained dry, of a people duped
and betrayed.[7] If at times the exaggeration is almost ludi-
crous in its enormity, we need to remember that Cicero
was addressing an excitable, ignorant crowd and not a bench
of Lords Justices of Appeal.

That is one side of the coin, but there is another. It would
be rash to assume that the authors of the bill were selfless,
disinterested men with no object but to increase the happiness and well-being of the deserving poor. Rullus himself is a
shadowy figure, 'a tribune without antecedents, and so
insignificant that his name never re-emerges in a period
offering so many chances to able adventurers'.[8] This may be
overharsh, for early death or a disabling illness might account
for the same facts; but there were more powerful men than

[6] Ibid. 84–9.   [7] *de leg agr.* II. 20–1; 29; 32; 39 ff; 49 ff; 76 ff.   [8] Hardy, 69.

Rullus involved. 'What security', Cicero asks the Senate, 'will remain for you once Rullus and *those whom you fear far more than you fear Rullus*, with all their gang of villainous desperadoes, with all their soldiers, with all their silver and gold, have got possession of Capua and the cities round about Capua?'[9] Cicero's colleague Antonius supported the bill, and it was probably not until the summer that Cicero bought him off by resigning his own claim to Macedonia in Antonius' favour.[10] Antonius' candidature for the consulship had been strongly backed by Crassus and Caesar. The people, too, are warned of the sinister and powerful figures who lurk behind Rullus, 'the authors of these plans', 'these greedy men who so often complain that every country and every sea has been handed over to Pompey'.[11] The optimate opponents of the Gabinian and Manilian Laws were certainly not behind Rullus' schemes: the finger points at Crassus, as it does too in the rhetorical question, 'Is there a ha'penny so well hidden that the architects of this law have not sniffed it out?'—if a modern historian at once thinks of Crassus, it is not fanciful to suppose that Roman senators did too.[12] Some people stood to gain a lot by the Rullan bill: in political support, in *clientelae*, in hard cash—which could in itself buy the first two.

Less than two years before, Crassus as censor had shown a marked interest in the enormous riches of Egypt. His attempt to make the country tributary to Rome was thwarted by his colleague Catulus. Crassus was supported by Caesar, who was aedile in 65 and who is said by Suetonius to have tried to use tribunes to get himself appointed to administer Egypt.[13] It was maintained by some that the late Pharaoh

[9] *de leg. agr.* I.22 (cf. I.16).

[10] Plutarch (*Cicero* 12) dates this transaction now, but in fact the surrender of Macedonia to Antonius almost certainly took place some months later. See below, p. 101.

[11] *de leg. agr.* 20 and 46.

[12] Ibid. I.11.

[13] Plutarch *Crassus* 13; Suetonius *DJ* 11. Alluded to by Cicero in *de leg. agr.* I.1. and II.44. In a non-extant letter referred to by Suetonius, Cicero wrote of Caesar that 'as consul he established that monarchy of which he had dreamed as aedile'. On Egypt, see further below, p. 197.

had bequeathed his kingdom to Rome. The prize glittered, fascinating a generation of Roman politicians. Money could unlock all doors. Before he left for his ill-fated expedition against Parthia in 55 Crassus had been worth perhaps as much as 8,000 talents. Yet Pompey could have bought him out and scarcely noticed it. He had distributed 16,000 talents to his Asian veterans alone. In Asia one king, Ariobarzanes of Cappadocia, owed Pompey in 51 a sum of between 1,500 and 3,000 talents.[14] The accumulated treasures of the Pharaohs, the great royal estates, the rich revenues of the Nile Valley, could redress a balance so disproportionately in Pompey's favour in the middle and late sixties, and offer scope for patronage on a staggering scale. In 65 Cicero himself spoke against the Egyptian project in the *de rege Alexandrino*, a speech whose meagre fragments include one plain reference to Crassus' grasping greed.[15] In 63 he returned to the attack. The Rullan Commission would be able to claim Egypt for the property of the Roman People. Crassus and his friends had failed to make good the straight course to Egypt; they now hoped to slip into Alexandria under cover of darkness and fog.[16]

With only Cicero's evidence to go on, we have to be wary. But there is no good reason to doubt that he and others were genuinely worried about what was afoot. It is safe to assume that Crassus and Caesar were behind Rullus; that they had their eyes on the vast potential of Egypt; that they were trying to gain control of resources both political and financial to match Pompey's. They would have been far less able and successful men than they were had they failed even to try. Cicero was a supporter of Pompey. His instincts were against what he saw as calculated bribery of the Roman electorate; his own interests could be served and Pompey and the *boni* pleased at the same time. The Rullan Commission threatened a side-tracking of the normal processes of

[14] See E. Badian, *Roman Imperialism in the Late Republic*, chapter VI, esp. pp. 72–5. [A talent was worth 24,000 sesterces at the official exchange rate.]

[15] *Scholia Bobiensia*, pp. 91–3 (Stangl): *Si hercle in nostris rebus tam acres ad pecuniam, tam adtenti, tam avari soleremus esse.*

[16] *de leg. agr.* II.44.

government by giving to ten men chosen by popular election vast powers and vast resources throughout Italy and the Empire for five years. Perhaps Cicero exaggerated the danger; he did not invent it. 'The three speeches [against Rullus] should be studied by all politicians who aspire to become proficient in the art of misrepresentation.'[17] They were certainly misleading and unfair; yet they were at the same time fundamentally sincere.

First blood in 63 went to Cicero and the opponents of reform. There is no record of the Rullan bill having even come to a vote. No doubt the declaration of Caecilius Rufus that he would use his veto was a serious deterrent. To attempt to trample over the veto as Tiberius Gracchus had done, and Gabinius too in 67, or as Caesar was to do in 59, would have been desperate and foolhardy in 63 in face of a tough and determined consul who, as events later in the year proved, was ready to employ the full reserve powers of his *imperium*; and the reformers lacked the backing of the sort of forces that Pompey could provide in 67 and 59. But we must allow full weight too not merely to Cicero's determination but also to his brilliant speeches which did much to discredit the bill and minimize its appeal and condition public opinion to its rejection. Cicero took the opportunity to make his position quite plain. In his speech to the Senate on 1 January, he announced that he was not going to seek a province or any other special distinction or advantage that could expose him to tribunician blackmail. And gazing round the assembled senators he issued a clear warning: 'If anyone here is led on by the hope that he can set his sails for office by a course of violence and revolution, let him abandon that hope so long as I am consul.'[18] Here at any rate in a public speech Cicero was being completely honest with his audience.

Crassus and Caesar and their friends were not easily intimidated. The challenge Cicero threw down was flung back in his face. Gaius Rabirius was prosecuted for a murder

---

[17] Rice Holmes, *The Roman Republic*, I. 249, note 2.
[18] *de leg. agr.* I.25 and 27.

he was alleged to have committed thirty-seven years earlier, when Cicero was six years old.

The murder was that of Saturninus. Late in 100 his explosive tribunate erupted in open fighting. The Senate passed the 'Ultimate Decree': the consuls Marius and Valerius Flaccus, assisted by the loyal tribunes and praetors, were to take all necessary steps 'to safeguard the power and majesty of the Roman People'.[19] Saturninus and his ally, the praetor Servilius Glaucia, were entrenched on the Capitol with their supporters. Marius put paid to their chances, and Saturninus surrendered, but along with a number of his supporters he was subsequently lynched. It was for this crime that Rabirius was now arraigned.

This was no routine prosecution. The age of the defendant, the long time that had elapsed since the alleged murder, both guarantee that. So too do the circumstances in which the charge was brought, the manner of its bringing, and the issues that it raised, so directly relevant to the situation in early 63. Briefly, Caesar dramatically and deliberately revived an archaic procedure which was believed to go back to pre-Republican days. The charge was *perduellio*—very roughly, 'high treason'—and was to be heard by two Commissioners chosen by lot from a list drawn up by the Urban Praetor. (The lot strangely fell on two Caesars: Caesar himself and his kinsman Lucius, the consul of 64.) The penalty laid down was scourging followed by crucifixion. The necessary legislation to effect all this was carried by the tribune Titus Labienus, later to be Caesar's second-in-command in Gaul. His was an appropriate role, for his uncle had died with Saturninus.[20]

The issue at the centre of this case was one of enormous importance. 'The object of this prosecution is quite simply that there should be from now on no public council of state at Rome, no union of hearts among honest citizens to confront the insane and unrestrained schemes of scoundrels, no refuge or safe stronghold in our country's hour of peril.'[21] More objectively, we may put it that this prosecution raised

[19] *pro Rab. perd.* 10.   [20] Ibid. 14 and 22.   [21] Ibid. 4.

the whole question of the employment of the *senatusconsultum ultimum*—the 'Ultimate Decree': its validity, its limitations, its place in the Roman constitution and in Roman Law.

In every country, a situation may arise in which the fabric of society and the rule of law and the normal working of constitutional government are threatened by movements which draw their strength from illegality, violence, and terrorism. Confronted by such challenges, or by their imminent threat, governments may find that the normal processes of law-enforcement are inadequate—too slow, too cumbrous, too hedged about with safeguards and caveats. The more enlightened and civilized a country is, the more likely is this to be the case, for its citizens enjoy a constitutional and legal system designed to check as far as possible the abuse of power or wealth or position. In an emergency it may become necessary to suspend the customary rules of law if revolution is to be averted or defeated and the government secured against overthrow by violent and illegal methods.

Sometimes a state specifically provides by law for emergency action in such a crisis.[22] In Great Britain we have the so-called Riot Act, which can in certain circumstances for a particular time and at a particular place authorize action to control or suppress a civil commotion by the use of methods which would normally be illegal. But even such specific provision in advance of emergencies does not remove all difficulties. Questions remain. Was the situation really such that extraordinary measures were called for, or did those in authority panic too quickly? Was more force used than was strictly necessary to restore order? Was the period of emergency prolonged beyond the time needed to cope with the trouble? These and many similar questions will always be asked, and will never find any ready or universally accepted answer; for the answers will be coloured by the political sympathies or social conscience of those who give them. In such situations things are done in a hurry, snap decisions

---

[22] On this, and the question at large, see the magisterial discussion by H.M. Last in *JRS* 33 (1943), 93-7.

have to be made, information is patchy and confused, tempers are high, nerves and judgement are strained taut, subordinates err. And subsequent questionings are much concerned with what the grammar-books call 'unfulfilled conditions in past time': we can never be sure what *would* have happened had Hannibal marched on Rome. It is therefore ridiculous to demand of the civil authorities that in such a situation every action taken shall be flawless. The only question worth asking is whether their conduct was such that a reasonable man can accept that it was by and large justified and untainted by partisanship, vindictiveness, or unnecessary brutality.

Rome had no Riot Act, nor anything like it. In a civil emergency which had passed the point at which legal methods could cope with it the authorities had to assume powers to deal with it. And 'about the action taken by the agents of society during such an interruption it is futile to ask whether it was legal; for legality means conformity to law, and when law has ceased to run there is no law to which to conform.'[23] But the resources of the consular *imperium* at Rome were vast, and in their origin monarchic. Custom and precedent had cocooned its deployment, laws had cased it in a shell of constraint. But in a crisis custom and precedent can be ignored; and the laws against the arbitrary exercise of the *imperium* had not deprived its holders of their powers but only menaced them with retribution if they exercised them contrary to the laws. Thus Gaius Gracchus' enactment that 'no one might pass sentence of death on a Roman citizen without the explicit authority of the Roman People'[24] meant, not that a consul could not pass and execute such sentence without such authority, but that if he did he could subsequently be prosecuted on a capital charge.

Essentially, then, it fell to the consuls to decide whether a crisis of such magnitude as to require extraordinary counter-action had developed or was threatening to develop. They could hope subsequently to justify their action as unavoid-

---

[23] Ibid. 94.
[24] *pro Rab. perd.* 12: *ne de capite civium Romanorum iniussu vestro iudicaretur.*

able: in Cicero's own words, *salus populi suprema lex esto*—'the safety of the People must be the highest law'.[25] But consuls would be rash men indeed if they did not see to it that their judgement had authoritative support and could not be represented as arbitrary and dictatorial. This brings us to the 'Ultimate Decree', the *senatusconsultum ultimum*. By passing this decree instructing the executive 'to see to it that the state take no harm', the Senate recorded its opinion that an emergency had arisen, or was impending, which called for extraordinary measures to be taken by those in executive authority. And if later their extraordinary action was challenged, the consuls could argue that their judgement had not been private and partial but had been shared by the members of the Senate itself, the *consilium rei publicae*. The 'Ultimate Decree' could not *authorize* the consuls to do anything illegal, but it reinforced their strictly illegal action and strengthened their resolution.

But it is one thing to cut down men who are in armed rebellion and even occupying fortified positions. It is quite another to kill men who have surrendered and are in custody and can in due course stand trial. Under cover of the Ultimate Decree it was always possible for the *boni* to carry out a sort of *pogrom* to liquidate their opponents and intimidate survivors. The *popularis* leaders could scarcely challenge the contention that the state had the right in certain circumstances to meet force with force, and there is no reason to suppose that the prosecution in 63 did challenge it. But they could properly contend that the 'Ultimate Decree' could and should not be treated as a justification for lynch-law. In prosecuting Rabirius in 63 they were not directly challenging consular authority. The consul most active in suppressing Saturninus had been Marius, and they had no wish to slight the name of the greatest *popularis* consul of recent times; in 65 Caesar had as aedile ostentatiously restored Marius' victory monuments.[26] Cicero, too, made great play in his defence with Marius' name. Rabirius, however, was

[25] *de legg.* 3.8.
[26] Suetonius *DJ* 11. Marius had been the husband of Caesar's aunt Julia.

and had been a private citizen. The prosecution had a double purpose. It was in itself a popular move, designed to convince the people that the men who were trying to bring Rabirius to book were true champions of the sacrosanctity of tribunes and of the rights of citizens under the law. In addition, it deprecated the *abuse* of executive authority under cover of the 'Ultimate Decree'. When some months later Cicero ordered the execution without trial of the captured fellow-conspirators of Catiline, he had been warned.

Of one thing we can be sure. The trial of Rabirius and the issues later raised by the execution of the conspirators were related by no mere accident. The *popularis* leaders can have been under no illusions when 63 opened that they were in for a rough passage and that the situation might get out of control. They had failed to get their own pair of consuls in. Their one successful candidate, Antonius, was far less resolute and dependable than Catiline; and, as it turned out, he was bought off and overawed by his colleague Cicero. Cicero himself had seized the earliest opportunity to make his own position clear: he was going to fight the reform programme, and he was ready to deploy the full force of his consular power. Caecilius Rufus announced his intention to interpose his veto against the Rullan bill. All in all, things were going sadly awry. Catiline could try again to win a consulship for 62, and if he succeeded much might be salvaged from the wreck; but if he failed, Crassus could not be expected to go on throwing good money after bad. Catiline would be desperate and ready for perilous adventures. Many hopes had been raised by the reform programme: hopes of land distribution, of the restoration of civil rights to those deprived of them by Sulla, of debt reform. It needed no inspired prescience to see in the early months of 63 that the extremists and desperate men might split off and be driven to open violence by the failure of great hopes, or to guess that ebullient *boni* might seize the pretext to carry out once again under the banner of a national emergency the sort of *pogrom* which in 133 and 121, in 100 and in the late eighties, had sliced a broad swathe through the *popularis* ranks.

This is why the Rabirius business has detained us so long. It was not its intrinsic importance, nor the brilliance of Cicero's speech for the defence—indeed it has some claim to be the poorest effort of his which we have. Happily we can excuse ourselves from turning over in detail the many awkward technical questions which bedevil this trial.[27] The attack on Rabirius was a showpiece trial, designed to focus public attention and to raise constitutional and legal issues of immediate relevance; a chance for the *populares* to state their position and thrust it on the attention of People and magistrates, a chance too for Cicero to riposte by making his own position and resolve clear—a test of nerves on both sides. Saturninus and Glaucia and Uncle Labienus were long dust and ashes, Rabirius a helpless old man. In 63 living men were worried about the next twelve months, and what might happen to themselves before the year was out. Once the issues had been given a public airing, the trial of Rabirius was interrupted and abandoned by a device as archaic and irrelevant as the *perduellio* procedure itself.

The *populares* did score one resounding success. Predictably, it was won by the most determined and gifted and dangerous of their number, Gaius Julius Caesar. After Catiline's defeat at the polls in 64 he had been prosecuted before the *quaestio de sicariis* on charges relating to murders committed in Sulla's time. Caesar was president of the court; but for all that he was distinguished in his presidency for his insistence on treating as murderers the killers of those proscribed by Sulla, Catiline was acquitted, which prompts the suspicion that Caesar was deliberately shielding a political associate.[28] Caesar played a conspicuous role in the Rabirius affair; he was undoubtedly involved in the fortunes of the Rullan bill. There is then no question where Caesar stood politically. This was the man who now came forward as a candidate for the office of Pontifex Maximus, made vacant by the death of its holder at the end of 64. The office was important not

---

[27] For a discussion of these, see Heitland's edition of the speech and Rice Holmes, op. cit., I.452–5 and the works there cited.

[28] Suetonius *DJ* 11; Dio 37.10.2; Asconius 90–1 C.

8—c.

only for its prestige but also because as chairman of the college of pontiffs and head of the state religion the Pontifex Maximus enjoyed considerable influence in the decision of questions of religious law, and at Rome such questions were frequently political questions. If auspices had not been properly taken, if technical hitches had occurred in the religious rites which accompanied so many actions of state, executive actions and legislative proceedings might be declared invalid, appointments might be cancelled. As we shall see, the consecration of Cicero's property by Publius Clodius after his exile in 58 and the amount of compensation Cicero could or should receive for it after his return, and whether it could properly be given back to him at all, were questions essentially political which fell to the college of pontiffs to decide, and the decision was likely to turn at any rate to some extent on that body's reaction to Cicero's political behaviour. He drew back and held his peace (always a difficult thing for Cicero) until the pontiffs should announce their decision: *nos tacemus, et eo magis quod de domo nostra nihil adhuc pontifices responderunt.*[29]

Thus the office of Pontifex Maximus was an important one for a politician to win. It was customarily held by senior politicians of their day, and Caesar (already a *pontifex* since 73) was not yet even a praetor and had as rivals for the election Publius Servilius Vatia Isauricus (consul in 79) and Quintus Lutatius Catulus (consul in 78), the latter the acknowledged leader of the *boni* and grand old man of the nobility until his death in 60. Caesar's election was a demonstration of the political influence which he personally, and his political associates with him, exercised in the popular assemblies, a demonstration all the more remarkable in view of his junior position on the ladder of public office. If the *popularis* leaders could follow Caesar's success with another and bring Catiline home to victory in the consular elections, there would still be a very good chance for reform.

Reform and redress of grievances were very much in the air. Land distribution, debt legislation, the rights of the

[29] *ad Att.* IV.1.7 (Sept. 57); below p. 196.

'sons of the proscribed', have already been mentioned. The 'Transpadane Question' was very much a live issue as well. The *Transpadani* were the communities in Italy north of the River Po (Padus). As a consequence of the Social War the rest of non-Roman Italy had received full Roman citizenship, but they had not. Their inferior position rankled, while their wealth and numbers made them worth cultivating by ambitious politicians. Pompey's position there was strong, since it was his father, Pompeius Strabo, who had effected the grant of Latin rights, a sort of half-way-house to full citizenship, as consul in 89.[30] Caesar is alleged to have become interested in them as early as 67 when he passed that way on his return from his quaestorship in Spain; hostile and hence unreliable sources had it that he planned to start an insurrection north of the Po as part of the 66 conspiracy.[31] However uncertain this report, Caesar's interest in the political potentialities of the area must have been real enough. In 65 it was Crassus' turn, and as censor he tried to secure the citizenship for the Transpadanes.[32] His colleague Catulus managed to effect a stalemate, and both resigned. Precisely how sincere Crassus and Caesar were may be questioned. Neither in 59 nor in any of the subsequent years when he and his partisans were dominant politically did Caesar try to carry enfranchising legislation in favour of the Transpadanes, and this suggests that he preferred to keep the issue simmering—once enfranchised, they might settle down to a quiet life. Only in 49 did he give them their long-awaited prize. But, of course, in 49 his opponents might have tried the same trick to win Transpadane support for themselves.

When on top of all this we recall the widespread social distress in Rome and Italy, the deep gulf that separated the few 'haves' from the uncountable 'have-nots', the ranklings of the communities (in Etruria especially) who had had their

[30] Asconius 3C.

[31] Suetonius *DJ* 9: *per Ambranos et Transpadanos*. The *Ambrani* are puzzling: C. E. Stevens' suggestion of *Marianos* for *Ambranos* is attractive. Cf. Suetonius *DJ* 11.

[32] Dio 27.9.3.

lands confiscated by Sulla, the restlessness and poverty of
many of the old Sullan colonists themselves, the crushing
burden of debt, then we can easily understand how the
reform movement of 63, with its specific social and economic
aims and its generally radical air, stimulated hopes and bred
desperation. Even the gentle Plutarch describes the position
as being on a razor's edge: 'All Etruria was strung up ready
for rebellion, and much of Cisalpine Gaul. Rome herself
was ripe for revolution because of the vast inequality of
wealth ... It needed only a small tilt in the balance to
overturn everything, and any bold adventurer might topple a
commonwealth which was rotten at heart.'[33]

While there is no reason to suppose that Caesar and Crassus followed Catiline into extremism in the latter part of 63,
there is equally no reason to doubt that they continued to
back his candidature up to, or nearly up to, his defeat at the
polls in the summer. He stood for the same sort of programme
of social and economic reform as they had associated themselves with. Cicero naturally enough was anxious to paint
Catiline in the most lurid colours and to depict his final
eruption into armed insurrection as the culmination of plans
and ambitions going back well before 63. In his *First Catilinarian*, delivered in the Senate on 8 November 63, he charged
that Catiline had been trying to have him murdered ever
since he (Cicero) had become consul designate;[34] and at the
elections in 63 as presiding officer he ostentatiously displayed
a cuirass beneath his toga, although later he rather in-
genuously explained that this was designed more to impress
the electors than to afford physical protection against cold
steel.[35] Sallust too would have his readers believe that a
conspiracy for the violent seizure of power was initiated in
June 64. Whether in thus antedating the inception of the
coup Sallust was misled by Cicero, or seduced by an artistic
impulse to simplification or moral instruction, or merely

[33] Plutarch *Cicero* 10.

[34] *in Cat.* I.15.

[35] *pro Murena* 52: *cum illa lata insignique lorica, non quae me tegeret ... verum
ut omnes boni animadverterent.*

being grossly careless, his account must be rejected. It was the double defeat at the polls that left Catiline with the grim choice between impoverished obscurity and a violent seizure of power.[36]

Apparently, Catiline continued to place hopes in Antonius and in certain undertakings (*promissa*) which the latter had given.[37] It was only now that Cicero won Antonius over by resigning to him the province of Macedonia, potentially more lucrative and offering greater chances of military glory than Cisalpine Gaul, the province originally assigned to Antonius. At any rate, Sallust places the arrangement at this time, which makes good sense. Plutarch dates it earlier; but it is hard to see how in this case Catiline could have continued to entertain hopes of Antonius.[38]

Thus, right up to, or almost up to, the elections Catiline continued to enjoy the support of leading *populares*. So long as he could still entertain hopes of a consulship he would have been a fool to spoil everything by plans of murder and rapine, of arming slaves and gutting Rome. He no doubt also enjoyed the support of the common people of Rome, whom Cicero later frightened off by his lurid depiction of plans to burn down the city and unleash a horde of savage Gauls and armed slaves. He stood for social and economic reform: land distribution, civil rights, the remission or abolition of debts. That legislation to do something about the crushing burden of debt formed part of Catiline's later revolutionary programme is undisputed.[39] Dio records debt reform as part of the programme of Antonius and some of the tribunes in the earlier part of the year,[40] and Catiline surely before his defeat was looked to by interested parties as of similar mind.

It has often been assumed or argued that if Catiline had stood openly for debt reform he could not have enjoyed the support of Crassus, for that multi-millionaire financier stood

---

[36] Sallust *Cat.* 17, 23–5. Syme, *Sallust*, 75–7.
[37] *pro Murena* 49.
[38] Sallust *Cat.* 26; Plutarch *Cicero* 12. Dio Cassius (37.33) is no help.
[39] See for example *in Cat.* II. 9 and 18; *ad Att.* II.1.11; *ad famm.* V.6.8.
[40] Dio 37.25.

to lose far too heavily. The assumption is ingenuous, the argument unsound. Catiline as consul might well, like Caesar many years later, have been a good deal less revolutionary in tackling the problem of debt than sanguine supporters had been simple-minded enough to believe. In any case, for Crassus, as for all Roman politicians, what mattered more than anything else was to have a hand on the levers of power. Given political control, monetary gains would follow. A consul of Catiline's verve and toughness might yet see Crassus dipping his hand deep in the riches of Egypt, for instance. The money that Crassus expended on men like Catiline and Caesar and Clodius was not intended to produce a safe investment at a guaranteed 5 per cent. The investments were political; if they paid off, as happened so magnificently with Caesar, the profits were enormous. And if some relaxation of the usury laws was likely to produce the right kind of political support, Crassus was not so small-minded as to flinch at the prospect.

Where else did Catiline look for support? Many men had been proscribed by Sulla and deprived of their civil status. Their sons fell under the same ban. Earlier in 63 a tribunician proposal inspired by Caesar to remove the political disabilities of these 'sons of the proscribed' had been defeated. Cicero himself opposed the move.[41] Such men were desperate and saw in Catiline the hope of better days.

At the end of November, Cicero drew a picture of Catiline's entourage as it had been as election time drew near:[42] Catiline himself, full of energy and gaiety; his faithful troupe of gilded youths; his informers and bravoes; an army of old Sullan veterans from Arretium and Faesulae; and, in sharp contrast, other men who had been shipwrecked and broken by the tempests that had accompanied Sulla's victory twenty years earlier. It was in the ranks of these tough and disillusioned men from the country, ex-Sullan soldiers and ex-Sullan victims alike, that Catiline found his staunchest and most dependable followers. For these 'rough

[41] *ad Att.* II.1.3; *in Pis.* 4; Quintilian *Inst. Or.* 11.1.85; etc.
[42] *pro Murena* 49.

countrymen, needy and impoverished'—*agrestis homines,
tenuis atque egentes*—Cicero had little time;[43] but it was their
distress, their grievances, their fears and hopes that provided
most of the fuel for the fires of political upheaval in the late
Republic. For Cicero, Catiline threatened social stability,
the rule of law, the rights of property. His own way with
debtors was short and sharp; 'Send in the broker's men and
sell them up.'[44] But the threat to established wealth was itself
a measure of the hopes that inspired Catiline's supporters. In
addition to the endemic factors already noted as breeding
social unrest in Italy, the turmoil and destruction and confiscations of the eighties, the civil war of 78–77, the persistence
of brigandage in the years that followed, the effects of piratical
depredations until Pompey swept the corsair fleets from
the seas in 67, the warfare in the East—all these bred distress
and poverty and debt. The slave uprising led by Spartacus
in the late seventies caused great damage and greater insecurity; the ineffectiveness of the government in coping
with it was witness to the chances of success that a well-
organized, well-led, and widely supported insurrection might
enjoy.

Cicero later asserted that the incidence of debt had never
been greater than in 63—adding that it had never been
more efficiently and speedily dissipated once his own firm
action had killed all hope of avoiding payment.[45] Although
often hard pushed himself to cover his obligations, Cicero
had a horror of debt-defaulting which no doubt owed a
great deal to his own solid municipal background and up-
bringing and to his lawyer's training and temperament. He
looked for support to the equestrian interests, which were all
for firmness in this matter. He is accordingly distinctly
unsympathetic in his account of what lay behind the agitation, and overemphasizes the importance of those debtors
who were in fact men of considerable property and had run
up extravagant debts which they were not prepared to meet
by selling off their patrimony. Such men certainly existed,
and had high hopes of debt reform; but to suggest, as Cicero

[43] *in Cat.* II.20.   [44] Ibid. 18.   [45] *de off.* 2.84.

does, that *all* debtors were victims of extravagance or incompetence or laziness or viciousness, is nonsense. For him the disaffected *Sullani* were those weaker brethren whose good fortune had gone to their heads, unused as they were to affluence. They built houses on an over-grand scale, kept too many servants, indulged in lavish furniture, and finished up so deeply in debt that 'their only hope of rescue is to raise Sulla again from the dead'.[46] No doubt this was true of some of them, enough to lend colour to Cicero's picture. But many had simply fallen victim to the adverse conditions which weighed so heavily on the Italian peasantry as a whole; and Lepidus is made by Sallust to assert in 77 that many of them had been fobbed off with marginal and unproductive land.[47] The letter sent by the ex-centurion Manlius on behalf of the rebels in Etruria has a ring of truth:

We call Heaven and mankind to witness that we have taken up arms against our own country not to create danger for others but to protect our own persons from injustice. Wretched and in want, thanks to the brutality and cruelty of the money-lenders many of us no longer have a fatherland, and all of us have lost all standing and substance. None among us was allowed our ancestral right of legal remedy; with the loss of our possessions we were reduced to bondage—such was the ferocity of the money-lenders and the judges.[48]

The cancer was not confined to Etruria. There was not a corner of Italy so remote but it had its debtors who looked to Catiline for rescue. There was unrest in the Cisalpine province, in Picenum and Umbria and Campania, in Apulia and Bruttium and the Paelignian territory: 'it is almost a catalogue of the recruiting areas for the Roman legions', not surprisingly since the legions drew their most numerous and best recruits from the tough inhabitants of a poverty-stricken countryside for whom military service with all its brutality and hardship offered one way of escape.[49]

Shortly before the elections a new law on electoral cor-

[46] *in Cat.* II.17, 20–1.
[47] Sallust *Oratio Lepidi* 23.
[48] Sallust *Cat.* 33.
[49] *in Cat.* II.8. The quotation in the text is from P. A. Brunt, 'The Army and the Land in the Roman Revolution', *JRS* 52 (1962), 69–86, q.v.

ruption was hurried through with Cicero as its sponsor. The *lex Tullia de ambitu* was designed to strengthen existing legislation by harsher sanctions: for convicted candidates a term of ten years' exile was added to the existing penalties, and (an innovation) recipients of bribes were also to be punished. But the measure was not aimed specifically or directly at Catiline. Cicero says that the senate was not happy about the law, and that although he himself steered it through he acted unwillingly; the move was forced on Senate and consul by Servius Sulpicius.[50] Sulpicius was stalking his rival candidate Lucius Licinius Murena. Murena, a former lieutenant-general under Lucullus and recently governor of the conjoined provinces of Transalpine and Cisalpine Gaul, was strongly backed by Lucullus' veterans who were assembled at Rome to celebrate Lucullus' long-delayed triumph, and he was spending money freely to win election. So convinced was Sulpicius, together with his friend Cato, of the nakedness of Murena's guilt that he as good as gave up canvassing to concentrate his efforts on assembling evidence for a prosecution which he believed must succeed and leave a vacant consulship for himself.[51]

The day before the elections Catiline in a private address delivered himself of some 'thoughts for the times'. He spoke of the *miseri*, a word difficult to translate but with connotations of poverty, oppression, desperation, and general ill-luck. Nobody could be trusted to champion the cause of the *miseri* unless he was one of them himself. The wounded and the distressed must not put their faith in the promises of men who were themselves secure and happy. To be free from fear, to lack all worldly goods, these were the qualities required of the man who was destined to be the commander and standard-bearer of the legions of the lost—*minime timidum et valde calamitosum esse oportere eum qui esset futurus dux et signifer calamitosorum.*[52] On Cicero's motion the Senate decreed that the elections be postponed so that it might discuss this report. Plutarch and Dio have it that Cicero's real reason for seeking postponement was that he had got wind of a plot to murder

[50] *pro Murena* 46–7.   [51] Ibid. 37–8, 43 ff.   [52] Ibid. 50.

him in the excitement and movement of the elections. But it is clear from Cicero's own account in the *pro Murena* that the grounds were Catiline's inflammatory words, and Cicero can scarcely have lied about the facts so soon after the event. Plutarch has it that Cicero did not bring up the murder plot at the time because he lacked convincing proof, but there was no reason why he should have been inhibited from bringing this out into the open in late November when Catiline was an outlaw. Probably the story in Plutarch and Dio is a construction from Cicero's wearing a breastplate at the actual elections.[53]

Catiline however was not overawed. The Senate was packed, and Cicero challenged him to explain the reports of what he had said. Unabashed, Catiline acknowledged them. Warming to his theme, he said that the state had two bodies: one was weak and with a feeble head, the other was robust and headless, but so long as he was alive if it put its trust in him it would have the head it needed. The Senate groaned, but failed to pass a decree of a severity worthy of this monstrous insult (so Cicero). Catiline swept out of the Senate-house gay and triumphant. His behaviour matched the bold front he had shown a few days before. Cato had been denouncing him and threatening him with prosecution (probably on the occasion of the debate on the electoral corruption bill), and Catiline rounded on him and warned that any attempt to send his fortunes up in flames would be quenched not with water but by pulling the house down over all their heads.[54]

Reading between the lines of the *pro Murena* discloses that Cicero received a rebuff from the Senate, which was not impressed by what he had to say, and took no action. As the year wore on he emphasized more than once that he was hampered in his struggle against Catiline by the 'softness' of a number of senators who refused to believe in the danger.[55] Some were naturally torpid and timid. Some

[53] Ibid. 51–2; Plutarch *Cicero* 14; Dio 37.29. Plutarch and Dio's version is accepted by E. G. Hardy, *The Catilinarian Conspiracy*, 41–2.

[54] *pro Murena* 51.

[55] Cf. *in Cat.* I.30: *mollibus sententiis.*

probably had the sense to appreciate that social and economic remedies were needed. Some were temperamentally suspicious of executive power. Some were in debt to Crassus. Not a few nursed resentment for this municipal upstart of a consul so full of his own importance, so ready to trumpet his achievement in scaling the walls of aristocratic privilege, so recently an advocate of reform, so lately an outspoken champion of the Pompey they feared and hated so much. Catiline was no saint, but he was a patrician and a *nobilis*, one of themselves, and a man of great charm and magnetism; the *invidia* which many of the *nobiles* had for a brash *novus homo* is a constant complaint of Cicero's over the next six or seven years.

Cicero may well have hoped to get sufficient support from the Senate for a long delay, long enough to see off many of the poorer country voters who had come to Rome to back Catiline but could not afford too long away at such a busy time of the year. It was not to be. So he strapped on his famous cuirass, arranged his toga over it carefully so that all the world could see that he had it on, and set off for the Campus Martius with a powerful volunteer bodyguard.[56] (The Senate had not seen fit to vote an *official* bodyguard as had been done for the incoming consuls of 65.) Decimus Junius Silanus had all along been regarded as a certainty for one consulship, the real fight being for the second place. According to Cicero, Sulpicius' preoccupation with his intended prosecution disheartened his supporters, who in face of the prospect of Catiline as consul rushed to back Murena.[57] Silanus and Murena were elected. Just how much Cicero's scare tactics had affected the result it is impossible to say. No doubt they helped, but Lucullus' veterans, Murena's lavish bribery, and the apprehension generally felt by many about Catiline's radical talk and wild promises, must have counted for a good deal more.

Thus far, Cicero had contrived to head off any serious attempt at social and economic reform. Nothing had been done for the landless, for those without civil rights, for the

[56] *pro Murena* 52.   [57] Ibid. 52–3.

Transpadanes, for those burdened or broken by debt. Egypt was still beyond Crassus' grasp. Rabirius had not been convicted, but the issues raised at his trial had yet to be tested in practice. Antonius had been bought off, Catiline repulsed. Caesar however was Pontifex Maximus and praetor-elect for the coming year. Italy was swelling with discontent and disappointment. Catiline was not yet ready to give up. There was little on the positive side. Cicero had reluctantly steered through the law on electoral corruption. He had also tackled the old scandal of *liberae legationes*, which allowed individual senators to travel abroad at the expense of the provincials for no specific public business, a system frequently abused; he tried to abolish them altogether, but was blocked by an obstructive tribune and had to settle for a reduction of their duration.[58]

Cicero had also successfully defended Gaius Calpurnius Piso on a charge of extortion and violence in his provincial command.[59] As consul in 67 Piso had shown bitter and stubborn hostility to Pompey and to the tribunes Gabinius and Cornelius. It might seem odd that a professed Pompeian should take on such a brief and bring to it all the authority of a consul. But Cicero had owed a lot to optimate support in winning his consulship, and he still needed that support as consul. We have no details, but his defence of Piso was surely part of that complex of *quid-pro-quos* which loomed so large in Roman political life. In particular, we saw how in the middle of 65 Cicero was thinking of availing himself of Piso's good offices to spend a few months in Cisalpine Gaul to consolidate electoral support there. Piso's offer left Cicero with a debt to repay. Further, the prosecution was inspired by Caesar as part of his Transpadane agitation. That Cicero should oppose Caesar in this matter was consistent with his general posture, and not at all likely to upset Pompey.[60]

[58] *de legg.* 3.18. Only the year is given, but the first half seems likelier than the second.

[59] *pro Flacco* 98.

[60] *ad Att.* I.1.2. For Caesar's part in this, see Sallust *Cat.* 49. In this connection it is worth noticing that M. Pupius Piso, consul in 61, gave to this same Piso, the consul of 67, who was his kinsman, the highly valued honour of being called

Cicero also claimed a leading part in helping Lucullus to his long-blocked triumph.[61] This too has a bearing on Pompey, on Pompey's reactions at the time and after his return to Rome eighteen months later. But such matters are not simple, and are best deferred for later examination. It is time to turn now to the final act in Cicero's struggle with Catiline.

first to speak in the Senate on 1 January 61. Yet Pupius had been a legate of Pompey's from 67 to 62, and had stood for the consulship with Pompey's strong support (Plutarch, *Cato Minor* 30). If Pupius could honour an obligation in this way, why should not Cicero have done the same? Neither can be assumed to have offended Pompey simply because he and Piso had been on bad terms in the past; Roman public life does not admit of this crude sort of analysis, which has marred a number of recent studies (on this see the brief and cogent comments of Sherwin-White in *JRS* 46 (1956), 1–2). On the particular matter of this note, see *ad Att.* I.13.2, and Balsdon in *Historia* 15 (1966), 66.

[61] Cicero *Lucullus* 3. See further below, p. 149.

VI

CATILINE

THE IMMEDIATE course of events following Catiline's defeat at the polls cannot be determined with precision: his plans were secret, his movements cautious.[1] What we can be sure of is that he had now nothing more to hope for from normal political action. But the mere seizure of power at Rome could be only a beginning, not an end. Given good leadership, good planning and good luck, it was not beyond his grasp. But what next? Leading senators would escape overseas, and rally their *clientelae*, while the provincial governors themselves would overwhelmingly stand by established government. Most important of all Pompey, with his huge army in the East and the command of the seas, was hardly to be expected tamely to acquiesce in a *fait accompli*. Perhaps Catiline hoped that he might be able to do a deal with Pompey. Perhaps the truth was that he had no precise long-term plan at all. Historians are by nature and profession addicted to neatness and precision, given to looking a lot further ahead than people (including themselves) do in real life. What happens accidentally can easily by hindsight be assigned its place in a predetermined pattern. At least, we can be sure that such worries about long-term problems did not inhibit Caesar from ordering his soldiers across the Rubicon, or deter an eighteen-year-old Octavian from throwing himself head-first into the maelstrom of Roman politics and war. Had Catiline been successful, we should not lack historical demonstrations of why he had been likely to win. So we had best abandon long-term and perhaps misguided speculation and give our attention to Catiline's immediate objectives.

[1] For some notes on the chronology, see Appendix A.

Unluckily for Catiline, his associates were clumsy, indiscreet, and inefficient. That is no cause for wonder. Successful and prosperous men were not likely to get themselves involved in such plans. His leading supporters were casualties of the Roman political fight: misfits, failures, disappointed men. If we are astonished by their blunders, we need to remember that more efficient and effective men would never have found themselves embroiled in so desperate a venture. Perhaps Catiline was not merely unlucky, but unwise; but he had to take what he could get.

The most prominent senatorial adherents of Catiline were Lentulus, Cassius, Cethegus, Autronius, Curius, Vargunteius, Annius, and Laeca. Of Quintus Annius and Marcus Porcius Laeca (in whose house the famous meeting was held on the evening of 6 November) there is little to report beyond their names. Of the others more can and will be said.

On paper the most distinguished was Publius Cornelius Lentulus Sura, a scion of one of the numerous branches of the great patrician house of the Cornelii. He had been consul in 71. Expelled from the Senate by the censors of 70, he had rehabilitated himself by again climbing the ladder of elective office. In 63 he was praetor: equipped with *imperium*, he was a powerful weapon in the revolutionary armoury, at the least as a 'front man' whose office and powers might serve to give a sheen of respectability to a political take-over. (In 49 another praetor, the future triumvir Lepidus, was employed by Caesar to clothe his assumption of constitutional authority with a show of legality.) Alas, his pretensions and person far outdistanced his native capacity. He had an imposing presence, a graceful carriage, a powerful and pleasing voice; these superficials concealed a slow wit and a lame delivery— so Cicero assessed him as an orator, and the assessment will serve for the man as well. He was a 'sleepy-head' and no cause for alarm: *non mihi esse P. Lentuli somnum pertimescendum.* It is no surprise to discover that this limited but pretentious man cherished an oracle that foretold that three Cornelii would rule Rome: he was to be the third in succession to Cornelius Cinna and Cornelius Sulla. His credulous mind

also saw significance in the fact that the year 63 marked
the twentieth anniversary of the burning of the Capitol,
and put faith in the constructions which soothsayers placed on
this accident of chronology.[2]

Lucius Cassius Longinus was the undistinguished bearer of
a distinguished noble name. He had been praetor in 66 along
with Cicero and Antonius. In this office he had had charge of
the *maiestas* court, before which the ex-tribune Cornelius
was arraigned, but had failed to put in an appearance on the
day he had himself appointed for the hearing of the case—
Asconius suggests collusion with the defence. In 64 he had
been a consular candidate with Cicero, but at the time was
reckoned stupid rather than disreputable—*stolidus tum magis
quam improbus videretur*. Quintus Cicero had dismissed him from
serious consideration as a consular candidate. He was also
remarkably corpulent: 'a barrel of lard', Cicero called him—
L. Cassi adipes.[3]

Weighty names but lightweight men. Gaius Cornelius
Cethegus presents us with a second patrician Cornelius.
Cornelii Cethegi occupy consulships and praetorships in the
late third and early second centuries, then disappear from
view. Our Cethegus is merely on record as a member of the
Senate in 63. Happily Sallust fills out the portrait.

Cethegus was forever complaining of the sluggishness of his associates.
By their hesitations and procrastination they were squandering great
opportunities. Actions not words were what the emergency called for.
Give him a few helpers and while others held back he would storm the
senate-house. A wild and forceful man, he held that speed was everything.[4]

His end had an appropriate touch of melodrama: his own
brother is said to have been among those in the Senate who
voted for the death penalty.[5]

Publius Autronius Paetus we have met before, unseated
from his prospective consulship in 66 with Publius Sulla and
frequently named in accounts of the 'conspiracy' of 66/65. A

[2] *Brutus* 235; *in Cat.* III. 9 and 16; *pro Sulla* 70; Sallust *Cat.* 47.
[3] Asconius 59–60, 82C; *Commentariolum* 7; *in Cat.* III. 16.
[4] Sallust *Cat.* 43.
[5] Ampelius, *lib. mem.* 31.

daring, impudent, and debauched man—*semper audax, petulans, libidinosus*—in defence of his sexual excesses he did not hesitate to use the filthiest language or even punch and kick.[6] Lucius Vargunteius likewise is alleged by Cicero to have been involved in the earlier 'conspiracy'. He had been condemned for electoral corruption, very likely in 66, the same year as Autronius. He was to be one of the two men told off to assassinate Cicero in his own house on the morning of 7 November.[7]

Another disgraced man brings up the rear. Quintus Curius while still only of quaestorian rank was expelled from the Senate in 70 for scandalous living. Again Sallust comes to our aid:

Of very respectable birth, he was deeply sunk in crime and debauchery. And his effrontery was equalled by his vanity: he could not hold his tongue about anything he was told or even make a secret of his own misdoings—indeed he did not care a feather what he said or what he did.

Which brings us to the lady in the case:

He had as his mistress a noblewoman called Fulvia, and the affair was of long standing. Just when he was beginning to be less attractive to her, because his lack of money made him less able to buy her presents, he suddenly began to brag and promise her the earth and sometimes to threaten to murder her if she were not submissive to him, and in general to be wilder and more excitable than he had been.

It did not take Fulvia long to find out the explanation for this sudden change and pass the information on.[8] Most of Curius' money (the lack of which first upset Fulvia, who had little confidence in the wild promises of her desperate lover) had gone on gambling. He was notorious for it, and the poet Calvus called him 'a savant of the dice-box'—*et talos Curius pereruditus*.[9]

Shallowness, pretension, unimaginative stolidity, impetuosity, debauchery and filth, obsessive gambling and

[6] *pro Sulla* 71.

[7] Ibid. 6 and 67. Syme, *Sallust*, 88.

[8] Sallust *Cat.* 23. The fact that Sallust antedates the inception of the conspiracy need not invalidate his narrative of Curius and Fulvia; it merely requires that we move his story up some months later.

[9] Asconius 93C.

love-crossed indiscretion, public disgrace and infamy—it is a sorry catalogue however much we allow for hostile distortion and posthumous vituperation. Yet these were the men on whom Catiline was relying for the success of his venture.

After the elections Catiline's agent Gaius Manlius was sent out to Faesulae in Northern Etruria (about five miles north-east of Florence) to organize forces there. He worked on the poverty-stricken and restless peasantry, at the same time enlisting brigands (plentiful in that area, a sure sign of social desperation) and Sullan veterans who had fallen on hard times. Further agents were dispatched to Picenum, to Apulia, and to other likely places.[10] Catiline stayed on in Rome to concert everything and allay suspicion. The first plan was for Manlius and his forces to concentrate within striking distance on 27 October, ready to move on Rome the next day.[11] Under cover of the confusion and relaxation attending the commemorative celebration of the Sullan Victory Games, concerted action by Manlius' troops and Catiline's supporters within the city (who included hired gladiators) would remove Cicero and seize control.

Cicero was probably informed of this by Fulvia, but she may have been able to give him no more than rather vague intelligence. There was also a dramatic intervention by Crassus. Rousing the consul from his bed he handed over a bundle of letters which had been delivered to his house addressed to himself and other leading men; Crassus' letter warned him of an impending massacre and advised him to leave Rome. It is a mysterious business. It has been suggested that Cicero had the letters forged and delivered as a test of Crassus' integrity, or that it was a device of Crassus' to exculpate himself. What we know about Catiline's co-revolutionaries makes it likeliest that one of them was indiscreet enough to warn a favoured few to make for cover. A meeting of the Senate was promptly summoned, but produced nothing beyond encouragement to raise levies and hold enquiries. Shortly afterwards an ex-praetor, Quintus Arrius, reported the gathering of troops in Northern Etruria

---

[10] Sallust *Cat.* 27–8.   [11] *in Cat.* I.7; Sallust *Cat.* 30.

and added that Manlius was hovering around the cities in that area with some considerable forces waiting for a signal from Rome. Cicero addressed the Senate again on 21 October, forecasting that Manlius would openly take the field on the 27th, and that a massacre was planned at Rome for the 28th. The Senate passed the Ultimate Decree.[12]

Whether Cicero was really as precise as he made out may be doubted. In his *First Catilinarian* he claims he named these dates in his speech on 21 October. But the *Catilinarians*, like his other major political speechs of 63, were written up for publication three years later. He may then have been tempted to turn what was originally a general forecast into a firm prediction. On the other hand, it remains possible that he had got the information from Fulvia.[13]

With the Ultimate Decree in his pocket Cicero moved with firmness and authority. The companies of gladiators lodged in Rome were broken up and distributed to Capua and other towns. A force of vigilantes was impressed and officered by the minor magistrates to secure the capital. Praeneste, apparently the planned jumping-off point for Manlius' assault on Rome, was strengthened with specially raised levies.[14] A few days later, about 1 November, a Lucius Saenius read to the Senate a letter he had had from Faesulae announcing that Manlius had taken the field with a large force on 27 October. There was news of other movements, of gatherings, of arms being transported, of slave risings at Capua and in Apulia. Again prompt and decisive action was taken. Two former consuls were outside the city, Quintus Marcius Rex and Quintus Metellus Creticus. They had for some time been waiting in the hopes of being allowed to

[12] *in Cat.* 1.7; Plutarch *Cicero* 15, *Crassus* 13; Dio 37.31. Plutarch and Sallust (*Cat.* 29) talk of only one meeting of the Senate, that of 21 October. It seems from Dio that there may have been two, following in close succession.

[13] *in Cat.* I.7. For the publication of the 63 speeches, see *ad Att.* II.1.3 (June 60).

[14] *in Cat.* I.8. (Praeneste); Sallust *Cat.* 30 (gladiators and vigilantes). 'Sallust places these steps after the news from Etruria, but . . . as there was information of a massacre planned for the 28 th., no time would have been lost, and Cicero explicitly states that he prevented the massacre by means of his guards (*in Cat.* I.8)' —so Hardy, *Conspiracy*, 58.

celebrate triumphs for provincial wars. Being technically *cum imperio*, they were given authority to take control in Faesulae and Apulia respectively. Capua and Picenum were entrusted to the praetors Quintus Pompeius Rufus and Quintus Metellus Celer, who were also given emergency powers to levy soldiers.[15]

According to Sallust Rome fell victim to panic.[16] Cicero himself in the famous opening sentences of his *First Catilinarian* speaks of the *timor populi*. No doubt credit was destroyed and property sales impeded. It may well have been at this moment that a banker, Quintus Considius, who had huge sums out on loan, ostentatiously declined to press for settlement and earned a laudatory resolution from the Senate.[17]

One man who did not panic was Catiline. Young Lucius Aemilius Paullus entered a prosecution against him for public violence (*de vi*). Catiline coolly offered to place himself in the custody of Cicero himself.[18] He remained at large and even attended the Senate. Cicero did not have sufficient evidence against him. To wait for a complete chain of proof before acting at all would have been criminally stupid; to move against Catiline himself called for caution. Cicero was aware of mistrust, suspicion, and envy. He had been rebuffed earlier in the year in the matter of the postponement of the elections. When nothing happened on 28 October it must have seemed to some a false alarm; the penalty of sound precautions was that the things guarded against did not happen. Communications were poor and slow, reports conflicting. There was always the risk that Cicero would be seen as an alarmist. But with firm moves being taken outside Rome Catiline was under considerable pressure to leave and take direct command of the forces of insurrection. Manlius might be capable and efficient, but he lacked the presence and magnetism and authority of Catiline. With Catiline gone, the other plotters at Rome would become less formid-

---

[15] Sallust *Cat*. 30.
[16] Ibid. 31.
[17] Val. Max. 4.8.3. Rice Holmes, op. cit., I. 261.
[18] Sallust *Cat*. 31; *in Cat*. I.19.

ble. It was a battle of nerves, and one which Cicero won. He held his hand, refused to be panicked, and forced Catiline into the open.

An attempt to seize Praeneste under cover of darkness on 1 November was deterred after the defences had been put in a state of readiness by Cicero. A final meeting of the leading conspirators was held on the night of 6 November in Laeca's house in Sicklemaker's Street. Catiline had now made up his mind to leave Rome. Area commanders were named for various regions of Italy—Apulia, Etruria, Picenum, Cisalpine Gaul; others, headed by the praetor Lentulus, were to stay in Rome to concert action there. A final attempt was to be made to remove Cicero. His determination and resource, and the efficiency of his measures of prevention, were a major obstacle. With him out of the way, his colleague Antonius would be left as sole consul, and his past associations with Catiline would count heavily in Catiline's favour. Thus for Catiline the assassination of Cicero was vital. While others held back, Vargunteius and a knight named Gaius Cornelius volunteered to make a formal call on the consul early the next morning and taking him by surprise cut him down in his own home. But by now Cicero's intelligence service was working very smoothly. Curius, who was himself now playing a double game, warned Fulvia to warn Cicero. When the assassins arrived, they found the house barred to them.[19]

The following day, 8 November, the Senate was called to the temple of Jupiter Stator on the Palatine Hill, a venue easier to secure than the Senate-house itself. The building was ringed by guards. Catiline himself appeared, defiant in his isolation as other senators edged away from the seats around him.[20] And Cicero launched into the most famous of all his speeches, the *First Catilinarian*: *Quo usque, tandem, abutere, Catilina* . . . . As rhetoric it is magnificent and overwhelming.

---

[19] Sallust *Cat.* 27–8; *in Cat.* I.8–10. II.6; *pro Sulla* 18 and 52. Sallust is alleged by some to have antedated the meeting in Laeca's house by up to three weeks, placing it before the meeting of the Senate on 21 October. But Syme demonstrates (*Sallust*, 79–81) that a careful reading of Sallust here shows nothing of the kind, and that his account is perfectly in line with the date of 6 November.

[20] *in Cat.* I.16, II.12.

The great drum-roll of his oratory beats on the ear. The approach is direct and violent, the syntax crisp and incisive. For all that, the superb manipulation of the Latin language cloaks a hollow centre, and occasionally skirts dangerously close to mere bombast. Cicero set out what happened at Laeca's house, exposed the abortive murder attempt of the previous morning, revealed the gathering of an army in Etruria. He claims to know all and see all, but we must remember that the published version was written up three years later. He asserts (quite erroneously) that the Ultimate Decree passed on 21 October empowered him to have Catiline arrested and executed, and that this is the course he ought to take.[21] But he did not take it. Why not?

It looks as if Catiline had planned to leave Rome on the night of 7 November. Primed by his spy-network, Cicero may have banked on addressing the Senate on 8 November with Catiline off and away, confessing guilt by the very act of flight. He still lacked real proof. The mere word of Fulvia and Curius was nowhere near enough: it could forewarn Cicero but not convict Catiline. Catiline's appearance in the Senate may have disconcerted Cicero and thrown him off balance. A triumphant paean over a fugitive had to be adapted to something less decisive. For all his braggadocio he knew that to have Catiline executed would be an act of madness.

There are not a few members of this order who either fail to see what is in store or pretend that what they do see is other than it is; who have nurtured Catiline's hopes by the flabbiness of their opinions; who by their disbelief have built up and strengthened his nascent conspiracy; whose authority is such that had I dealt with this man many people, not just wicked people but ignorant people too, would say that what I had done was cruel and tyrannical.[22]

Catiline must go, he must assume the command of the forces of insurrection; only then would all the world know that Cicero was telling the truth.

If Cicero hoped that the Senate would rise as one man and demand that the consul act, he was disappointed. 'Put it to

[21] Ibid. I.1–6.   [22] Ibid. I.30.

a vote', Catiline drily interjected at one point: '*Refer*
inquis '*ad senatum*'. Cicero prudently declined the offer.[23]

When Catiline rose to reply, his head was lowered and his
tone modest and appealing. He begged the Senate not to be
too hasty. He was a gentleman, a patrician, born and educated to high ambitions. Why should he want to destroy the
Republic which he and his ancestors had served so well?
And who was claiming to 'save' the Republic? Marcus
Tullius, a mere 'naturalized immigrant'—*inquilinus civis
urbis Romae*.[24] Five centuries of gentle birth was claiming its
due from its equals against a jumped-up nobody from a small
Volscian country town, Roman only by Rome's granting,
and at that for barely a hundred years. It was a wicked,
wounding phrase, and twisted in the wound by Cicero's
knowledge that even those nobles who were on his side
would savour and repeat it.

The victory went to Cicero none the less. He owed it not
simply to his oratory but to his courage, dedication, efficiency, and dogged persistence. Catiline could delay no longer.
Plans had miscarried, Cicero still lived. He must himself take
the field before his followers lost heart and dispersed. The
night following the meeting in the temple of Jupiter he
slipped out of Rome *en route* for Etruria, stopping for a few
days near Arretium to arm and organize insurgents there.
He went not as an exile, but as an *imperator* to join his army,
with the rods of office and the Eagle standard that had once
been carried before the soldiers of Marius.[25] (Catiline's first
wife had been a Gratidia, sister of Marcus Marius Gratidianus.[26]) He was claiming to be heir to the tradition of the great
popularis, the darling of Italy—ironically, another parvenu
from Arpinum.

[23] Ibid. I.20. Adcock in *Cambridge Ancient History*, IX, 499 combines this
passage with a fragment of Diodorus (40.5a) and thinks it probable 'that
Cicero was actually baited by Catiline into putting a motion for his banishment,
but was received in stony silence by the Senate, and was hard put to it to explain
away this rebuff.' In view of the silence of our other sources and the highly
rhetorical colour of the Diodorus fragment, this is a rash suggestion.

[24] Sallust *Cat.* 31.
[25] Ibid. 32 and 59.
[26] Sallust *Hist.* I.45; Syme, *Sallust*, 86.

According to Sallust, Catiline made one last attempt to blur the issues, writing to leading men at Rome to claim that he had been maligned and cheated, that he was yielding to ill-fortune and going into exile at Marseilles—not for any crime he had committed but to secure peace and quiet for his country.[27] The purpose must have been to gain a little time, to discredit Cicero, to impede his preventive measures by arousing doubts about their necessity. He wrote also to Quintus Catulus. Catulus read the letter out to the Senate, and Sallust claims to reproduce the actual text. It is the true Catiline we hear, the aristocrat addressing one of his own kind, the patrician doyen of the *boni*:[28]

Goaded by injustice and abuse, robbed of the reward of all my hard work and effort, failing to gain my due rank and dignity in the state, I was true to my character and embraced the public cause of the poor and the wretched. . . . I saw office and honour conferred on men unworthy of them and felt myself shunned through groundless suspicion. So I have pursued what in my unhappy plight is the perfectly honourable hope of preserving what remains of my *dignitas*. I had wanted to write more, but I have news that forces are gathering against me. Now I commend my wife Orestilla to you, and entrust her to your honour. Keep her safe from harm, I beg you by your own children. Goodbye.[29]

Cicero was triumphant. The next day, 9 November, he addressed his *Second Catilinarian* to the *populus*. Catiline was gone: *abiit excessit, evasit erupit*.[30] He explained why he had refrained from having Catiline arrested and executed: because of all the doubters and disbelievers and even secret sympathizers. He related how he knew the whole plot, the plans for risings all over Italy, for massacre and arson at Rome. He told of the arrangements he had made to counter them. Murder, plunder, rape, the burning of Rome are dangled before his audience's eyes to terrify them.

About the middle of the month news reached Rome of Catiline's assumption of imperatorial insignia and his arrival in Manlius' camp. The reaction was prompt. The

[27] Sallust *Cat.* 34.
[28] Syme, *Sallust*, 72.
[29] Sallust *Cat.* 35. Orestilla was presumably a near relation of the tribune Mucius Orestinus (above, p. 80).
[30] *in Cat.* II.1.

Senate outlawed Catiline and Manlius. To the mass of their supporters it offered a free pardon if they laid down their arms within a stated period. The consuls were empowered to hold a levy of troops and Antonius was to lead an army against Catiline with all speed while Cicero remained at Rome in charge of its security. Yet such was the magnetism of Catiline and the loyalty he inspired, such the distrust of the government, such the desperation of the insurgents, that not one man came forward to accept the rewards offered for information, or took advantage of the proffered amnesty.[31]

The commons in the city were still restless, and Lentulus and his collaborators were still at large. Cethegus was all for striking quickly, but Lentulus had enough sense to see that the best hope lay in concerted action by the revolutionary forces within and outside Rome. The plan now was that a tribune, Lucius Calpurnius Bestia, should convene a public meeting on December 16 and attack Cicero and stir up public indignation against him as having wilfully provoked a dangerous war without due cause. Then on the night of the 17th, under cover of the Mardi Gras excitements and confusions of the Saturnalia, the city was to be fired in twelve places, Cicero was to be ambushed and killed at his house, and other leading men assassinated. They would then break out of Rome to join Catiline, who would be near Rome at the head of his army ready to seize the initiative.[32]

In the midst of all these excitements Cicero was called back to the bar. The consul-elect Murena was an experienced general and was seen by Cicero as the man on whom he and Rome could rely to take the field against Catiline and beat him if the uprising continued into the year 62. It was therefore embarrassing that Murena should now be charged with

[31] Sallust *Cat.* 36.

[32] Ibid. 39 and 43; *in Cat.* III.10. According to the text of Sallust as we have it, Catiline was expected to have reached Faesulae with his army by the night of 17 December. But Faesulae had been the rallying-point of the insurgents since October at latest, and it was about 150 miles from Rome as the crow flies, far too far for Catiline to pounce on Rome. We must assume a slip of the pen by Sallust or his copyists; the best suggestions are that for *in agrum Faesulanum* we should read *Falerianum* or *Aefulanum*. Falerii was under 30, Aefula less than 25 miles from Rome—both within a hard day's or night's march.

electoral corruption. It was all the more embarrassing that
he was patently guilty, that the law under which he stood
charged had only recently been written into the statute book
and stood in Cicero's name, and that the prosecutors were
not malcontents or revolutionaries but Servius Sulpicius
Rufus and Marcus Porcius Cato. Sulpicius was an old friend
of Cicero's and a man of the highest public reputation, a
respected and learned jurisconsult. Cato, though still little
over thirty years old, had already achieved that moral
ascendancy in the Senate which was to last him all his life
and in the end cost him his life and win him immortality as
the martyr saint of the Republic. The force of his ascendancy
we shall soon be able to judge.

Cicero admired Cato's immense probity and in general
shared his political views; but he judged him an inept politician, impetuous and blind to the harsh realities of life. All
too often for Cicero Cato was the idealist who argued 'as if
he were living in Plato's ideal state and not in the cess-pit of
Romulus'.[33] This (somewhat less bluntly expressed) was the
burden of his speech in Murena's defence. National security
demanded that Murena should assume his consulship on 1
January. Sulpicius had his virtues, but they were the virtues
of an academic lawyer, little use against Catiline. Indeed
Cato and Sulpicius were very much giving aid and comfort
and hope to the common enemy. If Catiline were the judge,
he would condemn Murena, execute him if possible. If
Murena were removed, it was far from certain that a second
consul would be chosen to take his place: tribunician veto
might leave the other consul, Silanus, alone and unsuppor-
ted.[34]

Just how honest all this was is open to question. Catiline
was as good as beaten before the year was out. Even as sole
consul Silanus would have been well supported by the army
commanders in Italy. Cicero himself was no warrior consul.
No doubt the government (if one may call it that) would
have been discomfited had a consul-elect been unseated for
gross bribery; but did anyone see the 'establishment' of the

[33] *ad Att.* II.1.8.   [34] *pro Murena* 82–3.

late Republic as a paragon of moral rectitude? It would be kind to suppose that Cicero was over-anxious about the state of affairs and genuinely believed that Murena was needed to keep the country secure. More probably, he was defending established interests and arrangements. Murena was a protégé of Lucullus, to whom as a leading optimate Cicero must have been indebted for assistance in his own election, and whom Cicero had been forward in assisting to his long-delayed triumph. It does not tax the imagination to guess at the kind of mutually useful understandings that had been reached between a consul and his designated successor, understandings which Cicero would be understandably reluctant to upset. Nor should we assume that Murena, wealthy and well-supported, would have been convicted had Cicero not defended him—Hortensius and Crassus were also retained as defending counsel. Had Cicero declined to accept the brief, or even appeared for the prosecution, and had Murena been acquitted, Cicero would have been in an unhappy position in 62 with a hostile consul in office and his own actions in 63 challenged.

Happily Cicero did accept the brief—happily, since this is the most delightful and entertaining of all his forensic performances. Curiously enough, E. G. Hardy judged the *pro Murena* 'the dullest of dull speeches'.[35] One can only surmise that his assessment was coloured by indignation at the irresponsibility of Cicero's assault on established conservative values, or perhaps simply by lack of a sense of fun. For the *pro Murena* is in parts uproariously funny. Cato himself turned to his neighbours with a smile: 'What a comic we have for a consul'; and even granted that the remark was a *double entendre*, Cato recognized the effect of the speech on the court.[36] Little if anything is advanced in relevant rebuttal of the formal charges against Murena—presumably Crassus and Hortensius had had more to say on these heads—and what little is said is to the critical ear weakly a-prioristic, though rhetorically highly effective. There is much that is pure gold about the circumstances surrounding the elections

[35] *Conspiracy*, 73.   [36] Plutarch *Cato Minor* 21.

in mid-63, the unwritten rules of the Roman political game, the technique of a campaign, the moods of the electorate. But the chief delight of the speech remains its sparkling comedy and wit, the sheer ebullient gaiety of the passages where Cicero counter-attacks and quite irrelevantly carries the fight into the enemy camp. The mumpsimus of Roman legal jargon, the unwordly tenets of Stoic philosophy, Cato's ill-advised attack on the private morality of Murena—all these provide the wittiest Roman of his generation with a wonderful field for ridicule and ironic reproof. It is superb artistry, and it leaves the distinguished prosecuting pair slashed to ribbons and exposed as laughable amateurs quite out of touch with the stern realities of life as they are understood by Cicero and his fellow practical citizens who constitute the panel of *iudices*. Perhaps Murena would have been acquitted anyway, but Cicero's speech surely made acquittal certain and somehow respectable, for it appealed to the deep Roman prejudice in favour of the practical and effective man of affairs as against the theorist and the philosopher, to the belief that what mattered most was the result and not any subtle or schematic niceties which might impede its attainment.

Yet, it would be a mistake to judge Cicero's behaviour as unprincipled or directed merely to personal gain. He was, it is true, a very practical man and, like other politicians, constricted by past obligations and future needs. It remains that he honestly saw Catiline's movement as a threat to law and order and stability—we are not called on to sympathize with or share his attitude, only to understand it and accept that it was (at a conscious level) sincere. Murena *was* a very experienced general; if he had been guilty of bribery and corruption, others had committed the same offence before and others would do the same in the future; his chief fault was that he had been both more lavish and more careless than was usual. To unseat a consul-designate was a momentous thing to do. Apart from Sulla and Autronius a few years earlier, it was virtually without precedent. The effect would have been to ruin Murena for ever. Murena was rich and

nfluential; his friend Lucullus was even richer and far more
nfluential; his brother Gaius Murena had been left in Gaul
as acting governor and was dealing with the revolutionaries
n those parts. With his hands full with Catiline, we may
readily comprehend Cicero's reluctance to see a man in
Murena's position driven to contemplate desperate remedies.

Not that things were going well for Catiline. There were
risings in North Italy; in Picenum; in Bruttium and Apulia
n the deep South. But his agents were reckless and un-
balanced. Their nocturnal meetings, their carting about of
arms, and their general hurly-burly frightened people without
n fact presenting any real danger.[37] In the Apennine
regions the praetor Metellus Celer apprehended and im-
prisoned large numbers of insurrectionaries, and Gaius
Murena did likewise in Cisalpine Gaul. At Capua the energetic quaestor Publius Sestius bundled out the Catilinarians
and by December Campania was sufficiently quiet for him
to be transferred north in support of Antonius in Etruria.[38]
Metellus Creticus seems to have dealt with the threat in the
south, for we hear no more of trouble there. Only in Etruria,
the heartland of the revolutionary movement, did serious
opposition continue. By his efforts on the spot Catiline increased his strength from the 2,000 raised by Manlius to the
equivalent of two legions, about 10,000 men. But only one in
four was properly armed and equipped, the rest made do
with whatever came to hand, light hunting-weapons or
even sharpened stakes. It was not much with which to meet
the government forces with their full panoply of armour
and weapons and ancillary services. But Antonius, who had
now taken over command from Marcius Rex in this key-
sector, even with the assistance and prompting of the egreg-
ious Sestius proved singularly ineffective. Catiline manoeuv-
red cleverly to elude him and gave no chance of a battle to
his sluggish opponent, while all the time he hung on in the
hope that if his associates at Rome did their part his forces
would quickly swell in number. Meanwhile he prudently
refused to enlist in his army the large numbers of slaves who

[37] Sallust *Cat.* 42.   [38] *pro Sest.* 9–11.

had fled to his camp, since he was worried about the effec
this might have on the appeal of his movement to citizens.³

Unfortunately for Catiline, his hopes proved to be dupes
His associates at Rome embarked on a gratuitous and fool
hardy intrigue which gave Cicero the chance he had been
waiting for so long and so patiently. Harassed by the depre
dations of Roman financiers, who were backed by the Roman
provincial administrators, the south Gallic tribe of the Allo
broges had sent a mission to Rome to seek some redress. They
obtained none. As they were getting ready to go back home
they were approached by Lentulus who expected to be able
to take advantage of their disgruntled mood. In return for
promises of help they were to rise in support of the con
spiracy. At this distance, and through the fog of partisan
reporting, it is impossible to say just what their role was to be
Cicero painted a garish picture in his *Fourth Catilinarian* of a
horde of wild Gauls picketing their horses in the fire
blackened desolation that had once been Rome, though in
his earlier speech to the people he had spoken less luridly.⁴
It may be that the Allobroges' task was confined to creating a
diversion in southern Gaul and distracting the forces of the
two Gallic provinces above and below the Alps from joining
in the operatiòns against Catiline in Etruria. It may be that
they were to send at least a detachment of cavalry—an
arm in which Gaul was strong and Rome weak—into Italy
to operate with Catiline. But with the fearful memories
deeply embedded in Roman and Italian minds of the Gallic
sack of Rome early in the Republic's history, and the fresher
recollection of the German savages who had poured over
southern France and into north Italy barely a generation
earlier, Cicero was presented with a theme that was like a
gift from Heaven. Small advantage for Catiline to be
scrupulously eschewing the enlistment of fugitive slaves,
because of the effect this would have on public opinion,
when his friends at Rome were busy enrolling long-haired
Gauls!

A certain Publius Umbrenus, who had been active in

---

³⁹ Sallust *Cat.* 56.   ⁴⁰ *in Cat.* IV.12; III.4 and 9.

business affairs in Gaul, made the first contacts on Lentulus' behalf. Having sounded the Allobroges out, he brought in Gabinius—Publius Gabinius Capito, a leading conspirator of equestrian rank, not to be confused with Aulus Gabinius, the tribune of 67 and future consul of 58. With almost unbelievable stupidity the Allobrogians were given details and names. For some time they were in two minds, weighing their grievances against the uncertainties of the undertaking, but finally they poured out the whole story to Quintus Fabius Sanga whose family were the hereditary patrons of their tribe. Fabius told Cicero, who at once saw his chance. The Allobrogians were told to continue their dealings with the conspirators, simulate collaboration, and lead them into a trap.[41]

The conspirators rushed to their undoing like so many Gadarene swine. Prompted by Cicero, the Gauls demanded and received promises signed and sealed by Lentulus and others. Late in the evening of 2 December they left Rome escorted by Titus Volturcius, taking the deadly documents with them. Volturcius was to introduce them to Catiline, to whom he carried a personal message from Lentulus, partly in writing and partly oral. (The gist of it was that things were now critical, and Catiline must stop being squeamish and enrol slaves in his army; all was ready at Rome, the date was fixed, and Catiline should lose no time in closing in on the city, ready to pounce.) The party were filing across the Mulvian Bridge when the trap was sprung. On Cicero's orders, and under a tight security black-out, two of the praetors, both experienced military men, had concealed soldiers in the houses on both sides of the Tiber. They closed in in the darkness from both ends of the bridge and after a brief scuffle it was all over. The praetors took possession of the letters, and these and the prisoners were delivered to Cicero just as dawn was approaching. All unsuspecting, Gabinius, Lucius Statilius (an equestrian like Gabinius), Cethegus, and somewhat belatedly (he had been up all night) Lentulus were separately summoned to an audience

[41] Sallust *Cat.* 40–1.

with the consul and detained. By now rumours were flying
and leading senators came hurrying along. They urged
Cicero to open the letters, but Cicero refused—he knew
their contents and he wanted the seals intact when they were
broken in the Senate to avoid any suspicion of tampering
and to achieve a dramatic effect. An urgent summons went
out for a meeting of the Senate at full strength. Meanwhile on
a tip from the Gauls another praetor was dispatched to
search Cethegus' house, where he discovered and removed a
quantity of daggers and swords.[42]

The Senate met. Volturcius was examined first, and after a
brief attempt at evasion turned state's evidence in return for
immunity. He revealed the whole story about the message
to Catiline. Then the Gauls were brought in and they told
of the oaths and the letters and the projected use of their
cavalry and of Lentulus' talk about Sibylline oracles and his
destined power. Then the dénouement: the letters were
produced. First Cethegus acknowledged his seal; Cicero
broke it and read out the letter, in which in his own hand
Cethegus confirmed to the Allobrogian nation that he would
carry out the promises he had made to their envoys. Earlier
Cethegus had tried to bluster about the cache of arms discovered at his house, claiming that he had always been a
connoisseur of fine weapons. The recitation of his letters
shocked and disheartened him, and he could find nothing to
say. The pattern was repeated with Statilius; he confessed.
Next Lentulus acknowledged his seal and heard his own
letter read. He began with denials and rounded accusingly
on the Gauls and Volturcius. They held their ground, and
Lentulus suddenly broke and confessed. Then the letter
from Lentulus to Catiline was produced, seal and hand
verified by a now violently disturbed Lentulus: 'You will
know who I am from the bearer of this message. Be a man,
remember how critical your position is. Consider what you
must now do and enlist aid wherever you can find it, even
from the meanest.' Finally Gabinius received the same
treatment, began with brash denials, then crumpled and

[42] in Cat. III.4–8; Sallust Cat. 44–5.

confessed under the weight of the evidence. There was now
no sliver of doubt. The testimony of the witnesses, the letters,
the seals, the handwriting, the confessions, all pointed un-
waveringly at a truth underlined by a demeanour of the
accused, who stood dumbly gazing at the ground with
occasional furtive glances at each other.[43]

There is room for scepticism, but no profit to be gained
from it. Exactly what the Allobrogians had been promised
and were expected to do in return was not set down in writing
in the sealed letters, which did no more than confirm what
had been agreed orally. Widely separated fires to be set off
at Rome to enhance confusion are not the same as a general
conflagration. Cicero may have put words into the mouths
of the Gauls and exaggerated other features of the situation
to heighten the effect and frighten the commons. But whatever it was that the Gauls were called on to do does not
alter the fact that the conspirators were engaging in treason-
able activities; and in Cicero's Rome with its high wooden
buildings and tight-packed blocks a conflagration could
easily become general and catastrophic. The conspirators'
guilt was and is patent. Even Caesar did not dream of deny-
ing it.

The events in the Senate were retailed to the people by
Cicero in his *Third Catilinarian*, delivered later the same day,
indeed so promptly that the Senate's decree had not yet
been written out and had to be quoted from memory. Cicero's
anxiety to kill any support from the masses for Catiline by
the revelations about a 'slave war' and a barbarian in-
cursion into Italy and the firing of the city is evident and
understandable; and it was only prudent to exhibit the
firmness and resolve of the authorities and their control of
the situation. Lentulus was an awkward problem; as praetor
holding *imperium* there were serious technical difficulties in
dealing with him. It was resolved that he should first abdi-
cate his office and then be held in custody. Happily the now
shattered and unnerved praetor did as he was told and saved

---

[43] *in Cat.* III. 8–13. Sallust (*Cat.* 46–7) does little more than paraphrase
Cicero.

Cicero and the Senate the worry of having to strip him of his powers. Cethegus, Statilius, and Gabinius were similarly placed under arrest. All four were handed over to individual senators for safeguarding (Rome lacked a prison for such purposes), Statilius and Gabinius being entrusted to Caesar and Crassus respectively. The Senate also authorized the apprehension of other conspirators involved, notably Cassius, Cæparius, Publius Furius, Annius Chilo, and the freedman Umbrenus who had been the original go-between with the Gauls. Finally they decreed a *supplicatio*, a solemn thanksgiving to the gods, the first time such a thing had happened since the foundation of Rome in honour of a magistrate not in exercise of a military command. All this Cicero told the assembled people, and they responded by swerving away from sympathy towards Catiline to extravagant enthusiasm for the consul who had saved them from murder and destruction.[44]

It was a great moment for the new man from Arpinum. From first to last his handling of the crisis cannot be faulted. Patience, determination, restraint, tireless attention to detail, careful organization, courage, suppleness, and (not least) sheer craft had reaped their reward. Cicero was a happy man. But he was also a worried man. Sallust, whose political and historical judgement can vary from the banal to the acute, puts his finger on the spot with sure precision: the news of the successful completion of the ambush at the Mulvian bridge brought Cicero an immense wave of both joy and concern: *ingens cura atque laetitia simul occupavere*.[45] The reason for the joy is evident. The concern was over what to do with the arrested men. Their execution would be his responsibility, his the odium if anyone chose to exploit it, his too the blame if failure to take stern action should result in danger and loss to the state. The large issue raised by the arrest and manifest guilt of the Roman conspirators has already been examined in connection with the trial of Rabirius.[46] Here there is no

---

[44] *in Cat.* III.13–5; Sallust *Cat.* 47–8.
[45] Sallust *Cat.* 46.
[46] Above, p. 92.

need to do more than repeat that the sort of conjunction of events foreseen as likely by both sides on that occasion had in fact materialized.

Cicero resolved to put the responsibility onto the shoulders of the Senate. That body accordingly reconvened on 5 December to debate what was to be done and advise accordingly. Cicero's own speech that day is extant as the *Fourth Catilinarian*. But Sallust supplements this with a version of the debate in which the dominating roles are given to Caesar and Cato, whose opposed speeches engross his account. As Syme insists, this is not partisanship or long-cherished personal rancour against Cicero. Sallust's treatment of Cicero throughout his monograph is balanced, fair, even generous. His merit for us is that he helps us escape from the understandably self-centred writings of Cicero to a more objective view, and that he does so without minimizing Cicero's contribution.[47]

According to Sallust, the critical debate on 5 December was sparked off by attempts to raise forces of personal servants and dependants and hired ruffians to rescue Lentulus and Cethegus.[48] Other interesting things had been happening too on 4 December. A certain Lucius Tarquinius had appeared before the Senate, claimed that he had been entrusted with messages for Catiline, asked for and received immunity, and told his story. Basically he did no more than regurgitate what Volturcius had already said, but then he dropped his bombshell. He had been sent by Crassus to tell Catiline not to be dispirited by the arrests but to make the greater haste to reach Rome to restore confidence in his supporters and rescue his friends.

The Senate exploded in uproar. Some refused to believe such a story. Others found it credible enough, but judged it wisest to avoid provoking Crassus into a violent reaction. Many were personally in his debt. All joined in demanding that Tarquinius be kept in fetters and given no opportunity

---

[47] Sallust *Cat.* 50–5. Syme, *Sallust*, 110–20.
[48] Unless specially noted, the account of the debate is based on Sallust. For some controversial details, see Appendix B.

to say anything further unless it were to reveal the author of the lie. It is a very odd business. One explanation current at the time was that Publius Autronius engineered the whole thing, aiming to involve Crassus so that his great political influence would shield the conspirators with whose peril he would thus be linked. Others said Tarquinius had been put up by Cicero to embarrass Crassus and stop him exploiting the situation to his own political advantage. Sallust tells us how he was himself present when Crassus later openly declared that this disgraceful affair was Cicero's work. But what the soldier said is not necessarily evidence, and it is hard to believe Crassus in this. It would have been remarkably foolhardy of Cicero gratuitously to antagonize Crassus at such a moment.

Quintus Catulus and Gaius Calpurnius Piso also tried to exploit the situation. Both hated Caesar. Catulus' pride had taken a heavy blow when the young Caesar had robbed him of the office of Pontifex Maximus a few months earlier. Piso still smarted from the prosecution launched against him earlier in the year. They used every resource of entreaty and influence to induce Cicero to implicate Caesar by rigged evidence. Cicero would have none of it, but all the same they set to spreading lying rumours themselves with some success: as Caesar was leaving the Senate-house (probably after the debate on 5 December) some of Cicero's volunteer equestrian guard had to be restrained from threatening him.

Catiline was a desperate man. Crassus and Caesar were far from desperate, and neither can for one moment have even toyed with the idea of joining so forlorn a venture. Yet both of them had been prominently associated with the reform issues of the mid-sixties, and many of these were championed, specifically or implicitly, by Catiline and his fellows. There was much material for plausibly linking Crassus and Caesar with the aims of the Catilinarians and hence with the movement itself; guilt by association. With the forces of conservatism ebullient and scenting victory, it was always possible that others not involved in the conspiracy would be victimized. Crassus was probably too rich and influential to suffer much damage, and many nobles may have discerned in him a latent but basic conservatism. Caesar was younger and poorer and still with his way to make; Catulus and Piso were prompt to try to involve him and break him. It says much for Caesar's courage—and for his political 'nose'—that while Crassus (from pique perhaps, but most likely because of his natural caution and proneness to the waiting game) absented himself from the crucial debate on the fifth, Caesar not only attended but spoke so firmly and well that he came close to carrying the day.

The *Curia* was ringed with guards when Cicero put the question to the house: what should be done with the arrested men? The Senate had already decreed that they had committed crimes against the state, but this was too vague for Cicero's comfort. As consul it was for him to take action, and he wanted specific backing. The first speaker called was the senior consul-designate, Junius Silanus. Silanus moved that the arrested conspirators be put to death, along with Cassius Longinus, Furius, Umbrenus and Annius if and when they were apprehended. His fellow consul-designate Murena and no fewer than fourteen ex-consuls all added their weight to his motion.[49] Then came Caesar's turn as praetor-designate. His arguments were 'firm, subtle, and insidious'.[50] He did not challenge the guilt of the conspirators, rather he argued that no punishment could be too severe for their crimes. He took his stand on the rule of law and the danger of establishing a fatal precedent. History showed how other regimes had begun with the best of intentions, peremptorily removed scoundrels with universal acclaim, and then slipped into less discriminating tyranny. 'I have no fear of this from Marcus Tullius nor at this time, but a great nation embraces a wide range of different types of men. It could be that at another time, with another consul, a consul with an army at his call, a lie might be mistaken for the truth. If by our present example a consul unsheathes his sword by the Senate's decree, who will lay down a limit for that future consul, who will hold him in check?'

[49] *ad Att.* XII. 21. 1 (March 45). [50] Syme, *Sallust*, 109.

Caesar proposed that the arrested men be sentenced to life imprisonment in various Italian towns—a novel suggestion, for Rome knew of no such penalty at law. There is no reason to suppose that the suggestion won much support, but the speech had undermined confidence. An ex-praetor, Tiberius Claudius Nero (grandfather of the future Emperor Tiberius), proposed that a decision be postponed and the men kept under stronger guard until Catiline had been beaten and more detailed information was available.[51] Silanus abandoned his earlier draconian motion and announced that he would vote with Nero. Uncertainty prevailed, with a variety of opinions being expressed, until it came to the turn of the tribunes-designate and among them Marcus Porcius Cato.

His speech (Sallust no doubt preserved its gist while shaping and condensing it into Sallustian Latin), was determined and powerful. He brushed aside Caesar's suggestion as sophistic and dangerous. If there was a risk that the prisoners might be rescued from detention at Rome, how much greater if they were transferred to Italian towns, where the defences were weaker and hired bravoes no harder to come by? Revolution was a unique crime. Other crimes could be punished after they had been committed; with this one, if you did not scotch it before it happened, appeal to the courts would be in vain. The Senate must come to its senses and summon up its nerve. What were the facts? Men of the noblest stock had entered into a conspiracy to fire Rome; they had summoned wild Gauls to their aid; Catiline was in the field at the head of an army ready to move against Rome. Yet still the Senate hesitated and procrastinated about what to do with those of the enemy who had been taken in the city. What mercy would these men have shown? If they had cared a farthing for anything of value they would never have formed such plans. Their crimes were capital; they had confessed; they must die.

[51] Appian *BC* 2.5. Appian 'misplaces' Nero's contribution to the debate, but is far clearer about what Nero actually proposed than Sallust, who is irritatingly elliptical. See further, Appendix B.

Cato's force and authority and his succinct analysis were decisive. As he resumed his seat all the ex-consuls and the great part of the Senate burst into praise and applause, deriding each other's timidity.

Of course, Cicero himself spoke in the debate (*the Fourth Catilinarian*) apparently last, as befitted his position as president of the Senate. Sallust ignores the speech, but not unreasonably. His is inevitably a condensed account, and he gave his space to the two contributions he judged vital. Cicero's speech—in its published form—is balanced and undogmatic. It rehearses the arguments already advanced, and then leaves the decision to the Senate. If Cicero also leaves little doubt that he favours the sterner motion, and declares that personal risk will not deter him from putting it into effect, he does not explicitly back it, and his treatment of Caesar is studiously courteous. It was a very proper speech for a presiding officer to make, but it was not just a concern for propriety that influenced its form and content. It was essential for Cicero as far as possible to put the responsibility for any executions fairly and squarely on the broad shoulders of the Senate, so that subsequently he could claim that he had done no more than implement the freely and clearly expressed directions of the great council of state.

Cicero deserves our sympathy. For the moment he was overwhelmed with praise and honour. Catulus and Cato entitled him 'the father of his country', and the former censor Lucius Gellius moved that he be granted the *corona civica*, a coveted military decoration awarded for saving a citizen's life in battle.[52] The Senate was enthusiastic. But just over four years later Cicero was left to face the consequences alone while the *boni* either warily 'passed by on the other side' or looked on with a certain malicious satisfaction. Already in December 63, the tribune Metellus Nepos, who entered office on the 10th of the month, was to declare at a public meeting that a man who had executed others without trial should not himself be permitted to speak. And when

[52] *in Pis.* 6; Plutarch *Cicero* 23; Aulus Gellius 5.6.15. Caesar had won the *corona civica* in Asia Minor as a young man (Suetonius *DJ* 2).

Cicero prepared to deliver the customary valedictory address to the people Metellus used his power to insist that Cicero confine himself to making the required oath that he had fulfilled the duties of his office. Though Cicero turned the tables by taking the oath in a novel form and declaring that he had in truth saved the state and done his duty, the leaves were already beginning to rustle at the approaching storm.[53]

Controversy about the rights and wrongs of Cicero's actions in carrying out the execution of the conspirators is inevitable. There is no need to go over ground already covered in the discussion of the issues raised by the Rabirius trial. Those who sit in judgement on Cicero cannot be wholly objective in a matter where total objectivity is unattainable. Their varying temperaments are bound to colour their interpretation of the facts, about which there can be no dispute. To cite just one example: Theodore Mommsen charged Cicero with 'an act of the most brutal tyranny'; this in Mommsen's youth—in later works he held Cicero legally justified.[54] The change in his assessment owed more to the maturity and largeness of view that come with increasing years and wider experience than to any advance in scholarship.

We need to be clear about some features of the Roman legal system to understand what was involved. In Cicero's Rome the death penalty had to all intents and purposes been abolished for citizens. Probably this was not true of common criminals—cut-throats, highwaymen, and such. As so often, history leaves us largely in the dark about the lower orders of society, and certainty here is not to be had. No doubt such miscreants, even if they were freeborn Romans, were summarily executed without any fuss being made. Many would be cut down *in flagrante delicto*, many would flee to the life of an outlaw or a brigand. However it was, we are not concerned with them. The respectable criminal was another matter, particularly if he was a senator. This is not the place to examine in detail how this development had come to pass:

---

[53] *ad famm.* V.2.7–8.
[54] Cited by Rice Holmes, op. cit., I. 278, who reviews other opinions.

by and large it was the work of the tribunes, who could use their blocking powers to thwart executive action by preventing arrest or enforcing release from custody.[55] But come to pass it had, with the result that in effect the worst punishment a guilty man would suffer for a capital offence was retirement to some nominally independent town outside the jurisdiction of Rome—a retirement which need not be disagreeable. Only against this background can it be grasped how startling it was that men of the class of Lentulus and his friends should actually be sent to their deaths at the hands of the public executioner.

That, then, was part of the dilemma. To reserve the arrested men for later trial would have two serious drawbacks. First, there was the risk of rescue by violent means. Secondly, to bring them in due course to trial and see them pack their bags for what could prove a comfortable exile did not seem the proper course with men who had planned armed revolution and been foiled only by their own ineptitude. Such a compromise could lend strength to the rebels still at large, while sterner measures would underline the determination of the government and discourage Catiline's supporters. Lentulus and the rest were rebels. Had they been assailed with arms in their hands there would have been no question of the justice and legality of killing them. What penalty but death was appropriate to the magnitude of their crime?

But the heart of the dilemma was this: the proceedings in the Senate, for all that they might present the appearance of a trial (especially conjoined with the examinations of the witnesses and the accused two days earlier) did not and could not constitute a trial in strict law. No decree of the Senate could override statute law, which guaranteed all Roman citizens the right of trial before sentence could be executed on them and enjoined that a magistrate who put a citizen to death without due process of law was guilty of a capital offence. The Senate had no power to order the death of the conspirators. Cicero had, and in exercising it ran the risk of

---

[55] For a full discussion, see Strachan-Davidson, *Problems of the Roman Criminal Law*, I. 160–4.

falling foul of the august laws governing the right of appeal.
His only defence could be, not that the Senate had ordered
him to do something the Senate had no power to order,
but that the safety of the state had required him to act as he
did, and that he had had the support of the Senate's authoritative opinion in so acting. The responsibility remained his,
however unfair it may seem that it should. A less resolute
consul would have declined to carry out the executions, or
not even have initiated the discussion in the Senate. For all
his circumspection, Cicero showed himself both resolute and
courageous.

It is not surprising that later on Cicero should have been
upset at the adulatory stress laid on Cato's part in the debate.
In the *Fourth Catilinarian* Cato's name does not feature anywhere. The two motions discussed as being at issue are those
of Caesar and Silanus—technically correct since Silanus
had been the first to move for death, but none the less misleading. Nearly twenty years later Cicero was put out by
Brutus' treatment of the affair in his *Cato*, a work devoted to
the glory of Brutus' now dead uncle and father-in-law. He
wrote to Atticus about it in March 45:

Brutus is shamefully ignorant on this point: he thinks Cato was the first
to come out with the proposal for the death penalty. Every previous
speaker had advocated it before Caesar. And although Caesar's proposal
(he spoke at the time with a praetor's priority in the debate) was itself
so harsh, Brutus thinks that those of the ex-consuls were more lenient—
Catulus, Servilius, Curio, Torquatus, Lepidus, Gellius, Volcatius,
Figulus, Cotta, Lucius Caesar, Gaius Piso, Manius Glabrio, apart from
Silanus and Murena the consuls-designate. Why, then, was it Cato's
motion that was voted on? Because it said the same thing in more resounding and ampler phrasing. Then he praises me for bringing the
matter before the Senate—*not* for exposing everything, *not* for giving a
lead, *not* for making up my own mind before consulting the Senate! It
was because Cato had in fact lauded all this to the skies and moved that
it be officially recorded that it was on his motion that the vote was
taken.[56]

Obviously it remained a sore point for a long time. Injured pride or faulty memory may have misled Cicero in this

[56] *ad Att.* XII.21.1.

letter to play down the effect of Cato's speech. But the faults may not all be his: other versions 'may derive from authorities who loved Cato better than Cicero or truth—perhaps Brutus himself':[57] the kind of posthumous panegyric that Brutus composed on Cato was traditionally permitted great latitude with the details of fact by ancient opinion—piety was not to be constricted within the same rigid canons of accuracy as formal history (witness the patent example of Tacitus in his *Agricola*, another posthumous account of a father-in-law). To take just one point: Plutarch records that after Caesar had finished his speech the first to attack him was the formidable Quintus Lutatius Catulus. There is no reason at all to doubt this, but Sallust skims over the interval between Caesar's speech and Cato's by simply saying that 'different people took different positions'.[58] Sallust may have used Brutus' *Cato* as a source of information, and a desire for artistic and dramatic effect could well have led him to be careless of detail in the pursuit of broader aims.

He advances Caesar and Cato as the twin titans of the death struggle of the Republic, encapsulating in their persons the opposed ideals and characters of the age. 'For long years Rome produced scarcely any truly great man. But within my memory there were two men of immense character but quite divergent temperament, Marcus Cato and Gaius Caesar'— *sed memoria mea ingenti virtute, divorsis moribus fuere viri duo, M. Cato et C. Caesar.*[59] With such a theme, the Catilinarian debate was a severe temptation to point a moral or adorn a tale.

The truth is simple. Cicero was the man to whom the chief credit (or blame) was due, the consul who (regardless what view we take of the merits of the case) showed resolution and intelligence in every aspect of his conduct and in the end shouldered the final responsibility, which could be his and his alone, for ordering the executions. But there is room

---

[57] Shackleton-Bailey, *Cicero's Letters to Atticus*, V.316–17.
[58] Plutarch *Cicero* 21, *Caesar* 8; Sallust *Cat.* 52.
[59] Sallust *Cat.* 53.

enough for both Cicero and Cato to be given each their due
without detriment to either.

The rest of the story is soon told.

Cicero resolved to waste no time now that he had the
Senate's decree advising the death penalty. He wanted to
give no opportunity for a last-minute bid to rescue the prisoners; not even a single night must intervene. The consul himself escorted Lentulus, the rest were brought by the praetors.
One after another, the two patrician Cornelii first, they were
lowered into an enclosed dungeon—coincidentally called the
Tullianum—and garrotted. Cicero emerged and announced
to the assembled throng that the conspirators' lives had
ended. In Latin one terse word sufficed: *Vixere*.

When the news reached Catiline's camp, it had the desired
effect. Unnerved, the more casual of Catiline's supporters,
those who had had hopes of quick booty and excitement,
slipped away and dispersed. Catiline himself made ready for
one last throw. Jettisoning all designs in Italy and at Rome,
he planned to feel his way by a circuitous and difficult
route and escape across the Alps into Gaul. There a leader
of his calibre at the head of a tough and disciplined Italian
force might carve out a principality of his own; the recent
example of Sertorius in Spain showed what might be done.
But Metellus Celer in Picenum, anticipating such a move,
broke camp and quickly moved into a position where, aided
by information from deserters, he lay in wait for Catiline
at the exit from the mountains where his march to Gaul
must take him. Antonius was not far away, like Celer able
to make better speed than Catiline over easier ground.

Catiline had no choice but to risk everything on a battle.
His temperament pushed him the same way. He elected to
fight it out with Antonius rather than Celer. One can understand his decision, but his hopes were disappointed even here.
Antonius developed trouble with his feet, and handed over
his command to his lieutenant, Marcus Petreius, a tough and
experienced military man who had seen over thirty years of
service.

After a few words of encouragement, Catiline drew up his line of battle on a narrow front, its flanks resting on mountains and rugged rocky terrain.[60] As a gesture to inspire solidarity and confidence, he sent away all the horses. His first line consisted of eight cohorts, perhaps some 4,000 men, which he stiffened by drawing from the rear formations centurions, non-commissioned officers, veterans, and the best and best-equipped of the line soldiers—three-quarters of his original two legions, it will be recalled, were only sketchily armed and equipped. The ordering of his battle-line he supervised personally and on foot. Manlius commanded his right, an unnamed man from Faesulae his left. He himself took up position in the centre, attended by his closest personal followers, clustered around the Eagle of Marius.

Petreius, too, formed his front from his best soldiers, the veterans who had been recalled to the colours for the emergency, with the remainder in reserve. When he signed to the trumpeter to sound the advance, he warned his men to take it slowly. The enemy moved slowly to meet him. But when the two armies came within missile distance, they suddenly raised a great shout and charged head-on, javelins discarded, swords clashing. It was a bitter and bloody affair, as the veterans of Petreius found themselves evenly matched. Catiline was everywhere, bolstering weak points, bringing up fresh soldiers to close gaps, fighting and killing with his own hand. Petreius was surprised by a violence of resistance he had not anticipated. He ordered up the crack praetorian cohort and flung it at the enemy centre. The blow struck home; Catiline's men were thrown into disorder, and one by one they fell, still fiercely resisting. Then Petreius collapsed the opposing wings, whose commanders fell in the front ranks. In the ruin of his fortunes Catiline threw himself into the thick of the enemy and fought till he was cut down.

Of Catiline's whole force no freeborn citizen was taken alive, so savage was their spirit. No ground had been yielded,

60 The battle was fought near Pistoria, some twenty five miles north-west of Florence.

each man held in death the post he had been assigned. A few of those in the centre had been scattered by the shock of the charge of the praetorians, but all their wounds were in front. Catiline was found at some distance ahead of his men, still breathing faintly and still showing in his face that ferocity of spirit which had marked him in life.[61]

[61] Sallust *Cat.* 55–61.

VII

CONSULARIS

CICERO was a very intelligent man, and a 'new man' who had made his way by his own natural talents. His family was well-to-do and of local consequence; but it lacked any senatorial noble tradition to form or warp his character and outlook into that narrow and cruel and selfish mould which characterized many of the *nobiles*. His answer to the question 'How is the Republic to be defended against attack?' was his well-known doctrine of *concordia ordinum*. What this amounted to was a union of men of property and settled respectability in defence of the established order of society, a union of the Senate and the members of what can be loosely termed the equestrian order. If they could be got to co-operate in the courts and at elections they could be counted on to defeat radicals and reformers, who would either fail to secure election or be checked and disciplined by the courts when they tried to break through the wall of constitutional obstructions which the conservatives would throw up to contain them. In 63 Cicero was dazzled by the overwhelming success of his *concordia*: Senate and knights and the municipal ruling-classes of Italy had rallied to the side of their consul to reject the reform programme and crush Catiline. Cicero himself was overwhelmed with honours and praise. It is no surprise that the whole business should have gone to his head; and the brilliance left his sight impaired for the next six or seven years. It had been a remarkable achievement, and Cicero was the last man to play down in his own mind his own unquestionably central importance.

In the years that followed, in moments both of elation and

of disillusion, Cicero was much given to recalling the successes of his consulship and the chances of redeploying his
'army' of 63. Undoubtedly such a combination as he envisaged should have been powerful enough to hold the line
and even to counter-attack into the bargain. The combined
wealth and influence and voting power of his conjoined
'orders' would have been decisive. He saw too that continuing cohesion required an agreed leader who could
impart direction and control. The literary expression of this
idea has to wait for the years after 56, when Cicero in virtual
retirement from politics has leisure to compose treatises like
the *de re publica* of 52. Much of this work is now lost, but
writing to Atticus in February 49 Cicero has occasion to
refer to it and to what he had to say therein about his 'ideal
statesman', his *moderator*.[1] The hero of the dialogue is Scipio
Aemilianus, the great statesman of the forties and thirties
of the preceding century, who is introduced in conversation
with members of the 'Scipionic circle', the most notable of
whom was Laelius. Already in the letter he wrote to Pompey
in April 62 Cicero was expressing the hope that when Pompey
gets back to Rome 'you will readily allow me, who am not
so much a smaller man than Laelius was, to be associated
both in matters of state and in friendship with you, who are
far greater than Africanus' [i.e. Aemilianus].[2] Cicero had
enough sense not to cast himself for the role of *moderator rei
publicae*, but clearly he was toying with the idea of playing
Laelius to Pompey's Scipio, influencing the *moderator* himself
with sage advice and political wisdom.

Such, somewhat baldly, was Cicero's political thinking at
this time. But trouble arose in putting it into practice. Men
who could be got to rally against the threat of violent
revolution and expropriation of property might differ considerably amongst themselves about what they would like the
shape of the Republic to be: remove immediate threats, and
Senate and knights could readily fall to quarrelling amongst

[1] *ad Att.* VIII.11.1; *de re pub.* 5.8. See Appendix C.
[2] *ad famm.* V.7.3. (In July 59, he chose 'Laelius' as a cryptic pseudonym:
ad Att. II.19.5.)

themselves. Nor were men like Caesar and Crassus blind to the political importance of equestrian support, and they would work hard and unscrupulously to get it by offering the right price. The *boni*, over-confident and sometimes over-scrupulous, might and did neglect to do as much. Pompey had a record that was not calculated to endear him to the nobility, who understandably feared and distrusted him; and his thinking about the Republic was not on all fours with Cicero's, and he could not be relied on to take kindly to the idea that Cicero should set himself up as his guide and mentor in such matters. Politics is the art of the possible. Theories are of little use unless they can be translated into practice. At this period of his life Cicero's elating experience in 63 seduced him into minimizing the practical difficulties that stood in the way of implementing his ideas.

Underlying everything else was the truth that in 63 the danger had been averted, but not obliterated. All the social and economic ills remained to bedevil the Roman body politic. Politicians were bound to continue to try to remedy or exploit them. The nobility remained exclusive and unimaginative. In this Cicero proved as blind as any of them. He never grasped the fundamental fact that it was only by curing these ills, by taking positive steps to alleviate misery and disgruntlement, that the weapons could be dashed from the hands of the enemies of his Republic. His conscience was never stirred by the spectacle of the plight of the poor and disaffected, either to pity or to anger. At bottom he had the rich bourgeois's contempt for the poor, or perhaps 'disregard' is a better word. No doubt something could be done one day, but there was no urgency. As for political opportunity, he was himself the best example one could have of the sort of career that was open to anyone with ability and determination enough to try.

However, remembering that the success or practicability of Cicero's ideas was yet to be decided by events, let us return to 62 and to the critical question of Cicero's relations with Pompey.

After the suppression of Catiline, Cicero wrote what became a notorious letter to Pompey to tell him all about it. Unfortunately the letter is not among those that have survived. It was a very long letter, 'almost as big as a book' (*ad instar voluminis*). We first hear of it in the speech *pro Sulla*, delivered later in 62, where we learn that the prosecutor irritatingly persisted in reading out extracts from it to prove his case from Cicero's own pen. Eight years later another forensic opponent also threw it in Cicero's face. A commentator describes the letter as 'somewhat high-handed' (*aliquanto insolentius*), which fits in well with Cicero's ebullient mood at the time.[3]

This is the background to the extant letter from Cicero to Pompey of April 62, a letter written after the Senate had received Pompey's formal victory dispatch. Pompey had also written privately to Cicero, stiffly and without warmth:

As for your private letter to me [writes Cicero], although it contained scarcely any indication of your goodwill towards me, still I should like you to know that it gave me pleasure. For there is nothing makes me so happy as my personal conviction that I have done my duty. If sometimes this does not meet with a like response from the other party, I am quite content that the balance of obligation (*officium*) should remain with me. This I do not doubt—even if my own loyal exertions on your behalf have sufficed little to link you to me, public affairs will be sure to reconcile and unite us. And so that you may not be unaware of what it was that I missed in your letter, I shall write frankly, as my own nature and our friendship demand. I have achievements to my credit for which I expected some word of congratulation both in view of our close personal ties and on patriotic grounds . . .

And he ends up by looking forward to playing Laelius to Pompey's Aemilianus.[4]

Why this coolness between Pompey and Cicero, who had been so prominent a supporter of Pompey from 66 onward, whose election campaign had so largely rested, as Quintus Cicero put it, 'on your glorification of Pompey, your acceptance of the brief for Manilius, your defence of Cornelius'?[5]

---

[3] *pro Sulla* 67; *pro Planc.* 85; *Schol. Bob.*, p. 167 (Stangl).
[4] *ad famm.* V.7.2–3.
[5] *Commentariolum* 51.

One answer often offered is: Catiline. Pompey failed to clap Cicero heartily on the back over his record in 63. When later Pompey was back in Rome, he addressed the Senate in February 61 and studiedly neglected to dilate on the same subject. As he sat down, he turned to Cicero and said he thought he had said enough 'about those affairs of yours' (*de istis rebus*). Cicero disagreed, and when Crassus rose and waxed Ciceronically eloquent on the subject of Cicero's great services to the state Cicero confessed that it quite warmed his heart to hear it.[6]

As we have seen, Cicero's relations with Catiline from 65 onwards were not all of a piece. It is impossible to be certain what was happening in 66/65 in the matter of the alleged 'conspiracy'; Catiline may have had Pompeian connections at the time. In a sense it could be maintained that in 63 Cicero himself produced the Catilinarian uprising by his damming of the river of reform and his embittered opposition to Catiline himself. It is conceivable that Pompey was annoyed about the way in which a possible sympathizer, able and energetic, had been driven first into the arms of Crassus and then into desperate revolution. Further, it has been contended that Pompey had looked to be summoned home to deal with the insurrection, and was understandably annoyed when Cicero did not suggest it. All this is conceivable, but on examination not very plausible. Men of the stature and character of Cicero and Catiline, and others one could name, were more than mere hirelings to be ordered about by party 'bosses' and disciplined for failure to do as they were told. In 65 Catiline was in serious trouble; a conviction in the courts would have meant political extinction. If Crassus appeared with political and financial support, Catiline could not be expected to spurn the offer; both men had a lot to offer each other. Pompey was far away in the East, in no position to intervene directly, even had he wished to.

It is true that Metellus Nepos left Pompey's staff early in 63 to return to Rome to stand for the tribunate in some sense

[6] *ad Att.* I.14.2–3.

as Pompey's candidate. Cato's decision to stand as well is said
to have been taken because of the dangers he apprehended
from Nepos as an agent of Pompey. Nepos lost no time in
attacking Cicero, and the two men clashed in the Senate in
January 62, giving rise to an awkward exchange of letters
between Cicero and Nepos' brother, Metellus Celer. (Celer
had as praetor in 63 succeeded to the province of Cisalpine
Gaul which Cicero declined to take after his exchange with
Antonius, and Cicero claims that he and Antonius had
'arranged' that the lot should fall on Celer.) Nepos also
proposed that Pompey be recalled to Italy to deal with the
insurrection, and followed this up with a proposal that the
honour of dedicating the rebuilt Capitoline temple should be
transferred from Catulus to Pompey. The resultant uproar
and rioting led in the end to the Senate's suspending Nepos
and the praetor Caesar from their offices (Caesar had backed
Nepos in both proposals); and though Caesar behaved with
such circumspection that he was soon reinstated, Nepos
left Rome to return to Pompey's side.[7]

It would however be very wrong to suppose that whenever we read of Nepos' doing or saying something we can
quite simply substitute Pompey's name for that of Nepos.
If Nepos left Asia in time to conduct even a short canvass
before the elections, he can hardly have left later than
March or April 63 at the outside. Thus any news Pompey
had of affairs at Rome which could form the basis of discussion and briefing before Nepos set off for home can
scarcely have been fresher than the beginning of 63, when we
allow for the time taken for messengers to reach Asia Minor
and locate the commander-in-chief. We need to keep this
time-lag well in mind. The time taken for a letter or messen-
ger from Rome to reach Pompey in the East cannot be calculated exactly; it would depend on the weather, the state
of the seas and the roads, the location of Pompey's headquarters. But on average the time taken for information to
reach Pompey, be digested, and produce a considered reply

[7] Plutarch *Cato Minor* 20, 26–9; *Cicero* 23; Suetonius *DJ* 16. The exchange of
letters: *ad famm.* V.1 and 2. The ballot-rigging: *ad famm.* V.2.3.

back at Rome for anyone to act on must have been very considerable, certainly not much less than three months and sometimes longer.[8] Events moved fast, and by the time all this was completed the situation had changed radically. Thus for much of the time Nepos had to play things 'by ear', and guess what Pompey would want done. He could easily have guessed wrong. Pompey was subtle and flexible and cautiously close, while Nepos was clumsy and crude. To take one example: Nepos' proposal to transfer the Capitoline dedication from Catulus to Pompey outraged conservative opinion. When Pompey was back in Italy he was at great pains to conciliate the *boni*, and even offered Cato a marriage alliance. Seen in this light, Nepos' action was distinctly embarrassing. (In fact, Pompey divorced his wife Mucia, half-sister of Nepos, on his return from the East.)[9] As for Caesar, apart from any other considerations, by backing Nepos he was helping to diminish the chances of a possible reconciliation between Pompey and the *boni*, something that could have been disadvantageous to his own prospects.

It would have been ridiculous for Pompey to expect a serious insurrection to be kept simmering for months until he himself could be called home, and there is no reason to suppose that he was so unreasonable. It is most unlikely (to put it mildly) that it would have suited Pompey if Catiline with Crassus and Caesar behind him, had been elected consul for 63 or 62 and carried a reform programme. Possibly the three of them would have done a deal with Pompey on his return, but they would have been bargaining from a stronger position than Pompey can be expected to have relished. If Cicero needed optimate support to keep Catiline out and reject reform (and he did need it), he could not be blamed for seeking it from men like Lucullus who were in the best position to deliver it. And matters like Cicero's

---

[8] Writing to Atticus from Laodicea early in May 50 Cicero says that he has copies of the *acta urbana* only up to 7 March; that is, he is two months behind-hand (*ad Att.* VI.2.6). Yet Cicero had a good communication service.

[9] Münzer, *Römische Adelsparteien*, 349–50.

defence of Pompey's former enemy Piso turn out on closer examination to be more complex than a simple description would suggest.

In seeking the explanation of Pompey's coolness towards Cicero we need a finer-meshed and wider net. A few years earlier, Pompey had bestridden the world like a colossus. Associated with the vital reforms of 70 (above all the restoration of the full powers of the tribunate), the idol of the *populus*, the sympathiser with and backer of men like Cornelius and Gabinius, the hero of the knights, resistance to his will was doomed to failure and his two great commands could not be blocked however much optimates like Catulus and Hortensius and Piso tried. Ambitious men flocked to solicit appointments to his staff: posts which promised financial profit and valuable experience and perhaps even some small fame. Things were very different on his return to Italy late in 62. He remained unquestionably the most powerful figure in Roman politics, but the earlier dominance was gone. The political balance had begun to swing away from him in his absence. The optimates were in a buoyant mood. Largely thanks to Cicero they had thwarted very dangerous moves towards reform; after the defeats of 70 and 67 and 66 they had begun to win victories again; the knights had rallied to their side. Caesar and Crassus had made serious inroads into Pompey's near-monopoly of popular support. Pompey's gestures of friendship towards the *boni* met with no response; Cato would have nothing of a marriage alliance. When Pompey tried to secure the formal ratification of his eastern settlement he met with stubborn and successful resistance in the Senate. When he tried to push through a tribunician bill for land-distribution which would provide his time-served veterans with their expected reward the whole affair proved a damp squib. It was a far cry from the great days of 70 and the heady triumphs of the Gabinian and Manilian laws.

Set against this background, Pompey's lack of warmth and enthusiasm is comprehensible enough. After all, Cicero was publicly a Pompeian. He had fought his election in great part on this platform. He had been consul. He ought to have seen to Pompey's interests in the great man's absence; if Pompey's situation had deteriorated sharply, Cicero could plausibly be held to be partly to blame. But far from approaching Pompey with his tail between his legs, Cicero ran up expecting to be patted on the head; far from apologizing and seeking to excuse what had happened, Cicero wrote a 'rather high-handed' letter to Pompey and sulked when Pompey did not fall over himself to congratulate him on his achievements. He even proposed to set himself up as a sort of guide, philosopher, and friend to help steer Pompey through the delicate maze of Roman politics. If anyone is to blame for the breach, Catiline is far less good a candidate for responsibility than Cicero himself, whose success not only dazzled him but also thickened his skin and blunted his sensitivity.

Cicero had a fair case to make in his own defence, if he had chosen.

What had Crassus and Caesar been doing in Pompey's absence? Mommsen and his followers stressed the 'counterpoise theory': an attempt to get some area like Spain or Egypt as a *point d'appui* against Pompey. But that Piso or anyone else could repeat in Spain the success of Sertorius is hard to believe, especially as Pompey had built up a strong political base there during the seventies; and the strategic value of Egypt depended on sea-power—and the seas were held by Pompey. Above all, there is the supreme difficulty that any clumsy or overt attempt to do Pompey down by such means might give him an excuse to follow in Sulla's footsteps, or (more realistically) leave him with little option but to do so in self-defence. Too direct a threat to Pompey carried the dangerous seeds of its own destruction. Crassus and Caesar were not desperate men; they had no need to take desperate risks.

Considerations such as these have led some moderns to react against Mommsen's view, but they seem to have gone too far the other way. Their views suggest or imply that the great *populares* knew, presumably from their reading of

Pompey's character, that Pompey would not try to seize supreme power by force on his return, and hence they could proceed without concern on that score. But there is no good reason to assume that Crassus or Caesar or anybody else *knew* what Pompey was or was not going to do. Quite the reverse; Pompey was something of an opportunist, and notoriously poker-faced. More than once Cicero and other contemporaries emphasize this aspect of the man: 'It is difficult to know whether he wants something or doesn't' (a letter of Cicero's from 54); or, 'I have been here with Pompey. He has talked to me about public affairs a great deal, very dissatisfied with himself, *so he said*—one must always remember to add *that* when talking about Pompey' (a letter of 55).[10] Crassus and Caesar were not the men to throw up their hands and do nothing but sit quietly and wait for something to happen. Like most politicians (*pace* some historians), they lived in the present and chanced the long-term future. The fact that they could not *know* when Pompey would be back, how successful he would be, what the situation would be like at Rome, what he would do, did not and could not inhibit them from taking action. Pompey was a long way from Rome, preoccupied and out of touch; meanwhile there were valuable profits to be gained by those who knew how to work the political machine, for example in Egypt, where vast treasures and wide patronage might be acquired. Even if they achieved nothing positive, by their championing of popular causes they went far to persuade the Transpadanes, the urban masses, the poor countrymen, the children of the proscribed, and dissatisfied men in general that they were their friends, winning their support and favour and sapping Pompey's popular monopoly.

For Cicero it was an awkward situation. Not to oppose the reform programme of 63, as well as forfeiting the favour of the *boni*, would have allowed Pompey's old enemy Crassus and a dangerous newcomer like Caesar to secure great political advantage; but opposing the programme marked Cicero as a champion of reaction. By the wide use he understandably

[10] *ad QF* III.8.4; *ad Att.* IV. 9.1.

made of the popular name of Pompey and his own position as
a loyal Pompeian to defeat this programme he dragged
Pompey's reputation along with him and so weakened
Pompey's popular support, while his own success strengthened optimate morale.

It is hard to see any happy way out of this dilemma.
Pompey himself was far away and unable to intervene in
person to intrigue and influence, to buy concessions from the
boni as the price of his support or perhaps steal the opposition's clothes. It is noteworthy that never again did Pompey
stray far from Rome until driven out of Italy altogether in
49; noteworthy too that it was in parallel circumstances,
viz. during his preoccupation with the Gallic revolt and
Vercingetorix in 52–51, that Caesar lost contact with affairs
at Rome, and with loss of contact lost control and suffered
political defeat at the hands of the man on the spot, Pompey.

How much blame we assign to Cicero is a moot point.
Pompey was probably none too objective in his assessment,
and Cicero did nothing to help by his own bumptious attitude. Added to this, we can rely on it (and the events bear
this out) that Pompey needed time to feel his way into a
radically changed situation, and was not disposed to accept
at once and with becoming gratitude the ready-made
answers which Cicero was only too eager to propound. Of
course, when Pompey sent off his cool letter to Cicero and
Cicero replied in his letter of April 62, much of this had still
to happen. Pompey did not land in Italy until the end of
the year. But the Asian episode was now over, the formal
dispatch had been sent to the Senate and People of Rome,
and during his long and leisurely preparations for his return
Pompey had ample opportunity to revolve in his mind
schemes and possibilities for the future. The neutral tone of
his early letter is maintained in the months after he is back in
Italy.

Cicero's two extant forensic speeches of 62 are the *pro
Archia* and the *pro Sulla*. Archias we met early in Cicero's
life. Born in Antioch, he became part of the academic and

professional Greek 'brain drain' to Italy, where he gained great notoriety as a literary figure, poet, and teacher. As such he had been among the important early influences on Cicero's education. He was now charged before a court presided over by Quintus Cicero (one of the praetors of 62) with the crime of exercising Roman citizenship without proper title.

Archias was a protégé of Lucius Lucullus. It is therefore widely assumed that the prosecution aimed to attack Lucullus indirectly through his friend, and that Pompey was behind the attack, hoping to prick the balloon of Lucullus' new-found prestige consequent upon his long-delayed but magnificent triumphal display and the election of his old lieutenant Murena to a consulship. Had this been so, Cicero's defence of Archias would have been an overt act of opposition to Pompey. But that it was so is pure specu-lation, and quite unfounded. Pompey was not the only enemy Lucullus had. The name of the prosecutor, Gratius, is otherwise unknown, so that nothing can be deduced from it about his possible political connections. Neither in Cicero's speech nor in the observations of the ancient commentator on it[11] is there any hint or suggestion that the giant figure of Pompey may loom behind Gratius. That Cicero should in his speech make something of the importance of his client's patrons, the Luculli, and have little or nothing to say about Pompey, is entirely natural. We need only remember Cicero's own personal ties with Archias, and note too that this dis-tinguished poet (who had already composed works on Marius' Cimbric War and Lucullus' exploits in Asia) had now embarked on a poem celebrating Cicero's own consul-ship, to perceive that there is no reason to start any hares to explain why Cicero should have accepted this particular brief.[12] No more is it reasonable to suppose that Pompey should have been seriously upset that he did.[13]

[11] *Schol. Bob.*, pp. 175–9 (Stangl).

[12] *pro Archia* 20–1; *ad Att.* I.16.15; 20.6.

[13] The Archias case has been over-discussed; the evidence is minimal, the weight of speculation preposterous. For some recent comments, Taylor, *AJP* 73 (1952), 62–70.

Cicero's defence of Publius Sulla was a very different matter. The early months of 62 witnessed the tidying up of the loose ends of the Catilinarian business. Vargunteius, Autronius, Laeca, Gaius Cornelius, and others were proceeded against by due process of law. Cicero gave evidence against all of them, and it seems they were all convicted.[14] But when, probably about July, Sulla was arraigned on a similar charge, Cicero appeared for the defence along with Hortensius. The prosecutor was Titus Manlius Torquatus, son of the consul of 65 who had replaced Sulla after Sulla (together with Autronius) had been unseated for bribery. It was young Titus who had prosecuted successfully on that earlier occasion. At this trial he was assisted by the son of the convicted Catilinarian, Gaius Cornelius.

Sulla was charged with complicity in both conspiracies, the supposed one of 66/65 and the 63 affair. As we have already seen, the earlier business both is now and was then so befogged by rumour and wild partisan charges that the truth is and was unascertainable. Hortensius and Cicero so divided their roles as defending counsel that Hortensius concentrated on the earlier charge while Cicero himself dealt with the events of 63, and delivered the final emotional plea to the court, an art of which he was the acknowledged and unchallenged master. This division of duties Cicero justified in part by alleging that he was no expert on what had happened in 66/65, 'I suppose because I was not yet at the heart of politics, and had not yet attained the goal which I had set myself' [the consulship].[15] This is fraudulent and disingenuous. He was praetor in 66, and had in 65 seriously considered defending Catiline and running in harness with him for the consular elections. In other speeches he had not felt himself inhibited by ignorance from making sweeping and definite statements about the earlier 'conspiracy'. The true explanation is no doubt that, as so often, Cicero had talked too much, that he had in speeches like the *in toga candida* and elsewhere committed himself to a line which left

[14] *pro Sulla* 6.
[15] Ibid. 11–12.

him little room for manoeuvre, so that it was wiser to leav
the talking to Hortensius.

Even as it was, Torquatus tried to use the famous 'book
length' letter to Pompey to argue that Cicero's own word
proved the guilt of Sulla in respect of the earlier 'conspir
acy'.[16] But overwhelmingly we are ignorant of the charge
and evidence relating to the earlier affair since Cicero
avoided dealing with them and neither Hortensius' no
Torquatus' speech is extant. Cicero relies heavily on his own
central position in 63 for his defence on the later charge
stating firmly that he had never had any suspicion of Sulla
nor any evidence against him.[17] Sulla's connection with
Autronius was suspicious.[18] Although he was not at Rome
but at Naples in Campania for most of the relevant periods (a
point Cicero makes much of), Campania was a great train-
ing-ground of gladiators, and Sulla (working with his cousin
Faustus, son of the dictator) had collected a troop of gladiators rather hurriedly, ostensibly for a public show in honour
of the dictator's memory.[19] There was tension between the
old inhabitants of Pompeii and the new veteran colonists
planted there by the dictator: Publius Sulla was a patron of
the colony, and was suspected of manipulating the situation
in the interests of Catiline.[20] Publius' half-brother, the
tribune Caecilius Rufus, had been forward in trying to secure
the restoration of Publius' public status which he had lost
as a consequence of his conviction in 66.[21] Sulla had awkward connections with a colourful and shady adventurer
called Publius Sittius who was suspected of Catilinarian
links.[22] When the conspirator Lucius Cassius had been asked
by the Allobroges whether Sulla was in the plot, he had
neither confirmed nor denied it, but merely said that 'he

[16] Ibid. 67 ff.
[17] Ibid. 14.
[18] Ibid. 71.
[19] Ibid. 53–4.
[20] Ibid. 60 ff. Cf. *ad famm.* VII. 1.3 (Oct. 55, to M. Marius) for a probable
allusion to trouble involving gladiators there.
[21] Ibid. 62.
[22] Ibid. 56.

did not know for sure'.[23] The son of the conspirator Cornelius produced evidence of some sort at second-hand from his father.[24]

All the same, it looks as if the prosecution had no really hard proof, and had to rely on circumstantial evidence and inference. Probably the answer is that Sulla had been sitting on the fence in 63, possibly giving secret aid or encouragement to Catiline and Autronius, ready to collect any profit that might accrue, but far too wily to commit himself.[25] Cicero's authority exercised in his defence was decisive. Torquatus knew this only too well, and attacked Cicero head-on and brutally, accusing him of tyrannical behaviour, of setting himself up as judge and jury, of being 'the third foreign king of Rome since Tarquin and Numa'; it was intolerable, Cicero was abusing his influence to shield a guilty man.[26] So violent and disturbing was the attack that Cicero felt obliged to devote over a third of his speech to a defence not of his client but of himself.[27]

Why did Cicero defend Sulla? Apart from the embarrassments already noticed, young Torquatus was a particularly close friend, as Cicero admits in his speech—later he was given a speaking part in Ciceros' dialogue *de finibus*, where he is assigned the defence of Epicureanism.[28] Again, Cicero detested the Sullan proscriptions. In this speech he asks rhetorically who at that awful time had surpassed Publius Sulla in gentleness and mercy, claiming that his client had saved the lives of numberless worthy and distinguished men; but years later he spoke of him as having 'eagerly brandished the bloody spear of his uncle's proscriptions'.[29]

Explanations are not far to seek. Sulla was an immensely influential figure, at the centre of one of the greatest nexuses of the nobility, and a man of enormous wealth. Cicero was in

[23] Ibid. 36–7.
[24] Ibid. 51.
[25] So J. S. Reid: see p. 20 of his excellent edition of the speech.
[26] *pro Sulla* 21 ff.
[27] Ibid. 1–35.
[28] Ibid. 2 and 34; *de fin.* 1.28 ff.
[29] *pro Sulla* 72; *de off.* 2.29.

no position to undervalue the support of men like Sulla and his friends and relations, or to incur their hostility. Then there was Sulla's half-brother, Caecilius Rufus; as tribune in 63 Rufus had placed his veto at the disposal of the opponents of the Rullan bill, and this sort of service was not easily to be forgotten. Lastly, we know from a later source that Cicero had borrowed a very large sum of money from Publius Sulla to buy from Crassus a fine and expensive town house on the Palatine. (The news leaked out, and Cicero had some embarrassment in living the story down.)[30]

On the whole, apart from the death flurry of Catiline and the brief excitements of the demonstrations of Nepos and Caesar, there was not much happening at Rome in 62 that need detain us. For much of the year men were waiting for the return of the victorious Pompey from the East. His immense political power, exercised no longer over a wide gap of time and space but directly and in person by one of the shrewdest and most opportunistic politicians of the late Republic, was certain to shape the pattern of affairs at Rome. Cicero had already been treated to something of a rebuff. Despite the studied courtesy of his reply to Pompey's letter, the pique he felt can be read between the lines (as he meant it to be). With Pompey back in Italy at the end of the year, the pique is still very apparent; Cicero's assessment of his old hero is bitter and ungenerous. His first report on the returned Pompey is contained in a letter written to Atticus in January 61:

To come to that friend of yours (You know who I mean? The man of whom you wrote to me that 'he began to praise once he dared criticize no longer'), he makes out that he is enormously fond of me, is all over me and full of affection, and sings my praises openly while secretly—but it shows all the same—he is jealous. There is no grace in the man, no straightforwardness, no largeness of political view, no sense of honour, no courage, no frankness.[31]

Not long afterwards, on 13 February, Cicero reports on Pompey's first public appearance. Pompey was invited on to a public platform by the tribune Fufius Calenus. It was a

[30] Aulus Gellius 12.12.2.   [31] ad Att. 1.13.4.

sort of press-conference, and Fufius wanted to elicit Pompey's views on the burning question of the day, the *Bona Dea* scandal and the proposed trial of Publius Clodius. According to Cicero, Pompey was so non-committal as to satisfy nobody: 'there was nothing to give hope to the poor, nothing to encourage the scoundrels; the rich were not pleased, and honest men found it thin. So it fell flat.' When Fufius asked Pompey point-blank for his opinion about the Clodius trial jury, Pompey launched into a long, rambling lecture (*et id multis verbis*) on the authority of the Senate and its sanctity. And when the consul Messalla quizzed him in the Senate on the same subject, Pompey again took refuge in vague generalities.[32] Clearly, he was still hopeful of reaching some sort of understanding with the *boni* and thus securing his immediate aims of land-settlement for his veterans and the formal ratification of his eastern dispositions; at the same time —for we must remember that Pompey had scarcely had time to unpack his bags since his return to Rome—he was still feeling his way cautiously, not yet willing or ready to commit himself to a firm line which he might come to regret on fuller knowledge of the current political situation.

This is not the place to go into the details of the *Bona Dea* scandal, which can easily be studied in any history of the period.[33] Briefly, one night in early December 62 a company of ladies of high birth, including the Vestal Virgins, were celebrating the discreet rites of the *Bona Dea* in the official residence of the Praetor Urbanus and Pontifex Maximus, Gaius Julius Caesar. From these rites men were rigidly barred, yet Clodius (it was alleged) had insinuated himself into the house. There seems little doubt that Clodius was guilty, but of little more than a young man's wild prank. However, his political enemies seized their chance to exploit the affair in order to break him. Prominent among these would-be destroyers were Lucius Lucullus, Hortensius, Gaius Piso, and the consul Messalla;[34] and the reason for

---

[32] Ibid. I.14.1–2.
[33] And see Balsdon's article '*Fabula Clodiana*', *Historia* 15 (1966), 65–73.
[34] *ad Att.* I.14.5.

their hostility is not far to seek; they had not forgotten the part played by Clodius in undermining his brother-in-law Lucullus' position in Asia Minor and helping to pave the way for Pompey's take-over of the command against Mithridates. Most prominent among Clodius' supporters were the other consul of 61, Marcus Pupius Piso, the tribune Calenus, and the two Curiones, father and son. The eye of the storm settled around whether Clodius should stand trial before a panel of jurors selected in the usual way or before one hand-picked by the presiding praetor—the latter being what Clodius' enemies insisted on to secure against the risk of a bribed jury. In the end, the delaying tactics of Clodius' friends and the fear of Calenus' veto forced Hortensius and his friends to give way and accept a bill of indictment providing for a normal jury. This, so Cicero declared, was to sell the pass, for the composition of the court was all-important: *in eo autem erant omnia*. While Hortensius claimed that he could cut Clodius' throat even with a sword made of lead, Cicero (perhaps wise after the event—he was writing in July 61 after the acquittal of Clodius) thought it would have been better to have dropped the charge and left Clodius under a cloud rather than risk, and incur, a public defeat.[35] Defeat there was, for Crassus stepped in and briskly squared the jury to such good effect that thirty-one voted for acquittal against twenty-five for conviction.[36]

What is most important for us to notice in connection with the Clodius trial is this: in 61, both Pompey and Cicero saw Clodius lying bruised and battered and passed by on the other side. Clodius had deserved Pompey's gratitude by his activity a few years earlier against Lucullus: in 63 he had been a volunteer member of Cicero's bodyguard at the

[35] Ibid. I.16.2.

[36] Ibid. I.16.5. The identification of the 'paymaster' here is disputed; Cicero's description is allusive. Wiseman has argued (*CQ* 60 (1968), 297–9) in favour of the orator Calvus. I find his arguments unconvincing; in particular, I cannot see where Calvus could have found the large sums needed, and I am also influenced by the closeness of Crassus to Clodius in the years that follow. So I hold to the long accepted view that Crassus is meant here by Cicero: for the arguments in favour, see the notes ad loc. of How and Shackleton-Bailey.

height of the Catilinarian crisis. By rights, Cicero and Pompey ought to have fought hard for him in this hour of need. But Pompey looked the other way, and Cicero actually gave evidence to break Clodius' alibi. Both of them were betraying Clodius to get in with, or keep in with, the influential *boni* who were ranged against Clodius.[37] Understandably, Clodius neither forgave nor forgot. Conviction would have meant the end of public life for an ambitious and gifted young noble of the great Claudian house. We must always keep this in mind when considering Clodius' attitude to Cicero and Pompey in the years that followed; he had no love for them, and fought them all along the line; conversely, his political and personal ties with Crassus must owe something to Crassus' action in saving him. It is possible to question whether Clodius' acquittal was due to nothing but bribery, as Cicero alleges; but the fact remains that Crassus was energetic in lending his powerful aid to Clodius in his hour of need.

The whole affair went sour for Cicero. Clodius was acquitted, despite Cicero's testimony, and so survived to be his tormentor and destroyer. But for the moment Cicero was able to salvage a crumb of comfort from a brisk passage of arms with Clodius in the Senate, which ended up as follows:

'What about this house you've bought?' said Clodius [the fine house on the Palatine bought with the large loan from Publius Sulla]. 'Anyone would think you were saying', said I, 'that I'd bought a jury.' 'The jury didn't credit you though you were under oath,' said he. 'No,' said I, 'twenty-five of them did give me credit, but thirty-one gave you none—they insisted on cash in advance.'

The roars of delighted applause from the assembled senators forced Clodius back to his seat in baffled silence.[38]

Another comfort to Cicero was the fact that he and Pompey began to draw closer. In January 61 he wrote to Atticus that 'it is generally agreed that Pompey is very friendly

[37] Balsdon (art. cit. 73, note 53) follows Munzer and Gelzer in rejecting as absurd Plutarch's story (*Cicero* 29) that Cicero's wife Terentia nagged him into joining the attack on Clodius because she suspected an affair between her husband and one of Clodius' sisters.

[38] *ad Att.* I.16.10.

towards me';[39] but this is a rather jejune statement, and a later letter of 13 February has no suggestion of any close familiarity.[40] Now, in July, the Roman commons believe him to be 'the apple of Pompey's eye'; and 'certainly we have been united by much delightful personal contact', so much so that the young bloods had begun to nickname Pompey 'Gnaeus Cicero'.[41]

It looks as if by July Pompey had begun to change his tack, giving up hope of an accommodation with the *boni*. He was spending money like water to secure the election of his old lieutenant, Lucius Afranius, to one of the consulships of 60. Afranius turned out to be ineffective; moreover the other consul, Quintus Metellus Celer, whose half-sister Mucia Pompey had divorced on his return from the East, proved an active and bitter opponent of Pompey. Pompey was probably also behind the election of one of the only three tribunes active enough in 60 for their names to have come down to us—Lucius Flavius, who proposed a land bill to settle Pompey's veterans and even went so far as to throw the consul Celer into jail for his opposition. Pompey was cultivating Cicero in summer 61 in the hope that his influence with the knights and his oratorical skill and mastery of public persuasion might be enlisted in support of his aims in 60.

Early in 60 Flavius produced his bill, which aimed to secure land grants for Pompey's veterans and, by providing for other needy persons, to win general popular support. But the event makes it clear how much of the old Pompeian magic had been lost. Not only did the Senate as a body oppose the bill (fearing, says Cicero, that some new position of power was being sought for Pompey); it was resisted by the well-to-do in general ('my old army', Cicero calls them). Cicero himself argued publicly against the bill almost *in toto;* all he was prepared to support was the proposal that the new revenues deriving from Asia Minor over the next five

[39] Ibid. I.12.3.
[40] Ibid. I.14.
[41] Ibid. I.16.11.

years should be used to purchase land for distribution. In the end Pompey was compelled to call Flavius off and the bill was abandoned.[42]

All this Cicero reports in a letter of March 60. He has been rendered cautious by disillusion. The '*immortalis gloria* of the Nones' has brought with it, he now recognizes, 'jealousy and many enmities'. There had ensued the scandalous and dangerous acquittal of Clodius, which had confirmed the 'fickleness and unreliability of the courts', and which marked the beginning of the end of his hopes of a *concordia* between Senate and knights. He sees too that 'certain rich gentlemen, I mean those fish-fancier friends of yours, do not trouble to hide their jealousy of me.' 'So', he goes on, 'I have decided that I must look about me for some greater resources and more dependable support'; Pompey is to be his bastion against the 'unreliability of the *boni*, the wickedness of my ill-wishers, the hatred of the scoundrels'. He means to tread softly, keep his head, and trust nobody.[43]

Pompey was not going to be satisfied by such half-measures. Cicero had failed to support Flavius' bill as a true friend of Pompey's should have. Already, when it was clear that Flavius was not going to get it through, Pompey must have been rethinking his position and looking about for other allies. The truth is that Cicero was being rather stupid and placing far too high a value on himself, despite his professed realism. In June he writes to assure Atticus that 'I would not have you suppose that it was for my own protection that I drew close to Pompey'; no, it was rather that, as things stood, any open difference between himself and Pompey might have involved Rome in serious political upsets (why this should be so is not at all clear!); he had never had any intention of abandoning his own policy, but rather of wooing Pompey to it, to 'get him to reform and temper somewhat his flirtation with the masses'. Indeed, not content with improving Pompey, he hopes he may do as much for Caesar: 'Suppose I can reform Caesar as well, for whom the

---

[42] Ibid. I.19.4.
[43] Ibid. I.19.6–8. (The 'Nones' are, of course, the Nones (5th) of December 63.)

winds are now set so fair, am I really such a nuisance to my country?'[44]

It is easy to see that between March and June 60 Cicero had forgotten his own sound self-administered advice to prudence and scepticism, and had been (as so often) becoming a little too sure of himself and displaying his endearing or exasperating Micawberish hope that 'something would turn up'. He had lost the backing of the nobility, made enemies by his opposition to reform, and seen his cherished hopes of a *concordia ordinum* fast running aground on the reefs of quarrels over the issue of jury-bribery and the Asian tax-contract. Yet he had neglected to keep in with Pompey. He was soon to find out that Pompey was not prepared to act as Cicero thought best for him. Unfortunately, we have no letters from June to December 60; but it was in these months that the balance of political forces at Rome was finding a new and epoch-making alignment that was to lead to the collapse of the Republic as Cicero understood it—*Motum ex Metello consule civicum. . . .*[45]

The *concordia* of which Cicero had had high hopes had run into trouble before the end of 61. In a letter of 5 December he wrote to Atticus:

I assume you have heard that our friends the knights have virtually broken with the Senate. In the first place they were very seriously put out by the promulgation by senatorial decree of a bill to institute an inquiry into the conduct of jurors who had taken bribes. It happened that I was not present when the decree was passed, but sensing that the knightly order was unhappy about it though saying nothing in public, I took the Senate to task in what I thought a most authoritative fashion, and spoke with considerable weight and eloquence in defence of a none too honourable case. And now along have come the knights with another dainty dish, which is really almost too much! But not only have I stomached it, I have even garnished it for them. The tax-farmers who bought the contract for the Asian taxes from the censors have complained to the Senate that falling victim to over-eagerness they bid too high a price, and they have asked for the contract to be voided. I took the lead in backing their claim—or rather, I followed up, for they were egged on to make this bold demand by Crassus. It is a wretched business, a disgraceful demand to make, a confession of impudence. But there was a

[44] Ibid. II.1.6.   [45] Horace *Odes* 2.1.1.

very grave danger of an open breach with the Senate if they were simply refused. Here again it was I who principally came to the rescue, and I arranged things so that on 1 December and the following day they were faced with a very well attended Senate in a very generous mood, when I had a lot to say about the prestige and the harmony of the two orders. Not that the business has been settled yet, but the Senate's inclinations were clearly to be seen. The only man who spoke against was Metellus, the consul-designate. Our hero Cato was expecting to speak against too, but the brief daylight ended before it came to his turn.[46]

Though Cicero was hopeful, he was also wary, for he concludes by saying: 'So I am defending as far as I am able that *concordia* which I myself cemented. But all the same, seeing that it is so shaky . . .'. Shaky it was, and it took more than the brief daylight of December to muzzle Cato.[47] Cicero's expectation that the Senate would come round to his view was proved wrong, and by June 60 the quarrel had reached an open breach. Cato had won the day, and this was a bitter blow for Cicero. In January he had lamented that the year just past had seen the overthrow of the two buttresses of the Republic which he had himself erected as consul in 63, the 'authority of the Senate and the alliance of Senate and knights'.[48] In 60 Cato was at the head of the wrecking gang, getting the Senate to persist in demanding the trial of equestrian jurors suspected of corruption and refusing to negotiate a new contract for the Asian taxes.

What [asks Cicero] could be more reasonable than that a man who has accepted a bribe as a juror should be brought to trial? Cato moved to this effect, and the Senate agreed. So the knights have declared war on the Senate—not on me, for I dissented from Cato. What could be more barefaced cheek than the tax-farmers' repudiation of their contract? Nevertheless, we should have made the sacrifice to keep the whole class on our side. But Cato stood his ground and won through. And so now we have a consul shut up in gaol, a continual series of riots, and not one of those whom I and my successors as consuls used to count on to rally to the defence of the state has stirred a finger to help. 'Well then,' you will say, 'are we to pay these friends of yours for their support like hired mercenaries?' What else are we to do, if there is no other way?[49]

[46] *ad Att.* I.17.8–9.
[47] Decrees of the Senate made before sunrise or after sunset were invalid: Aulus Gellius 14.7.8 (citing Varro).
[48] *ad Att.* I.18.3.   [49] Ibid. II.1.8.

Cicero differed from Cato, not in failing to agree that the knights were in the wrong, but in holding that other factors needed to be considered than the justice and morality of their claims. Cato was a utopian: 'He makes speeches in the Senate as if he were living in Plato's Republic instead of in this cesspit of Romulus.'[50] The prime consideration was to hold the knights on the side of the Senate in defence of the existing order. Cato's success meant a fatal break between the financiers and the *boni*, and to no avail in the long run, for the knights swung their backing behind the anti-*boni* group. We hear no more of trials of corrupt equestrian jurors, and early in 59 Crassus negotiated a new and better contract for the tax-farmers. The support of the powerful financial and business interests was lost to the *boni* at a critical moment. Caesar was a favourite for election to one of the consulships of 59.

Cicero had been labelled by some as a 'trimmer'. In an important sense this is true, in that he sometimes did trim his sails to the prevailing political wind (though by no means always). But it is not true that Cicero was devoid of political principle; rather, as here, he was ready to sacrifice lesser principles to greater. His main object was to preserve the Republic against domination by men who would use methods and pursue ambitions which might destroy what he believed in. We are under no obligation to share his prejudices or premisses, or even sympathize with them; but we must try to *understand* them. He stood broadly for the maintenance of the rights of property, the rule of law, the free working of Republican institutions; he was opposed to *dominatio*, whether of one man or one group. He was perhaps too much concerned with form rather than with content. He recognized that much was amiss with the existing state of the nation, but he preferred it to what he saw as the alternative—absolute and arbitrary rule. Rome was not a Platonic Utopia, but a dirty, messy midden—*faex Romuli*. If one side did not keep the knights happy, another would be only too ready to try. Nothing was to be gained by high-minded

[50] Ibid.

pposition on principle, and much could be lost. It was not a noble creed, but it was a practical one. Cato was to take his own life at Utica rather than sue for pardon from an all-powerful Caesar. He became a legend, and perhaps he was happier to have it thus; but he might never have found himself at Utica had he and his friends paid greater heed to Cicero's realistic advice.

In 60 Cato 'stood his ground and won through'. Cicero was understandably acutely unhappy, and while he was in his mood of disillusionment Caesar baited a tempting hook. For Cicero, granted that he so often overestimated his own importance, was a very powerful ally to have on one's side. He must not be underestimated simply because he falls short of his own excessive valuation. His influence with the upper-classes of Italy, his extraordinary gifts as an orator, were well worth enlisting. Perhaps Caesar was even a little wary of him. We ought not to forget the considerable trouble that was gone to to muzzle and (when this proved impossible) to get rid of Cicero in 59 and 58, nor his very remarkable achievement in stopping the reform programme of 63 dead in its tracks. Cicero sometimes behaved in what seems to the cool northern-European an abject and hysterical manner (this is especially true, as we shall see, of his exile); but he was also a bold, even a rash man, thanks to his great self-confidence and a belief in his own importance which never long deserted him and quickly recovered from the most grievous blows. This trait in his character made him dangerous to opponents as well as to himself. For all the pro-fessed realism of his political theory, his practice was often emotional and hot-blooded; he might run amock and start serious trouble when cooler-headed men preferred to lie low or compromise.

Caesar could appreciate his potential, both for help and hindrance; and Caesar was an old friend, whose relations with Cicero are always tinged by warmth and an unbounded admiration for his literary genius. In December 60 Cicero writes to Atticus about the prospects for the coming year, in which Caesar is to be consul:

Either I am to put up a brave resistance to the agrarian law [which Caesar was planning to introduce], which will mean a stiff fight but a very honourable one; or I must keep quiet, which pretty well amounts to burying myself in some country retreat; or I can even turn to and help, and this they tell me Caesar has not the slightest doubt I shall do. For Cornelius has been to see me, Cornelius Balbus I mean, Caesar's crony. He kept assuring me that Caesar would be guided by me and Pompey in all matters, and would work hard to reconcile Crassus to Pompey. So here we have it: the closest collaboration with Pompey, if I choose, as well as with Caesar; reconciliation with my enemies, an armistice with the masses, a secure old age.[51]

It is clearly to these same overtures that Cicero referred in a speech over three years later when he claimed that Caesar had wanted to include him in an alliance with Pompey and Crassus.[52] The bait was tempting, but Cicero resisted it: 'I don't think that I can hesitate to stick to my old opinion that there is "One omen that prevails: to fight for fatherland".'

Cicero chose to reject Caesar's advances—as he was to do again ten years later. Nor did he favour 'keeping quiet'. The 'trimmer's' choice fell on 'a brave resistance'. Early in 59, with Caesar now consul, he defended Gaius Antonius, his old colleague of 63, and in the course of his speech had 'certain complaints to make about the state of public affairs which I thought were relevant to poor Antonius' case. But some scoundrels reported these remarks of mine to certain powerful men in a very distorted form.'[53] It was all very well for Cicero to speak thus depreciatingly in a speech delivered after his return from exile when he was under promise to Caesar to behave himself; we may doubt that he was as gravely misreported as he makes out. At any rate, it is probably to this speech in defence of Antonius that Suetonius refers when he says: 'When Cicero was deploring the state of affairs at some trial or other, Clodius, Cicero's enemy, who had for some time been vainly trying to be transferred from patrician to plebeian status, was given the necessary author-

[51] Ibid. II.3.3.
[52] *de prov. cons.* 41.
[53] *de domo* 41.

ity by Caesar at three o'clock that very same day.'[54] On the afternoon of the day on which Cicero spoke out in his defence of Antonius, Clodius was 'adopted' into a plebeian family at a ceremony presided over by the Pontifex Maximus, Gaius Julius Caesar, and thus became eligible for the potentially explosive tribunate of the plebs.

Caesar began his consulship with some calculated gestures of constitutional propriety, but a clash was inevitable. Cato's obstinacy forced Caesar to take his land bill direct to the people with no preceding senatorial decree. Since the bill provided at long last for land for Pompey's veterans, and enjoyed Pompey's backing, the necessary force was available to convoy its passage into law; when Caesar's colleague Bibulus, supported by Cato and some tribunes, tried to block it by constitutional manoeuvres, they were forced to flee for their lives—Bibulus' *fasces* were smashed in the mêlée. The tax-contractors also got their revision of the Asian contract, which gained for Caesar not merely their political friendship but a bonus in share-certificates as well.[55] Even more money was forthcoming from Ptolemy XI, 'the Fluteplayer', in payment for his official recognition as Pharaoh of Egypt; among the Roman bankers who funded this deal was Gaius Rabirius Postumus, who was rewarded by being appointed by Ptolemy as his finance secretary (Cicero defended him successfully in 54). Caesar and Pompey themselves were said to have pocketed the stupendous sum of nearly 150 million sesterces.[56] Pompey also at last saw the ratification of his arrangements in Asia Minor, which, apart from being highly efficient and long-lasting, had firmly established his political influence in that area by binding to him the petty dynasts and local political groups he had put in power.

By the end of the spring Caesar was in complete control. His colleague Bibulus retired to his house for the rest of the year, keeping up a barrage of verbal attacks and taking such

[54] Suetonius *DJ* 20.
[55] *in Vat.* 29. In general, for Caesar's activities in 59, see Gelzer, *Caesar*, chapter 3.
[56] Suetonius *DJ* 54.

action as would provide abundant legal ammunition against Caesar in the future. Others followed suit, including Cicero, who left Rome for his country estates. When the tribune Vatinius carried the law which granted Caesar the provinces of Cisalpine Gaul and Illyricum for five years, fears that Caesar had come to stay were shown to be only too well-founded.[57]

Round about this time it is against Pompey that Cicero's bitterness is chiefly directed. In December 60 he calls him *Epicrates* ('The Conquering Hero'); in April he is *Hierosoly-marius* ('The Jerusalem Wallah'); in May *Sampsiceramus* and *Arabarches* ('The Pasha' and 'The Sheikh of Araby'), all of them malicious nicknames.[58] But Pompey seems to have been no happier about the company he was keeping than Cicero was. Despite his opportunistic and (in his early days) bloody past, he was curiously, almost primly, averse from open flouting of propriety. Though anxious to see Caesar's meas-ures passed in his own interest, he was uncomfortable about the violent methods Caesar was using. Cicero gives a caustic report of Pompey's behaviour on a public platform which is a good example of the way he tried to sidestep awkward questions.

Yes, I approve of Caesar's laws. His methods?—*Caesar must answer for those himself.* Yes, I liked the agrarian law. Was the exercise of the veto made impossible?—*That is none of my business.* I was glad that something was being done at last about Egypt. Was Bibulus observing the portents at the time or not?—*That was not for me to inquire.* As for the tax-con-tractors, I wanted to oblige that body of men. What would have hap-pened if Bibulus had come down into the forum? *I really cannot begin to guess.*

And so on. It is cleverly done but, as Cicero remarks, it is mere 'casuistry'. He imagines himself joining in the question-ing: 'Come along, about this agrarian law, Pasha: how are you going to secure it?'; and he imagines Pompey's reply: 'I shall hold you down with Caesar's army.'[59]

---

[57] Gelzer, *Caesar*, 78.   [58] *ad Att.* II.3.1; 9.1; 16.2; 17.3.
[59] Ibid. II.16.2. I take *exercitus Caesaris* here at its face-value, viz. the army of Cisalpine Gaul. See Shackleton-Bailey's note ad loc.

We have here what is obviously a reflection of the incident reported by Plutarch when Caesar put Pompey up onto a platform early in 59 to answer questions: 'Do you approve of my laws?—*Yes*. If anyone were to use force against my laws, would you come to the aid of the people?—*I would meet force with force*.'[60] Cicero's paraphrase is bitterly pithy, especially the implication that Pompey will be dependent on Caesar's Gallic legions; but it is not grossly unfair.

It is worth emphasizing again here the great difference between 63 and 59, Cicero's consulship and Caesar's. In 63 the reform programme had failed because in the last resort its champions had not dared to risk an open fight. Those who aimed to pass controversial measures had always to be prepared either to ignore or to override constitutional obstructions, but this could be done only if they had the assurance of superior force on their side. In 70 the Sullan constitution had been laid to rest; the political support for its dismantling had been there for years, but it was only the threat of Pompey's and Crassus' forceful intervention that made repeal a practical possibility. In the early sixties Pompey's tribunes had been able to force through their measures because in the last resort they could rely on Pompey to save them from the fate of the Gracchi. In 63 the reformers, lacking this sort of backing, could not push their attack to the limit. But now in 59 Pompey was behind Caesar, which meant not only a great addition of political power but also the vital factor of Pompey's veterans.[61] So Caesar and his associates were able to brush aside technical opposition; their opponents dared not bring matters to the point of open violence, for they were hopelessly outgunned. In fact, it was only on very rare occasions such as in 49, when both sides thought they had the chance of winning by open war or one or the other was driven into a corner, that civil war actually raged. Usually, although there might be a good deal of ugly brawling in the streets, the balance of power lay so obviously

---

[60] Plutarch *Pompey* 47.

[61] Not long after his public answers to Caesar's questions, Pompey 'flooded Rome with his soldiers and controlled everything by force': Plutarch *Pompey* 48.

with one side that the other shrank from going to the limit.

Looking back, it is easy to see that the refusal of the *boni* to accommodate Pompey on his return from the East led first to Pompey's trying to go it alone and then, when that attempt failed, to his coalition with Caesar and through Caesar with Crassus. We can see that that combination, buttressed with the support of the great financial interests whom the Senate had offended, proved irresistible, and set in train shifts of power which led by a direct road to the collapse of the Republic and the autocratic rule of Caesar. So it is clear that the *boni* miscalculated, as too did Cicero. But the miscalculation was not palpably crazy, as is sometimes implied. Cicero's consulship had seen the rout of the reformers, and the knights rallying firmly to the Senate's side. On his return Pompey had not attempted to use the threat of force to secure his ends. His old political dominance was gone, his popular support in particular seriously undermined. His demand that his eastern arrangements should be ratified *en bloc* without detailed discussion was extraordinarily high-handed, and the Senate had good reason to refuse to give in to him in this. That he would ally himself with his inveterate enemy Crassus was almost unthinkable (and, as events were to show, even Caesar could not get the two of them to work smoothly in harness). That he would lend his power to exalt Caesar was not the likeliest of guesses.

Again, the instability which the so-called 'First Triumvirate' was prey to during the first few years of its existence is itself a warning not to assume too readily that in the years from 62 to 60 men at Rome should have planned with the likelihood of such a coalition in mind. In any case, what was the practical alternative open to them? The picture Pompey presented to the eye of the Roman noble at the time was of the 'young butcher' of Sulla's *pogroms*,[62] the unprincipled and untrustworthy opportunist exploiter of changing situations, a blackmailer, a man who had dominated the Roman political world and might do so again if his temporary weakness were not exploited to the full. And who can say what would have

[62] *Adulescentulus carnufex*: Val. Max. 6.2.8.

happened had the *boni* responded to Pompey's advances on his return from the East, any more than what would have happened had Pompey and not Caesar won the civil war that began in 49? There is no reason to suppose that Pompey, whatever his ultimate aims may have been, had in the years after his return lost that versatility and cunning in political manoeuvre that had marked his astonishing rise to power in his middle years and were again to be displayed in his political activity in the fifties. Now, as ten years later, he may have been planning to use the *boni* to re-establish his own position; certainly, any of the *boni* could have believed this without the belief being foolish. Cicero was a highly intelligent man, an expert in Roman politics, a shrewd observer and excellently informed; yet neither he nor anyone else, as far as we can see, foresaw the 'First Triumvirate'.

Another danger we have to watch out for is that of being taken in by words or slogans. The Roman constitution, thanks to the haphazard nature of its growth, was a tangle of contradictions, and offered boundless chances for the legal obstruction of attempts to introduce changes. When, as in 59, these obstructions are brusquely shouldered aside, the other side naturally and automatically cries out that the august authority of the consular office, the sacred rights of tribunes, are being trodden underfoot. To this the reply comes pat: 'This obstruction of yours is not to use but to abuse the constitution; these are no true tribunes but the paid hirelings of a selfish oligarchy; it is not genuine religious conviction that inspires Bibulus to search the heavens for portents with an anxious eye (would he do the same if Cato were proposing some anti-Caesarian measure?); no, it is the *boni* who are in the wrong in seeking to thwart the will of the People by unprincipled manipulation of the machinery of the constitution.' But again there is a rejoinder available to the *boni*: 'What is this *populus Romanus* of which you talk so grandly? Not the solid, cautious, dependable, self-confident and self-reliant yeoman peasantry which once constituted the legions and assemblies of the Republic; this is the wretched starveling apology for a *plebs*, the scum of the earth, a rootless,

un- or under-employed mob of proletarians and ex-slaves
who can be bought for a few shillings or intimidated by
gangs and ward-bosses; by what right do they claim to
speak for Italy and the Empire?' To which Caesar and his
friends could retort: 'By what right do the *boni* claim to act
as if they and their friends in the Senate were that "assembly
of kings" which had awed the ambassador of Philip of
Epirus, men of proved worth and experience, freely chosen
by the people and ultimately answerable to them; not a
collection of nobles who owe their high position in the state
to the mere chance of their birth and the material advantages
their birth has brought them?'

The issues were other than these. Whoever won, Rome
was not going to become a democracy; the *populus Romanus*
was scattered far afield over Italy and the West and was not
to be reconstituted within the city limits of Rome. Nobody
on either side thought seriously for one moment of handing
over sovereign power to the unrepresentative population of
the capital city. Its function was to provide pawns for the
game, not to control it. The struggle was for political power,
and it was waged by a handful of 'top people'.

Not of course that the struggle was for power *simpliciter*,
fashionable though that doctrine may once have been; no
sane man seeks power for its own sake. Power is a means to a
variety of ends, and the motives which move men to seek it,
and the uses to which they wish to put it, are as varied as the
men themselves: fear, cupidity, pride, cruelty, a conviction
of administrative vocation, a desire to see things done better,
an impatience with inefficiency, even occasionally a sense of
duty, feelings of compassion for the underdog, love of
country, hatred of waste or muddle or injustice. Of those
who joined or opposed Caesar many no doubt were moved by
selfish considerations of material advantage; but some were
minded otherwise. In the end we can judge these men only
by their deeds, not by their words. We must see what they
did, and form an opinion of what they were likely to have
done had they had the chance, and then make up our minds
which we prefer. Taken by and large, it is for this reason

that one's preferences incline, if they do so incline, to men like Caesar and Pompey and Augustus. To see them in modern dress as so many Hitlers or Stalins is to be guilty of unpardonable anachronism: there was no social-democratic party waiting in the wings ready to provide fair democratic government if only the dictators were removed. The choice was between dynast and oligarchy, king and barons, not between dictator and democrats; and neither Cicero nor Caesar nor (most skilful tempter of all) Tacitus should make us for one moment believe otherwise. What Cicero's Roman world needed was a strong, stable, and efficient central government, capable of enforcing the law and pursuing long-term policies without preoccupation with short-term gain. And this is something which the ruling oligarchy of the late Republic with its selfishness, its inefficiency, its corruption, its hostility to outside talent, and above all its lack of cohesion and unity which led to and combined with an invincible distrust of individual power, could no more provide than the factious nobles of pre-Pisistratid Athens or pre-Tudor England.

Many things might have happened in the last years of the Republic. What did happen in the end was the arrival in Rome in 44 of an eighteen-year-old, somewhat sickly, youth who had come to claim his inheritance, and who proceeded smoothly to outmanoeuvre Cicero, Brutus, Cassius, Antony, Lepidus, and the rest, achieved supreme power at the age of thirty-two, and died peacefully in his bed a month short of his seventy-sixth birthday having exercised that power without serious challenge for forty-five years. Even on reflection it remains the unlikeliest of chances.

VIII

EXILE

IN THE LETTER (early May 59) in which he was so bitter
about Pompey's casuistic support for Caesar's programme,
Cicero went on to tell Atticus that he had had enough of
politics.[1] But the mood was short lived. In late June or early
July 'indignation is beginning to overmaster fear'. Caesar
has offered him an official position on his staff; but, although
concerned about the danger from Clodius, he none the less
declines the security which this appointment would afford.
Something is raising Cicero's volatile hopes again: 'I have no
wish to run away, I am thirsting to fight. Everyone is very
excited. But I say nothing definite; you must keep this to
yourself.'[2] It is hard to see what was cheering Cicero up if it
was not the prospect of a rift in the triumviral lute. As early
as April he had referred to the possibility: 'Our one hope
of salvation is that they should quarrel among themselves,
and that this might be beginning to happen was the impression I got from young Curio.'[3]

The background to this is to be found in an interesting
clutch of letters written in April and early May. They are
addressed to Atticus, who is in Rome, from various of Cicero's
country houses, and they refer constantly to the tit-bits of
news and gossip which Atticus purveys to Cicero from the
city.[4] There were rumours that Pompey and Crassus might
run for the two consulships of 58; however well- or ill-foun-

---

[1] *ad Att.* II.16.3. Unless otherwise indicated, the following references down
to p. 184, n. 29 are all to the Atticus correspondence.
[2] II.18.2–3.
[3] II.7.3.
[4] II.4–II.16.

led, they at least show that people were thinking that the
'Triumvirate' might need to put out a large show of strength
to hold their ground.[5] Then there was trouble with Clodius.
This had arisen out of a proposal to send Clodius on an
official mission to King Tigranes of Armenia; Clodius was
far from enthusiastic, especially since a more lucrative
mission to Egypt which had been promised to him was being
kept for someone else. 'Why, poor fellow,' says Cicero,
alluding to the *Bona Dea* scandal, 'he hasn't even been found
a place on the agrarian commission of twenty, though he
was once the only man in Caesar's house.' He urges Atticus
to work on Clodius: 'Stoke him up, I beseech you, as much
as possible'—then follows the remark about 'our one hope of
salvation'.[6]

In this same letter we learn of discreet and guarded hints
which Atticus has been dropping about the possibility of
disagreements within the 'Triumvirate': 'I am anxious to
know what lies behind your obscure hints about what some
members of the agrarian commission themselves are saying.
What on earth is it? If there is anything in it, it is better
news than I imagined.' Though he at once goes on to dis-
claim any appetite to become involved himself, and says
that he would rather watch the shipwreck from *terra firma*,
it is clear that his interest is beginning to quicken.[7]

On 18 April young Curio (a close friend and supporter of
Clodius in 61) has been to call on Cicero and 'what he had
to say about Clodius was in striking agreement with what
you have written'.[8] Atticus himself is having private conversations with Clodius, and a split between Clodius and the
'Triumvirs' is very much in the air: 'if he is going to fall
out with them, it will be ridiculous for him to attack me.'
Cicero thinks that 'they' are losing popular support; people
may have disliked the rule of the Senate, but what is going
to happen when they find that power has been transferred
not to the people but to three ambitious men? 'So let them
bestow consulships on anyone they choose, let them even

5 II.5.2.   6 II.7.3.
7 II.7.3–4.   8 II.8.1.

drape that scab Vatinius with the purple robe of a priest, before long you will see the triumph not only of those who have never put a foot wrong but even of the arch-sinner Cato.'[9]

A day or so later there is a suggestion that Clodius is not a plebeian after all (and so not qualified for the tribunate). 'Are they going to deny that Publius has become a plebeian? This is naked despotism and not to be tolerated? Let Publius send me a list of the witnesses. I will go into court and swear that our friend Gnaeus [Pompey] told me that he was present at the ceremony.' Curio has come running down from Rome, and asks Cicero if he has heard the latest news: '"No", said I. "Publius", he said, "is going to stand for the tribunate." "What's that?" I said. "Yes," he said, "ane he is bitterly opposed to Caesar and talks of rescinding all his acts." "And Caesar?" said I. "He is saying", said Curio, "that he had nothing to do with his adoption."'[10]

Cicero was understandably fretting for news.[11] On 23 April he reports how unpopular Caesar and his friends are down at Formiae, largely on account of their agrarian proposals. And he is now beginning to worry seriously about Pompey's reaction if Caesar and his tribune Vatinius should come to grief: 'There is nothing at the moment which I think ought to alarm us more than the possibility that our friend the Pasha, once he realises that no one has a good word to say for him and sees that what has been done can easily be reversed, may begin to run amock.'[12] And almost at once we are back to Clodius, with Cicero writing on about 28 April: 'Believe me, our hope lies in Publius. I pray he becomes tribune.'[13]

Finally we come to the beginning of May, Cicero has heard about the proposal to annexe the public lands in Campania for additional allotments. His reaction is mixed: relief, that the proposal is less momentous than he had feared

[9] II.9.1–2.
[10] II.12.1–2.
[11] II.11.
[12] II.14.1.
[13] II.15.2.

it might be from Atticus' guarded hints; consolation, in that he believes that this will produce only about 5,000 allotments so that a large number of the urban poor are going to be disappointed and alienated (in fact, if other sources are to be believed, Cicero was wildly out and 20,000 families benefited); and comfort, since he sees the proposal as upsetting the financial interests who are beneficiaries of the public leases of the Campanian land which will now be terminated.[14]

Even allowing for Cicero's natural inclination to look on the bright side, it does seem that Caesar and his partners were running into difficulties. We can understand why Caesar got Pompey to make it plain that he was prepared to use force if need be to defend Caesar's position. Clodius, with his well-organized gangs, was here of great importance. Some have seen in Clodius' behaviour an attempt to lull Cicero into a false sense of security, but it is hard to see with what object.[15] Possibly Clodius was being used by Crassus to put on pressure for some reason of his own; or it may have been a trick to encourage the opposition to think that the coalition was near rupture so that they would be less ready to make overtures to Pompey, while Pompey would at the same time be persuaded of the need to maintain unity in defence of the common programme. But all these suggestions are a little far-fetched. It is easiest to take events at their face value and accept that there genuinely was a coolness, to put it no higher, between Clodius and Caesar. Clodius was putting on a bold and independent front to secure what he believed to be his true value. It may be that Caesar was a little frightened of his potential and independence of mind, and that Clodius had to exert himself to secure not merely his tribunate but also a comparatively free hand in legislation.[16]

---

[14] II.16.1. Suetonius *DJ* 20; Vell. Pat. 2.44.4. Cicero was perhaps influenced in his calculation by the proposal of the Rullan bill of 63 to settle 5,000 *coloni* at Capua: *de leg. agr.* II.76–7.

[15] Tyrrell and Purser, I.298, note 3.

[16] For a full discussion of Clodius' position at this period, see Lintott, *Violence in Republican Rome*, 190 ff.

By the beginning of July, however, if not a little earlier, Cicero is talking of the need for some defence against attack from 'Pretty Boy', which indicates that he no longer has any hopes of Clodius; and this is underlined by his ceasing to call him 'Publius'—an amiable address—and reverting to the pejorative diminutive 'Pulchellus'.[17] This is confirmed about a fortnight later when we read that 'Clodius' threats and the bitter struggles which impend do not worry me very much.'[18]

This same letter mentions the famous scene in the theatre at Rome when the actor Diphilus was encored over and over again for his shaft against Pompey at the Apolline Games in the second week in July: 'By our misfortune thou art Great' [*Magnus*]. Caesar entered the theatre to a very lukewarm reception from the audience (*mortuo plausu*); while young Curio, the hero of the anti-Caesarian forces, was rapturously received. We cannot doubt the truth of Cicero's reporting; he is writing a private letter to Atticus, not making a speech. And the upshot of the affair was obviously a matter of common knowledge:

Caesar is upset. It is said that letters are flying off to Pompey at Capua. They are bitter against the knights who gave Curio a standing ovation; they are at war with everybody; they are threatening to repeal the Roscian Law [which gave the knights front seats at the theatre] and even the Corn Law [which provided for regular cheap distribution of corn to the populace at large]. There really is a tremendous to-do![19]

Despite, or perhaps because of, the renewed open threats from Clodius, Cicero was offered a place on Caesar's agrarian commission when one of the members died; and the offer of an appointment on Caesar's staff was either renewed or still open. Still Cicero would not accept: 'I prefer to fight.' It looks as if Caesar had made his peace with Clodius and was planning either to get Cicero on his side or silence him through fear. Cicero's importance was still considerable: his golden tongue, his influence with the well-to-do and the

17 II.18.3: Clodius was, of course, a Claudius Pulcher, whence the diminutive.
18 II.19.1.
19 II.19.1–3.

financial interests, not least his relations with Pompey. For Pompey was once again making up to Cicero, who was an obvious intermediary between him and the *boni*. All this, and Cicero's propensity to rashness, combined to make his behaviour matter very much to Caesar. And Cicero was in a pugnacious mood: 'Trouble is looming up . . . I think that I can certainly count on the backing of my old consular army of patriots, even of lukewarm patriots.'[20]

Pompey is the key figure in all this. On his return from Asia Minor, his immediate political future hinged on securing the ratification of his political arrangements there and providing his veterans with the plots of land to which they looked forward on discharge. Hence he was driven,when the *boni* did not respond to his overtures and after he himself had failed to 'go it alone' with Afranius and Flavius, to come to an arrangement with Caesar, and through Caesar with Caesar's ally Crassus. But Pompey was desperate for results, and he had to pay a high price for Caesar's help: it meant giving Caesar great and dangerous power, and co-operating with Crassus, whom he hated and distrusted (the feelings were reciprocated). Yet, although temporarily embarrassed, Pompey was in the long term playing from strength. Caesar's position had two grave weaknesses. In the first place, once he had given Pompey what he wanted, Pompey would have no compelling motive to go on supporting him. True, the political alliance of Pompey and Caesar had been cemented by the marriage of Pompey to Caesar's only child, Julia; but divorce was easy and common, and the marriage itself was not likely to be a lasting bond if Pompey considered his reasonable pretensions were not being satisfied—and Pompey's record for opportunistic turn-arounds was difficult to match and could scarcely inspire confidence. Secondly, there was the ever present risk that the *boni* might cut their losses and pay Pompey's price—which was being paid by Caesar anyway—in order to win him over and bring down Caesar and the rest of his programme. In short, Pompey held the better hand because his need of Caesar was

[20] II.19.4–5.

temporary and soon satisfied, and could be satisfied by others, while Caesar's need of Pompey was more enduring and his projects and ambitions of a kind which could never hope to win the support of the *boni*. The programme of 59 was necessarily carried through with violence and technical illegalities; all that was needed to destroy it was the acquisition by the *boni* of sufficient force to back up their legal arguments. Such force lay in Pompey's gift, and he would surely prefer to work with the *boni*—his original choice—rather than continue to buttress the position of his chief political rivals. 'The First Triumvirate' has long served as a convenient shorthand term to describe the coalition of Pompey, Caesar, and Crassus. The chief drawback to using it lies in the presumption of solidity which the words convey; it has too much of an air of permanence and tidiness. There is nothing in our evidence to suggest that anything more specific was envisaged than the satisfying of certain aims by the programme of 59. Each of the three must have been well aware that the others were moved by self-interest, that he could not blindly trust them if something better offered. And the fact is that from at least the latter part of 58 down to the summer of 56 only the eye of unquestioning faith can discern any 'Triumvirate' in existence at all.

The next three extant letters from Cicero to Atticus cannot be precisely dated; they were written sometime between late July and the early autumn. They tell of Pompey's increasing familiarity with Cicero and his repeated protestations of support for Cicero against Clodius. Cicero is not sure just what Clodius has in mind—and he inclines to suspect that Clodius is no more sure than he is.

Now this is how things are: he rushes here and there like a madman, quite unpredictable, hurling denunciations at all and sundry. It looks as if he will be guided by the way things chance to fall out. When he observes the hatred people feel for the present régime, he seems on the verge of launching an attack on those responsible for it; but then again, when he reflects on how rich and powerful these men are and on the size of their armies, he does an about-turn and attacks the *boni*.[21]

Nothing, Cicero reports, is more popular than hatred of

[21] II.22.1.

the popular leaders.[22] The defiant and scurrilous edicts of Caesar's fellow-consul Bibulus, which he posts up regularly outside his house, are so popular that one cannot pass along the street for the crowds reading them.[23] When Bibulus used his consular authority to postpone the elections, usually a predictably unpopular act, Caesar tried to incite a public meeting to march in protest to Bibulus' house, but failed to raise a single cheer. Pompey was thoroughly displeased with himself: he could see that advance was dangerous, retreat a confession of weakness; the *boni* were his enemies, the popular leaders were not his friends.[24]

At last Pompey comes out into the open. Probably in August, Cicero writes to Atticus: 'First of all I want you to know that our friend the Pasha is very unhappy about his position and longing to be put back onto the pedestal from which he has toppled. He tells me how distressed he is, and sometimes openly asks for a remedy.'[25] So Pompey is putting out feelers to Cicero, hinting that he is willing to reach an accommodation with the *boni* if this can be arranged. 'But', Cicero continues, 'I don't think any remedy is available.' Indeed, he believes that the 'Triumvirate' is about to die a natural death without outside assistance. Clearly, if this view was at all widely shared by the *boni*, there was little chance that they would be ready to discuss Pompey's terms for deserting a sinking ship.

Onto this interesting scene there now steps the (in more than one sense) intriguing figure of Vettius.

Nobody can deny that the Vettius 'conspiracy' came at a most opportune moment for Caesar and turned out to his advantage. Pompey has been getting restless, even to the point of making overtures to Cicero. The 'Triumvirate' has been sinking into a trough of unpopularity. Now along comes a plot to murder Pompey which bears all the signs of being an optimate plot. Pompey is frightened back into Caesar's arms, convinced that there is no hope of an accommodation with the *boni*. Cicero himself had been talking a

[22] II.20.4.   [23] II.21.4.
[24] II.21.3–5.   [25] II.23.2.

trifle too glibly about the 'bloodthirsty young men' among
the nobility, whose leader and hero was young Curio, with
whom Cicero was on excellent terms and who had told
Cicero back in April that 'the younger men were very angry
and not prepared to put up with the "proud Kings" whom
Curio hates so bitterly'.[26] Curio was now named by Vettius
as the ringleader of a plot to murder Pompey, and Pompey
was warned to beware of danger in Cicero's own house. In
contrast with his recent warm relations with Cicero, Pompey
grows distinctly cool towards him, with disastrous results for
Cicero's safety.[27] It does look like a cunning and successful
plan on Caesar's part to keep Pompey in line. Caesar was
certainly behind the *exposé* of the affair, encouraging Vettius
to tell all he knew, as is clear from Cicero and Suetonius—
though Suetonius does not say that the murder plot was
rigged by Caesar, only that Vettius was bribed by Caesar to
turn informer and that some of the names he then produced
were 'not without some suspicion of a fraud'.[28]

Cicero is quite definite on the point. Vettius was an *agent-
provocateur* with instructions from Caesar to frighten Pompey
and discredit young Curio.[29] But can we believe him?
Tyrrell and Purser speak of 'the strange plot revealed by
Vettius, the true character, object, and source of which are
profoundly uncertain'. Indeed, there are aspects of the affair
which lead one to suspect with Merivale that there may have
been a genuine plot after all.[30]

Cicero later alleged that Vatinius as Caesar's agent did not
suborn Vettius until *after* Vettius had first laid his information before the Senate.[31] Secondly, Vettius claimed that the
young bloods had planned to stab Pompey at the gladiatorial
games given by Gabinius and that 'Aemilius Paullus was the
leader in this'. Nonsense, says Cicero; everybody knew that

[26] II.7.3; 8.1.

[27] II.24; *pro Sest.* 41; *de domo* 28; Plutarch *Cicero* 31.

[28] Suetonius *DJ* 20.

[29] II.24.2.

[30] Tyrrell and Purser, I.279; Merivale, *A History of the Romans*, I. 197. Rice
Holmes, *The Roman Republic*, I.479–82 has a full discussion of the evidence.

[31] *in Vat.* 24–6.

Paullus was in Macedonia at the time. How then did Vettius and Caesar not know this?—the Roman upper-class world was a very small one. But the Latin *principem fuisse* naturally refers not to the man who was to strike the first blow but to a ringleader in the plot, which is quite another matter.[32] Further, we may ask why Pompey's personal enemies, Bibulus and the two Curiones, father and son, should want to warn him that his life was in danger. Yet they did, and their action suggests that they had something to worry about, and were taking out an insurance policy.[33] Most important is the behaviour of Pompey, who must have weighed the possibility that it was all a Caesarian trick; but his reaction was to cleave closer to Caesar and grow cooler towards Cicero—so Pompey did not believe Cicero's version, whatever his views may have been about the reliability of every detail of the information Vettius had come out with.

Certainty is unobtainable; but it must remain a distinct possibility that there was a plot against Pompey's life, and that it involved some of the 'bloodthirsty' and 'tyrant-hating' young nobles. Both Marcus Brutus and Aemilius Paullus were named as conspirators by Vettius. They were two of Pompey's most bitter personal enemies. Paullus' father was the consul of 78, Aemilius Lepidus, whom Pompey had betrayed and driven out of Italy to die miserably in Sardinia; Brutus' father was the Brutus whom Pompey had treacherously murdered at Mutina during the same uprising. Brutus had further cause for hatred of Pompey: he had been betrothed to Caesar's daughter Julia until her marriage to Pompey robbed him of this brilliant match.[34] And of Brutus it cannot be said that he did not have it in him to be a tyrannicide.

Before there could be any judicial enquiry, Vettius was found dead. 'Caesar's work,' cried the *boni*. But the question *Cui bono?* suggests the answer that those who stood to gain most from silencing Vettius did not include Caesar and Vatinius. That Cicero had any part in a plot to kill Pompey

[32] *ad Att.* II.24.3.
[33] Ibid. 2–3.
[34] Syme, *RR*, 34.

is incredible, for all that at about this time he was writing letters to Atticus in cypher.[35] But he had compromised himself in Pompey's eyes by his intimate association with young Curio, his opposition to the 'Triumvirate', his cool response to Pompey's appeal for help, and (we can take it for granted) by his usual weakness for talking too much and too eloquently. Pompey could no longer trust Cicero, or at least look to him for any positive political co-operation. Caesar had made Cicero generous offers, only to have them rejected. Clodius was out for Cicero's blood, and with the tribunate of 58 assured him, and backed by wide popularity and organized gangs of rowdies, he was too valuable and dangerous for Pompey and Caesar to thwart him openly—and why should they wish to when Cicero was stubbornly prepared to offer them absolutely nothing in return for their support and protection?

If Cicero would not actively join Caesar, or agree to keep quiet, he was better out of the way. If he would not act as a loyal agent for Pompey, there was little inducement for Pompey to take risks in protecting him. In losing the backing of Pompey and rejecting Caesar's offers Cicero threw away that firm support which, in an earlier moment of clarity, he had discerned himself to stand in need of.[36] All that remained for him to rely on against Clodius' attack was the support of the *boni*, the very men he had then judged to be unreliable. Unpopular the dynasts might be; they had not fallen apart as Cicero had suspected they would, for their broad community of interest (at any rate in the short term) and the absence of alternatives held them together. The more unpopular they were, the greater the dangers they faced, the more necessary was it to muzzle Cicero and appease Clodius. Cicero never woke up to the fact that, for him personally, a really secure 'Triumvirate' was much safer than an insecure one.

In a letter to his brother Quintus, written about November

<hr/>

[35] *ad Att.* II.19.5 (mid-July 59): *Si obscure scribam, tu tamen intelleges. In iis epistulis me Laelium, te Furium faciam; cetera erunt ἐν αἰνιγμοῖς.*

[36] *ad Att.* I.19.6 (March 60).

59, Cicero showed himself mistakenly confident of the future:

If Clodius brings in an indictment, the whole of Italy will rally to me, so that I shall leave the field with my glory enhanced; if on the other hand he tries to use brute force, I hope that we shall meet force with force, thanks to the enthusiastic support not only of my friends but of others as well. Everybody is generous with promises—of himself, friends, dependents, freedmen, slaves, and money. My old band of loyalists is burning with enthusiasm and devotion . . . The tribunes-designate are friendly towards me [later in 58 eight of them were to propose an abortive bill for Cicero's recall]; the consuls-designate are making an excellent showing; among the praetors-designate I have four supremely energetic and friendly patriots in Domitius, Nigidius, Memmius, and Lentulus—others are reliable but these are outstanding. So be sure to keep your spirits high and your hopes firm.[37]

The bubble soon burst. Clodius assumed office on 10 December, and at once promulgated four bills: one provided for free distributions of corn to the urban populace, one set a limit on the censors' untrammelled power to expel members from the Senate, a third put severe checks on the sort of manipulation of the auspices and religious devices which Bibulus had practised against Caesar in 59, and a fourth legalized the formation of clubs and associations (*collegia*) which had been ruled illegal five years before. All four bills became law on 4 January 58. He wasted no time in forming *collegia* as a 'front' for the organization of gangs, and even established a sort of armoury in the Forum. According to Dio Cassius, Clodius had managed to trick Cicero into inactivity by false promises; certainly, both Cicero and Atticus formed the odd idea that the legalizing of *collegia* was to Cicero's advantage—perhaps they imagined that it might facilitate the mobilization of his own supporters if need arose.[38]

No further letters are extant until we come to April 58 when Cicero is already on the road to exile. What happened in the interval we have to learn from Dio Cassius and Plutarch, and from the speeches Cicero made after his return—

[37] *ad QF* I.2.16.
[38] Dio 38.14; *ad Att.* III.15.4. On Clodius' activity, see Lintott, op. cit., chapters 6 and 7.

speeches in which he is not always to be relied on for the truth and in which he is understandably very bitter and unfair to some individuals, particularly to Piso, who he reckoned had as consul in 58 let him down very badly. But the main facts are not in dispute, whatever we think of Cicero's interpretation of them.[39]

The new praetors Memmius and Domitius Ahenobarbus sought to impugn the legality of Caesar's legislation. This did Cicero no good. Caesar was faced with a hostile Senate—all the more reason not to antagonize Clodius. Pompey too had an interest in safeguarding Caesar's legislation and was not likely to view with any warmth the prospect of an optimate *révanche*. The praetors got nowhere, and early in February Clodius promulgated two new bills: one proposed to outlaw anyone who had put Roman citizens to death without trial, the other assigned desirable provinces to the two consuls— Macedonia to Piso and Cilicia (later changed to Syria) to Gabinius. Thus the support or acquiescence of the consuls was bought, and the two bills were synchronized to prevent any possibility of backsliding.

The former bill was aimed straight at Cicero, though he was not specifically named. The Senate appealed to Gabinius, and getting no satisfaction went into public mourning— only to be sharply compelled to desist by a consular edict. Cicero's friend Lucius Aelius Lamia set about organizing demonstrations and protests by the knights, and was promptly banished two hundred miles from Rome by Gabinius. A deputation of prominent senators waited on Pompey, who referred them correctly but unhelpfully to the consuls. Piso murmured darkly of the probability of bloodshed if Cicero did not go quietly; when Cicero appealed to him personally, he seems to have expressed the view that it was every man for himself. Clodius dangled the threat of violence in the face of the Senate. He held a meeting at which the consuls publicly expressed their disapproval of the execution of citizens without trial; Caesar agreed, though, for what it was

---

[39] Dio 38.12–17; Plutarch *Cicero* 30–1; Cicero *pro Sest.* 26–9, 32, 41; *in Pis.* 11–12, 14, 17–18, 21, 23; *post red. in sen.* 12–13, 17, 32; *har. resp.* 47.

worth, he deprecated any direct action against Cicero.

Cicero yielded to Clodius' threats and left Rome under cover of darkness probably about 20 March.[40] To begin with he hovered near Rome, but Clodius rushed through a bill exiling him by name and confiscating his property. Cicero headed south, speeded on his way by the news that penalties were fixed against anyone who harboured him. He stayed on the outskirts of Brindisi for the last fortnight of April, taking ship on the 29th. It is convenient here to anticipate his later movements. He reached Salonika in Macedonia on 23 May; there he stayed till late November, owing much to the kindness of his good friend Gnaeus Plancius, who was serving as quaestor in Macedonia in 58—a kindness he was later to repay by a brilliant defence of Plancius in the courts. At the end of November he moved back to Dyrrhachium (Durazzo) on the Adriatic coast, partly to be nearer Italy and news from Rome, and not a little to keep out of the way of Piso when he arrived as governor of Macedonia. At Durazzo he stayed until his return to Italy.

Cicero had been dazzled by the 'immortal glory of the Nones'. His justifiable pride in his achievement as consul, his vanity, his ambition, had overcome good sense and induced him throughout much of 59 to believe that the united front which he had formed and led in 63 might be revived and even become an enduring force. His references at this time to another *concursus bonorum omnium*, to his 'old army of loyalists', are frequent. The writing was on the wall, but it was only in very rare moments that he could read it, and it was soon sponged from his memory. Generally, his natural optimism (what he himself called his εὐελπιστία[41]) led him to overestimate his own admittedly considerable importance and to believe that he could reform men like Pompey and Caesar and teach them to walk in his ways.[42]

The first effect of exile was shattering. Cicero thought of suicide, or so he claimed later, He gave way to a 'Latin'

[40] Shackleton-Bailey II, Appendix I, for these dates.
[41] *ad Att.* II.17.2.
[42] Ibid. II.1.6.

indulgence in flamboyant emotions and wild tears. He be-
wailed the disgrace and ruin he had brought on friends and
family; he berated Atticus and other friends for having 'let
him down' by failing to give him the right advice—for he
was not long in convincing himself that he should have stood
his ground and fought Clodius toe to toe. Overwhelmed by
abject despair, pessimism, and self-pity, he remained blind
to the true reasons for his disaster; there is no sign in his
letters that he diagnosed his earlier faults correctly, and his
actions after his return show that the lesson had been at best
only partially learned. Making every allowance one can for
his understandable shock and dismay, it must be admitted
that Cicero in exile reminds one of a petulant and emotion-
ally self-indulgent child. Some of the letters have a note that
can be described only as 'whining'.[43]

Atticus showed exemplary patience in putting up with his
friend's charges and complaints. Pompey too was a predict-
able target of Cicero's bitterness. Pompey had betrayed him
into the hands of his enemies: in a letter of June 58 Pompey
is a 'deceiver'; in August his inaction had been an 'abrupt
desertion',[44] But there is a certain lack of conviction in his
condemnation of Pompey; he must have recognized that the
faults were not all on one side. In any case, Pompey soon
emerged as the one man on whom centred all his hopes of
return, and his most acid reproaches were reserved for the
boni, particularly Hortensius, who had turned out to be such
false friends.

It is clear that Pompey (whether from genuine remorse, or
from a conviction that Cicero was much too useful to be discarded, or because of growing hostility between himself and
Clodius and Crassus) lost little time in setting about bringing
Cicero back. Of this fight for restoration there is no need to
chronicle every detail. We may content ourselves with the
main features.

The first move came as early as May 58 from Marcus

---

[43] For the moods and reactions described, see esp. *ad QF* 1.3 and 1.4; *ad Att.*
III.7–III.20.
[44] *ad QF* I.3.9, 4.4. Cf. *ad Att.* X.4.3 (April 49).

Terentius Varro, historian and scholar as well as politician, and Publius Plautius Hypsaeus; both were intimates of Pompey.[45] But for the remainder of 58 Clodius succeeded in holding up all such moves. His organized gangs often gave him virtual control of a city which lacked any police force. Clodius clashed with Pompey when he released from custody and then aided to escape from Rome a prisoner of Pompey's, Tigranes, son of the King of Armenia. The consul Gabinius, an old henchmen of Pompey's, also brushed with Clodius, raising a gang of his own which fought with Clodius' men in the streets (not that Cicero thanked him for it, for his hatred of Gabinius remained unabated).[46] On 1 July the tribune Ninnius, encouraged by Pompey, proposed in the Senate that Cicero be recalled; nobody dissented, but another tribune, Aelius Ligur, put down a veto. When Quintus Cicero returned from his province of Asia, he was accorded a widespread and sympathetic reception.[47]

By early September Cicero had heard that Pompey was definitely moving and was in correspondence with Caesar about the matter.[48] Clodius cleverly played on Pompey's morbid fear of assassination, and Pompey retired to the safety of his country houses for the remainder of the year.[49] But the fight went on. Cicero's son-in-law, Gaius Calpurnius Piso, tried hard to win over his kinsman, the consul Lucius Piso; he declined to go to his province as quaestor in order to devote himself to working for his father-in-law's interests. (Cicero had a deep affection for him, but unhappily he died before Cicero returned to Rome.) Another young friend, Publius Sestius, tribune-designate for 57, went to see Caesar in Gaul, but seems to have got a cool reception.[50]

The elections had gone well. Of the two consuls-designate, Lentulus Spinther was a good friend and Metellus Nepos (a cousin of Clodius) was persuaded to forget his old quarrels with Cicero. Eight of the ten tribunes-elect turned out to be on Cicero's side, including the powerful and tough Titus

[45] *ad Att.* III.8.3.   [46] Asconius 47C; *in Pis.* 27; Dio 38.30.
[47] *pro Sest.* 67–8.   [48] *ad Att.* III.18.1.
[49] *pro Sest.* 69; *har. resp.* 49; *in Pis.* 28–9; Asconius 46C.
[50] *pro Sest.* 54, 68, 71; *post red. in sen.* 38; *ad famm.* XIV.1.4, 3.3; *Brutus* 272.

Annius Milo. Encouraged by this, eight of the existing tribunes tabled a bill on 29 October for Cicero's recall. Cicero
quibbled peevishly about its loose drafting. and it was vetoed
by Aelius Ligur, still working with Clodius. But it was a
straw in the wind, and Clodius' tribunate had only about six
more weeks to run.[51] Not long afterwards, Cicero left Salonika
and moved west to Durazzo. The swelling tide of support
for him, though it still left him pessimistic about his chances,
fed his conviction that he had been wrong to run away and
that his friends had advised him badly.

Cicero's pessimism was not ill-founded. On 1 January 57
Lentulus Spinther moved in the Senate for Cicero's recall.
Nepos did not oppose him, and the praetor Appius Claudius
Pulcher (Clodius' elder brother) held his peace. Lucius
Cotta (consul in 65) went further, and argued that Cicero
ought to be not merely recalled but publicly honoured.
Pompey agreed, cautiously but sensibly noting that any
resolution ought to be confirmed by a vote of the people.
Then things went awry. Two of the new tribunes were
against Cicero, and one of them, Atilius Serranus, remained
adamant. Tribunician machinations held up a resolution for
the rest of January. On 25 January, the day fixed for putting
the proposal to the people, a friendly tribune, Quintus
Fabricius, proceeded to the Forum before first light only to
find it occupied by armed gangs. A violent affray developed,
blood flowed freely, and Quintus Cicero had a narrow escape
from serious injury or death: 'The Tiber was choked with
corpses, the sewers blocked, blood had to be mopped up
from the Forum with sponges.' Cicero's gloom is understandable in the face of this fresh demonstration of Clodius'
power.[52]

Gang warfare raged. Sestius and Milo recruited gangs of
their own to fight fire with fire, Milo's including a squad of
trained gladiators. Milo also tried, though without success,
to bring Clodius to trial for riot. The tide began to stand in
Cicero's favour; all other considerations aside, the Senate

[51] ad Att. III. 22.2, 23.1–3; ad QF I.4.3.
[52] pro Sest. 72–7; cum senatui 5–9; in Pis. 34–5; Dio 39.7; Plutarch Cicero 33.

had to assert its authority in face of gang-law. On the motion of the consul Lentulus Spinther, he was commended to the protection of provincial governors, and a call went out to citizens throughout Italy to come to Rome to vote for his recall. Quintus Cicero gave a pledge that his brother would behave himself; thus able to reassure Caesar and secure his neutrality, Pompey plunged into the fight, speaking in the Forum and travelling tirelessly from town to town to enlist support. Cicero, he declared, had saved his country; and a packed Senate, with a single dissentient vote, ordered that this sentiment be entered in the public record. The following day, the house ruled that anyone hindering the vote for Cicero's recall should be deemed a public enemy.[53]

The day fixed for the popular vote was 4 August. It was to be taken, most unusually, in the centuriate assembly, for there the wealthier voters had a greater influence. Rome was packed tight as citizens flooded in from the municipalities of Italy. (Clodius later blamed Cicero for the subsequent food crisis on the grounds that this had been caused by the massive influx into the capital.) Lentulus Spinther moved the bill. Milo was at hand with his armed men, but now that Pompey had come out so openly Clodius must have seen that resistance was useless. The bill passed into law.[54]

Cicero had anticipated the outcome. He sailed from Durazzo on 4 August, landing next day at Brindisi to a tumultuous reception. A few days later he received confirmation of the vote at Rome and headed north. The communities along his route besieged him with congratulatory deputations and addresses. As he neared the capital, 'everybody who was anybody' (so he puts it himself) made a point of coming out to meet him. On 4 September he made a triumphant entry at the Porta Capena, and the crowds and the cheers accompanied him to the climax of his arrival at the Forum and the Capitol, packed to bursting point with his welcomers. The exile had come home.[55]

[53] *pro Sest.* 84–8, 117, 129; *ad Famm.* I.9.9; Dio 39.8.
[54] *de domo* 90; *ad Att.* IV.1.4; Dio 39.8.
[55] *ad Att.* IV.1.4–5.

IX

CAPITULATION

CICERO was well aware that without Pompey's powerful help his return would not have been effected, or effected as and when it was. In the end, it was the guarantee of Pompey's backing that alone could give free rein to the forces and individuals pressing for his recall. Even to Spinther, who had as consul played a central role, Cicero later wrote that 'my greatest debt was to Pompey, as you yourself openly testified.'[1] In his speeches Cicero proclaims his gratitude and is lavish in his praise: 'Can I ever,' he asks, 'ever hope to repay in full the debt I owe him?'[2] It is likely that Pompey had in mind particular services which Cicero could render in helping to secure for him the great command or appointment which he considered his natural due and for which he seemed now to be yearning more than ever, especially in view of Caesar's striking successes in Gaul. Yet Cicero did not give him much help. But before we condemn him, we must give his side of the case a hearing.

On his return, Cicero was at once plunged into two exciting political issues: the food crisis of autumn 57 and, soon to follow, the thorny business of Egypt. Here was his chance to begin to repay his debt, and he took the lead in proposing the creation of a special commission for Pompey to deal with the food crisis. This was within a week of his arrival back in Rome. He made his triumphant entry on 4 September, delivered his speech *post reditum ad Senatum* on the 5th, and proposed the corn-commission on the 7th.

[1] *ad famm.* I.9.6.
[2] *post red. in sen.* 5 and 29; *post red. ad Quir.* 16.

The Senate accepted Cicero's motion, and he later addressed the People on the subject—for a law was needed to
implement the senatorial decree.[3] But he was (perhaps
studiedly) vague about the precise details of what he was
proposing. The situation was tricky; of some twenty *consulares* available, only three, of whom Cicero was the senior,
attended the meeting on 7 September; the others declared
that it was not safe for them to attend, but this was only an
excuse to cover their unwillingness to commit themselves one
way or the other. Next day there was a full house, including
the *consulares*, and the consuls, Spinther and Metellus Nepos,
duly produced a proposal giving effect to Cicero's motion
which had been carried the day before. According to Cicero,
this gave Pompey everything he was asking for: the enormous establishment of fifteen *legati* or lieutenant-commis-
sioners (Pompey put Cicero's name at the head of the list and
said he would treat him as his *alter ego* in all things), and
supreme control of all grain supplies throughout the world
for five years. But the action of the tribune Gaius Messius
suggests that Pompey in fact wanted more than he was
prepared openly to ask for. For Messius proposed as an
alternative to the consular proposal one which gave Pompey
an open cheque on the state treasury, a fleet and an army,
and *maius imperium*, i.e. an authority latently superior to that
of all provincial governors.[4]

Compared with this the consuls' proposal (said Cicero)
now seemed 'a modest one': Messius' was 'intolerable'.
Pompey publicly professed his preference for the consular
measure, but his cronies said that he really wanted the
commission on Messius' terms. The *consulares*, now present
in force and representing the embattled interest of the
'establishment', were boiling. What was Cicero to do? 'I am

---

[3] *ad Att.* IV.1.6.
[4] *ad Att.* IV.1.7. Balsdon, *JRS* 47 (1957), 16–18. Given the activity which
Pompey's intimate supporters were soon to display in trying to secure him the
Egyptian commission, one is bound to suspect that Messius (and Pompey) were
thinking of the *cura annonae* as a possible springboard from which Pompey could
establish himself in Egypt. Egypt was a very important source of grain; and an
army and a fleet and *maius imperium* would be indispensable for such a venture.

keeping quiet', he tells Atticus. Having sown the wind, he had no taste for reaping the whirlwind that followed. He surely knew that Pompey's commission must involve the use of ships and troops, and that (in view of the need to post deputies in the various maritime and corn-growing provinces) it would probably give rise to jurisdictional disputes and conflicts of authority between Pompey and individual governors. So Pompey would need a fleet and an army, and his position vis-à-vis the governors would have to be clarified if a repetition of the bickering that had gone on during Pompey's Mediterranean-wide pirate command ten years earlier was to be avoided. This must have been clear to many besides Cicero; there were numerous senators who were unwilling to come out openly against Pompey but reluctant to see him presented with too rich a prize.

Cicero was awkwardly placed. His original proposal that a corn commission be established and entrusted to Pompey was highly unpopular with the leading nobles, so much so that he felt obliged to devote the first quarter of his speech *de domo sua ad pontifices* (delivered on 29 September) to a defence of his action. The proposal of Messius, with its sweeping powers, was anathema to the oligarchs, and Cicero simply could not afford to outrage them so soon after his return by associating himself with it. So, 'I am keeping quiet, and all the more so because so far the pontiffs have come to no decision about my house'.[5]

Cicero's property had been confiscated by Clodius, and some of his country houses pillaged. In particular, his fine town house on the Palatine had been demolished and part of the site dedicated by Clodius with ironic humour for a shrine to *Libertas*. It fell to the College of Pontiffs to decide whether the consecration could be annulled, and the pontiffs were not simply religious officials but also leading politicians; in 57 the eighteen pontiffs included seven ex-consuls (including the absent Julius Caesar), the consul Lentulus Spinther, two future consuls, two ex-praetors and two future praetors. It is not certain whether Crassus was one

[5] *ad Att.* IV.1.7.

of the pontiffs, but they certainly included in their number notorious enemies of Pompey like Marcus Lucullus (consul in 73) and Quintus Metellus Creticus (consul in 69), and the seventy-seven-year-old Publius Servilius Isauricus (consul in 79). On 29 September they did decide in Cicero's favour, and arrangements were made for him to be reimbursed for the damage done to his town house and villas. But during the week or two after his return he was clearly worried about the possibility of offending the political views of important members of the College.[6]

Clodius was far from a spent force. His gangs worked hard to interrupt the rebuilding of the Palatine house, and in 56 Cicero had to fight off another attempt to use religion against him. Subterranean disturbances were interpreted by the *haruspices* as indicating that holy places had been defiled. Clodius claimed that this was Cicero's fault for rebuilding on a consecrated site, but in his speech *de haruspicum responso* Cicero won the Senate over to his side, arguing that the true blame lay with Clodius himself. As is the habit with their tribe, the soothsayers had in their report leaned more heavily towards magniloquence than precision.[7]

The Egyptian question also found Cicero not a free agent, for he was bound by the strong claims of his friend and helper in 57, Lentulus Spinther.

The struggle that now flared up had a long history in Roman politics. Egypt had by the latter part of the second century added to its external impotence the further disadvantage of internal strife. This was accompanied by sporadic rebellions in the course of which appendages like Cyrenaica and Cyprus became separate entities from the rest of Egypt under rival royal claimants. In 96 Ptolemy Apion had died and bequeathed his realm of Cyrene to Rome, though it was not until 74 that it was converted into a Roman province. In 80 Sulla bestowed the throne of Egypt on one of the rival claimants of the day. The new king was lynched

[6] For the list of Pontiffs in 57, see Broughton, *Magistrates of the Roman Republic* II, sub anno.

[7] *har. resp.* 8 ff; 20 ff; 34 ff; 56.

before his reign was three weeks old. He was alleged to have left a will bequeathing Egypt to Rome, but whatever Sulla's original intentions may have been he took no steps on the death of his nominee Pharaoh. As we have already seen, in the sixties Crassus revived the dormant claim and backed a proposal to annex Egypt, first openly as censor in 65 and then covertly in connection with the agrarian bill of 63.[8] In 59 Caesar had managed to secure something on account: in return for a generous consideration he had Ptolemy Auletes recognized as king of Egypt and friend and ally of the Roman People. The following year Clodius turned Auletes' brother out of Cyprus and annexed the island to Rome. Two birds were killed with one stone, for he had Marcus Cato sent out to organize the new territory, thus keeping that formidable individual out of Rome and out of Clodius' way until 56.

Roman interest in Egypt is readily comprehensible. For all that its economy had been going steadily downhill for years, it retained immense reserves and immense potential.[9] And the dynastic tangles and rivalries, coupled with the arguable claim of Rome herself under a Pharaoh's will, offered the leading politicians of Rome both inducement and excuse to try to get their hands on the enormous loot and patronage that were there for the taking. By the same token, any attempt would be fiercely contested by jealous and apprehensive rivals; for if any one man or group could secure firm hold on Egypt and exploit it they would throw the balance of Roman politics—so closely geared to money and patronage—right out of true. The business was revived now because Auletes, whom Caesar had put on the throne in 59, had been unseated and was appealing for help to get back on. In 57 Spinther had carried a motion in the Senate that Auletes be restored, and restored by the governor of Cilicia. This was not as disinterested as it may sound, for Spinther was himself governor-designate of Cilicia. But things were not going to be settled as simply as that. Other names were canvassed, and the position was further complicated when

---

[8] Above, pp. 89 ff.

[9] On Augustus' special treatment of Egypt, see Tacitus *Ann.* 2.59.

Gaius Cato produced a Sibylline oracle which declared that no army might be used to effect the king's restoration. Gaius Cato is not to be confused with Marcus Cato; Gaius was a supporter of Crassus and a friend and collaborator of Clodius. Probably Crassus was trying to insure that even if Pompey did get the Egyptian command it would not be of military importance; indeed, given the vigorous turbulence of the Alexandrians, which was later to give an overconfident Julius Caesar a rude shock and a narrow escape, it is not easy to see how without an army the job could be done at all.

Cicero was naturally under an obligation to support Spinther, and he took the lead along with Hortensius and Marcus Lucullus—though they recognized that they must give way on the religious point if they were to have any chance of success; intervention would have to be diplomatic, not military. By mid-January 56 a variety of proposals had been laid before the Senate. Apart from that of Spinther's friends, they were as follows. Crassus proposed a commission of three men selected from among those who held *imperium*; this did not exclude Pompey since he had *imperium* in virtue of his corn commission, but it ensured that if chosen he would not have a free hand. (Crassus may also have calculated that if the commission were chosen from those already vested with *imperium* no special legislation and hence no special powers would be required.) Bibulus agreed, but with the proviso that the three men should be chosen from among those *not* at present holding *imperium*; this cut out of consideration both Pompey and Spinther. Crassus was probably not disagreeably surprised by this modification, and all the other *consulares* expressed their agreement with Bibulus with only three exceptions. These three were the grand old man Servilius Isauricus, who moved that they resolve not to restore Auletes at all; and Volcacius Tullus and Afranius, who both supported the proposal of the tribune Publius Rutilius Lupus that Pompey should be commissioned to restore the king.[10]

[10] *ad famm.* I.1.3.

What did Pompey himself think? According to Cicero, he was all for Spinther, to whom he was indebted not only for invaluable help in securing Cicero's recall but also as the author of the law to give him his corn commission. On 13 January 56 Cicero writes to tell Spinther how things stand:

As for Pompey, I never stop pushing and begging him, even openly accusing him and warning him that he must avoid ruining his reputation for fair dealing. But really he renders all my appeals and warnings superfluous. Not just in his private conversation but also in his public declarations in the Senate he presses your claim with unsurpassable eloquence and weight and vigour, warmly citing your services to him and his own deep affection for you.

All this we must take with a large pinch of salt, as Spinther must have done; Pompey was notorious for his habit of saying one thing while thinking something else. His intimates certainly thought that they knew what Pompey really had set his heart on—and it was *not* the appointment of Spinther. 'All the energetic and anything but secret to-ing and fro-ing of Libo and Hypsaeus and the exertions of all Pompey's intimates have produced a general belief that Pompey wants the appointment for himself. Those who are against Pompey are no friends of yours either, because of your past services to him.'[11]

The proposal to send Pompey to Egypt stemmed from the pro-Pompeian tribune Lupus. It was supported by Afranius, who was almost comically pro-Pompeian, and by the two tribunes Scribonius Libo and Plautius Hypsaeus—the former the father-in-law of Pompey's son Sextus, the latter an old quaestor of Pompey's who had served under him in the East and who was to be strongly backed by him for a consulship in 52[12]—to say nothing of all Pompey's other close friends. Nobody believed that Pompey could not have stopped all this had he really wanted to. 'When I am with him and listening to him, I at once acquit him of all suspicion of self-seeking'—so writes Cicero to Spinther on 15 January. 'But when I see his intimates of every class, I realize what is now

[11] Ibid. 2–4.
[12] Below, p. 218.

plain to everyone, that the whole affair was rigged long ago.'[13]

On 13 January the Senate settled down to debate the issue, but most of the day was taken up by a procedural squabble between the consul Lentulus Marcellinus and the tribune Caninius Gallus (another Pompeian supporter, who was later to try to get the people to accept a bill for Pompey to restore Auletes). Next day they settled down again to take the various proposals one by one. The house agreed with Bibulus about the religious bar on the use of an army, but rejected the rest of his proposal by an overwhelming majority. Hortensius' motion (with which Cicero and Lucullus associated themselves) was next on the agenda, but now the trouble began. The tribune Lupus demanded that his motion be taken first. He knew that many senators would not want to see the job go to Pompey, but would be scared of openly voting against his motion. They could get out of their dilemma by voting for Hortensius' motion, which Pompey was ostensibly supporting, before Lupus' turn came around. But Lupus meant that they should stand up and be counted. The consuls, Marcellinus and Lucius Marcius Philippus, had themselves favoured Bibulus' motion, and saw that Hortensius' motion, if put, would be carried by a large majority. Hence, though for different reasons, they were happy to join in the game with Lupus and allow the rest of the session to be frittered away by a tiresome discussion of his point of order.[14]

All the time the political moves were going on against a background of mounting civil disorder. Cicero gives a vivid picture of this in a letter of 23 November 57. Armed rowdies of Clodius had driven off the workmen from the Palatine site and damaged the portico of Catulus next door. Quintus Cicero's house nearby was stoned and set on fire. A week later the gangs launched a sudden attack on Cicero himself in the *Via Sacra*, and Cicero had to retreat smartly into a nearby

---

[13] *ad famm.* I.2.3.

[14] Ibid. 1–3. Crassus had apparently withdrawn his motion, presumably in favour of that of Bibulus. Otherwise Crassus' motion should have been taken first.

house. A day or two later Clodius set up headquarters in the house of Publius Sulla and launched an incendiary attack on Milo's house. A counter-attack drove him off with heavy losses. Attempts to get some action from the Senate were frustrated by the obstructive tactics of Clodius' cousin, the consul Metellus Nepos, and his brother, the praetor Appius Claudius. Clodius was hoping to be elected aedile (thus gaining immunity from the prosecution Milo was threatening him with), so Milo settled down with his hired bravoes to occupy the Campus to thwart him. Cicero presciently noted that if Clodius gave Milo the chance, Milo would kill him: 'He has no scruple about doing it, makes no bones about it. He is not frightened by what happened to me.'[15]

Clodius succeded in being elected and hit back with a prosecution of Milo. Pompey was backing Milo, and when he put in an appearance on 7 February to speak for him at a preliminary hearing he was howled at and abused throughout his speech. When Clodius got up to reply, he was given a dose of his own medicine as the opposing claque exercised their lungs and talents for abuse, ending up by gaily chanting filthy songs about Clodius and his sister Clodia. White with rage, Clodius began a counterpoint with his followers: 'Who's starving you all to death?' he screamed. 'Pompey!' they roared back at him. 'Who wants to go to Alexandria?'—'Pompey!' 'Who do *we* want to go?' —'Crassus!' they all yelled. All this had now been going on for about four hours. Tempers rose, men began to jostle each other. The Milonians charged, drove off the Clodians, and tumbled Clodius himself off the speakers' platform. At this point Cicero decided to make himself scarce before he got hurt.[16]

Pompey was having trouble with the *boni* as well. Hortensius, Bibulus, Curio and company had no time for Pompey, for his past tergiversations or his present soaring ambitions. When Gaius Cato launched a set attack on Pompey in the Senate on 8 February he harped on his betrayal of Cicero in 58 and was listened to in attentive silence. Pompey responded

[15] *ad Att.* IV.3.   [16] *ad QF.* II.3.2.

with vigour, hinting very plainly that he thought that Crassus was planning to have him assassinated; he gave public warning that he was taking due precautions. He told Cicero in private that there was a plot against his (Pompey's) life, that Crassus was behind Gaius Cato and financing Clodius, and that both were being encouraged by his enemies among the *boni*. The commons, he declared, were pretty well alienated from him, the nobility hostile, the Senate biased, the young nobles restless. To words Pompey added deeds: the call went out, and loyal followers were summoned from his 'barony' in Picenum. In the general confusion and excitement the Egyptian question slipped out of sight.[17]

It looked as if Pompey had been foiled again. He had got his corn commission, but not in the form his friends contended he had really wanted. He had not got Egypt, and his treatment of Spinther further reinforced his reputation for double-dealing. On neither occasion can Cicero be said to have given of his all. We have seen his difficulties. In order to avoid an open display of ingratitude he took refuge in the discrepancy between Pompey's real wishes and his expressed views, professing to take the latter at their face value. (In this he was no worse than Pompey himself, who pretended to back Spinther but made no attempt to restrain his own supporters from wrecking Spinther's chances.) Pompey was much given to this sort of duplicity, and with his superb 'poker-face' and air of surprised innocence he was physically well-equipped for the role.[18] His deviousness was often remarked by Cicero and other contemporaries. 'It is difficult to know what he wants and what he doesn't want'; 'You know how cautious and tight-lipped the man is'; 'It is his habit' (writes Caelius Rufus) 'to think one thing and say another'; and he goes on, 'But he is not clever enough to hide what he really wants.' And here we approach the crux of the matter: it was up to Pompey's intimates to look behind the public façade to divine the true wishes of their leader,

[17] Ibid. 3–4.
[18] See the frequently reproduced portrait bust now in the Ny Glyptothek, Copenhagen.

and act accordingly. Cicero knew this, for he often admits that one can never rely on it that Pompey means what he says. Thus (in a letter of April 55 to Atticus): 'I have been here with Pompey. He has had long talks with me about politics, very upset with himself—*so he says*. . . in my opinion, whenever we talk about Pompey, we have to keep adding "*so he says*" like a refrain in an old song.'[19]

Pompey was a devious man. But Cicero's own letters make it plain enough that he too was capable of thinking one thing and saying another, and so too surely would the private letters of other leading politicians of the time, if we had them. It was Pompey's habit never to ask for anything openly; should he fail to get what he wanted, he would not openly lose face. (It would not do to minimize for one moment the importance to the leading men of Rome of this question of 'face', of *dignitas* as they termed it.)[20] Pompey's behaviour did nothing to absolve his friends and supporters from their obligation to try to get him what he really wanted. In electing to act on the basis of Pompey's overt declarations Cicero cannot be acquitted of ingratitude simply on the ground that he was misled by what Pompey himself said. His real excuse was that he was not a free agent. His chief fault—surely venial—was that he let himself get carried away in his purple passages about Pompey in his post-exile speeches. This was an abiding failure: as he once wrote to Atticus, 'You know how thick I lay it on.'[21]

To pick up the threads again, what was Pompey's position now? A good deal better than might appear at first sight. Once again, as in the late sixties, he had failed to get what he wanted from the Senate and the *boni;* but, as before, there was still Caesar. Pompey could put pressure on Caesar, if he chose, for Caesar's security (as was very clearly to be shown a few years later) rested on the assurance of Pompey's co-operation. If this were withdrawn, or if its withdrawal were

[19] *ad QF* III.8.4; *ad famm.* I.5B.2; VIII.1.3; *ad Att.* IV.9.1.

[20] Thus Caesar declared (*BC* 1.9): *sibi semper primam fuisse dignitatem, vitaque potiorem.*

[21] *ad Att.* I.14.3: *nosti illas* ληκύθους.

threatened, Caesar's enemies would be snapping at his throat. What lies behind the political activities of the months before the Conference of Lucca, and what precise part Cicero played, has been variously reconstructed by modern scholars, and the answers depend in part on careful examination of textual clues. To rehearse this polemical detail would be out of place here. The account that follows is by no means idiosyncratic, but other views are held.[22]

By early 56 the growing evidence of dissension among the 'Big Three' was plain for all to see: the riotous scenes at Rome, Clodius' anti-Pompeian demonstrations, Pompey's open quarrel with Crassus, his fear of assassination and his summoning of armed retainers from the country to reinforce Milo's rowdies. All this is hard fact, related to Quintus in a private letter. It is not surprising that Cicero should add his own conclusion that some really big development was in the offing: *itaque magnae mihi res iam moveri videbantur*. Crassus and Pompey were in open and brutal confrontation.[23]

Late in February Cicero's advocacy secured the acquittal of his friend and Pompey's, Publius Sestius, who was charged with riot in connection with the disturbances in 57 when as tribune Sestius had worked vigorously for Cicero's recall and later to try to prevent Clodius' election as aedile. The speech (*pro Sestio*) survives. Cicero earlier, during the course of a speech in defence of Lucius Bestia, had slipped in some apposite comments relevant to Sestius' case, and he had been greatly encouraged by the reaction of the court. During Sestius' trial Cicero savaged the prosecution witness Vatinius (tribune in 59 and factotum then to Caesar), 'cutting him to ribbons just as I pleased'. Pompey was present in court listening to all this (he had come to give a formal testimonial on Sestius' behalf), and he heard Cicero turn his cross-examination of Vatinius into a general indictment of what had been done in 59, speaking freely about the violence, the disregard of religious proprieties, the buying and selling of kingdoms. He even went so far as to declare how much more

---

[22] For a detailed discussion, see Stockton, *TAPA* 93 (1962), 471–89.
[23] *ad QF* II.3.4.

highly he rated the fortune of Caesar's colleague Bibulus to any victories and triumphs won in the field—a clear dig at the brilliant successes of Caesar in Gaul. Nor did Cicero confine his comments to the courtroom, for he kept harping on the same themes in the Senate as well. The consul Lentulus Marcellinus, he told his brother in a letter of March 56, was acquitting himself splendidly in opposing Gaius Cato and blocking pro-Caesarian legislation. The only fault Cicero has to find with him is his asperity towards Pompey, but he remarks that the Senate does not at all mind this. The continuing unpopularity of Pompey with the Senate is also shown by Milo's narrow failure to secure a verdict of guilty against Sextus Cloelius, one of Publius Clodius' leading helpers; the senators on the jury voted overwhelmingly for acquittal, thanks in some measure to their dislike of Pompey.[24]

Cicero had clearly regained his old ebullience. On 5 April he secured the Senate's assent to his motion that the question of the Campanian Land be put on the agenda for discussion at a full meeting of the house on 15 May. It was the high-water mark of his anti-triumviral activity since his return: 'Could any more serious attack have been launched against the citadel of that party? Could I have shown greater un-concern for my personal security, greater concern for my past glories?' Yet he goes on to observe that Pompey gave no indication that he was put out by his action, and Cicero's boldness was clearly stiffened by his belief that Pompey was behind him.[25]

This belief was not foolish. The question of the Campanian Land had been raised earlier, in December 57, and signifi-cantly by a new tribune, Publius Rutilius Lupus, soon to be active in pressing Pompey's appointment to Egypt, and Cicero had given a report to his brother at the time. The initiative in the matter came from an adherent of Pompey, who took the opportunity to direct a number of barbed

[24] *ad QF* II.3.1 and 4; II.4.1; II.4.4–6; *ad famm.* I.9.7. For Sextus Cloelius, see Shackleton-Bailey, *CQ* 54 (1960), 41 ff.

[25] *ad famm.* I.9.8.

remarks against Caesar, but finished by saying that he would not call for a vote because he did not want to embroil the Senate in responsibility for starting a serious row. He added that both past experience and the mood in which the Senate had listened to him told him what the Senate thought about the matter. Milo also spoke. Finally Marcellinus, consul-designate and the man who would have to bear the brunt of leading the Senate in the new year, wound up the proceedings: 'I should not want you, Lupus, to divine from our silence what at this moment we either approve or disapprove. To speak for myself, but I believe I am speaking for everybody else as well, the reason why I remain silent is that I do not think it suitable to discuss the question of the Campanian Land in the absence of Pompey.'[26]

It looks as if Lupus was 'flying a kite', and certainly the Senate realised that Pompey's attitude was crucial. Just what the proposals about the Campanian Land were we are not told.[27] But, whatever they were, it is plain that they were likely to affect Caesar adversely, but not Pompey. Though Pompey had benefited from Caesar's agrarian legislation in 59 by getting land-allotments for his veterans, they must long have been settled and it is inconceivable that any motion emanating from Lupus or Cicero envisaged dispossessing them.

Two and a half years later Cicero told Spinther that Pompey had given no sign of being put out by his motion on 5 April.[28] The truth of this is confirmed by a contemporary letter to Quintus. Early in the morning of 8 April Cicero scribbled a hurried postscript:

Yesterday I dined with Crassipes [just betrothed to Tullia]. After dinner I was taken in my litter to see Pompey at his place in the suburbs. I had not been able to see him during the day because he had been away. I wanted to see him because I was leaving Rome today and he was off to Sardinia himself. I did meet him, and I asked him to send you back home to us as soon as possible. [Quintus was serving as legate to Pompey in charge of the corn commission in Sardinia.] 'At once,' he said. He was

26 *ad QF.* II.1.1.
27 For a reasonable conjecture, see M. Cary, *CQ* 17 (1923), 103 ff.
28 *ad famm.* I.9.8.

due to leave, so he told me, on 11 April, intending to take ship at Labro (Leghorn) or Pisa. So, brother mine, as soon as he arrives be sure to take the first boat home, provided the weather is fair.

The tone and circumstances of the letter leave no room for doubt that less than two days after Cicero spoke in the Senate about the Campanian Land relations between him and Pompey were perfectly amicable.[29]

Yet, when Pompey did leave Rome, he went first to Lucca, and there met Crassus and Caesar in secret conclave. When he emerged, he sent to tell Cicero to take no further action about the Campanian affair until his own return. When he did reach Sardinia, 'The very man I want to see,' he said to Quintus; 'nothing could have been better timed. If you don't deal carefully with your brother Marcus, you will have to answer to me about the undertaking you gave me on his behalf.' Pompey was reminding Quintus that agreement to Cicero's recall had only been gained by a promise that Cicero would behave himself.[30] Cicero had little choice. He stayed away from the Senate on 15 May, the date fixed for the Campanian debate by his own motion, and the business was not taken. 'I am up against a brick wall,' he told his brother: *in hac causa mihi aqua haeret.*[31]

Pompey is too often represented as a good general and administrator, but lacking in political finesse, blundering about in the delicate maze of Roman politics like a powerful but clumsy carthorse. Yet it cannot be contested that Pompey came away from Lucca better off than when he arrived. Soon there was to be a second consulship and (in addition to his corn commission) a five-year command in Spain with the right to govern in absence through legates while himself remaining in Italy—all the advantages of position, power, and patronage without the sacrifice of close involvement with affairs at the centre. Anyone who can believe that Caesar and Crassus conceded this much to Pompey 'for the sake of his beautiful blue eyes' can believe

[29] *ad QF* II.5.3.
[30] *ad famm.* I.9.9–10.
[31] *ad QF* II.7.2.

anything.[32] Pompey had a strong bargaining position—he could offer to stop being awkward and line up squarely with Caesar to face the dangers that threatened. He did not have to wait for Caesar and Crassus to point it out to him to be aware that Cicero was misbehaving. He must have known that Cicero believed that he was not upset by what Cicero was doing. Yet he made no move to silence Cicero until after the conference at Lucca; then he shut him up firmly and promptly.

Caesar was in an awkward position. He had been compelled to cut legal corners to carry his programme in 59, which was one of the main reasons why he had needed Pompey's para-military support. But if the balance of force should shift, Caesar would be in a dangerous position, liable to recall and prosecution by his enemies. Pompey could not be expected to go on backing Caesar forever if it was not made worth his while. Already by 58 serious differences had emerged, with Pompey working for Cicero's recall, Clodius and Crassus blocking, and Caesar dragging his feet. By autumn 57 Pompey and Crassus were in open conflict, with Clodius, Gaius Cato, Gellius, Milo, Lupus, and the rest all joining in the mêlée. Little was left holding the partnership together but Pompey's marriage to Julia, and this could hardly prove a lasting or sufficient bond if Pompey felt that his reasonable aspirations were not being satisfied. Plutarch says[33] that Quintus Terentius Culleo, one of the tribunes of 58, urged Pompey to divorce Julia and ally himself with the Senate against Caesar; but Pompey was too wily to take such a precipitate step before he could count on getting his own terms from the Senate. His needs, urgent enough a few years earlier, had been met in 59. His eastern settlement had been in operation *de facto* since 62 at latest, and *de jure* since 59; his veterans had been settled on accessible farms in Italy and nobody was likely to be rash enough to try to evict them. Pompey's continuing interest in defending the author of the acts of 59 was decidedly thin.

[32] This seems to be what How supposed: *Cicero Select Letters*, II.151–2.
[33] *Pompey* 49.

But the Senate, or rather the old guard among the senatorial inner circle, was still reluctant to trust Pompey, and some were ready to go to almost any lengths in their vituperative hatred of him. What Crassus' intentions were is obscure; it may be that he allowed his personal detestation of Pompey to blind him to other considerations, but it may also be that he was taking a calculated risk to forestall any possible deal between Pompey and the *boni* by precipitating a public breach. Certainly, whether Crassus meant it or not, the consequence of his clashes with Pompey was to make such a deal less tempting.

Pompey's response was to turn to the offensive, attack Crassus openly, back Milo against Clodius, summon retainers from the countryside. Everybody becomes very excited, Cicero included, and with good reason. The 'Triumvirate' is in ruins, and the hunt is after Caesar. Domitius Ahenobarbus, the immensely powerful and almost certainly successful candidate for a consulship for 55, an inveterate enemy of Caesar, begins to publish his intention if elected to secure Caesar's recall from Gaul.[34] Cicero, recognized by one and all as being in Pompey's confidence and certainly in no way restrained by Pompey, follows Lupus in raising the explosive question of Caesar's agrarian legislation. The *boni* were in a truculent mood, and Pompey was apparently not unhappy about the prospect of an attack on Caesar. Crassus posted off to see Caesar at Ravenna. Pompey was invited to Lucca.

Cicero had made grave errors. He had thought that the 'Triumvirate' had broken beyond repair. To all outward seeming it had; and that an open split between Pompey and Caesar was always a possibility is shown by the fact that one did occur a few years later. But Pompey was not yet ready for an open confrontation with Caesar—he lacked a strong enough power base such as he had in the late fifties, with armies in Spain and friendly governors in all the provinces outside Gaul, and he had not been able yet to impose himself on the *boni*. But neither was Caesar ready for a fight. He had

[34] Suetonius *DJ* 24.

behind him only two seasons in Gaul: his legions had not yet been welded into the veteran, supremely confident, and devoted army of 49, and Gaul was far from pacified and properly organized. This is not to say that Caesar would not have fought in 56 if he had been driven to it, as he did in 49; but there was room for manoeuvre, and agreement would be preferable to a violent solution. Pompey artfully used an unsuspecting Cicero to send out storm-warnings to Caesar. But Cicero was not the whole picture; Ahenobarbus, Marcellinus, Milo, Lupus, Clodius and others played their part. Where Cicero went wrong was in not allowing sufficiently for the flexible realism of Caesar and Pompey, or the selfishness and lack of purpose and cohesion of the *boni*. Of them he was to write to Spinther in July: 'Those who enjoy superiority in wealth, in armies, and in power [*viz.* Caesar, Pompey, and Crassus] seem to me thanks to the stupidity and weakness of their opponents to have gained the superiority in prestige (*auctoritas*) as well.'[35]

There was little Cicero could do, except what he was told. Pompey and Caesar had their uses for him, for he remained an unrivalled advocate and a respected figure with the propertied classes. He was forced to make his peace with Caesar, composing a 'palinode' as he called it, a recantation to make amends for his past misbehaviour. Whether this palinode is to be sought in a public declaration like his speech *de provinciis consularibus* of summer 56 (a speech urging Caesar's claims to stay on in Gaul and full of praise of him) or in a formal semi-public letter addressed to Caesar, we cannot say. Probably a letter,[36] but it matters little; the *amende* was offered, the words eaten. And, after so many false dawns in the past, Cicero settled down to his new role of 'Cicero the realist', resigning himself more and more to the position of observer and commentator and beginning a retirement

---

[35] *ad famm.* I.7.10.

[36] This seems the obvious inference from *ad Att.* IV.5.2 if one accepts the very probable emendation '*tacerem*': *Dices eatenus te suasisse qua tacerem, non etiam ut scriberem.* One would not expect *scriberem* in opposition to *tacerem* if a speech were in question.

from which he was not to emerge for a dozen years. He sums up the new Cicero in a letter to Atticus of about June 56:

I was a little bit ashamed of my palinode. But goodbye now to honest dealing, to candour, to honour! It is hard to credit what traitors these 'leaders' of ours are—'leaders!', that is what they would like to be, and could be too if they had one shred of loyalty in them. I had experienced it, known it all before; they led me on, abandoned me, threw me to the wolves. Yet despite everything I wanted to see eye to eye with them in politics. They are the same as they have always been. Now, at long last and thanks to you, I have come to my senses. . . . Let there be an end to it! Since those who have no power do not choose to love me, I must see to it that I win the affections of those who do have the power. You will say 'If only you had done it long ago!' I know you wanted me to, and that I have been a perfect ass—*scio me asinum germanum fuisse.* [37]

Cicero was to stick to his decision with surprising consistency. But it was a cruel cross for him to bear, for his nature was extrovert and impetuous, and he was a proud man. From his mid-thirties he had played a very active part in public affairs, from the age of forty he had been a leading figure. Now at fifty it was all over. He had known triumph and disaster, and (more painfully) further triumph and humiliation. His return from exile had been marked by unprecedented senatorial decrees and wildly cheering crowds. The compensation voted him for the damage to his property he had thought less than generous.[38] but he had at once resumed a leading place in politics, moving important decrees, speaking his mind in public at political trials. He saw as clearly as ever the dangers that threatened his Republic: the violence that Caesar had unleashed in 59 and the impotence of the constitution when confronted by naked force. Unshaken by his exile, but rather heartened by his welcome home, he had faced these dangers boldly, as in the past, calling in aid all his personal influence with the settled classes and all his oratorical genius. This last was seldom

[37] *ad Att.* IV.5.1–3. Wiseman (*JRS* 56 (1966), 114–15) suggests that Cicero's acquiescence may have been bought with a promise of freedom to attack L. Piso. I find this far-fetched. Cicero's letters are redolent of abject capitulation, not of a 'deal'.

[38] *ad Att.* IV.2.5.

exercised with greater brilliance. The spring of 56 saw his superb *pro Caelio*,[39] if not his greatest surely his most dazzling speech. In defending his young friend Marcus Caelius Rufus he found a case dear to his own heart. The prosecution was inspired by Clodia, the 'Lesbia' of Catullus, Clodius' sister. Cicero assailed her with a *tour de force* of wit, sarcasm, irony, vituperation, slapstick-comedy, and sheer forensic brilliance. His tongue rolled lovingly around the Latin language, he purred and slashed at Clodia and her associates: *libidines, amores, adulteria, Baias, actas, convivia, comissationes, cantus, symphonia, navigia*; he called up the ghost of the great censor, Appius Claudius the Blind, to excoriate his debauched descendant—poor Clodia, already saddled with the brilliant nickname Caelius had coined for her: '*quadrantaria Clytemnestra*'.[40] The contemporary *pro Sestio* was a grimmer and a greater speech, and in it he passed in magisterial review his own public career from his consulship to his return from exile, restating as lucidly as anywhere his own political philosophy. Although in its published form it has evidently (like the *in Vatinium*) been worked over to tone down its anti-Caesarian colour, it remains a frank attack on what Caesar stood for; and the unanimous acquittal of Sestius by the large jury suggests that Cicero's point of view was shared by many typical members of the senatorial and equestrian classes.

Henceforth, the egotism and the impetuosity were to be restrained, the pride humbled, the oratorical genius exercised at the instructions of his masters.

What [he asks Atticus in a letter probably to be dated in Spring 55] could be more degrading than the life we lead, above all the life I lead? If I say what ought to be said on political subjects, I am thought a madman; if what is expedient, a slave; and if I keep quiet, a cowed prisoner—how miserable am I bound to be? Just as miserable as in fact I am, and what makes it worse is that I cannot even *be* miserable without seeming ungrateful to you. And what if I take a fancy to give up and

---

[39] For the date, see R. G. Austin's edition of the *pro Caelio* (Oxford, 3rd ed. 1960), Appendix IV.

[40] *pro Caelio* 33–5, 62. For the identification of Clodia Metelli as Lesbia, see Austin's edition of *pro Caelio*, Appendix III; Fordyce *Catullus*, xiv–xvii.

seek the haven of retirement? No use—no, I must gird on my armour and join the battle. Must I then be a private soldier, I who refused to be a war-lord? Needs must—for I can see that you advise it. Oh, if only I had always taken your advice! All that remains is the old tag: 'You have drawn Sparta; make the best of it.' Well, I can't.[41]

In summer 56 Cicero was put up to argue in the Senate against proposals to allocate either or both of Caesar's Gallic provinces to the future consuls of 55. The importance of the debate lay in the fact that under its special procedure the decision of the Senate could not be vetoed; hence a simple majority could turn Caesar out. By Vatinius' law of 59 Caesar was guaranteed Cisalpine Gaul until 28 February 54; but by a strange quirk of circumstance Transalpine Gaul, which had turned out to be the seat of war, he held only in virtue of a later *senatus consultum*, and there was no technical obstacle to this being over-ridden by a later decree of the Senate. Moves were made to secure the assignment of each of the two provinces, and Cicero duly countered them.[42] Some crumbs of comfort could be found, for he took his chance to savage his old enemies Gabinius and Piso, and suggest that their provinces of Syria and Macedonia were ripe for new governors.[43] As it turned out, Caesar's position was easily preserved;[44] and in any case 55 was to see Pompey and Crassus consuls and special legislation passed to secure extraordinary commands for all three dynasts.

Similar tasks followed. Later in 56 the defence of Cornelius Balbus, protégé of Pompey and quartermaster-general to Caesar, who acted also as Caesar's political secretary. Who inspired the prosecution we do not know; perhaps enemies of Pompey and Caesar who had launched their strike before Lucca and were now left with a forlorn case. Crassus and Pompey both appeared for the defence, though to Cicero was reserved the master's place of speaking last;[45] and Balbus

---

[41] *ad Att.* IV.6.1–2. For the dates of *ad Att.* IV.4–IV.12. see Shackleton-Bailey, II, Appendix II.

[42] *de prov. cons.* 36–8.

[43] Ibid. 1–17.

[44] *ad famm.* I.7.10.

[45] *pro Balbo* 2 and 17.

was acquitted. Then there was Vatinius. Cicero defended
him in a case which came to court in August 54; the pressure
Pompey and Caesar put on Cicero is clear from a letter to
Spinther at the end of 54.[46] But the worst blow of all was
without question having to undertake the defence of Gabinius, a man Cicero really hated, the man who flung the brutal
word 'Exile!' in his face in front of the Senate.[47] Pompey
began the task of sapping Cicero's entrenchments in autumn
54. Gabinius, just back from Syria (where he had settled the
Egyptian question by restoring Ptolemy Auletes to his
throne at Pompey's instigation and on his own authority),
was threatened with prosecutions for *maiestas* and *repetundae.*
'Pompey has been working very hard to effect a reconciliation, but so far he has made no progress, nor will he so long
as I retain a single particle of freedom.' This to Quintus, and
again to Quintus a few days later Cicero wrote that, so far
from being prepared to defend Gabinius, he would have
given a very great deal to lead for the prosecution.[48] He was
soon to learn the bitter truth that he did *not* retain a single
particle of freedom. The pressure was too much for him, and
he appeared for Gabinius.

Later, in a public speech, Cicero declared:

My reason for defending Gabinius was simply friendship. We had
adjusted our differences and shaken hands. If you think I did it reluctantly to please Pompey, you are vastly mistaken about both Pompey and
me. He would not have asked such a sacrifice of me, nor would I have
made it. I am too clearly the champion of everybody's independence to
resign it in my own actions.[49]

In fact, the defence of Gabinius was the final humiliation, the
negation of everything he had stood for. His wretchedness at
this time is well expressed in a letter to Quintus at the end of
October 54 in which he excuses himself from writing some
verses:

[46] *ad famm.* 1.9.19. Cicero's defence of Caninius Gallus in 55 is probably
another example: *ad famm.* VII.1.4.
[47] *ad QF* III.2.2.
[48] Ibid. 1.5; 2.2. (For Pompey's instigation of Gabinius, see Dio 39. 55–6.)
[49] *pro Rab. post.* 33.

I would do it if I could, but (as you know only too well) to write a poem calls for a certain gaiety of spirit—*alacritas animi*—of which circumstances altogether rob me. I do indeed withdraw myself from all political interests and give myself to literature; but I must reveal to you something which, as Heaven is my witness, I particularly wished to keep from you. I am in torment, dear brother, in torment—*angor, mi suavissime frater, angor;* there is no Republic, there is no justice; and this period of my life, when I ought to be at the summit of my authority in the Senate, is frittered away in the courts or sustained by my private writings; and what I have longed to do since I was a boy

> All men to excel, to be a prince of men

—all this has crashed in ruins. I have not attacked my enemies, some of them I have even defended. I am not free to think, I am not even free to hate.

And this was written *before* he had yet been driven to defend Gabinius.[50]

This is not the place for a detailed examination of the fortunes of the 'triumvirs' at this time, but the Gabinius trials remind us that despite Cicero's capitulation they were not having things all their own way. In 56 Ahenobarbus and Cato had fought on, and it was not until 55 had begun that the consular elections were at last held, six months late, and Ahenobarbus defeated by Pompey and Crassus, and then only with the help of violence; attempts were made in summer 56 to allocate one or other of Caesar's provinces to somebody else; Cornelius Balbus and Vatinius were attacked in the courts. Now it was Gabinius' turn. At his first trial (for *maiestas*) he was acquitted by a narrow margin—38 votes to 32.[51] This boded ill, and sure enough at his second trial (for *repetundae*) he was condemned and forced into exile, despite the strong backing of Pompey and Caesar and the advocacy of Cicero. There is good reason to believe, despite the smears of Cicero, that Gabinius had been an excellent governor of Syria, at any rate in protecting the provincials against the Roman financial interests (thereby living up to his record as tribune in 67).[52] It was the financial interests which combined with optimate hatred to bring Gabinius

[50] *ad QF* III.5.4.
[51] Ibid. 4.1.
[52] Syme, *RR*, 66–7.

down. Syme believes that Pompey could have saved him but 'was probably desirous of conciliating the financial interests at this time'. Yet it is clear from Cicero's letters that Pompey was working hard for Gabinius, and Dio adds that Caesar addressed a special letter in support of Gabinius to be read out in court.[53] It matters little, however, whether the financial interests were powerful enough to beat Pompey and Caesar, or whether they were powerful enough to compel the sacrifice of one of their chief collaborators.[54]

Domestic Roman politics continued turbulent. The year 55 began with an *interregnum* until Pompey and Crassus became consuls after Ahenobarbus had been driven from the election-field by armed force. In the same year, at the election of the aediles, there was riot and bloodshed; Plutarch records that Pompey was drenched in blood, and that when his wife Julia, Caesar's daughter, who was pregnant at the time, saw the servants bringing his stained clothes home she fainted from shock.[55] By the middle of 54 it was becoming clear that there was going to be trouble over the consular elections for 53. In June Cicero wrote to Quintus: 'There is some hope for the elections, but it is uncertain; there is some hint of a dictatorship, but that isn't certain either. Nothing stirs in the Forum, but it is the quiet of a country growing old and tired, not acquiescent. My own contributions to senatorial debates are such as to win the agreement of others rather than myself.' At the same time there came to light an electoral scandal of heroic proportions between two of the candidates for the consulship of 53, Memmius and Domitius Calvinus, and the two consuls of 54, Domitius Ahenobarbus and Appius Claudius Pulcher.[56]

By the end of October there was once again a 'smell of dictatorship in the air'. All the consular candidates were being indicted for electoral corruption. In November Pompey's hanger-on Lucilius Hirrus came out into the open in

---

[53] Dio 39.63.

[54] Ironically, Gabinius was clearly guilty of the charge on which he was acquitted, and almost certainly innocent of that on which he was convicted.

[55] Plutarch *Pompey* 53.

[56] *ad QF* II.14.5, 15.4. *ad Att.* IV.17.2.

advocating that Pompey be appointed dictator. Pompey was playing his old game: 'It is hard to tell whether he wants it or not; but with Hirrus behind it he will not convince anybody that he doesn't.' Memmius was pinning his hopes on Caesar, whom he expected soon to take up winter quarters south of the Alps from where he could take a more immediate hand in Roman politics.[57] There was much that needed his attention—apart from the turbulence we have noticed, Julia had died in childbirth in September (her baby soon followed her); and Crassus' vast experience as a political manager was no longer available, for Crassus was far away in Syria, where he was soon to destroy himself and a Roman army at Carrhae.

The confusion continued well into 53; it was not until July, just one year late, that Domitius Calvinus and Valerius Messalla were elected consuls and at once assumed office. Things did not get any better: they deteriorated, as might have been expected with Milo standing for the consulship at the same time as Clodius was standing for the praetorship (both of 52). Milo was a very strong candidate, for he enjoyed the support of the *boni* and of the *populus* (thanks to widespread largesse and astronomical sums poured out on public shows and games). Milo's rival candidates were Plautius Hypsaeus, Pompey's old quaestor, and Pompey's newly acquired father-in-law, the blue blooded and polyonymous Quintus Caecilius Metellus Pius Scipio Nasica. Pompey was backing these two against Milo, once his powerful helper against Crassus and Clodius but since Lucca the optimate opponent of the 'triumvirs'; while Clodius was backing Pompey's candidates against Milo, seeing that his own praetorship would be valueless if Milo were consul. Cicero was for Milo, partly out of gratitude for his help in 57, partly because of his continuing fear of Clodius. Young Curio, champion of the optimate cause, was supporting Clodius out of personal friendship against the optimate candidate Milo.[58]

[57] *ad Att.* IV.18.3; *ad QF* III.8.3–4.   [58] Asconius 31 C.

Rome was a cockpit of gang warfare. When 53 ended
neither consuls nor praetors had been elected. The confusion
was heightened when Pompey had his agent, the tribune
Munatius Plancus, veto the appointment of an *interrex*,
thereby depriving Rome of any holder of *imperium*.[59] But
there soon followed the fatal 18 January which saw the clash
near Bovillae of the escorts of Milo and Clodius and the
killing of Clodius. At once an *interrex* was appointed (the
future triumvir Marcus Lepidus); but the Clodian mob
burned down the Senate-house, and the factions of Scipio
Nasica and Hypsaeus besieged Lepidus' house insisting on
immediate elections (which was unconstitutional), hoping
to profit from a revulsion of feeling against Milo. Milo's
supporters soon turned up with the same demand, for if
elected Milo would escape the danger of prosecution. The
two mobs fell to fighting each other, and Lepidus got clear.
But the *fasces* were stolen from his house, and carted around
to the houses of Scipio and Hypsaeus, and then on to
Pompey's house with cries of 'Pompey for consul!' and
'Pompey for dictator!'. Terror and chaos reigned until
finally the *boni* bowed to the inevitable and called in Pompey
to restore order. The 'Ultimate Decree' was passed 'that the
interrex and the tribunes of the *plebs* and Gnaeus Pompeius,
who was outside the city with proconsular authority, should
see to it that the state took no harm; and that Pompey should
levy troops throughout Italy.' Pompey was home and dry
at last; on the fifth day before the first of March in the inter-
calary month of 52, on the motion of Bibulus, the interrex
Servius Sulpicius created Pompey sole consul.[60]

Julia was dead, Crassus was dead, and with him his
brilliant younger son (it was young Publius Crassus' widow
that Pompey had recently married). Caesar's two invasions
of Britain had been spectacular, but unproductive and
hazardous. Gaul, so often pronounced 'pacified', was at this
moment on the brink of the most convulsive and dangerous
upheaval of them all. Preoccupied with the eighteen-month
revolt of Vercingetorix, held north of the Alps throughout

[59] Ibid.   [60] Ibid. 33–4, 43C.

the winter of 52 to 51, Caesar's grip on Rome faltered and loosened. Pompey, free from worries about Clodius, soon got rid of the equally dangerous Milo, ensconced his father-in-law Nasica in the second consular chair, and settled down to weave the web that was in the end to leave Caesar with no option but to burst out of it by war.

All these events found Cicero on the sidelines, an observer and reporter, save when he was called on to defend a 'triumviral' partisan or deliver a prepared brief in the Senate. We have seen how unhappy he was. Yet in the letter already quoted in which he told Quintus of his 'torment', he had gone on to say that Caesar alone loved him as much as he wanted to be loved; and in other letters to Quintus at this period he speaks of Caesar with warmth and respect. Since early in 54 Quintus had been a legate to Caesar in Gaul and Britain, and letters between the two brothers would normally be carried by the regular official dispatch service of Caesar or his deputy, Labienus; it follows that Cicero needed to be circumspect in what he said about Caesar.[61] However, even allowing for this, it does seem that Cicero was free from bitterness towards Caesar, and at one point he becomes quite excited about the possible fruits of their relationship.

The original motive for Quintus' transfer to Caesar's staff had been to gain his friendship and political protection. Cicero's worries about the danger from Clodius did not evaporate after his recall in 57. Letters after that date contain a number of allusions to his continuing apprehension, and this played an important part in his estimation of the value of keeping in with Pompey and Caesar. Thus in July 54, for example, he tells Quintus that he expects the coming year to bring him peace or at any rate security, 'because I am well in with Caesar and with Pompey. This gives me reassurance. But if that madman [Clodius] should break out in a frenzy, all is ready to hand to break him.'[62] However, as the old friendship with Caesar warmed to life again, something more positive seems to have emerged. In June Cicero refers to a letter he has had from Caesar, 'which was all respect

[61] *ad QF* III.8.2.   [62] *ad QF* II.15.2.

and attentiveness and charm. These marks of his goodwill
are of great value, no, rather of the *greatest* value, for they
are a potent force for renown and the highest distinction.'
And he goes on to talk of Caesar's great affection for him
'which I value higher than all the honours which he wishes
me to look for from him.' In September he expresses keen
pleasure at the prospect of a visit from Caesar's confidential
agent Balbus, who is to have a serious discussion with him.
Late in October or early in November there is another
reference to 'promises' from Caesar. A few weeks later Quintus went through a brief bout of irritation and complaining
brought on by his distaste for campaign life, and his brother
tells him to hang on and reminds him:

We were looking for the secure protection which could come from the
goodwill of a great and good man for our whole standing in public life.
There is hope of more than we ask for; let any profit be put aside to cover
our outlay ... And let me add this advice too: don't write anything in
your letters which we should regret if it were divulged. There is a lot I
prefer to be ignorant about if being told about it involves some risk.[63]

What Caesar was promising, what Cicero thought he was
promising (which was not necessarily the same thing),
what additional profit Cicero thought looked like emerging
from their association, this we do not know. The letters are
cautious and elliptic; there were few letter-carriers, Cicero
knew, 'who can carry a letter of any weight without lighten-
ing the burden by perusing it'.[64] We often encounter this
barrier in the correspondence, and it is to be surmounted (if
at all) only by informed speculation. Here there is the added
difficulty that no letters survive from Marcus to Quintus
later than December 54 to help us follow the matter further.
In 53 Cicero was to be elected to the place in the College of
Augurs made vacant by the death of young Crassus, on the
nomination of Pompey and Hortensius, though Lucilius
Hirrus was a competitor and Mark Antony also had some
hopes.[65] Membership of one of the two greatest priestly

[63] *ad QF* II.14.1; III.1.12, 5.3, 6.1–2.
[64] *ad Att.* I.13.1.
[65] *Phil.* 2.4; *ad Att.* VIII.3.1. Cicero had told Atticus in spring 59—and only
half in jest—that the 'triumvirs' might have bought his support then for the

colleges was a rich plum, and Cicero was always inordinately proud of the honour. Of course nobody could know in 54 that Crassus would die in 53, but a promise from Caesar that he would use his influence to secure the next vacancy that became available for Cicero might well account for Cicero's hopes in 54. Yet there may have been more in prospect than that. It was accident that delayed Caesar's second consulship until 48, the unexpected turns that events were to take—the deaths of Julia, Crassus, and Clodius, the long and bitter revolt in Gaul, and the advantage to which Pompey turned all this. Caesar may in 54 have had his eye on the possibility of a consulship in 52 or 51, and Cicero was not without attractions as a running-mate. Certainly Caesar never underestimated his worth: in 49 he exerted all his considerable charm and persuasiveness to woo Cicero to public support for his position, well aware of his value as a spokesman and as a man ideally suited to give to his actions a powerful *imprimatur* of respectability.[66]

This however is speculation, not fact. All we can say for certain is that by late 54 Cicero had come to look for some valuable material advantage from Caesar beyond mere protection.[67]

Cicero's withdrawal from the centre of affairs at this time is underlined by the paucity of the surviving letters; only thirteen from 53, and these a lightweight collection, inconsequential and unexciting; the next year, 52, even leaner, producing only four letters, of a trivial character.[68] But Cicero was active in other fields: his boundless energy could

price of an augurate (*ad Att.* II.5.2). In October 57 he had contemplated standing at the next censorial elections, but nothing had come of it (*ad Att.* IV. 2.6).

[66] Below, pp. 257–9.

[67] Wiseman (*JRS* 56 (1966), 108–15) suggests that Cicero was hoping for a consulship for his brother Quintus. This is possible, but to me the tone and language of the letters in question fits far better a hope of advancement for Cicero himself. Cf. particularly *ad QF* II.16.1: *Tamen ex hoc labore magnam gratiam magnamque dignitatem sim conlecturus*—here we get away from the ambiguity of the first person plural to the precision of the first person singular. Further, Quintus' impatience and Cicero's attempts to assuage it suit better a context in which Marcus is to be the chief gainer from Quintus' labours.

[68] The letters of the year 53 are nos. 166–78 in Tyrrell and Purser, II, those of the year 52 are nos. 179–82.

not be contained in the dull routine of estate-management or dilettante pursuits or the empty formalities of public life. It had to find an outlet, and find an outlet it did in activity which was in the long run to contribute far more than his political activities to his influence and reputation with posterity.

From these years of political retirement flowed his works on philosophy and rhetoric. The three volumes of the *de Oratore* were finished about the end of 55. This was a full scale dialogue, dedicated to his brother Quintus, concerning the art and essence of oratory; and it was soon followed by a briefer and simpler essay, *Partitiones Oratoriae*, which took the form of a dialogue with his young son. Still in the same vein, the *de Optimo Genere Oratorum* appeared in 52. The following year saw the publication of the six volumes *de Republica*, while the *de Legibus*, though probably published posthumously, seems to have been begun in 52; these works served as vehicles for the expression of Cicero's thinking about the state and its organization. A further and even broader flood was to mark the years from 46 to 44—essays and dialogues, historical and biographical, on philosophy, life, and morals. Apart from the evidence they provide of Cicero's continuing intellectual energy, it is almost impossible to exaggerate the influence these writings were to have on western civilization. In them, more even than in his speeches, Cicero took firm hold of the Latin language, and from it fashioned a magnificently lucid and supple instrument. By careful experiment and constant discussion with his friends, particularly Atticus, he laboured to adapt Latin to the expression of abstract ideas, and by so doing minted the basic vocabulary of abstract thought which is the continuing legacy of the languages of western Europe.[69] As a thinker and theorist, Cicero was neither original nor profound; but these essays are usually distinguished by a massive common-sense and practicality, and they were often the vehicle by which Greek thinking was transmitted at second-hand to later centuries which knew little or no Greek. Many of the qualities of these

[69] Cf. L. R. Palmer, *The Latin Language*, 128 ff.

writings are those which are commonly thought of as truly and best Roman; and their avoidance of theoretical schematics and their empirical bias, allied to the lucidity and charm and supple brilliance of the language in which they were expressed, gave to them a greater appeal and a wider range of readers and a more pervading influence than many subtler and more original but more abstract works have commanded.

These productions must be noted, but a political biography is not the place to examine them in detail, although of course it was not merely posterity that set a high value on them. Contemporaries recognized their worth, and the brilliance of Cicero's achievement—not least Caesar, himself a considerable man of letters, whose admiration for Cicero's literary achievements was genuine and unbounded (both men shared a distaste for the more florid and archaizing styles that were increasingly in vogue). Unfortunately, Cicero could win only a literary success with his most important forensic speech at this period.

Pompey was frightened of Milo, or pretended to be. And certainly, with Clodius dead, the danger that this immensely determined and violent man might challenge Pompey's dominance at Rome was a very real one. Necessity can make strange bedfellows, and between an active and powerful Milo and a Caesar in need of fresh support at Rome an alliance is not unthinkable. There is no reason to suppose that Pompey was yet moving towards a break with Caesar, but there is equally no reason to suppose that he did not have a keen eye for future possibilities. The attack was launched with Clodius' young nephews (the sons of his dead brother Gaius) to the fore, but with the weight of Pompey behind them. Milo was charged with *vis* and other offences. Special precautions were taken to guard against bribery of the *iudices* by careful selection, re-selection, and tight timetabling. Cicero's loyalty to his old helper and enemy's enemy was sternly tested; but he persisted in standing by Milo. He planned to base his defence on a plea of accidental death. When the final day of the trial came he got to his feet to close for the defence, but at the last he faltered. The howls of the Clodians, the packed ranks of Pompey's soldiers, the atmosphere of crisis, all proved too much for him. The speech *pro Milone* that we now read is the speech he meant to deliver; Asconius judged it perhaps the finest of all Cicero's speeches. But he never delivered it. Harassed and nervous, his actual performance, as Asconius politely puts it, lacked his customary *constantia*.[70] Milo went into exile. The story of his reply to Cicero after reading a copy of the speech Cicero had meant to deliver is too good not to repeat. It was just as well (he said) that the court had not heard it, for if it had he would never have had the chance to savour the excellent sea-food for which Marseilles was already famous.[71]

Among Pompey's legislative activities in 52 were new regulations for the government of the provinces. Electoral bribery was endemic at Rome, but recent years had seen it reach new heights. It fed on many sources, but the most important was the opportunity a successful candidate had of recouping his expenditure or repaying his debts at the expense of the province to which he would proceed at the conclusion of his year of office at Rome. A year earlier the Senate had resolved that no consul or praetor might go out to a province until five years after the termination of his period of office; it was hoped thereby to reduce electoral corruption, since a man would think long and hard about spending his patrimony, and creditors about making large loans, when there would be so long a time to wait for the chance of recovering the money. The Senate's resolution was not implemented, but Pompey now had legislation passed to enforce it.[72] The result was to open up a gap until the first five-year period should elapse and a new regular succession of appointments could begin. To fill the gap former consuls and praetors who had not governed provinces were called on. The first two consulars to be so employed were Cicero

[70] The full and exciting background to the trial of Milo is admirably set out by Asconius 30–42C.
[71] Dio 40.54.
[72] Dio 40.30 and 56.

and Bibulus. Bibulus was allotted Syria, and Cicero Cilicia. So he was forced to break the promise he had made himself nearly twenty-five years earlier when he had returned from his quaestorship at Lilybaeum in Sicily.[73]

[73] *pro Planc.* 64–6; above, p. 14.

X

CILICIA

'CONTRARY to my wishes and quite unexpected': so Cicero described his appointment.[1] He was never happy to be away from the bustle and excitement of Rome, even though he was no longer a directing force; and from 51 onwards events were moving towards a crisis as the pressure began to mount on Caesar, with Pompey and the *boni* drawing erratically but increasingly closer. To have to quit Rome and rely for information and informed gossip on letters two months or more old grieved him greatly,[2] and this sense of frustration and resentment is a constant theme in his own letters home. 'How little this business suits my character,' he tells Atticus. '"What (you will say), grumbling already? You haven't even started yet!"—How well I know it, and I believe there is worse to come.'[3] Or again: 'Words cannot express how I am on fire with longing for Rome, how hard it is to bear the insipidity of everything here'—and this in a letter written from Athens before he has even reached his province![4] Already before leaving Italy he had begun bombarding his friends with appeals to do all they could to ensure that his year of office was not extended,[5] and the bombardment continued throughout his absence. There was good reason for his apprehension, for the manoeuvres of Caesar's enemies and the counter-moves of Caesar's supporters threatened to lead—and did lead—to a blockage of

[1] *ad famm.* III.2.1.
[2] Above, p. 149, note 8.
[3] *ad Att.* V.10.3.
[4] Ibid. 11.1.
[5] See, for example, *ad Att.* V.1.1 (written from Minturnae, early May 51).

provincial appointments. Cilicia itself confirmed his fears: provincial administration bored him, he felt that his gifts were wasted on it. His departure at the end of his year found him unrepentant: 'Rome, my dear Rufus, Rome! Cling fast to it and live in its light! All foreign service, as I realized long ago when I was young, is dingy and sordid for a man who has it in him to cut a figure at Rome. Believe me, I would exchange all the advantages of a province for one little stroll together, one chance for us to talk.'[6]

We, however, have reason to be grateful to Pompey's law, even if Cicero was not. The letters from Cilicia throw a light on the contemporary system of provincial administration no less valuable, and more revealing and reliable, than that thrown by Cicero's great public speeches. And there is the added bonus of Caelius, man-about-town, and letter-writer extraordinary.

Marcus Caelius Rufus was over twenty years Cicero's junior. He set his sights on a political career and sat at the feet of Cicero as Cicero had earlier sat at the feet of Scaevola and Crassus. He fell under the spell of Catiline's magnetism and charm, and this was to evoke some splendid examples of Cicero's forensic brilliance and craft in the *pro Caelio* when this episode was dragged up against Caelius; but he was not involved in Catiline's downfall. He was gay, irrepressible, amusing, ambitious, witty, and not always responsible; but of his ability there can be no question, either as a student of politics or as a speaker. He was later numbered among the great names of this, the golden age of Roman oratory, though his forte lay in attack rather than in defence: he had, commented Cicero, 'a good right but a poor left'.[7] In 59 he prosecuted Cicero's old colleague Antonius, and the great critic Quintilian cites a passage from his speech as an unsurpassable example of persuasiveness, vivid aggression, and convincing realism: *nihil his neque credibilius fingi neque vehementius exprobari neque manifestius ostendi potest.*[8] In the late

---

[6] *ad famm.* II.12.2.
[7] Quintilian *Inst. Or.* 6.3.39.
[8] Ibid. 4.2. 123–4.

sixties and early fifties he entered the circle of Clodia, a lady who has had the signal misfortune of being best known to us through her enemies, Caelius, Catullus, and Cicero, three of the most accomplished character-assassins known to literature. Perhaps he succeeded Catullus in Clodia's favours and in her bed; two of Catullus' poems suggest as much, but do not prove it.[9] Her break with him, her attack on him, and Cicero's defence, we have already noted. He was tribune in 52, very friendly towards Milo and hostile to Caesar.

Such briefly was the man Cicero selected to act as his confidential correspondent; for he had never known anyone, he said, with a better nose for politics than Caelius.[10] His job was not to retail everyday news but to give Cicero the cream of informed speculation and interpretation.[11] And this he did, with a raciness of style, a command of slang, a mixture of metaphors, and an intimate knowledge of personalities that were all his own—and which he combined with a remarkable shrewdness. He knew everybody, saw and heard everything; and the letters he sent we can read over Cicero's shoulder.[12]

When Cicero left, Caelius was a candidate for the aedileship, and he meant to emulate Milo by putting on some really impressive public games—a useful investment for his political future. Accordingly, he asked Cicero to help by sending him some panthers for a wild-beast hunt. The appeals begin in June 51, and early in September, with Cicero barely a month in his province, Caelius writes: 'Patiscus [a Roman businessman in Cilicia] has sent Curio ten panthers; you ought to be ashamed of yourself if you don't send many times that number.' By February 50 Cicero's patience is wearing thin; another aedile (Caelius has been elected by

---

[9] Catullus *Carmina* 58 and 77. See R. G. Austin's edition of the *pro Caelio*, Appendix III.

[10] *ad famm.* II.8.1: πολιτικώτερον enim te adhuc neminem cognovi.

[11] Ibid.

[12] Cicero's letters to Caelius are collected in Book II of the *ad famm*; those from Caelius to Cicero in Book VIII. The Cilicia letters are printed in the third volume of Tyrrell and Purser, and the introductions to that volume are very valuable.

now) has asked Atticus if Cicero can get him some panthers as well, and Cicero writes that 'I am delighted that you told him you did not think I could. But in future, whenever there is any doubt, always give a firm No.' He tries half-heartedly to laugh the animals off, and tells Caelius that, disgusted at being the only creatures to be persecuted under his administration, they have all decided to emigrate.[13]

This business about panthers may seem trivial, and it *is* trivial. But it illustrates how in many small matters a governor was expected to use his office to help his friends and acquaintances. Panthers were not the only game that Caelius was after, for he coolly expected money to be forthcoming from the province to cover the expenses of his aedilician entertainments. Such demands were not uncommon, for Cicero had written to Quintus, then governor of Asia, on the subject of this so-called 'aedilician levy' (*vectigal aedilicium*) and commended him for refusing to allow it in his province. So Caelius was going rather far in suggesting it to Cicero himself, and not surprisingly he was sent away with a flea in his ear.[14] But the very fact that such requests were made, not to mention that they were not always refused, is witness to the times. As we shall see, there were others to whom Cicero could not say No quite so bluntly.

Cilicia covered an area of some 40,000 square miles in southern Asia Minor, bordering on Syria to the east; Cyprus also came under Cicero's jurisdiction. Within this region Cicero's will was law, *de facto* if not *de jure*. This was inevitable. Given the slowness of communications and the backwardness of technology, the men who governed Rome's provinces had to be allowed a great deal of independence and could not be forever referring back to the capital for advice and instructions. In any case Rome sent out to govern the provinces not political failures but her own praetors and consuls, men who had held the highest administrative posts at home, men who in theory had been chosen as the ablest and fittest by the Roman electorate. It has sometimes been

[13] *ad famm.* VIII.2.2, 9.2; *ad Att*, V.21.5; *ad famm*, II.11.2.
[14] *ad QF* I.1.26; *ad Att*. VI.1.21.

urged that what was wrong was Rome's failure to provide an adequate civil service. But this is a superficial criticism, and can be traced back to false analogies with modern colonial empires. The Roman empire was overwhelmingly an empire embracing civilized peoples, a world of city states and tribes and petty kingdoms, not of nations, and on these units Rome devolved the ordering of their own everyday affairs. Different *civitates* (to use the Roman word for these political subdivisions) might have different rights, based on treaties or special grants, but by and large they were alike in being entrusted with the charge of their own affairs. The business of the governor was to command in war, to maintain peace and security, to see that the taxes were paid, to arbitrate between the constituent *civitates* of his province, to deal with certain legal matters, especially those involving Roman citizens and businessmen resident in the area. It was not his job to appoint and supervise sewage engineers, or medical officers, or educators, or agricultural and forestry experts, and all the other numberless and necessary officers of a modern colonial service.

The governor could himself be expected to have military or legal and administrative experience already. He had his *legati* to make up any deficiencies in these fields—Cicero's four legates included his brother Quintus, ex-praetor and former governor of Asia for nearly three years; and Gaius Pomptinus, a man of considerable military experience who had been praetor in 63 and subsequently governed Transalpine Gaul where he suppressed a rebellion of the Allobroges. He had a quaestor to act as financial secretary. In addition he and his staff had trained slaves and freedmen at their service to process their papers, file their correspondence, check accounts, act as clerks of assize, see to their travelling arrangements, and so on. Many of these were their personal servants whom they took out with them, others might be taken over from a predecessor;[15] experienced and intelligent soldiers from the province's garrison could be seconded for

---

[15] S. Treggiari, *Roman Freedmen during the late Republic*, 155, 158.

headquarters duty. It was not a vast body of men, but it did exist and should not be disregarded.[16]

What was wrong with the provincial administration of the late Republic was not the system, but the way in which the system was perverted. Rules and regulations, frequently detailed and excellent in themselves, existed to control and limit a governor's conduct and provided severe penalties for transgressors. The difficulty arose in bringing offenders to book. Here the powerful network of marriages and *amicitiae* among the ruling nobility came into its own, as men of weight and influence banded together to save a friend or a brother. Courts could be bought with provincial profits or influenced in other ways by powerful allies. Pressures hard to resist could be directed against the provincials themselves, and it must often have seemed a daunting prospect to provincial communities to think of initiating a prosecution against their ex-governor, one of the great ones of Rome, armoured by influence and graft. The *patronus* system did something to mitigate this, for communities or whole provinces might look to individuals or families among the Roman ruling aristocracy for traditional protection; and in their own interests *patroni* would not want to be thought powerless to protect their clients. But usually whether an errant governor was punished for his misdeeds depended not on his guilt or innocence but on whether political enemies at Rome were interested in attacking him and strong enough to succeed. So all too often a governor was relatively free to disregard the rules with little risk that he would be any the worse for it. And the ever-increasing expense of politics at Rome, especially of the bribery and corruption-ridden electoral campaigns, made men look to the provinces as a source of supply or replenishment of their coffers.

Again, whatever the theory, in practice in Cicero's day advancement to high office was not simply a matter of convincing a self-confident electorate of your proven abilities, experience, and promise. High office was all too often the

---

[16] A. H. M. Jones, 'The Roman Civil Service', in *Studies in Roman Government and Law* (= *JRS* 39 (1949), 38–55).

reward of birth, wealth, and influence. And, as the level of competence of the urban magistrates declined, so too did that of the governors of the provinces, since they were the same people. The central government of Rome was weak, divided, lacking in continuity, and corrupt—indeed, it is questionable how far it is proper to talk of there being a 'government' at all in the usually understood sense. Given these faults at the heart, the administration of the provinces was bound to go wrong.

Not all governors were corrupt, cruel, and inefficient. Too many were. Something of the enormous damage a governor could do in pursuit of quick gains can be seen from Cicero's references to his predecessor, Appius Claudius Pulcher. Cicero has scarcely arrived before he is writing to Atticus about 'the wounds which Appius has inflicted on the province. I avoid opening them, but they are obvious and cannot be hidden.' The province is 'damned and virtually ruined for ever'; Appius himself is 'not a human being but some sort of horrible wild beast'.[17] Apart from the regular taxes (which had been sold to contractors since the personal exactions of Appius had prevented them being paid on time—a harsh act which considerably increased the taxpayers' burden), Appius had imposed for his own benefit a special poll-tax and a tax on doors.[18] He also practised extortion: towns were invited to pay large sums in return for a promise that they would not have troops billeted on them—the island of Cyprus alone paid just under five million sesterces in 'protection money'.[19] These exactions were not only wicked, but dangerous. When Cicero was faced with the threat of a Parthian invasion, he reported in an official despatch to the Senate and magistrates that he could not rely on the local provincial levies since 'thanks to the harshness and injustice of our rule they are either too weak to give much help or else so alienated that nothing can be expected from them or entrusted to them'.[20]

To his credit, Cicero set his face against such malpractices

[17] ad Att. V.15.2, 16.2.   [18] Tyrrell and Purser, III.328–9.
[19] ad Att. V.21.7.   [20] ad famm. XV.1.5.

and did what he could to repair the ravages of Appius. He cut his personal expenses to the bone, and despite their protests made his staff do the same. He made up his mind not to inflict any unnecessary expense on his province, and declined to exact even those supplies and services which were due to him: 'I refuse to accept not only fodder or the other things usually provided in accordance with the Julian Law but not even firewood, nothing in fact beyond a bed to sleep in and a roof over my head—indeed often enough not even a roof, for I generally stay in my tent.'[21] He tells Atticus that he is sure 'that you recognise that what I have professed for many years has now been brought to the test'.[22] He travelled extensively, being punctilious in the exercise of his judicial duties, and discovered that the Cilicians had suffered much from the dishonesty of their own local officials. He brought pressure to bear on them to make good what they had pilfered, and to such good effect that he was delighted to report that the province, which had paid no taxes during the current quinquennium, had now sufficient funds to pay off even the arrears from the previous one; this, he adds, has made him 'the darling of the tax-contractors'.[23]

Cicero was of course very careful in his handling of the Roman businessmen and financiers active in Cilicia, for he needed to preserve his standing with the financial and business class. An amusing example of his delicacy can be found in the history of a clause in the edict which he promulgated on assuming his appointment. He at first planned to publish his intention to uphold all business contracts between Romans and provincials 'provided that no force or fraud has been used to secure the contract'. One would have thought this harmless enough, but Atticus hastened to point out that the proviso implied a grave slight (*gravi praeiudicio*) against the class to which he himself belonged—in other words, it contained an unfortunate allusion to what happened only too often but was better not spoken about! So Cicero adopted a more tactful and periphrastic formula: 'provided that the

[21] *ad Att.* V.16.3.   [22] Ibid. 13.1.
[23] Ibid. VI.2.5.   [24] Ibid. 1.15.

contract has not been so entered into that it ought not in good faith to be upheld'.[24]

Cicero's attempts to deal fairly with the provincials had a number of unpleasant consequences. They annoyed his predecessor, and involved Cicero in a most irritating correspondence. The two men got off to a bad start. Cicero had gone to some trouble to ascertain Appius' plans in order to pay a courtesy call as soon as possible after arriving, but when he did arrive he found that Appius had taken himself off to Tarsus at the other end of the province. 'This was not the act of a gentleman', he told Atticus. He was even more piqued when Appius had the face to take him to task for having shown a want of courtesy![25]

As often happened, many cities were preparing to send extravagant delegations to Rome to honour their outgoing governor. Sensing Cicero's sympathy, their leading citizens told him that coming on top of Appius' ravages they could not afford the expense. When Cicero counselled them to keep within the limits laid down by law, Appius rounded on him with a charge of deliberate obstruction, and Cicero hastened to placate him: 'I did not so much *command* as *recommend* that the expenditure should as far as possible be kept within the limits prescribed by law. Even on this I did not *insist*, as the accounts of the towns will show.'[26]

Cicero was also accused of rescinding certain decisions of Appius, and in general Appius interpreted Cicero's liberal and sympathetic administration as a slight on his own. It was, and Cicero said as much to Atticus: 'What greater contrast could there be? When he was governor the province was drained dry by expenses and outlays, while under my rule not a penny is exacted from individuals or from communities.'[27] But his letters to Appius himself strike a different note. Never absent is the profession of deep friendship and admiration; the 'horrible wild beast', the scourge of Cilicia, suffers a metamorphosis into the gentleman 'than

[25] Ibid. V.16.4, 17.6; *ad famm.* III.7.4.
[26] *ad famm.* III.8.2–3, 10.6: *non tam imperavi quam censui.*
[27] *ad Att.* VI.1.2.

whom there would be no other more concerned to hand over the province to me in the best state and most free from trouble'.[28] 'But if there is anyone who does not like the policy I have adopted in the province and thinks himself injured by a certain dissimilarity between my policy and yours, for although each of us has acted correctly we have not both followed the same line, then I do not care to have that man for a friend.' A 'certain dissimilarity' (*quadam dissimilitudine*) is very rich; but we soon find Cicero assuring Appius that his 'liberality has been widespread through the province'.[29]

By his successor's hard work and self-restraint Appius was at last put into a more amiable frame of mind, and even induced to accord a grudging recognition of Cicero's patience and politeness. It was a pity that, though no fault of Cicero's own, fresh storm-clouds loomed up. His new son-in-law, Publius Cornelius Dolabella, indicted Appius on charges of *maiestas* and bribery. And while on his way back to Italy Cicero learned that his young friend Caelius had quarrelled bitterly with Appius; it seems that Appius had refused to honour certain obligations to Caelius (so Caelius saw it, anyway)—'that ape Appius', Caelius calls him.[30]

Apart from normal provincial business, Cicero found himself faced with the threat of an invasion by the Parthians, who had not so long before cut Crassus and his legions to pieces at Carrhae. There had been disturbing rumours even before he left Italy. In Cilicia he found no more definite news, but only reports (unfounded as it turned out) that some Roman cavalry had been badly mauled in neighbouring Syria.[31] It was a worrying situation. The military establishment in Cilicia was only two legions, and both were very much under strength and the three cohorts which did happen to be at full strength had become mislaid (this was Appius' fault) and 'where they are I don't know'.[32] The

[28] *ad famm.* III.2.1.
[29] Ibid. 8.7–8.
[30] Ibid. VIII.6.1, 12.1–2.
[31] *ad Att.* V.16.4.
[32] *ad famm.* III.6.5. Plutarch (*Cicero* 36) says he had 12,000 infantry, but no

local provincial levies were useless; and the neighbouring client-kings, who formed a sort of buffer-zone under Roman influence on the edges of the empire, were a doubtful factor. In September came the news that the Parthians had crossed the Euphrates in full strength.[33]

Happily the danger, which was taken so seriously at Rome that there was talk of sending Pompey or Caesar east to take command,[34] soon blew over, thanks chiefly to the skill and energy shown by Gaius Cassius at Antioch. (Cassius, later prominent as the leader of the Republican forces after the death of Caesar, was acting as governor of Syria in the absence of Bibulus.) Cicero too showed sound sense. Relying on the natural strength of Cilicia's mountain frontier to secure it against immediate danger, he concentrated on the defence of the exposed client-kingdom of Cappadocia to the north, and worked hard to keep the other local potentates loyal.[35] At a critical moment he moved up in support of Cassius, and the news of his approach at the head of his troops contributed to Cassius' success. The success was how-ever mainly Cassius', though Cicero characteristically claimed much of the credit for himself.[36]

With Cilicia safe from the Parthians for the winter, Cicero turned his forces against a troublesome bandit stronghold in the mountains, but its capture did little to satisfy his thirst for military glory. 'Pindinessus?' (he imagines Atticus asking) 'Who are these people? I have never heard of the place.'[37] Still, he had the satisfaction of being saluted 'Imperator' on the field by his troops, and the lawyer-politic-ian was anxious that his military exploits, sound if hardly resounding, should be recognized and rewarded. He set his heart on the Senate's voting him a solemn public thanks-

---

doubt he is simply assuming two legions at their full paper-strength of 6,000 each; *ad Att.* V.15.1 makes it plain that both legions were sadly under strength.

[33] *ad Att.* V.18.1.
[34] *ad famm.* VIII.10.2.
[35] *ad famm.* XV.2: an official despatch.
[36] Ibid. 2.8.
[37] *ad Att.* V.20.1.

giving (*supplicatio*), and even dreamed of the greater honour of a triumph.

This gave rise to an exasperating exchange of letters with Cato.[38] When the Senate debated the question of voting a *supplicatio* in recognition of Cicero's successes, Cato cast his vote against the motion. The motion was carried, and Cato wrote to Cicero to tell him that he was none the less delighted that this had happened. Cato was a past-master of this sort of convoluted paradox, his argument being that it was silly of Cicero to prefer that thanks be given for his successes to the immortal gods rather than take the credit to himself; and he went on to pour cold water on Cicero's hopes of a triumph. Cato's letter is a remarkable amalgam of pomposity, insensitivity, and downright rudeness, and its style awkward and insincere. To it Cicero, masking his annoyance behind a screen of ironic courtesies, returned an adroit reply. His comment that no doubt he would look at such things in a different light 'if, not everyone of course, but at any rate a fair number of our fellow-citizens were Catos' inevitably reminds us of other remarks he had made about Cato's utopianism. After all, he gently reminds him, one need not take the immortal gods too seriously; this sort of honour is hallowed by custom. In fact Cicero was very angry indeed with Cato. Cato had known perfectly well what Cicero's wishes were, for earlier Cicero had specifically asked him for his support in the Senate for the *supplicatio* and had made it plain that he saw such a public honour as some sort of salve for the wounds his public dignity had suffered in the past.[39] Writing to Atticus, he reveals his true feelings: 'Cato has treated me shabbily and spitefully. He bore witness in the debate to my integrity, my justice, my mildness, my honesty —which I did *not* ask for. What I *did* ask, he refused.'[40] Caesar himself wrote to Cicero commenting on Cato's monstrous behaviour.[41]

Cato is a difficult man to love: tortuous, involved, clumsy,

---

[38] Cato's letter and Cicero's reply: *ad famm.* XV.5 and 6.
[39] *ad famm.* XV.4.11 and 14.
[40] *ad Att.* VII.2.7.
[41] Ibid.

ungracious. But he does have a high reputation for integrity and honour. This he often deserved, but sadly not on this occasion, for when his own intimates were concerned he forgot the high-minded sentiments of his letter to Cicero, his contempt for empty honours. A *supplicatio* of twenty days was suggested for Bibulus, of whom Cicero wrote that 'as long as there was a single enemy soldier in Syria he didn't put a foot outside his own front door'. The proposal was moved by·Cato. It is perhaps small-minded to point out that Bibulus was the husband of Cato's daughter.[42]

Cato's letter tells us a lot about Cato. But undoubtedly the most intriguing of the Cilician letters are those that tell us a lot about 'the noblest Roman of them all', Marcus Junius Brutus.

Brutus was a nephew of Cato's and was also to become a son-in-law, for he later married Bibulus' widow; but at the time he was married to a daughter of Appius Claudius, a fact not unconnected with what follows. For he had large financial interests in Cilicia and Cyprus, and that these were in some sense related to his father-in-law's office and influence as well as his uncle's is not to be doubted (Brutus had accompanied Cato on his mission to organize Cyprus). At any rate, Brutus had gone to the trouble of giving Cicero a memorandum in which these interests were detailed for the governor's special attention.[43] One of the most important items was a large loan he had made to Ariobarzanes, the king of Cappadocia, and he never ceased to press Cicero to squeeze money out of this unfortunate monarch. This was not easy. The king was short of ready cash, and so long as the Parthian danger lasted it was not politic to press him too hard. In any case Brutus was not the only creditor, nor the most important; Pompey had lent the king even more, and 'hundreds' of his agents were busy dunning Ariobarzanes.[44] Pompey's claims were all the more to be respected in that he might soon appear in person to deal with the Parthians.

[42] Ibid.; *ad Att.* VI.8.5.
[43] Ibid. VI.1.5.
[44] Ibid. 1.3.

Cicero did his best; he got the king to pay Pompey about 800,000 sesterces a month on account, and this satisfied Pompey even though it did not cover the interest on the loan. Brutus did not get all that was due either, but he got more *pro rata* than Pompey himself. Still Brutus was not satisfied, and he continued to plague Cicero with rude demands to do better than this, until in the end it was only with difficulty that Atticus persuaded him not to wash his hands of Brutus' affairs altogether; 'for', said Cicero, 'why should I bother?[45]

Brutus does not come well out of this, but there is worse to follow. 'Your friend Brutus', wrote Cicero to Atticus, 'is on good terms with certain creditors of the town of Salamis in Cyprus, Marcus Scaptius and Publius Matinius, whom he commended to me warmly.' Appius had given Scaptius a commission as *praefectus* and some troops of cavalry, which Scaptius had used to terrorize the Salaminians; he had even besieged the local council in their Town Hall until five of them died of starvation. He asked Cicero to make him a *praefectus* too. Cicero refused, and ordered the cavalry out of Cyprus, promising however that he would enforce payment of the money due. Eventually Scaptius and the Salaminians came to Tarsus, and Cicero was astonished when the latter promptly offered to settle the debt. But, whereas Scaptius was demanding 200 talents, they calculated the sum due at 106. The difference arose over the rate of interest; Cicero had fixed the rate at the traditional twelve per cent (a figure recently confirmed by the Senate), but Scaptius wanted forty eight.

The whole business stank of corruption. The original loan had been made some years earlier at Rome—which was illegal; but Brutus' influence had secured two special decrees from the Senate legalizing the transaction. Cicero refused to go against his own edict, but would not give judgement *against* Scaptius at the twelve per cent rate. Then, a few days later, Scaptius produced a letter from Brutus confessing that he had lied to Cicero; Scaptius and Matinius were

---

[45] Ibid. 3.5; *Quid est igitur quod laborem?*

only agents, Brutus himself was the creditor. Cicero was shaken, but stood his ground:

My mind is quite made up. If Brutus thinks that I ought to have accepted forty eight per cent and so ruled, though I was working on twelve for the whole province and had so stated in my edict and secured the approval of even the toughest moneylenders; if he is annoyed at my refusing a praefecture to a businessman, as I did to our friend Torquatus in the matter of your Laenius and to Pompey himself with Sextus Statius; if he is put out by the withdrawal of the cavalry—well I shall be unhappy that he is angry with me, but even more unhappy that he is not the man I thought he was.[46]

We have seen what difficulties lay in wait for a governor who wanted to deal fairly with his subjects in the quarrels with Appius Claudius. Now we have seen more of them in this affair. There are powerful men about, men of great influence and wide connections, who need to be handled with care. No doubt Cicero expected such pressure from Appius Claudius, but Brutus genuinely surprised and saddened him. It is to his credit that to the last he would not budge from the figure of 12 per cent. But even so he could not bring himself to decide against Brutus, even if he could not decide for him. He evaded the responsibility by leaving the affair to be settled by his successor.

It is worth setting out the Salamis affair not only because of its intrinsic interest, or the glimpse it gives us into a dirty corner of Rome's imperial cupboard, but also because of the warning it contains. Some modern writing on the fall of the Republic is calculated to leave the reader with the impression that those who won the struggle were a gang of unprincipled rogues, and those who lost the core of what might almost have become a social-democratic party. It is tempting to seek a cachet of sophistication by blackening the successful men of history. We all know that they were not 'nice' people; that they committed crimes from which decent, humane men, untutored in power politics, would revolt. But one must try to be fair, and grant that their opponents were often no better, sometimes worse. To

[46] The substance of the Salamis affair is set out in *ad Att.* V.21.10–13, VI.1.5–6.

17—C.

describe Brutus, as Syme does, as 'a sincere and consistent champion of legality', to write of his 'firm character and Roman patriotism', to say of him that he 'did not believe in violence', is simply to adopt the old Tacitean or Tudor technique of deepening the blackness of those of whom you disapprove by applying liberal coats of whitewash to other selected characters. Brutus, Syme assures us, 'proclaimed a firm determination to fight to the end against any power that set itself above the laws', and 'would have known the true name and essence of the *auctoritas* of Augustus the Princeps.'[47] But when we recall his blatant lies to Cicero, his manipulation of his father-in-law's influence, his use of rigged *senatusconsulta* to evade decent and just legislation, his petulance when Cicero would not fall in with his wishes, and the misery of Salamis and its five dead town-councillors who were victims of his greed and disregard for legality; when we recall these things, we may be forgiven for supposing that we know the 'true name and essence' of what Brutus himself stood for, and for suggesting that very few people outside his own circle and class were sorry to see it go. Caesar was in the habit of saying about Brutus: *Quidquid vult, valde vult*—'When Brutus wants anything, he wants it in earnest.'[48] If Cyprian Salamis leaves Shakespeare's Brutus somewhat the worse for wear, it endorses the shrewder judgement of Brutus' victim.

Of course, 'it is not necessary to praise political success or to idealize the men who win wealth and honours through civil war'.[49] But no more need we praise political failure, or idealize the losing side. To be really cynical, one must adopt Acton's dictum and stick to it relentlessly: 'Great men are almost always bad men.' But then, of course, one may have to give up the idea of writing history; it is not surprising that it was Acton who was responsible for: 'Advice to persons about to write History:—Don't.' As Creighton pointed out, between black and white there exists a wide range of greys.

[47] Syme, *RR*, 148, 183–4, 320.
[48] *ad Att.* XIV.1.2.
[49] Syme, *RR*, Introd. viii.

All politicians will from time to time do what they know to be wrong, or not do what they know to be right, in the interests of party or country or personal advantage; but some worry about it less than others, some have better reasons or motives than others. It would be foolish to deny this. Cicero does not come out of the Salamis affair with clean hands; he did not insist on what was right, he allowed (however reluctantly) personal and party considerations to outweigh conscience. But his conduct is infinitely ·to be preferred to that of Appius Claudius or Marcus Brutus; we all know whom we should prefer to have as governor.[50]

Despite his many acts of liberality and his generally equitable management of affairs. Cicero's governorship cannot command unstinted praise. Exactly where the blame lies is a moot point. We have to judge his actions against the background of his age, as with anyone else: we do not call Dr. Johnson a brute because he saw nothing against public hangings. This does not mean that we shall end up approving of what Cicero did; but we may hope to understand him better. He was free from the commoner failings of many of his contemporaries: he was not rapacious, he had a natural humanity often lacking in the Claudiuses of his day (to be fair, we need also to bear in mind that, unlike Appius Claudius, he did not go out to govern Cilicia with a load of debts hanging around his neck). But, like every other politician of any consequence, Cicero was not free to go his own way. Other people's interests had to be considered, the rules of the Roman *quid-pro-quo* had to be observed. Men like Appius and Brutus were not to be ridden over roughshod, and were expecting of Cicero what many others would give them with little or no demur. And Cicero himself was ever active in writing to provincial governors soliciting their good offices for business friends of his own, clearly in the expectation that something beyond bare and ordinary justice would be accorded to them.

[50] I have used the Acton-Creighton correspondence as reproduced on pp. 328–45 of *Essays on Freedom and Power by Lord Acton*, ed. Gertrude Himmelfarl (Thames & Hudson, 1956).

Cicero, it has now been pointed out often enough, was no Utopian. He knew perfectly well that, even if he wished it, a system consecrated by tradition and buttressed by powerful interests was not to be altered by his single effort and example. Brutus and his agents were unpleasant, Appius was a brute; both were very influential men, both belonged broadly to the class of men who wanted to see the Republic continue and 'Caesarism' eschewed—as did Cicero. For Cicero political life would have been impossible had he not been ready to ignore the moral failings of those who shared his constitutional views. Tax-contracting companies and moneylenders were often no better than wolves but they represented a powerful class in Roman society and politics on whose support Cicero had leaned heavily in the past and which he could ill afford to lose.

To have made a bold stand for justice and legality would have been a stirring gesture. It could have had no important or lasting effect; and if Cicero had been the man to make it he would never have advanced so far as to be in a position to do so. So the truth was only for Atticus' private ear. Clemency and generosity were restricted to matters which affected only himself and his subordinates; duties were carried out punctiliously, assizes held, local officials called to account. For this the province had good reason to be grateful. Yet even here our ear detects a hollow ring in the letters. It is hard not to conclude from reading them that Cicero is all the time thinking, not of the welfare of Cilicia, but of his own reputation. Appius' conduct is castigated, but principally in order that Cicero's may appear all the more fair; he never tires of praising his own virtues, while inviting Atticus to applaud from the sideline—'Look what an excellent governor I am!' What seems to shock him most about the Salamis affair is Brutus' wishing to make him dishonour his own edict and his past reputation: 'Please don't think, Atticus, that I have cast your exhortations to the winds—they are lodged in my heart. You wept as you urged me to look to my reputation—not a letter of yours in which you don't come back to it. So let who will be angry, I don't mind: "Right is on my side", especially since I have bound myself over to be of good conduct with six books as guarantors.'[51] The Parthians appear, not as a grave danger to provincial lives and property, but as potential bearers of military disgrace or glory. And the fundamental self-interest of Cicero is underlined when, eager to quit his province once his year is up, and with no successor yet appointed, he leaves Cilicia in the charge of his quaestor, a young man he himself recognizes to be quite unfitted for the responsibility and as unprincipled as Appius: 'Nobody thinks my quaestor worthy of the appointment, for he is shallow, profligate, and light-fingered.'[52]

Not that Cicero ever sought the job in the first place. Forced to take it on, his natural humanity combined with his vanity, and so he set out to live up to the reputation his speeches and treatises had won for him. We may condemn him or not, as we are inclined; it makes no difference to him now, nor to the facts. He was not a free agent, except in the widest sense that all men are always free in the end to do what they choose if they are prepared to be hanged for it. His own attempt to create a third force in Roman politics had failed. His choice had to lie between Caesar, the amiable revolutionary, with the threat of autocratic government which he instinctively and profoundly abhorred; and, on the other hand, Pompey and the *boni*, many of whom he disliked, distrusted, and despised, but whom he regarded as the lesser of two evils. Reasonably honest for his day and class, cultured, humane, jealous of his good name and with a natural taste for legality, he was a born middle-of-the-roader unlucky enough to live in a period of extremism. His experience in Cilicia is part of his general dilemma. To use his own words when confronted by the choice forced on him by civil war: *Ego vero quem fugiam habeo, quem sequar non habeo*— 'As for me, I know who to run from, but I have no one to run to.'[53]

[51] *ad Att.* VI.1.8. Cicero refers to the six volumes of his *de re publica*.
[52] *ad Att.* VI.3.1 (*levis, libidinosus, tagax*); VI.6.3.
[53] Ibid. VIII.7.2.

Cicero left Italy towards the end of April 51. He landed
there again on 24 November 50. A lot had happened while
he was away, and Caelius' letters not only add to the facts
at our disposal but—much more valuable—enable us to
follow them against the background of contemporary
opinion and gossip and reaction at Rome.

We left Pompey secure in the consul's chair with his new
father-in-law for a colleague, and Caesar drawn back north
of the Alps to grapple with what was to develop into the
most serious challenge to his hold on Gaul. In the course of
the year 51 the situation became threatening. In May there
were rumours that Caesar was planning to enfranchise the
Transpadani: they soon faded, but their mere existence
suggests that people found it plausible to suppose that he
would need to strengthen his political position. The war in
Gaul was still absorbing his attention, and the news from
there was uncertain and generally not encouraging. The
consul Marcus Claudius Marcellus, a bitter enemy of
Caesar's, had already begun to agitate for a successor to be
sent out to take over from him but had put back a positive
proposal until 1 June. There is no evidence that he did
anything on 1 June either—thus confirming his reputation
for sluggishness—but he was active in another direction.[54]

In July Cicero wrote to Atticus to comment on the action
of Marcellus in flogging (at Rome) a citizen of Novum
Comum (Como) in the *Transpadana*. Briefly, by taking this
action Marcellus was publicly demonstrating his anti-
Caesarism, and in particular his contention that Caesar's
enfranchisement of colonists at Como in 59 or 58 was vitiated
by those legal flaws which technically voided all the Caesarian legislation of 59 and what followed therefrom. But, as
Cicero remarked, whatever the legal issues involved, it was a
'disgusting' thing to do: the man was after all a Transpadane, not a savage.[55]

Marcellus' action illustrates two points. First, he was

[54] *ad famm.* VIII.1.2–4.
[55] *ad Att.* V.11.1. For a full discussion, see E. G. Hardy, *Some Problems in Roman History*, 126–49.

confident that he would not be called to account for his behaviour—or else that, if he were, he would be acquitted; and such confidence argues that Caesar was no longer sufficiently powerful at Rome to deter or punish Marcellus. Second, it warns us not to assume too readily that Pompey and the leading *boni* are yet working smoothly in double harness; for Cicero observes that Pompey will not like what Marcellus has done any more than Caesar—Pompey himself had oid and strong ties of patronage with North Italy.[56]

Soon followed a development the importance of which was not perceived at the time, but which was to be crucial in the crisis of 50. One of the tribunes-designate for 50 died, and young Curio suddenly decided to stand for this chance vacancy. His friend Caelius reckoned that he would be found on the right side, as was only to be expected in view of his past record: 'As I hope and should like, and as he himself has it, he will favour the *boni* and the Senate.' Caesar, says Caelius, has treated Curio with scant respect; and Curio's candidature was being opposed by Caesar's lieutenant, Mark Antony.[57]

The initiative still rested with Pompey; for the whole question of provincial allocations, involving of course the question of whether or not Caesar was to be superseded, hung on his decision. At the time he was due to leave for Ariminum (Rimini), just south of the Rubicon (a conjunction which tempts the suspicion that he may have been planning secret conversations with representatives of Caesar), and nothing could be settled till he was back, as the Senate agreed.[58]

The picture in late summer 51 is then this. Pressure is beginning to build up against Caesar, and moves to have him superseded soon are actually being mooted. If evicted from his provinces and stripped of the armour of his *imperium*, he will be open to attack in the courts. But as yet the *boni* and Pompey are not hand in glove. When at last the question

[56] *ad Att.* V.11.1.
[57] *ad famm.* VIII.4.2.
[58] Ibid. 4.4.

is openly debated in the Senate on the last day of September, it is clear that without Pompey the anti-Caesarians are powerless to move; and Pompey makes it plain that he is not prepared to do anything before 1 March 50. The upshot was that four proposals were laid before the Senate (Caelius gives them *verbatim*): (a) that the consuls of 50 must see to it that the Senate at once proceed on 1 March 50 to discuss the allocation of consular provinces with priority over all other business, and the magistrates were to see to the passing of any legislation then required to implement the will of the Senate; (b) that the tribunician veto be debarred from use during the proposed discussions and action after 1 March 50; (c) that the Senate should decide the question of demobilizing parts of Caesar's army on grounds of length of service or for other reasons; (d) a rather complicated proposal which boils down to this—that the only provinces available for consular assignment should be Caesar's provinces and Syria. (As it happens, even Syria might be held to be unavailable. Its present incumbent was Bibulus, who had been late to assume his command because—so some people said—he wanted to delay his departure.)[59]

The purpose behind all this is evident. Caesar's enemies aimed to produce a situation on 1 March 50 such that overriding priority must be given to a decision on provincial allocations; at least one of Caesar's provinces would have to be assigned to an ex-consul; and no tribune could obstruct a majority vote of the Senate. Pompey had said that he was not prepared to take a decision about Caesar's provinces before this date, but that after it 'he would not hesitate'. The best Caesar's tribunes could do now on this last day of September 51 was to veto all but the first of the four motions. It did Caesar no harm to have further discussions postponed for five months, and the vetoing of the three pendant motions meant that he did not have to face the Senate on 1 March naked and bound. But all these motions had received majority votes from the Senate, so Caesar was clearly going to meet strong opposition. Thus it is not surprising that

[59] For Bibulus' dilatoriness, see *ad Att.* V.16.4.

people should have thought that he might have been driven to do a deal with Pompey which would leave him with half a loaf rather than no bread, as Caelius tells us they were encouraged to think by certain remarks of Pompey. At the same time, the effervescent Curio was planning an all-out attack on Caesar in 50. Significantly, among those senators who publicly put their names down in support of the four motions were Scipio (Pompey's father-in-law), Hirrus (an active Pompeian tribune in 53), and Curio himself, as well as old enemies like Ahenobarbus.[60]

Everything was poised for a decision on 1 March 50. (This was, I myself would argue, the terminal date laid down in the *Lex Pompeia Licinia* for Caesar's Gallic command: but this is not the place to argue it.) Then early in 50 the scene was transformed, and the balance shifted. Curio, who had been elected to the vacant tribuneship, now defected to Caesar. This dramatic news was transmitted to Cicero in a last-minute postscript to a letter written by Caelius towards the end of February.[61] The explanation of this *volte-face* does not concern us here, but more than simple bribery was involved; what matters is that it was of vital importance, for apparently Caesar had as yet no tribune on his side, and we certainly hear of no other tribune active for him this year except Curio—indeed of the other nine tribunes only one is known to us by name.[62] This suggests that Caesar had been far too busy in Gaul to give sufficient attention to the election campaigns of the previous year—the attempt to get Mark Antony elected late in the year had not come off. Now Curio changes sides, producing one of those unlooked-for chances which Caelius had seen could happen at any time and which rendered accurate prognostication impossible; for he had written in November 51 that 'there are other things that can happen that I am blind to; time, I know, brings many

[60] All this information about the debate on 29 Sept. 51 is taken from *ad famm.* VIII.8.4–9.

[61] *ad famm.* VIII.6.5. (Note that the numbering of the letters in Book VIII does not necessarily follow the chronological order of the letters.)

[62] For an excellent analysis of Curio's tribunate, see Lacey, *Historia* 10 (1961), 318 ff.

things to upset the best laid plans'.[63] Instead of pressing inexorably on with their programme, Caesar's enemies ran up against the obstructionist tactics of Curio. He had his veto, he was resolute and immune to intimidation and blandishment, quick to spot a trap and avoid it. Nothing was achieved in March. In April Pompey offered a compromise: let Caesar agree to leave on 13 November. The offer looked generous, but Curio saw through it and flung it back in Pompey's face, and resumed his obstruction to any proposals that involved the appointment of a successor to Caesar. The strain began to tell, and Caelius believed that the Senate might crack under it: 'This I tell you: if they push Curio to the limit, Caesar will defend his tribune and his veto; if they get cold feet—and it looks as if they will—Caesar will stay as long as he pleases.'[64]

The issue was stark and precise. Caesar was determined to stay on in his provinces barricaded behind his army and his *imperium* until he could return to Rome to a consulship to which he planned to be elected in absence. Secure in this new *imperium*, he would again build up his strength at Rome. His enemies were no less determined that this was a consummation to be avoided at any cost; that now, while he was politically weak at Rome, Caesar must be extracted from his defences, brought back to Rome as a *privatus*, and duly dealt with. As Caelius put it about the end of April: 'What Pompey certainly does not want, and plainly fears, is that Caesar should be elected consul before resigning his army and his province.'[65] Both sides agreed on one thing: if Caesar left his province and returned to Rome without a consulship in his pocket, he would be finished. Again, Caelius puts it in a nutshell in a letter written in late September:

The point at issue is this, and it is over this that the men in power are going to fight: Pompey has made up his mind not to let Caesar be elected consul without his first surrendering army and provinces, while Caesar

[63] *ad famm.* VIII.10.4.
[64] Ibid. 11.3: *Si, quod videntur, reformidarint, Caesar quoad volet manebit.*
[65] Ibid.

is convinced that his personal security depends on his keeping his army
... So their old love-affair and their detestable alliance have not decayed
into furtive bickering but have erupted into open war.[66]

By the spring and early summer of 50 it was too late for
Caesar to try to get elected consul that year; he had not had
time to organize a powerful enough campaign, and in any
case his candidature could have been ruled out of order
under the law, which strictly required him to wait another
year before he could be eligible. But he would be eligible
to stand in the summer of 49 for a consulship in 48; he had a
special dispensation, granted in 52, to stand in absence;
Curio, and his successors in 49, could see to it that he was not
superseded until he chose; he had ample time to mount a
full-scale campaign to win election. So the year 49 must see a
resolution of the issue. Meanwhile, both sides paused for
breath and to wait on events. Caesar would not be wise to
precipitate a war against heavy odds while there was any
chance he would not have to fight at all. Pompey did not
underestimate Caesar's brilliance as a commander in the
field or the fighting qualities of his veteran legions, and time
could be well spent in organizing his own resources in men
and *materiel*. If Caelius was any judge, neither could be sure
of the Senate, and both could hope that it would in the end
take the right path, to weakness or to resolution. Meanwhile,
a vigorous war of words could be waged to convince public
opinion that each side was constitutionally in the right and
moved only by an unselfish concern for legality and the
public good; for neither side wanted to gain the reputation
among the important possessing classes of the Italian
municipalities that it was merely in quest of personal advantage and careless of legality.

This was the Italy to which Cicero returned in November.
He did not like what he found, as he made plain to Atticus:
the Senate had been too weak in handling Curio, he would
have cracked under sufficient pressure; the *publicani* were
unreliable; the bankers and landowners were for peace at

66 Ibid. VIII.14.2.

any price, concerned only for their property. Too much water had been allowed to flow under the bridge, but what was to be done now?

With Caesar either it must be war to the death or we must let him stand for the consulship. Better war than servitude—so *you* will say. But war for what? Defeat will mean outlawry, victory will bring servitude all the same. What then am I going to do? What cattle do; when they are lost they attach themselves to their own kind. As the strayed ox joins the herd, so will I join the *boni*, or those who are so called. I see plainly what is the best course in these sorry times. For while nobody can foresee what will happen when it comes to open war, anybody can foresee that if the *boni* are beaten Caesar will be as merciless to their leaders as Cinna was, and as greedy in plundering the rich as Sulla was. But I bore you with this politician's talk, and I would go on longer if my lamp were not failing me. To the point, then: 'What say you, Marcus Tullius?' 'I cast my vote with Gnaeus Pompeius—that is, with Titus Pomponius Atticus.'[67]

Curio's term of office expired on 9 December. Next day the new board of tribunes assumed office. Two of them were firm for Caesar: Mark Antony and Quintus Cassius Longinus (not to be confused with Gaius Cassius Longinus, the 'liberator', who was also tribune this year and was probably Quintus' cousin). They made it plain that they were going to continue where Curio had left off, and that the veto would be interposed to block any attempt to recall Caesar. The moment of decision had come. Cicero reached Rome on 4 January 49, though he did not enter the city because he still had hopes of a triumph. Caesar had written to him to ask him to use his influence for peace,[68] but, as he told his old friend Servius Sulpicius, 'I could make no progress. I had come too late, I was alone, I was thought unversed in the facts of the case, I had entered a madhouse full of men lusting for war.'[69] Much later, he said in a letter to Varro that 'I could see that our friends were eager for war, while Caesar was not exactly eager but not frightened at the prospect'.[70] On 5 January Caesar's father-in-law, Piso, received some support for a plea to go to Ravenna to negotiate with Caesar

---

[67] *ad Att.* VII.7.5–7.
[69] *ad famm.* IV.1.1. (April 49).
[68] *ad Att.* VII.21.3 (Feb. 49).
[70] *ad famm.* IX.6.2. (June 46).

but the opposition was too strong and the proposal was rejected. Two days later Antony and Cassius were advised that in the interest of their personal safety they should leave the Senate. They made their protest, and packed their bags; with Pompey's soldiers everywhere they had no real choice. With them out of the way, the Senate had recourse to the 'Ultimate Decree': the consuls, praetors, tribunes, and those proconsuls who were near the capital (a long-winded way of saying 'Pompey'), were to look to it that the state took no harm.

It was the parting of the ways for many people. Caelius was no admirer of Caesar, but he had decided none the less to throw in his lot with him. He had set out his thoughts to Cicero back in August:

As for me, on the one side I have both influence and close personal ties with the individuals concerned [Caesarian friends of Caelius' like Curio and Dolabella and Antony], while on the other I love the republican cause but detest its supporters. And this, I think, you are well aware of— that in a time of civil discord it is a man's duty to support the better side so long as the struggle is conducted by constitutional means and without recourse to arms; but when it comes to open war, he must support the stronger side, and equate virtue with security.[71]

Cicero was equally in a cleft stick, but his emotional and personal ties drew him in the opposite direction, towards Pompey. So he stayed where he was while Caelius headed north. On the morning of 11 January Caesar had crossed the Rubicon into metropolitan Italy, and the town of Ariminum was in his hands. There he found Caelius and Curio waiting for him, along with Mark Antony and Quintus Cassius. The war that had been so long feared had begun.

[71] Ibid. VIII. 14.3.

XI

CIVIL WAR

THE WAR cut a broad swathe through the ranks of Rome's
politicians. Caelius and Milo met their deaths trying to raise
Italy against Caesar. Curio died fighting in Tunisia. Bibulus
worked himself into his grave as commander-in-chief in the
Adriatic. Ahenobarbus fell on the field of Pharsalus, and
Pompey escaped only to meet a crude death on an Egyptian
beach. Scipio Nasica remembered his ancestors as he lay
dying: *Imperator se bene habet.* Cato inevitably chose death
rather than dishonour at Utica, gaining a *cognomen* and giving
birth to a legend. Many others perished: the ex-consuls
Afranius, Gabinius, Lentulus Spinther, Marcus Claudius
Marcellus, along with Cornelius Lentulus Crus, one of the
consuls of the fatal year 49.[1]

Many survived, and some prospered, thanks to an initial
correct choice of sides or a well-timed change. But Cicero
neither died nor prospered. He had too little faith to be a
martyr, too much to be an apostate. His decision to throw in
his lot with Pompey and the *boni* had more of resignation in
it than enthusiasm; and once the tide began to set strongly
in Caesar's favour, and Caesar himself showed that his fears
of a return of the days of Cinna and Sulla were ill-founded,
his main concern became to extricate himself from the mess
and be left alone. It is not an edifying story, and Cicero often
displays the same petulant self-pity and self-reproach that
had marred his months of exile; but given his position and
his helplessness, his reactions are understandable, and he
does deserve credit for his constant refusal of Caesar's offers.

[1] Probably Gaius Marcellus, the other consul of 49, as well; but the date and
manner of his death are uncertain.

Not then a hero of the resistance, neither was he a collaborator.

Caesar had to move fast to throw Pompey off balance. But
Caesar's *celeritas* was his most notable quality. He swept into
Italy and overran the north-east. Pompey left Rome on 17
January to join his two veteran legions in Apulia, and the
next day the consuls and other magistrates fled the capital in
such haste that the treasury was left intact. Ahenobarbus
ignored Pompey's urgent advice and thought to stand and
destroy Caesar at Corfinium. He was neatly netted, but allowed to go free; his men were formed into two legions and
with them Curio secured Sicily and crossed to Africa. Pompey was at a serious disadvantage in that he lacked that
supreme authority which Caesar had over his own army; he
could not issue orders to men like Ahenobarbus, for Ahenobarbus was a proconsul himself, appointed by the Senate to
succeed Caesar in Gaul. Many of the *boni* still mistrusted
Pompey, and not everybody understood his strategy, which
could be mistaken for weakness or suspected as potentially
treacherous. Early in March Caesar was outside Brindisi,
his army swollen by reinforcements and deserters to six
legions. Pompey's plan to hold Brindisi, contain Caesar in
Italy, cut off overseas supplies, and crush him by attack from
east and west (where in Spain his old lieutenants Afranius
and Marcus Petreius commanded seven legions and large
forces of cavalry and auxiliaries) had to be scrapped. On 17
March he retired across the Adriatic to Dyrrhachium
(Durazzo).

After patching up arrangements at Rome, Caesar moved
against Spain. In a campaign of startling brilliance, he won
control of the country and was back in Rome by early
December, receiving the surrender of Marseilles en route.
He had been appointed dictator in his absence, and now
had himself elected consul for 48. He stayed at Rome only
for eleven days, and by the close of the year he was back at
Brindisi. He managed to slip his troops across the Adriatic,
but Pompey out-manoeuvred him at Durazzo. There followed

a period of strategic movement until the decisive battle was fought at Pharsalus on 7 August 48. Pompey escaped from the ruin, and had he got clear away the war would have been far from lost, but he was murdered as he landed in Egypt.

Cicero met Pompey outside Rome on 17 January 49, and he was shaken to hear that Pompey was abandoning Rome and planning to retire before Caesar's advance (though Cicero calls it 'running away', *fuga*, not 'retiring'). It was as if, he told Atticus, 'the sun had gone from my universe'. The two friends spent the next few weeks in anxious correspondence: Cicero's resolution had never been strong to begin with, and as he came to appreciate that the war was not going to be a walk-over for Pompey or find a quick end in a compromise peace, it was easily sapped by his cautious friend. As early as 21 January Atticus was having second thoughts: 'we must see what Gnaeus [Pompey] does and where his plans are leading. If he leaves Italy, he will be acting altogether wrongly and, as I think, foolishly; but then we shall have to change our own plans.' Caesar's initial successes cooled his ardour, and set him to finding excuses for spilling some of the wind out of his own sails.[2]

Cicero himself, still vested with *imperium* as proconsul, had been put in charge of the Campanian coast, with responsibility for its oversight and for the raising of troops there. He spent a few days in limp execution of this commission— few recruits were forthcoming—and took part in an abortive council along with Pompey and the consuls which discussed a peace offer from Caesar but approved it only with an unacceptable proviso.[3] By the end of January he was back in his villa at Formiae, from which he scarcely stirred for the next two months; he did make one half-hearted attempt to join Pompey in Apulia, but having got no further than Cales (about ten miles north of Capua) the news that Caesar was outside Corfinium sent him back home.[4]

[2] *ad Att.* IX.10; cf. VII.7.7.
[3] *ad famm.* XVI.12.3. cf. Caesar *BC* I.10–11.
[4] *ad Att.* VIII.3.7.

Not that Cicero for one moment contemplated going over to Caesar and actively co-operating with him. Caesar, he said, talked a great deal about his *dignitas*, 'but what is dignity without a sense of honour? Is it honourable to have an army without any public authority, to seize Roman towns to pave the way for a return to Rome, to plan cancellation of debts and the recall of exiles and a thousand other wickednesses, "So to win Tyranny, greatest god of all"?'[5] Yet Caesar was making overtures; in March he appealed to Cicero to join him soon at Rome 'so that I may avail myself of your advice, influence, authority, and assistance in all matters'.[6] Caelius added his plea, writing to Cicero in April telling him not to be stupid, and urging him at least to wait to see how things went in Spain before committing himself finally to the *boni* and Pompey. Tullia, who was married to the vigorous Caesarian Dolabella, was also pressing him with the same arguments.[7]

It is easy to see why Caesar was anxious to win Cicero over. His own followers did not inspire confidence. Syme delineates them acidly: 'Deplorable in appearance, the lack of consulars, while precluding the personal rivalries that disturbed the camp and counsels of Pompeius, and strengthening Caesar's hands for action, gave his rule as party-leader a personal and monarchic character ... For the rest, elderly survivors, nonentities, neutrals or renegades. A few names stand out, through merit or accident, from a dreary background.'[8] For Caesar, then, Cicero would be a fine catch, giving to his actions and his cause a *cachet* of respectability and adding to his propaganda the most persuasive tongue in Rome. But Cicero would have none of it, and he would have none of Caelius' and Tullia's advice to wait on events in Spain either, as he tells Atticus on 2 May:

This advice would be sensible, so it seems to me, only if I meant to accommodate my plans to the outcome of events in Spain. But this I will not do. It must happen either that Caesar is driven out of Spain (which is what I should like best), or that the war there drags on, or

5 Ibid. VII.11.1.   6 Ibid. IX.7A.
7 *ad famm.* VIII.16; *ad Att.* X.8.1.   8 *RR* 61–2.

that he wins the Spanish provinces (as he seems confident he will). If he is driven out, and I then join Pompey, how gratified or impressed is Pompey likely to be, when I imagine that even Curio will be defecting to his side? But if the war drags on, what am I to wait for, and for how long? The only other possibility is for me to stay neutral if our side is beaten in Spain. But myself, I think quite the contrary. I think the time to abandon Caesar is when he has won, not when he has lost; while he is still uncertain, not when he is sure of himself. . . . Caesar's friends write to me that he is displeased that I have not attended the Senate. Am I to contemplate selling myself to him with the risk of rejection when I have declined to join him with the assurance of reward? And remember, this whole struggle is not going to be decided in Spain, unless you suppose that if Spain is lost Pompey is going to surrender. But Pompey's whole strategy is Themistoclean: he thinks that the man who controls the sea must be the master. . . . So he will sail, when the time comes, with his vast fleets, and arrive in Italy. And if I am sitting there, what will become of me? Neutral I shall not be allowed to be . . . I made a mistake; perhaps I ought not to have, but I did. I thought we should have peace; and, were this to happen, I did not want Caesar annoyed with me while at the same time he was friendly to Pompey. I knew how very like each other they were. It was fear of this that trapped me into procrastination. But I can make everything good if I hurry now, while if I delay I shall lose all. [9]

It was not only his expectations of an early peace or his unhappy memories of 56 that lay behind Cicero's hesitation. He certainly felt strong ties of personal gratitude to and respect for Pompey, and he did identify him and the *boni* as the champions of the Republic against the threat of autocracy. But apart from his concern at what seemed a lack of foresight and proper planning on their part, he was horrified at the thought of what they would do if they were victorious, of the bloody vengeance they would take on enemies and neutrals, of the ravaging that lay in store for Italy at their hands.

If it were only a question of running away, I would have done that right willingly, but I was horror-struck at the prospect of war in its most cruel and enormous form beyond men's expectation. What threats against the towns of Italy, against good decent men specifically named, against all indeed who should be found to have remained behind! How often that fatal *Sulla potuit, ego non potero?*—'Sulla could do it, why not I?'[10]

[9] *ad Att.* X.8.2–5.   [10] Ibid. IX.10.2–3.

Cicero had returned an honest answer to Caesar's letter, telling him that he would find no one readier than himself to help bring about peace and reconcile him with Pompey, but making it plain that he would not actively support him in any other way.[11] Caesar was not satisfied. The two men met face to face at Formiae on 28 March, and again Caesar urged Cicero to come to Rome.

We were mistaken [Cicero wrote to Atticus after the meeting] in supposing that he would be easy to deal with—far from it! He told me that my refusal was a vote of censure against him, that all the others would drag their feet if I did not come. I said that their situation was different. On and on, then finally, 'Come to Rome, then, and work for peace.' 'With *carte blanche*?', said I. 'Of course,' said he; 'who am I to dictate to you?' 'This', said I, 'is how I shall set to work: senatorial opposition to any expedition to Spain or to the transport of troops to Greece—and I shall have a lot to say in defence of Pompey.' Then he said, 'I certainly don't want that sort of talk.' 'I thought not,' I said, 'but *I* certainly don't want to be there because either I must say this and a lot more besides which I could not hold back if I were present, or else I had better not come at all.' The upshot was, since he apparently wanted to be finished, that 'I was to think it over.' I could not say No, and so we parted.[12]

Cicero's departure from Italy was imminent. He still talked occasionally and vaguely of neutrality, even of retiring to somewhere like Malta 'for the duration', but this was principally to mislead Mark Antony and other Caesarians—for he was closely watched.[13] He toyed with the notion of going to Sicily and doing something noteworthy there, and he was disgusted to learn that Cato had evacuated the island.[14] Since mid-February he had had a boat standing by at Caieta (just along the coast from his villa at Formiae) and another at Brindisi.[15] He embarked at Caieta on 7 June, and sailed away to join Pompey.[16]

The five months since the outbreak of war have bequeathed to us over one hundred letters to and from Cicero,

[11] Ibid. 11A.
[12] Ibid. 18.1. In April Caesar wrote again strongly urging Cicero at least to remain neutral: *ad Att.* X.8B.2.
[13] Ibid. X.8.10.
[14] Ibid. 12.2; 12A.2; 15.2.; 16.3.
[15] Ibid. VIII.3.6.
[16] *ad famm.* XIV.7.

startling proof of his mental turmoil as well as an intimate insight into his character and calculations. But for the rest of this year 49 there is not a single letter remaining for us to read. Even for the following year we have only a handful until his return to Italy after Pharsalus: five short letters to Atticus, one or two to Terentia and his family, one from Caelius and one from Dolabella—and the Atticus letters are almost all about money, and have little or nothing to tell us of politics.

Plutarch's biography must be called in aid.[17] Most people in Pompey's camp were pleased to see Cicero arrive, although Cato thought that it would have been better for Cicero to have stayed in Italy and worked for his friends and his country there rather than 'share in our danger without reason or necessity'. Cato held that he could not himself abandon his post with the party he had embraced from the very beginning, but clearly he saw that Cicero's attachment to the cause of the *boni* amounted to less than total dedication. Cicero was upset, and it did not help that Pompey found him no worthwhile job to do. He belittled Pompey's preparations, surreptitiously disparaged his plans, and could not resist exercising his scathing wit at the expense of the leading Republicans. Not that he was at all cheerful himself: 'he never laughed, and walked about the camp with a gloomy face, but he made others laugh even when they did not want to.' It was not the sort of laughter that lifted the heart, and his frequent 'wisecracks' engendered bitterness.

Cicero recalled these days in a letter three years later, when he remarked on the many things he found wrong when he arrived in Pompey's camp: 'First of all, his forces were neither large nor in good fighting spirit'—this is false, for whatever might be thought about the quality of Pompey's largely inexperienced troops they were not deficient in numbers—

Then, leaving aside the commander-in-chief and a few others (I am talking of the leaders here), the rest behaved like brigands in their conduct of the war, and their talk was so bloodthirsty that I shuddered at the very thought of victory. And these great gentlemen were up to their ears in debt. Why go on? The only good thing was the cause itself. Seeing all

[17] Plutarch *Cicero* 38.

this, and despairing of victory, I first of all began to advocate, peace which I had always worked for; then, when Pompey shied violently away from this suggestion, I set about persuading him to drag the war out. He was won over for a while and seemed likely to agree, and perhaps he would have were it not that as a result of a particular engagement he gained confidence in his troops [Pompey broke Caesar's over-extended lines and inflicted unpleasant casualties on his army][18], after which time this great man ceased to be a general.[19]

Probably little of this is wisdom after the event: it has a ring of truth, and chimes in well with what we know of Cicero, and with Plutarch's report. Caesar comments on the rapacity and cruelty Scipio displayed in Asia Minor.[20] The threats of many of the leading *boni*—*Sulla potuit, ego non potero?*—had long worried Cicero. That some of them saw the war as a heaven-sent opportunity to repair their personal fortunes and satisfy their greed is stated by Cicero in a letter to Aulus Caecina in autumn 46. But as early as March 49 he had asked Atticus whether he supposed 'that Scipio or Faustus Sulla or Scribonius Libo are going to hold their hands from any crime over there, now that their creditors are said to be meeting here? And what do you suppose they will perpetrate against Roman citizens, once they have won?' After his return to Italy at the end of 48 he told Atticus how there had been talk about 'proscription', and how Cornelius Lentulus Crus had earmarked for himself Hortensius' town house and Caesar's mansions at Rome and at Baiae.[21] As to his verdict on Pompey's generalship, Caesar took the same view, for while he recognized that Pompey had beaten him at Dyrrhachium, he believed that Pompey exaggerated the significance of this success and was led astray by it into over-confidence.[22]

Ironically, while Cicero was venting his frustration and disillusion in acid jokes and mischievous sniping, his friend Caelius wrote to him from Italy (in February 48) to tell him

---

[18] Caesar *BC* 3.62–74.
[19] *ad famm.* VII.3.2. (August 46, to M. Marius).
[20] Caesar *BC* 3.31–3.
[21] *ad famm.* VI.6.6; *ad Att.* IX.11.4, 6.2, 6.6 (Atticus himself threatened).
[22] Caesar *BC* 3.72.

how deeply he regretted his own decision to join Caesar. 'It is not that I have lost confidence in Caesar's cause, but, believe me, death is preferable to the sight of these people. If it were not for the fear of the cruelty of your friends, we should have been thrown out of here long ago. Apart from a few money-lenders there is not a man or a class here that is not all for Pompey.'[23] On the other hand, Cicero's son-in-law Dolabella advised him in May (in a letter whose execrable Latin reminds the reader how much the language owed to Cicero) to come over to Caesar;[24] but Dolabella was one of 'these people' whom Caelius could not stand the sight of. Caelius tried unsuccessfully to arouse public feeling against Caesar's debt-law, and finally moved to open insurrection, calling his old friend Milo to join him. Milo came—alone of the exiles he had not been recalled by Caesar, who hated and distrusted him too much. It was a forlorn hope; they could raise no solid support. Milo was killed by a sling-stone while attacking the walls of Compsa in Apulia; Caelius was murdered at Thurii by some of Caesar's Gallic and Spanish cavalry he was trying to bribe.[25]

All this time Cicero was worried about money, until a timely legacy restored confidence in his credit;[26] perhaps also about his wife's health. For some time before the battle of Pharsalus he was himself ill, and so was not present when Caesar won his decisive victory. A few days afterwards, Labienus reached Dyrrhachium with the news. The Pompeians crossed over to Corcyra (Corfu), and Cato invited Cicero as the senior consular present to take command of the considerable military and naval forces there. He refused the appointment, and Cato had to restrain young Gnaeus Pompeius (Pompey's elder son) and his friends from running Cicero through as a traitor. He then went to Patrae, at the western end of the Gulf of Corinth, where he had a quarrel with his brother, Quintus. By October he was back at Brindisi.[27]

So Cicero's decision to leave Italy and join Pompey had

---

[23] *ad famm.* VIII.17.1–2.   [24] Ibid. IX.9. Cf. chapter XII, p. 306, note 71.
[25] Caesar *BC* 3.22   [26] *ad Att.* XI.2.1.   [27] Ibid. 5.4; Plutarch *Cicero* 39.

been a leap 'out of the frying-pan into the fire'. Many anxi-
eties combined to make a sorry situation worse. There was
the quarrel with his brother, which may have been sparked
off by a squabble over money[28] but was not confined so
narrowly. Quintus' irascibility was notorious, and it was not
helped by the fact that he was in a highly strung state. With
his son he had gone to Caesar after Pharsalus to seek pardon
and rehabilitation, and they hoped to assist their cause by
blackening Marcus' character and putting all the blame on
him. Yet Marcus himself had written to Caesar absolving
his brother from all responsibility for and approval of his own
political hostility towards Caesar.[29] The quarrel dragged on,
causing Marcus much unhappiness, and it may be that it was
not until the summer of 47 that the two brothers made it
up.[30] Cicero's health continued poor and the bad climate of
Brindisi was notorious.[31]

Then, too, he began to quarrel with his wife. Again, money
was the ostensible reason, and Cicero was upset by certain
testamentary dispositions Terentia was said to be making.
This is in the summer of 47, but it looks as if things had been
going wrong well before.

As for Terentia, I say nothing of all the other countless incidents, isn't
this the last straw? You wrote to ask her to send me a bill of exchange for
12,000 sesterces, that being the balance outstanding. She has sent me
10,000, with a note that *this* is the amount outstanding. When she en-
gages in petty pilfering from a petty sum, you can see what she will have
been doing where a really large amount is involved.

It is no surprise that the two were divorced early the following year.[32]

His darling Tullia was as faithful and affectionate as ever,
but her husband was becoming a public scandal for his
vigorous amours; and on top of that Dolabella was playing

[28] Ibid. 13.4.
[29] Ibid. 8; 9; 10; 12.
[30] Ibid. 23.2 (July 47) suggests that they were now friendly again. There
was some trouble in August (Ibid. 21.1), but probably this arose from the late
discovery by Marcus of a letter which Quintus had written to Caesar before
July.
[31] Ibid. 5.3. (See 22.2 and Caesar *BC* 3.2. for the climate.)
[32] Ibid. 24.3 Cf. 16.5 and 23.1.

the extravagant demagogue and may even have gone so far as to set up a public statue of his hero, Publius Clodius— hardly calculated to please his father-in-law. Honour made a second divorce inevitable.[33]

Such, briefly, were the private distractions of a very up-setting year. But what chiefly nagged at Cicero's thoughts was a concern personal to himself. This concern took two forms. First, he was on tenterhooks about how Caesar would treat him after his earlier rejection of Caesar's advances. Secondly, he began to wonder whether the war *was* over. A number of the Pompeians had regrouped in Africa and Spain, and fought on; while Caesar had stirred up a hornet's nest at Alexandria, and for much of the winter of 48/47 was cut off under siege and attack by vastly superior forces. So the ever-volatile Cicero plunged deep into despair as he tortured himself with the prospect of an anti-Caesarian triumph after all, and convinced himself that his own pre-mature defection after Pharsalus would find no forgiveness.

Atticus stood by him, ever ready with help (especially in money matters), encouragement, and advice. Vatinius was kindness itself.[34] The admirable Gaius Matius, a close friend of Caesar's as well as of Cicero's, 'came flying' to see him at Brindisi; Quintus Lepta (Cicero's quartermaster-general in Cilicia) and Gaius Trebatius (a young lawyer friend and former protégé) visited him there in December 48; and Aulus Ligarius (another common friend of Caesar's and Cicero's) and Vatinius were loud in their reprobation of the shocking conduct of Quintus Cicero towards his brother.[35] But Cicero was in no mood to be easily comforted.

Soon after his return to Italy, Atticus advised him to move nearer Rome, travelling by night; but Cicero thought this not feasible.[36] He claims not to regret his decision for neutrality after Pharsalus, but he does express regret at

---

[33] Ibid. 6.4, 23.3. (The statue of Clodius is revealed by an inspired emenda-tion of Purser's.)

[34] Ibid. 5.4.

[35] Ibid. 27.4, 8.1, 9.2.

[36] Ibid. 5.2.

having returned to Italy; he should have settled down abroad and waited to be sent for. Oppius and Balbus, Caesar's confidential secretaries, had written with assurances of Caesar's goodwill and favour, but 'I should put more reliance in all this had I stayed behind. However, what's done can't be undone.' This same letter contains a curiously muted 'obituary notice' of Pompey, all the more sincere and moving for its low-pitched tone: 'I cannot but be grieved at his fate. I knew him as a man of integrity, decency, and high principle' (*hominem enim integrum et castum et gravem cognovi*).[37]

There ensued an upsetting muddle over Cicero's status. Caesar became disturbed at the prospect of haphazard returns to Italy of old enemies, especially since he himself was out of the country; so he wrote to Mark Antony, his deputy, barring from Italy all those whose cases he had not himself reviewed. Antony told Cicero politely that he had no option but to ask him to leave. Cicero replied that he had returned at the specific encouragement of Dolabella, who had written with Caesar's knowledge and authority. Antony promptly published an edict lifting the ban from Cicero (and Decimus Laelius) by name. This was *not* what Cicero wanted: 'I do wish he had not done that; the exemption could have been made without naming names.' Partly Cicero was ashamed, but partly he was worried about the course of the war. He has heard that many loyal Pompeians have gone to Africa and wonders what will become of him if they win after all. This is the major reason why he wishes he had retired to some neutral spot to await the outcome.[38]

The new year finds Balbus' letters 'growing more lukewarm every day', and Cicero pathologically worried by nightmares of what others might be writing to Caesar about himself. He is betrayed into maudlin sentiment: 'Today is my birthday (3 January 47). How I wish they had let me die that day, or that my mother had never borne a second son! I am too full of tears to write more.'[39] As the months

---

[37] Ibid. 6.2–5.   [38] Ibid. 7.2–4.   [39] Ibid. 9.1–3.

passed there was more disquieting news of the consolidation
of anti-Caesarian forces in Africa and Spain, of dissatisfaction
in Italy, unrest at Rome, and grumblings among Caesar's
soldiers.[40] Money worries persisted.[41] By mid-May Cicero
has almost convinced himself that the worst *is* going to
happen:

Caesar seems to be so cooped up in Alexandria that he is ashamed even
to write about his situation there, while these people from Africa look
like arriving at any moment, and the Achaean contingent and those in
Asia look like rejoining them or staying on in some neutral locality.
What do you think I ought to do? I see it is a difficult decision. For I
am quite alone, or alone but for one other,[42] in having no avenue of
return to them nor any glimmer of hope held out to me by these people
here.[43]

Not at all well, worried by his daughter's ill health and her
marriage, short of money, at odds with his wife, apprehensive
of a Pompeian victory, envious of those who had gone to
ground in Asia and Greece, Cicero was at his lowest ebb. He
did not know it, but some six weeks earlier, on 27 March,
Caesar had broken out of Alexandria and won a decisive
victory in Egypt.[44]

Caesar did not at once return to Italy, for he had to hurry
to Asia Minor where a son of Mithridates, Pharnaces, had
beaten one of Caesar's generals and was causing a lot of
trouble. He dealt with Pharnaces in five days of brilliant
speed: '*Veni, vidi, vici*'.[45] Only then was he free to turn for
home. In June Cicero had no news of his movements, and
planned to send his son Marcus, now nearly eighteen, to
Alexandria to see Caesar and make a personal appeal on his
father's behalf. But on hearing rumours that Caesar was still
seriously held up there, he changed his mind. Instead, he
begged Atticus to extricate him from Brindisi. He had now
been there for seven or eight months, very unhappy months

[40] Ibid. 10.2.
[41] Ibid. 11.2.
[42] The 'one other' was Decimus Laelius: see preceding paragraph.
[43] *Ad Att.* XI.15.1.
[44] [Caesar] *Bell. Alex.* 26–33.
[45] Suetonius *DJ* 37.

during which he had been a prey to fears and rumours and uncertainty, and he was desperate:

Absolutely any punishment must be lighter than having to stay on here. I have written to Antony on this subject, and to Oppius and Balbus. Whether there is going to be fighting in Italy, or whether it will be a naval war, either way it is highly inexpedient for me to remain here ... I now look forward to nothing whatsoever except something nasty, but nothing could be more god-forsaken than the situation I am in at present. So please talk to Antony and the other two, and arrange things as best you can.[46]

In August came what Cicero called a 'fairly generous' letter from Caesar, but it was couched in vague terms.[47] About this time too we have a letter from Cicero to Gaius Cassius, which is interesting as an explanation of what had gone wrong, as Cicero saw it. Like Cicero, Cassius had chosen Pompey's side, and had been given command of a fleet. But Cicero and Cassius had talked things over between themselves at Formiae in February 49, and both had agreed that it would be sensible to accept the decision of a single major battle. Like Cicero, Cassius acted on this decision after Pharsalus; he made his way to Caesar in Asia Minor, was forgiven, and taken into his service. What had followed Pharsalus, wrote Cicero, was such that

it is more astonishing that these things could have happened than that we should not have seen that they would happen and, being only human, failed to divine them in advance. For my part, I admit that my own reading of the situation was that once that battle, that almost predestined battle, had been fought, the victors would want to look to the safety of Rome and the vanquished to their own; and I believed that both these things hinged on the victor's acting with speed ... Who would have imagined that this long delay of a war at Alexandria would be added to our war, or that this Pharnaces or whatever you call him would terrorize Asia? As for us two, our plan was the same, but chance has treated us differently. The path you chose has enabled you to share in the councils on your side and, what is the best cure for anxiety, to gauge what is likely to happen. But I, having hurried back to Italy to see Caesar (as I thought) so that on his return with so many fine men still spared I might, so to say, spur on a willing horse towards the goal of peace—I

[46] *ad Att.* XI.16.1., 17.1; *ad famm.* XIV. 11, XIV. 15; *ad Att.* XI.18.1–2.
[47] *ad famm.* XIV.23; *pro Ligario* 7; *ad Att.* XI.18.1–2.

have been, and remain, separated from him by a vast distance. All around me are the groans of Italy and the unhappy complaints of Rome itself—things which each of us, I for my part and you for yours, might have been able to alleviate if only the man responsible had been here.[48]

At long last, about 24 or 25 September 47, nearly a year after Cicero's own return, Caesar landed at Tarentum and proceeded next day to Brindisi. Again, we have to turn to Plutarch.

Cicero hurried to meet him. He was not altogether without hope, but he was embarrassed at having to approach his victorious enemy in front of a crowd of witnesses. However he was not forced to say or do anything to cause him shame; for when Caesar saw him coming to greet him a long way ahead of all the others, he got down and embraced him and continued along his way for several hundred yards in private conversation with him. And from this moment on he continued to treat Cicero with respect and kindness.[49]

Cicero's long and tedious quasi-exile at Brindisi was over. He at once set out for Rome, and the first of October found him already at Venusia, well over a hundred miles on his way, writing to tell his wife to expect him at his estate in southern Tuscany on the seventh or eighth of the month, and to see to alterations to the bathroom. The letter is brusque and chilly; as Long remarked of it (and with justice), 'a gentleman would write a more civil letter to his housekeeper'.[50]

The Civil War had now lasted nearly three years, and it was not over yet. So Cicero did not find that his return to Rome coincided with the beginning of a period of settled administration or overhaul of the machinery of government. His letters are interesting for the insight which they give us into the attitude of an important section of the Roman governing class towards Caesar and his methods; on top of this, they provide valuable contemporary factual informa-

[48] *ad famm.* XV.15. The whole tone of this letter suggests that Cicero wrote it carefully in the expectation that Cassius would see to it that others read it as well. Nonetheless, it seems truthful as far as it goes.

[49] Plutarch *Cicero* 39.

[50] *ad famm.* XV.20. Long, *Plutarch's Lives*, IV.195n. (cited by Tyrrell and Purser, ad loc.).

tion and so furnish us with landmarks to help steer a way through the uncertain shoals of later accounts of Caesar, tainted as these are by partisanship, propaganda, romantic exaggeration, or sheer ignorance.

Caesar left Rome again late in November 47, and arrived in North Africa just before the end of the year. Here, after some close shaves, he brought the regrouped Pompeians to battle at Thapsus on 6 April 46, winning a decisive victory. Cato's suicide followed a few days later. Caesar was back in Rome by the end of July. But before the year was out he was again constrained to quit Rome and hurry to Spain to deal with the dangerous threat of Labienus and Pompey's sons, who after escaping there after Thapsus had made great head-way—much helped by the grave shortcomings of Caesar's deputies. The campaign that began near Corduba in December 46 was perhaps the toughest of the war, and it continued for three grim months until the last Pompeian army was shattered at Munda on 17 March 45. Only Sextus Pompeius of the principal Pompeian leaders escaped, to emerge later as a persistent thorn in the flesh of Octavian, who had joined his great-uncle in Spain. The time was fast approaching when the bloody feuds of the late Republic were to be bequeathed to the *diadochi* of a new generation.

Caesar now came back to Rome for the last time, early in October 45. He had six months to live.

For months after his own return to Rome Cicero lived in a kind of limbo. His detachment from public affairs is obvious and understandable, yet it seemed to drain the life-blood from him. His letters have an almost wraith-like quality about them, as if their writer were only half-alive, almost transparent. Being the man he was, Cicero could not be idle. As always, he sought a haven in literary activity, and there began a highly productive period which continued down to the latter part of 44; in the *Brutus* he passed in review the great orators of the last two or three generations, and this treatise was speedily followed by the *Orator*, which was also dedicated to Marcus Brutus. Both these works were written in early 46, and the next year saw the *Hortensius* (a plea for the study of philosophy which was greatly to influence St. Augustine), the first draft of the *Academica*, the *de finibus*, and the *Tusculan Disputations*. Before the end of 44 he had added the *de Natura Deorum*, *de Divinatione*, *de Fato*, *de Senectute*, *de Amicitia*, and *de Officiis*, not to mention other works which have not come down to us. The letters from this period are peppered with references to the solace which he got from his literary studies in the midst of his depression and pessimism about public affairs.

But for all his literary greatness, Cicero was essentially a political animal, and Caesar would have found a use for so experienced and influential a man had Cicero been ready to conform. However, Cicero's political convictions went deep, and both he and Caesar recognized that an active compromise was unattainable. The upshot was that he was neither 'flesh, fowl, nor good red herring'. Of the old Pompeians, many were dead, some were in disfavour, some still fighting on, and a number had made their peace with Caesar and were in active employment. Cicero attended meetings of the Senate, but did not speak. Both sides looked askance at him: the victorious party regarded him as one of the vanquished, while those who deplored the defeat of the Pompeians were sorry to see him still going on living. Yet he was kept in Rome by his own fear of what people would say if he left— that he was a coward or a traitor or, most leniently, too ashamed to look people in the face.[51] So he stuck it out, and left it to time to grow a protecting scab over his wounded pride. Though he expresses his readiness, if called on, to join in the work of rebuilding the Republic 'not as an architect but as a common labourer', his tone is not that of a man who really expects to be invited to do anything.[52]

The thin quality of his letters is partly explained by his feeling of having no firm ground under his feet; but partly it was dictated by prudence. 'It remains for me,' he writes to Papirius Paetus, 'to say or do nothing stupid or rash in opposition to those in power; this too, I think, is part of

[51] *ad famm.* IX.2.2.–3 (April 46, to Varro).   [52] Ibid. 2.5.

wisdom.'[53] And what he said in a letter to P. Servilius Isauricus in September holds good of all his letters at this time: 'If I do not write to you often about what I feel about the high affairs of state, it is because such letters are dangerous.'[54] He sought to rationalize his past course of action. He told Varro that he did not regret his decision because

I followed the path not of hope but of duty, and I abandoned the path not of duty but of hopelessness. Thus I acted with better conscience than those who did not stir from home, and with better sense than those who did not come back home when the game was lost. But I could not care less about the harsh judgements of the stay-at-homes, and however things may be I stand in greater awe of those who died in the war than to worry about these people who think I fall short because I am still alive.[55]

But the easing of an uneasy conscience was difficult when he spent so much time with, and was getting on so well with, the leading members of the victorious party—a circumstance which made his conscience all the more troublesome, and provided ammunition for those detractors whose judgement he professed to scorn.

In particular, he was seeing a lot of Caesar's confidential agents, Hirtius and Balbus and Oppius, under whose instruction he claimed rapidly to be turning into an expert gourmet.[56] He came to believe that Caesar's friends were genuinely fond of him, and Caesar himself treated him with studied courtesy and consideration.[57] In July he was giving lessons in public speaking to Hirtius and Dolabella, and taking lessons from them in the art of high living.[58] Yet a little while before this he had begun preliminary work on an appreciation of Caesar's enemy, Marcus Cato.

The writing of his *Cato*—the suggestion had come from Brutus—faced him, as he told Atticus, with a problem to tax the skill of an Archimedes: how to do justice to his subject without giving offence to Caesar.

The truth is that, even if I eschew reference to his public utterances and all his political conceptions and policies, and content myself with vague

[53] Ibid. 16.5. (July 46).
[54] Ibid. XIII.68.2.
[55] Ibid. IX.5.2.
[56] Ibid. 20 (August 46).
[57] Ibid. 16.2–4 (June/July 46).
[58] Ibid. 16.7.

praise of his strength of character and undeviating courage, this in itself will still ring hatefully in the ears of your friends. Yet, if Cato is to receive his true praise, one simply must speak eloquently of how he saw that what is now happening was going to happen, how he fought to prevent it happening, and how he died rather than live and see it happening.[59]

The problem proved unresolvable, and though the *Cato* was finished later that summer it was held back from publication to avoid giving offence. It is to Caesar's credit that when at last he read it his response was to take up his pen to answer it; but he made a grave mistake in allowing his personal irritation to lure him into a spiteful attack on Cato's personal morality which was so distorted that it backfired on itself, and so spiteful as to raise serious doubts about Caesar's famous *clementia*.[60]

More than once, Cicero tries to excuse Caesar by drawing a distinction between his own character and aims and his obligations to his party and the demands of circumstances.[61] War was still being waged in Africa, and Caesar did not return from there until July 46. So various Pompeian exiles can be written to in terms that, if not positively encouraging, hold out some slight hope of better days to come; when the war was at last over, Caesar might perhaps turn to the task of restoring ordered constitutional government.[62] His willingness to forgive and forget was reassuring; true, *clementia* was the virtue of an autocrat, but it was still a virtue (though perhaps an unwise one); and, if Caesar was an autocrat, it might be thought that this was an inevitable consequence of the existing emergency, a consequence that might itself disappear when the emergency ended. For Cicero himself, and many others, the high-water mark of these comforting hopes was the pardoning of Marcellus.

This was the Marcus Marcellus who had as consul in 51 launched the attack on Caesar that eventually drove him across the Rubicon. He was now in self-imposed exile at Mytilene, but moves were begun to effect his return to Italy. In September 46 Cicero wrote three letters to persuade him

---

[59] *ad Att.* XII.4.2. [60] See Gelzer, *Caesar*, 301—3.
[61] *ad famm.* IX.17.2—3; XII.18.2.; VI.6.8—10. [62] Ibid. XIII. 68.2.

to return, promising to do all he could to make this possible.[63]
Many others did as much, as is clear from Cicero's letter to
Servius Sulpicius at the end of the month in which he describes the scene in the Senate after Caesar, for all his dislike
of the 'bitterness of spirit' that Marcellus had displayed,
suddenly and unexpectedly declared that he would not stand
in the way of the wish of the Senate in this matter. The event
was particularly significant for Cicero, for it led him to break
a long silence. Lucius Calpurnius Piso (Caesar's father-in-law,
the consul of 58) introduced the question of Marcellus and
Gaius Marcellus[64] flung himself dramatically at Caesar's
feet, whereupon the Senate as a body rose and approached
Caesar in formal supplication.

Ask no further [writes Cicero]; so fair a day it seemed to me that I
thought I beheld the ghost of the Republic returning to life again. So
after all those who had been invited to speak before me had expressed
their gratitude to Caesar—except Volcatius, who said that he would not
have done what Caesar had done had he been in his place—when it
came to my turn I had a change of heart. For I had made up my mind,
not I swear through any sluggishness but out of regret for the loss of my
prestige of former days, to stay silent for ever. But this resolution of mine
was shattered by Caesar's magnanimity and the Senate's loyal constancy.
So I expressed thanks to Caesar at considerable length.[65]

When the greatest of Roman orators rose to speak in a
Senate which had scarcely heard his voice for over five years,
it was an event of some importance.[66] We can still read the
speech. It starts (judging it by Cicero's own high standards)
awkwardly and ponderously; but gradually he moves into
his old stride, and words and ideas begin to flow freely again
as he leaves the formal phrases of thanks behind him and
warms to his favourite theme of the *res publica* and the need
for constitutional reconstruction. He urges Caesar to think
beyond the moment and plan for a lasting settlement that

[63] Ibid. IV.7–9

[64] Consul in 50 and cousin of Marcus, he was married to Octavia, sister of
Octavian, and remained neutral during the Civil War. He is not to be confused
with the other Gaius Marcellus, brother of Marcus, who was consul in 49 and
had been a leading Pompeian supporter, and was now probably dead.

[65] *ad famm.* IV.4.3–4.

[66] *ad Att.* XV.3.1 reveals that Cicero had addressed the Senate at one of its
meetings early in Jan. 49 with a plea for moderation—probably only briefly.

will not be dependent on the life and power of one man. 'Day and night, as I am duty bound to do, I think of you and of all the chances of our human life, the physical ills that threaten us and the frailty of our common condition, and I am filled with fear, and I weep to think that our Republic, which should be immortal, should hang on the heartbeat of one mortal being.' And in a mood of sombre prophecy he continues: 'And if to these common human chances and the uncertainties of physical health is added the possibility of a criminal conspiracy to assassination, can we trust that any god could save the Republic, even if he so wished?'[67] The urgent task is, then, to put the Republic back on its feet again: 'Reconstitute the courts, restore confidence and credit, repress vice, increase the birth-rate, use stern laws to tighten and bind all that has come loose and dissolved.'[68] There is work to be done if the great name of Caesar is to survive as more than an object for empty wonder: 'Then it will be for you, if you wish, when you have paid your debt of duty to your country and yourself drained dry the cup of life, to say "I have lived long enough".'[69]

Of course, all this is vague, but the reader can still sense the live enthusiasm of Cicero's words. After nearly four years of arbitrary government, it is the idea of a return to constitutional forms that dominates, and this unpremeditated speech was not the occasion for spelling things out in detail. Certainly, Cicero was greatly encouraged. Not long afterwards he took up the cudgels on behalf of another man deep in Caesar's disfavour. Quintus Ligarius had been among those who had not given up after Pharsalus, and he had fought Caesar at Thapsus in 46. Though pardoned, he was forbidden to return to Italy.[70] Cicero sought an audience with Caesar along with Ligarius' brothers, and though they extracted no concession he reported that the outlook was encouraging.[71]

---

[67] *pro Marcello* 22-3.
[68] Ibid. 23.
[69] Ibid. 27.
[70] See the scholiast on *pro Ligario*: Stangl 291.22.
[71] *ad famm.* VI.14.2.

Meanwhile Quintus Tubero brought a formal charge against Ligarius in connection with his activities in Africa. Cicero spoke in his defence, a quiet and elegant speech. Caesar was moved to consent to Ligarius' return—if we can trust Plutarch, Cicero's words affected him so strongly that he broke down, overcome by emotion.[72]

Not long after this Caesar had to go to Spain, leaving the effective management of affairs once again in the hands of Balbus and Oppius.[73] Cicero still cherished hopes of a return to something approaching normal government, much encouraged by the leniency shown to Marcellus and Ligarius.[74] There were still things that irritated him—Caesar's high-handed attitude towards magisterial elections, and the production of fake senatorial decrees to order.[75] But in May 45 he began the composition of a 'letter of advice' to Caesar. Inevitably, it had first to pass through the sieve of the scrutiny of Balbus and Oppius. Their suggested modifications Cicero found intolerable: 'For God's sake,' he wrote to Atticus, 'let us be rid of the whole business, and at least be *half*-free!'[76] From this point onwards, he resigned himself to the hard and unalterable fact of absolutism.

Cicero's public disillusion followed on a traumatic personal shock. Though divorced from Dolabella, his darling daughter Tullia was pregnant. A son was born early in 45 but did not long survive. Tullia herself died in February, as a result of the childbirth. Her father's grief knew no limits, and he was quite beyond any consolation of friends or books. He sought refuge in solitude, in the composition of a treatise 'On the alleviation of grief' (*de luctu minuendo*), and in endless and pathetic concern with the erection of a shrine to Tullia's memory.[77] His grief made him turn savagely on his new young wife. At the end of 46 there had been considerable

---

[72] Plutarch *Cicero* 39.
[73] *ad famm.* VI.8.1.
[74] M. Marcellus never did return to Italy, for he was murdered at the Piraeus in May 45.
[75] *ad Att.* XII.8; *ad famm.* IX.15.3–4.
[76] *ad Att.* XIII.31.1. Cf. XII.40.2, XIII.28.3, etc.
[77] Shackleton-Bailey, V, Appendix 3.

activity among his friends to find him a wife in place of the divorced Terentia; Pompey's daughter had been suggested among others, but he finally settled on his ward Publilia, who was little more than a child. This did his reputation no good, for he was thought to have married her for her money under pressure of his debts. His old extravagance, particularly notable where houses were concerned, reared its head again late in 46 and set him toying with the idea of buying Publius Sulla's mansion at Naples. However, the new marriage was short-lived; he suspected Publilia of being secretly pleased at Tullia's death, refused to see her, and soon divorced her.[78]

The mood of deep pessimism that darkened the year 45 for Cicero darkened it for many others as well.[79] The carefully composed letter which his old friend Servius Sulpicius addressed to him to console him on the death of Tullia is well known.[80] Sulpicius was a genuine Republican. As consul in 51 he worked for moderation against his anti-Caesarian colleague Marcus Marcellus; he stayed neutral when war broke out, and left Italy; after Pharsalus he resumed his legal work until Caesar chose him to govern Achaea. Yet in this consolatory letter his blank despair at the seemingly irretrievable loss of the Republic is no polite pose. He had been expressing the same views in earlier letters.[81]

When a man [writes Boissier] as timid and moderate as Sulpicius dared to talk in this way, what must not the others have said and thought! One can appreciate this when one sees what sort of letters Cicero wrote to the majority of them. Even though he is addressing officers of the new government, he does not trouble to dissimulate his opinions; he expresses his regrets frankly, because he knows well that they share them. He talks to Servilius Isauricus, proconsul of Asia, as to one who has a distaste for the absolute power of a single man and who hopes that some limits may be applied to it. He tells Cornificius, governor of Africa, that things are going badly at Rome and that much is happening there that would wound him. 'I know what you think of the fate of the *boni* and of the misfortunes of the Republic', he writes to Furfanius, proconsul of

[78] *ad Att.* XII.11; Plutarch *Cicero* 41; Quintilian *Inst. Or.* 6.3.75; *ad famm.* IX.15. 3–5; *ad Att.* XII.32.1.
[79] G. Boissier, *Cicéron et ses amis,* 313 ff.
[80] *ad famm.* IV.5.
[81] *ad famm.* IV.3 (Sept. 46); IV.4 (Oct.).

Sicily, in commending an exile to him. Yet these personages had received important posts from Caesar: they shared in his power, they passed for his friends.[82]

What lay behind this increasing disillusion of Cicero and many others of his class and standing was the continuing arbitrariness of Caesar's rule, understandable and acceptable for a comparatively brief period of emergency but increasingly difficult to bear as time hardened it and bedded it deeper in the soil of the Republic. We have to try to put ourselves in the position of Cicero and his friends, and see things (as the letters allow us to) through their eyes. Looking back, we may come to the conclusion that the Republic was obsolete, that it had nothing more to offer to the people of Italy and the Empire, and that from the point of view of the mass of the inhabitants of the Roman world the constitutional liberties of the ruling class were light in the balance when weighed against the material advantages of a more personal regime such as Caesar promised and Augustus realised. But the ruling class itself saw things differently. Once again, it is not easy to improve on Boissier's analysis. He asks.:

Whence could come the baulks which the new government encountered among people who had after all agreed to take part in it? They sprang from various motives, which can easily be identified. The first, perhaps the most important, was that this government, even while it heaped honours on them, could not give them what the old Republic would have given them. With the establishment of a monarchy, an important revolution took place in all public offices: the magistrates became functionaries. Once upon a time the men elected by the popular suffrage had the right to act as they chose within the sphere of their duties. At all levels, a fertile initiative animated this hierarchy of Republican dignitaries. From aedile up to consul, all were sovereign in their own field. They could not continue to be so under an absolute government. Instead of running affairs on their own responsibility, they were nothing but so many channels, so to speak, along which the will of a single man circulated to the very ends of the earth.[83]

This is not the place to analyse in any detail the events which ultimately led up to Caesar's assassination. With the

[82] Boissier, 314–15. The letters referred to are *ad famm.* IV.5, XIII.68, XII.18 and VI.9.

[83] Boissier, 315–17.

victorious conclusion of the campaign in Spain and his return to Rome in September 45 came the last occasion on which he might have given clear signs that the present personal form of government was only a passing phase and that in due course changes might be made that would go some way to mollify the ruling class. But Caesar seems no longer to have cared, and his detachment had become such that he was constantly mistaken in his judgement of men. Fourteen years of supreme command in the field had imbued him with the habit of authority, accustomed him like the centurion in the gospel to say to a man come and he cometh, and go and he goeth. Fourteen years of success had fortified his confidence in his own judgement and good luck. The man who had once been so definite that his personal *dignitas* was of supreme importance and dearer than life itself[84] seems to have forgotten that such a sense of values was not an idiosyncratic whim but a general mark of the caste to which he himself belonged and in which he had grown up. Extraordinary honour was piled on honour, statues and regalia and robes followed one another in glittering succession. Whatever his ultimate aims, more and more did his aspect take on that of a monarch, a king. On the very last day of the year 45, almost casually, he delivered a body blow to the pride of the nobles when, with indecent haste and disregarding the due formalities, he took the chance presented by the sudden death of one of the consuls to appoint a suffect consul to hold office for less than a day—thereby conveniently and cheaply discharging one of the many obligations he owed to his partisans.[85] Cicero's disgust at this action released itself in a barrage of bitter jokes about the devoted vigilance of a consul who did not get a wink of sleep throughout his whole term of office—perhaps the best was when he said that Caninius' consulship was like the atoms of Epicurus, too small to be seen by the naked eye; the result was that Caninius could never be sure in whose consulship he had been consul.[86] Such

---

[84] Caesar *BC* 1.9. [85] Tacitus *Hist.* 3.37.2.

[86] *ad famm.* VII.30.1. Macrobius 2.3.6 gives a selection of the numerous 'wisecracks' which Cicero made on the subject.

witticisms served not to disguise, but to underline, the insult
the ruling class saw in this gross and offhand cheapening of
the supreme office of the Roman commonwealth. Not long
afterwards, in February 44, the man who had been dictator
before for fixed periods became *dictator perpetuus*.[87]

A month later, Caesar lay dead at the foot of Pompey's
statue. The assassins were a heterogeneous collection of men:
Republicans and Pompeians alongside prominent adherents
of Caesar himself. Their motives and origins were mixed,
their long-term aims non-existent or conflicting; what united
them was the despotic authority of Caesar, which they all
wanted to end.[88] A number of them were close friends of
Cicero, but he himself 'had not been asked to the party';
had he been, 'there would have been no left-overs'.[89] But
Antony survived, and it was against Antony that Cicero was
to measure himself when at last he emerged from his twelve-
year-old retirement and made an open bid for the leadership
of a new Republic. The conspirators, or 'liberators' as they
preferred to be called, lacked direction and cohesion and
force; these deficiencies Cicero resolved himself to make
good.

[87] On the accretion of Caesar's honours and outward shows, see Gelzer,
Caesar, 315–24.
[88] Syme, *RR*, 59–60.
[89] *ad famm.* X.28.1 (to Trebonius), XII.4.1 (to Cassius).

XII

'ADSUM IGITUR'

As MARCUS BRUTUS stood over the lifeless body of Caesar, he raised his dagger and cried out 'Cicero'.[1] But Cicero was slow to answer his cue. For several months he was conspicuous in public affairs only by his absence. His frequent letters naturally evidence a continuing concern with the course events were taking, and we learn often enough what he thinks other people ought to be doing. But on the whole he was resigned to sitting back and letting events take their course, seeing little prospect that he himself could direct them. His gaze often strayed from affairs of state—his son's education, money matters, wills, property are much in his mind, and much time was given over to literary composition. The *de divinatione, de fato, de gloria, de senectute, de amicitia, de officiis,* and the *Topica* belong to this period; and even granting the amazing speed with which Cicero worked—he polished off the *Topica* in a week[2]—these essays clearly occupied many of his waking hours.

Cicero left Rome on 7 April on a tour of his country properties: first south, settling at Cumae for the last half of the month; then Pompeii and Puteoli until mid-May; then on to Arpinum and Tusculum for most of June. He set off for Greece to see his son, planning to stay until the end of the year. Sailing from Pompeii on 17 July, he reached Syracuse on 1 August. Then news from Rome caused him to change his plans. He was back in Rome on 31 August, and two days later rose to deliver his *First Philippic*. The name of the speech may mislead, for he was still some way from moving to challenge Antony openly.

[1] *Phil.* 2.28.   [2] *ad famm.* VII.19.

Caesar's murder triggered off disorder, violence, and confusion. Antony took cover in his house. He was soon joined
by Lepidus, who as the dictator's deputy, *magister equitum*,
was able to collect some military force. The conspirators,
after a vain appeal for popular support, dug themselves in on
the Capitol. Brutus and Cassius were both praetors, and
Cicero urged them to seize the initiative and summon the
Senate.[3] His advice went unheeded; they were upset that the
Roman people did not share their enthusiasm at the death of
a tyrant, they realized how weak they were militarily. Next
day (16 March) Brutus again essayed a popular address,
but with no more success; his diction was stylish, but his
words lacked fire.[4] At daybreak Lepidus had occupied the
Forum, and Antony, recovering from his initial consterna-
tion, summoned the Senate to meet on the 17th at the
Temple of Tellus.

The Senate met. The 'liberators' were neither honoured
nor condemned. Caesar's acts were confirmed; too many
vested interests were involved for any other decision to be
feasible. Cicero made a plea for a total amnesty.[5] Next day,
Piso, Caesar's father-in-law, steered through the recognition
of Caesar's will and agreement to a public funeral, which
took place on the twentieth. Antony's speech, and more
particularly the announcement of Caesar's testamentary
liberality to the Roman commons, resulted in tumult as the
crowd took charge and burned the corpse in the Forum. An
altar and a column were erected on the spot, prayers were
offered to Caesar and oaths certified in his name. The
assassins barricaded themselves in their homes. As soon as it
was safe, early in April, they left Rome and hid themselves
away in small towns in the vicinity.

Cicero was disgusted, in a detached and fatalistic way. The
tyrant was dead, the tyranny lived on. The slaying had been
a noble deed, but only half done: the work of those who had
been men in courage but children in design (*animo virili,
consilio puerili*).[6] He was now sixty-two. In 63 Octavian had

[3] *ad Att.* XIV.10.1.   [4] Ibid. XV.1A.2: *Ego tamen . . . scripsissem ardentius.*
[5] *Phil.* 2.89.   [6] *ad Att.* XIV.12.1, 14.2, 21.3. Cf. XV.4.2.

been a newborn baby, the other chief *dramatis personae* boys
or beardless youths. He was effectively the senior statesman,
the doyen of the consulars. Lucius Cotta and Lucius Caesar
(an uncle of Mark Antony) were his seniors, but little was
seen of them, nor of Cicero's old colleague Gaius Antonius
(another uncle of Antony's). Lucius Philippus, step-father
of the young Octavian, and Gaius Marcellus, husband of
Octavian's sister Octavia, hovered in the wings. Piso and
Publius Servilius Isauricus were more prominent: Piso
robustly independent and working for compromise, Servilius
more devious, a relation of Brutus and Cassius and Lepidus
and destined to win the reward of a second consulship in 41.
The rest, leaving aside Lepidus and Calenus, are of little
moment.[7]

Everything hinged on Antony. That he at once began to
dream of, and work for, the succession to Caesar's supreme
position is not to be lightly assumed. His actions are better
explained by a desire to secure himself from danger and an
ambition to occupy a leading position in the state natural in
any noble, and especially in one with so distinguished a
record in war and administration.[8] Antony worked for
moderation and compromise, thus serving his own interests
and those of public order. By early April, Cicero could tell
Atticus that Antony had had a 'not unsatisfactory' interview
with Brutus and Cassius, all things considered; and a few
days later he reported that 'it is excellent news that Antony
is securing the approval even of our friend Brutus.'[9] Brutus
and Cassius were allowed a dispensation from their praetorian duties to enable them to stay outside Rome. Their fellow-
conspirator, Decimus Brutus, held the strategic province of
Cisalpine Gaul, Trebonius Syria. Dolabella had succeeded
to Caesar's consular chair—he would need careful watch-
ing, for he was ambitious and wilful. Lepidus was fobbed off
with the succession to Caesar's office of Pontifex Maximus,
and persuaded to leave for his province of Narbonese Gaul

---

[7] For a review of the consulars, Syme, *RR*, 135–7, 163–5.
[8] Syme, *RR*, ch. VII, especially 108–9.
[9] *ad Att.* XIV.6.1 (12 April), 8.1. (16 April).

(Provence). Antony himself was assigned Macedonia, where six of Caesar's best legions stood waiting for the eastern campaign that had never come.

So, well before the end of April, things seemed to be settling down. On the 21st Antony felt free to leave Rome for Campania to attend to the clamant needs of Caesar's veterans. But almost immediately a cat arrived to scatter the pigeons: Caesar's heir came to claim his inheritance.

From 7 April onwards Cicero was writing almost daily to Atticus. On the 11th he feels helpless, seeing on the one hand the military strengh of the Caesarians and on the other the weakness of the 'liberators'. Next day he can find nothing to be pleased about except the mere fact that Caesar is dead. Everything is topsy-turvey: the tyrannicides are praised to the skies, the tyrant's dispositions safeguarded: 'I can't begin to see how I can take any part in politics.'[10] The next week the theme is the same: the Ides of March had been the day of decision, by the time the Senate met two days later the initiative had passed to Antony.[11] Cicero was at Puteoli with Balbus and the consuls-designate Hirtius and Pansa when Octavius came to lodge in the neighbouring villa, and next day (22 April) they met. 'Octavius is here with me—full of respect and most amicable. His entourage address him as 'Caesar', but Philippus doesn't, so I don't either. I can't see how he can be relied on. He is surrounded by so many people who threaten death to our friends and declare that the present state of things is intolerable. What do you reckon is going to happen when he arrives in Rome?'[12]

But for the time being Octavius is forgotten. The 26th finds Cicero undecided, unenthusiastic, resigned. He does not know whether to stay in Italy or go to Greece. Antony has written him a letter of studied courtesy, to which he has returned an over-fulsome answer—Antony later upset him by reading it out in public, which was not the act of a gentleman! (To be fair to Cicero, he had privately found the

---

[10] Ibid. 5.2, 6.1–2.
[11] Ibid. 10.1.
[12] Ibid. 11.2, 12.2.

substance of Antony's letter 'dishonest, disgraceful, and wicked'.[13]) A few days later he heard that Antony was planning to exchange Macedonia for Cisalpine Gaul and 'Long-haired' Gaul (the *Comata*, which Caesar had conquered and reduced to a province)—this was effected by a plebiscite, probably on 2 June, which bestowed these provinces on Antony and gave Syria to Dolabella, in each case for a period of over five years.[14]

The first of May saw the sun shining brightly. Dolabella had taken vigorous action against the Caesarian rioters at Rome, and had pulled down the column erected in Caesar's honour. Cicero is ecstatic: 'Over the [Tarpeian] rock with them! Onto the cross with them! Down with the column, clear the site! Why, it's truly heroic!' Lucius Caesar, badly ill at Naples, offered Cicero his congratulations when he called to see him, declaring that had he as much influence with his nephew Antony as Cicero with Dolabella they might see an end of their troubles. Cicero addressed a long and enthusiastic letter to Dolabella, ending up by telling him that the fate of the Republic rested on his shoulders. Poor Republic! Pansa however did not at all care for what Dolabella was up to, and no more did Atticus. In this they were wiser than Cicero, who only saw the truth later.[15]

At this time Cicero was planning his trip to Greece, and Brutus too was thinking of leaving—to exile. Antony is working on the veterans and sounding them out. Things, so Cicero opines, are moving towards war. He does not want war, but that is not his business: 'let the young men worry.'[16] Early in May he had written Cassius a long complaint about Antony's goings-on: 'forged documents, grants of immunities, vast sums of money squandered, exiles recalled, fake decrees registered.' Cassius and Brutus ought to be doing something, not just sitting back and imagining that they had finished

---

[13] Ibid. 13.6. (Antony's letter and Cicero's reply: 13A and B. The reading out of Cicero's letter: *Phil.* 2.7.)

[14] Ibid. 14.4; *Phil.* 1.6, 5.7; *ad Att.* XV.11.4.

[15] *ad Att.* XIV. 15.1, 17A. 3 and 8, 19.2, 18.1.

[16] Ibid. 16.3, 18.4, 21.2–3; XV.4.1.

their task.[17] What they were supposed to be doing Cicero does not specify. When they wrote to him at the end of May to ask his advice he 'just did not know what to say to them'; he himself did not plan to attend the important meeting of the Senate announced for 1 June.[18] It is difficult to know whether to blame Cicero. Brutus and Cassius did seem in-effectual: witness a letter they wrote to Antony about this time in which they asked whether they could safely trust themselves to come to Rome, protested (rather plaintively) their faith in him, and pleaded that all they had ever wanted was 'peace, and freedom for all'.[19] But other people re-mained suspicious of them. The pair wrote to Cicero to ask him to use his influence with Hirtius in their favour. Hirtius in his turn asked Cicero to try to restrain them from doing anything 'too hot-headed'. Cicero told him to have no fears on *that* score, remarking to Atticus that Hirtius and his friends seemed still to be afraid that the liberators 'have more spirit than in fact they do have'.[20] But events were to show that Hirtius was right to suppose that Brutus and Cassius had it in them to precipitate a major conflict.

Probably it was his lack of responsibility for events that led Cicero to see things in a simple black-and-white contrast. Perhaps he had spent too long in the country among the conservative upper classes of the smaller towns—of whom, despite their 'optimistic and partisan proclamations', as Syme puts it, one may doubt whether they 'possessed the will and the resources for action, and eventually for civil war'.[21] Brutus was anxious to avoid war—Cassius was not so much a prisoner of tortured conscience and bookish idealism, but Brutus was the dominant partner. Whatever the reason, it is hard to see that the way out was quite as easy and trouble-free as Cicero suggests—a mere matter of Brutus and Cassius and their friends summoning up more energy and spirit.

---

[17] *ad famm.* XII.1.1–2.
[18] *ad Att.* XV.5.1–2.
[19] *ad famm.* XI.2.1–2.
[20] *ad Att.* XV.6.
[21] Syme, *RR*, 101.

About 7 June Cicero went to Antium (Anzio) to attend a conference of Brutus' family and friends. Among those present were Brutus' wife Porcia (Cato's daughter), his half-sister Junia Tertulla (Cassius' wife), and that great and formidable lady, his mother Servilia. Servilia was a woman of enormous ambition and influence: herself the half-sister of Cato, and ruthless in the employment of her three daughters in support of her dynastic policy, in younger days she had had a notorious liaison with Caesar.[22] Before long Cicero was launched into his favourite theme about the Ides of March, what opportunities had been let slip. It was never easy to shut Cicero up once he had got started, but Servilia did not find it difficult: 'Well really.' she said, 'I never heard the like!' That was enough: Cicero held his tongue, and Servilia got down to business and explained bluntly how she would see to it that things were 'arranged'—getting senatorial decrees amended was something she understood about.[23] While Cicero was crying over spilt milk, Servilia and Brutus and Cassius were carefully exploring the practical possibilities.

A few days later Octavian again makes an appearance in the correspondence, and one can see the first stirrings in Cicero's mind of the plan that was in the end to prove fatal to him. The young man, he wrote to Atticus, was not lacking in spirit or intelligence, and seemed to have the proper attitude towards the 'liberators'. 'But how much we can trust his age, his name, his inheritance—this calls for a lot of thought. His step-father (I saw Philippus at Astura) thinks he is not to be trusted at all. But all the same he ought to be nursed and—if nothing else—kept away from Antony.'[24]

As June wore on, Cicero's mood continued gloomy, defeatist, and unconstructive. On the fifteenth 'things seem to me to be pointing towards a massacre, and that not far off: I tell you, I don't feel at all safe'. Five days later he is in despair, and death is in his mind. Young Pompey is on the

[22] Syme, *RR*, 39, 69.
[23] *ad Att*. XV.11.1–3.
[24] Ibid. 12.2.

move in Spain, armies will soon be marching. Neutrality is impossible. Antony rules that out; but which side to choose? —'weakness on the one, wickedness on the other'. He writes to Tiro stressing his anxiety to retain Antony's goodwill. Brutus is 'all at sea' (this comment on 6 July); he is making preparations to quit Italy, but being deliberately slow about it in case 'something should turn up'. On 25 July Cicero himself is at Vibo (on the toe of Italy) en route to Syracuse and Greece, protesting that he is not running away and scouting the notion that any danger is to be apprehended before 1 January, when he means to be back. Then nothing more for over three weeks, until 19 August finds him back at Pompeii. As he had been waiting for a wind at Leucopetra on 6 August he had heard exciting news. It looked as if Antony and Brutus and Cassius would reach a compromise, with Antony resigning his Gallic provinces and the other two ready to leave Italy in the interests of peace and harmony. So Cicero turned round in his tracks, not knowing that there had been an angry and bitter exchange of letters between the three men, and that the Rome to which he was returning was near boiling point. Only when he reached Velia on 17 August did he meet Brutus and learn that a final breach had occurred between him and Antony. Still he continued on his way, and arrived in Rome on the last day of the month.[25]

The picture Cicero presents in these months is thus one of vacillation, timidity, recrimination, and absence of any constructive thought—understandable enough, even excusable, but neither edifying nor notably public-spirited. His influence on affairs was negligible, and Brutus and Cassius looked to him for useful advice in vain. Perhaps what strikes one most about him is his lack of a long perspective—itself a product of earlier discouragement and pessimism. He never sat down and soberly considered the practical options, a surprising defect in a politician once so concerned with the realities. Did he really suppose that firmer and more aggressive action on the part of the 'liberators'

[25] Ibid. 18.2, 20.2–3; *ad famm.* XVI.23.2; *ad Att.* XV.29.1, XVI.5.3, XVI.6.2.

would have led to the collapse of Antony and the other old Caesarians? Of course not; but he never let his mind dwell on such thoughts long enough. The facts were simple. Either Antony was going to pick up the pieces and build them into a position of dominating authority, or he must be stopped, and this would mean war. Cicero may have been right in holding it folly not to cut down Antony as well as Caesar; he was wrong in not putting this out of his mind and accepting that it had *not* happened. Never a man of war, he flinched from the brutal reality that there was no alternative to Antony *but* war; hence his mistaken because over simple and over-hopeful judgements of men like Dolabella and Octavian, whom he saw only as short-term counters to Antony, not as long-term dangers. On the kindest view, his experiences over the past twelve years had sapped his confidence: he could not bring himself to risk backing yet another loser.

There were other views held. Atticus and Pansa looked askance at Dolabella; Marcius Philippus saw the danger of trusting his stepson Octavian; so too did Brutus (as we shall see); Hirtius was not taken in by the temporary inactivity of Brutus and Cassius. They may not have seen a better way through the wood than Cicero—indeed perhaps there was no way through; but what Cicero saw as the desirable end did not seem so to all. Here the attitude of his old friend Gaius Matius is instructive.

Little is known of Matius, a knight and a friend of Caesar's, beyond what we can learn from his famous letter—but that tells us much. Back in April Cicero had been staying with him, and running him down in his letters to Atticus.

He really is the limit, says there is no solution—'for if Caesar with all his genius could not find a way out, who is going to find one now?' Why go on?—he says that we are done for (I rather think he is right, but *he* seems to revel in it) and declares that Gaul will be up in arms inside three weeks. Since the Ides of March he hasn't talked to anyone but Lepidus. In short, he doesn't think that this is all just going to come right again. How sensible Oppius is! He misses Caesar just as much, but says nothing any decent man could be upset by.[26]

In August there was an exchange of letters between the

[26] *ad Att.* XIV.1.1 (7 April). Cf. 3.1., 4.1.

two friends. Cicero had been making more spiteful remarks about Matius—his support for a law (probably that giving Antony the Gallic provinces), his underwriting the games given in Caesar's honour by Octavian. Trebatius effected a reconciliation, and Cicero wrote a grudging apology.[27] To this Matius returned a letter which seemed to Rice Holmes 'the noblest that has come from antiquity'; it certainly is superb evidence of the loyalty that Caesar could inspire in his friends even from the grave, and it shows us the other side of the coin from that which Cicero brings to our notice.[28]

How can I [asks Matius] who wanted everybody to go unharmed, not take it hard that the man who secured this has perished? Especially when the self-same men who caused his unpopularity also caused his destruction. 'You will smart for it then,' say they, 'since you dare to condemn what we have done.' What unheard of arrogance! They can glory in their crime, others cannot even weep for it unpunished. Why, even slaves have always enjoyed this much freedom—to be afraid, to be happy, to be sad, of their own choice and not at another's bidding. Yet this freedom your 'champions of liberty', so they keep on saying, are trying to wrest from us through terror. But they are wasting their time; no fear of danger will ever divert me from the path of gratitude and human decency . . .

You will say that it is my duty as a patriotic citizen to wish to see my country saved. That indeed *is* what I long for—but, if my life hitherto and my hopes for the future do not prove this without my having to say it, I do not expect to convince anyone by arguing. So I do earnestly beg you to let actions speak louder than words, and to believe that, if you agree that a man ought to be guided by his conscience, I can have nothing to do with blackguards. The principles that I set before myself as a young man, when I might have been excused for straying from them, am I to exchange them now for others in my declining years, and unravel the warp and woof of my life? I will not do it, nor will I do anything to cause offence, except that I do grieve for the heavy fate of one who was for me a very dear friend, as well as a very great man.[29]

Slogans and catchwords may rebound on themselves, giving rise to surfeit and suspicion. It is refreshing to hear the 'champions of liberty' bluntly termed blackguards and bullies, arrogant ingrates who had murdered the man who had generously pardoned them and advanced and rewarded

[27] *ad famm.* XI.27. Cf. *ad Att.* XV.2.3.
[28] Rice Holmes, III.349; *ad famm.* XI.28.
[29] *ad famm.* XI.28.2–5.

them. It is as well to be reminded that not everybody hailed the Ides of March as the dawn of freedom after the long night of tyranny, or saw the possible triumph of the 'party of the Republic' as an occasion for unreserved rejoicing. It is pleasant too to discover that virtue does not always go unrewarded. For Matius, who shrewdly observed that those who disliked him for his staunch loyalty to Caesar would rather have the likes of himself for a friend than their own sort,[30] did 'outlive this day and come safe home'. Loyalty to Caesar meant for Matius loyalty to Caesar's adopted son; honesty and principle led him to choose the side that fear or clever calculation might have warned him to shun. He chose Octavian, and lived to die old, and in peace.

It is time to take a closer look at Octavian.

Born Gaius Octavius, he was the grandson of Caesar's sister, who had married a prosperous banker of Velitrae in Latium. Their son, Octavian's father, entered politics and became praetor and governor of Macedonia. An early death robbed him of the consulship that would surely have been his. His son was Caesar's nearest male relative, and this, together with the promise that his great-uncle must have discerned in him, explains why in his will Caesar named Octavius to succeed to his personal fortune and his name. Thus he became Gaius Julius Caesar Octavianus—and as Octavian he is known to history until he becomes Augustus. He preferred to be called 'Caesar'; the magic of that name was too powerful to neglect. Already in April 44 his entourage was addressing him as 'Caesar'; his step-father and Cicero stuck to 'Octavius'—perhaps relying on the legal nicety that his adoption into the *gens Julia* had not yet been formalized by the necessary ceremonies; but if so, this was their pretext, not their true reason, for avoiding the new name.[31] No doubt Antony exaggerated when he addressed the young man as *puer qui omnia nomini debes*;[32] it remains true that only 'Caesar' could have become 'Augustus'.

[30] Ibid. 28.8.
[31] Above, p. 283, n. 12.
[32] *Phil.* 13.24.

Antony had seemed to be sailing into clear water by the third week in April. True, three of the conspirators had left for provincial commands: Decimus Brutus to the Cisalpina, Trebonius to Asia, and Tillius Cimber to Bithynia. In Spain, Sextus Pompeius was playing the role of Sertorius with some success, and the old Pompeian Caecilius Bassus was at large in Syria—or rather, not at large, for his smallish forces were 'pent up in Apamea. But Gaul had remained quiet (despite Matius' gloomy forebodings); Lepidus held Provence, and the Caesarians Plancus and Pollio Gallia Comata and Further Spain. Antony had been allotted Macedonia with its six fine legions, Dolabella Syria. Above all, Antony was consul, and his possession of Caesar's state papers and access to his private fortune were additional powerful cards which he knew how to play, to extend patronage and build a following. And before the end of April it was common knowledge that he would exchange Macedonia for Gallia Cisalpina and Comata, while transferring to his new command the vital Macedonian legions.[33]

Octavian was at Apollonia on the Albanian coast when he heard of Caesar's murder. He lost no time in reaching Brindisi, where he learned of his inheritance and adoption. He arrived at Naples on 18 April, about three days before Antony left Rome. Cicero was called on, and treated with becoming courtesy and deference; the nascent diplomatic skill found a good target for its early exercise.[34] By the beginning of May Octavian was in Rome, announcing his acceptance of Caesar's adoption and addressing the people by leave of Antony's brother, the tribune Lucius Antonius.

On 1 or 2 June Antony effected his exchange of provinces. On 5 June he got the Senate to fob Brutus and Cassius off with a commission to supervise corn supplies in Sicily and Asia. Cassius was indignant—he knew the difference between a favour and an insult.[35] Brutus hoped that the Games of Apollo on 7 July, celebrated at his expense as Urban Praetor though in his absence, would produce signs of support.[36]

---

[33] *ad Att.* XIV.14.4 (28/29 April).
[34] Ibid. 10.3, 11.2.
[35] Ibid. XV.11.1.
[36] Ibid. 11.2.

His hopes turned out to be dupes. Octavian saw his chance. With the assistance of wealthy friends, who included Matius and the financier Rabirius Postumus, he poured out money on the *Ludi Victoriae Caesaris* at the end of the month.[37] The loyalty of commons and veterans to Caesar's heir was manifested, and their enthusiasm heightened by the appearance of a comet which was seen as a sign of the reception of Caesar into the heavens as a god.

The inroads Octavian was making into Antony's Caesarian support led to the latter's engaging in further negotiations with Brutus and Cassius. He could see the danger of being caught between two fires. Cicero heard heartening news at Leucopetra on 6 August, but whatever was in the wind was dissipated in bickering and mutual recrimination. Antony was the prisoner of his own position; Caesar's soldiers compelled a formal reconciliation with Octavian. The Senate was induced to grant Brutus and Cassius the unmilitary provinces of Crete and Cyrene. Before the month was out, Brutus had left Italy, though Cassius still dawdled. Meanwhile, Cicero returned to Rome.

Antony summoned a meeting of the Senate for 1 September, at which he himself presided. Cicero absented himself, pleading weariness after a long journey; he had no appetite for a meeting whose main agendum was the voting of additional divine honours to Caesar. Antony attacked him furiously, threatening to send men to pull his house down over his head to compel his attendance.[38] Next day Antony had left Rome, and the Senate met again under the presidency of Dolabella.

This time Cicero came, and delivered his *First Philippic*, a restrained and thoughtful speech untarnished by cheap abuse and scabrous taunts. He reviewed the course of events since March, praising Antony for his early statesmanlike moderation. He saw the first of June as the day when Antony began to change for the worse; thereafter the Senate was treated with despite, armed force paraded, Caesar's memoranda and notebooks exploited shamelessly for patronage and

[37] Ibid. 2.3. [38] *Phil.* 1.12–13.

gain.[39] On 1 August Piso had been a lone consular voice in the Senate, with no one to support him; what he had urged Cicero does not say, but he speaks generously of his old *bête noire*.[40] His tone towards Antony is one more of sorrow than of anger. Criticism of his recent behaviour is balanced by an appeal to his honour and sense of duty.[41] No gauntlet is flung down, no vendetta started. The whole speech is a clear appeal to re-establish the compromise of March. It could not be done, because of the new factor that had entered the calculations: yet in the whole speech Octavian's existence is ignored, his name never mentioned. Antony's response was to hurl a violent attack at Cicero in the Senate on 19 September.[42] Cicero was not there to hear it (the Senate did not see him again till late in December, when he came back with a vengeance). Evidently Antony was shaken by Cicero's re-appearance and the attitude he had adopted, coming on top of Piso's independent stand on 1 August; he now had two senior and influential consulars ranged against him and working on opinion, reminding him of the insecurity of his position.[43]

Antony decided it was high time he made his loyalty to Caesar plain to the world. To a statue of Caesar he added the inscription, 'The Good Father of his Country': *Parenti Optime Merito*. As Cicero wrote to Cassius early in October, this was a deliberate slap in the face for the 'liberators' and their sympathizers. On 2 October Antony's bitter enemy the tribune Tiberius Cannutius called him publicly to account to explain his action; Antony obliged, with abuse of the 'liberators', declaring that Cicero was the sinister influence behind both them and Cannutius.[44] But he could not delay

[39] Ibid. 1.6. It was Cicero himself who jokingly entitled his speeches against Antony 'Philippics': *ad M. Brutum* II.3.4. (To avoid confusion, I have retained the traditional numeration of the letters to Brutus. The latest Oxford edition—W. S. Watt, 1958—renumbers them, but gives the old numeration in square brackets.)

[40] *Phil.* 1.10.
[41] *Phil.* 1.27–8, 31–6.
[42] *Phil.* 5.19.
[43] Syme, *RR*, 123.
[44] *ad famm.* XII.3.1; Vell. Pat. 2.64.3.

much longer—the end of the year was not far off, and with it the end of his consular authority. He left Rome on 9 October for Brindisi to collect four of the Macedonian legions, meaning, as Cicero thought, to lead them to Rome,[45] but in fact preparing to wrest the Cisalpina from Decimus Brutus.

Everything suddenly started happening at once. On 25 October Cicero heard from Servilia that Scaptius had arrived with secret news from Brutus, which she would pass on as soon as she had it. She had also heard from Caecilius Bassus in Syria: the legions at Alexandria had mutinied, and were inviting Bassus to come; Cassius was also expected there. Relating all this to Atticus, Cicero can scarcely suppress his excitement.[46] Things were moving fast: Syria might fall to Cassius, as well as Alexandria. Decimus Brutus had raised and trained new legions to add to the two he took over with his province. And in Antony's absence Octavian planned a coup of his own. He traversed Campania on a recruiting drive: personal magnetism, the name of 'Caesar', money, and promises produced results, including the invaluable veterans at Casilinum and Calatia. He wrote to Cicero to tell him what was happening:

He wanted to know [Cicero tells Atticus] whether to set out for Rome with 3,000 veterans, or hold Capua and block Antony's approach, or make for the three Macedonian legions which are marching up the Adriatic coast, who he hopes are his men. They refused to accept a bounty from Antony (so Octavian says), and jeered him, and walked away while he was trying to address them. And now Octavian offers himself as our general and looks to us to back him up. Anyway, I have argued that he should come to Rome. I think he will have the city rabble on his side, and even the decent people too, if he can win their trust. O Brutus, where are you? What a chance in a thousand you are missing! *This* indeed I did not foretell, but I thought something of this sort would happen.[47]

Just what Brutus could have done it is not easy to surmise. Octavian was a threat to Antony precisely because of his obvious appeal to the Caesarians. Had Brutus been in Italy,

45 *ad famm.* XII.23.2.
46 *ad Att.* XV.13.4.
47 Ibid. XVI.8.2.

and tried to take advantage of this division, almost certainly the young Caesar and Antony would have made common cause—the only conceivable alternative would have been a deal between Brutus and Antony, for an unholy alliance between Caesar's adopted son and Caesar's assassins was quite unthinkable. But a deal between Antony and Brutus would have cost Antony further loss of Caesarian support to Octavian.

Octavian fell in with Cicero's advice. On 4 November Cicero received two letters from him, asking him to go to Rome. Octavian was planning to work through the Senate, and wanted Cicero's help and counsel. But Cicero was circumspect: he was uneasy about Octavian's youth (he had only recently passed his nineteenth birthday) and puzzled about what was in his mind, and he was also far from writing Antony off as a powerful force to be reckoned with. At the same time he was afraid of missing something big. Octavian had considerable forces at his back, and Cicero thought he could perhaps get Decimus Brutus on his side.[48] For the time being, Cicero stayed on at Puteoli, relying for news on Atticus' letters from Rome. Octavian was writing to him every day,

to urge me to take a hand, come to Capua, save the Republic a second time, at least go to Rome at once. 'I blush to say No, yet I fear to say Yes.' But he has certainly shown, and is showing, a great deal of energy, and will reach Rome with a large force. Still, he is clearly only a boy. He thinks the Senate will meet forthwith—but who will attend? And if anyone does, who will risk a clash with Antony with everything so uncertain? He will perhaps be some protection on the first of January—or perhaps the battle will have been fought out before then. The boy is amazingly popular in the country towns. On his way to Samnium he visited Cales and stopped at Teanum. Wonderful receptions and enthusiasm! Would you have thought it? Because of this I shall be in Rome sooner than I had planned.[49]

Cicero meant to be in Rome on the twelfth, but swerved aside to avoid bumping into Antony, and settled down at Arpinum for a few days. Atticus was as usual urging caution: 'In reply to your letters . . . I do very much agree with you

48 Ibid. XVI.9.   49 Ibid. XVI.11.1 and 6 (5 November).

that if Octavian were to get much power the tyrant's measures would be a lot more firmly consolidated than they were
at the Temple of Tellus, and this would be to Brutus'
disadvantage. On the other hand, if Octavian is beaten,
you will find Antony intolerable, so you can't know which to
choose.'[50] Cicero wrote this about 12 November. Two days
earlier Octavian's soldiers had grounded arms in the Forum.

But Cicero had been right—the Senate did not meet.
Cicero might have given a lead, but he was lurking at Arpinum. The tribune Cannutius did give Octavian a chance to
address the populace, but his talk about 'his determination
to match his father's honours' and dramatic gestures towards
Caesar's statue led Cicero, when he heard of it, to write:
'God save me from such a saviour!'[51] The veterans had no
stomach for a fight against fellow Caesarians, and numbers of
them drifted away. Their disconsolate leader took himself
off to Ravenna and resumed the task of recruiting, soon
establishing a base at Arretium, where his friend Maecenas
was powerful. Thither, having weighed the toil of husbandry
against the attractions of military life and the gain it offered,
many of the veterans drifted back to him.[52]

Antony hurried back from Brindisi, where he had had
trouble with his troops, who had been tampered with by
Octavian's agents. The Senate was summoned for 24
November: the consul meant to punish Octavian's high
treason by having him declared a public enemy. But the
consul was diverted. The Martian Legion, one of those from
Macedonia which was marching up the Adriatic coast,
declared for Octavian and turned to join him. Antony intercepted their march, but failed to win them back. The Senate
met after dark on the 28th. A consular was ready, said Cicero,
with a motion against Octavian all prepared, but Antony
did not take it; another Macedonian legion, the Fourth,
had gone over to Octavian.[53] Antony changed his tack:
Lepidus was to be flattered by a special decree, Crete and

[50] Ibid. XVI.12.1, 10.1, 14.1.
[51] Ibid. XVI.15.3.
[52] Appian BC 3.42.
[53] Phil. 3.20. The unnamed consular was pretty certainly Fufius Calenus.

Cyrene were taken away from Brutus and Cassius, Macedonia was allotted to Antony's brother Gaius, who was one of the praetors. Next day he set out northwards: Decimus Brutus presented fewer problems than Octavian; he was one of Caesar's assassins and Caesar's legionaries would fight against him without demur. Before the year was out, he had settled down to besiege Decimus at Mutina (Modena). The war which Cicero had so long expected had at last begun.

Marcus Brutus was unfair to Cicero when he wrote to Atticus: 'We fear death and exile and poverty too much. For Cicero, so it seems to me, these are the ultimate evils, and so long as he has people who will give him what he wants and make much of him and flatter him, he is not the man to spurn servitude, provided it is honourable servitude—always supposing that there can be any honour in total and utter disgrace.'[54] This was to see part of Cicero, not the whole man. He was a curious amalgam of vices and virtues, strengths and weaknesses. Abject self-pity, a wary concern for his own skin born of bitter experience, and flashes of sober realism were intermixed with immense self-esteem and ebullience and a sense of a high calling which could lead him to courageous—often impetuous—action. After the Ides of March he could have run for cover and barricaded himself behind his books, to emerge in due course when the battles were over to make his peace with and lend his tongue and pen to the ultimate victor. But a genuine sense of duty towards his country and a deep thirst for personal glory—it is not easy to tell where the one stopped and the other began—battled with his hard-learned caution, and drew him spasmodically but steadily closer to involvement. Antony appreciated this, which is why he attacked him on 19 September to try to cow him into silence; Cicero was the one man who stood a good chance of giving to the scattered opposition the leadership it lacked and firing it with his oratory and spirit. But Antony's attack did not scare Cicero off; it set him to composing a reply, that model of vitriolic

[54] *ad M. Brutum* I.17.4.

diatribe which we know as the *Second Philippic*. Atticus tried to turn his friend's thoughts to the writing of history, and cautioned him 'neither to lead the van nor bring up the rear'.[55] But it was all in vain. Late in November, or early in December, this monument of invective was given to the world.[56] Partly a defence against Antony's charges, it moved to a vicious attack on Antony's private and public life. It is a tremendous piece of writing, of which it is hopeless to try to give the flavour—high class political scurrility is out of fashion these days. From Antony there could be no forgiveness. As Juvenal said, it would have been safer for Cicero if he had stuck to poetry:[57]

> 'O fortunatam natam me consule Romam!'
> Antoni gladios potuit contemnere, si sic
> omnia dixisset. Ridenda poemata malo
> quam te, conspicuae divina Philippica famae,
> volveris a prima quae proxima.

But the *Second Philippic* was not a speech, it was a pamphlet. The moment when Cicero stood forward to claim political leadership was still to come. He returned to Rome on 9 December. On the twentieth he reappeared in the Senate for the first time for three months. The consuls had left, Antony for the North, Dolabella for Syria. The new consuls were not yet in office. The tribunes summoned a meeting to discuss the provision of an armed guard so that the incoming consuls might be able to hold a meeting of the Senate on 1 January in safety. Cicero brushed this aside, or rather used it as a launching-pad for a speech, the *Third Philippic*, which dealt with the whole political situation. He ended by moving that Decimus Brutus be confirmed as governor of Cisalpine Gaul and Antony's appointment by the People be held invalid; and that Octavian, and the two legions which had gone over to him, be thanked and honoured for their loyalty to the constitutional government.

[55] *ad Att.* XVI.13B.2 (11 November); XV.13.1 (25 October).
[56] Copies were sent to Atticus and Brutus, and it is reasonable to suppose that many others read it too. See Rice Holmes, *The Architect of the Roman Empire*, 198–9.
[57] Juvenal *Sat.* 10. 122–6.

Cicero himself saw 20 December as the occasion when he threw his cap into the ring. In the *Fifth Philippic* he described it as the day on which he began the task of rebuilding the Republic (*ieci fundamenta rei publicae*), and he used the same phrase in a letter to Quintus Cornificius in March 43.[58] Clearest of all is his declaration to Trebonius early in February:

On the first occasion on which it was possible for the Senate to meet freely after Antony's disgraceful departure, I recaptured that spirit which I used to have in the old days, which you and that splendid patriot your father always talked of and loved. The tribunes had convened the Senate for 20 December, meaning to put another matter before it; but I embraced the whole condition of public affairs, and reviewed it searchingly, and more by moral force than by argument took hold of a dispirited and tired Senate and called it back to its traditional duty and courage. That day, and the energy of my delivery, first gave back to the Roman People the hope that liberty might be recovered. As for myself, since that day I have not allowed a moment to pass without my not only thinking about what has to be done, but actually doing it.[59]

Trebonius was an old friend, but perhaps even through the English the reader can detect a stiffness of diction and manner which is inescapable in the Latin of the original. It reminds us that we suffer a heavy blow as we move forward to follow the fortunes of Cicero's 'fight for the Republic'. Over one hundred letters survive from December 44 to July 43. Cicero's correspondents are numerous and important; they include Marcus and Decimus Brutus, Lepidus, Cassius, Plancus, and Pollio. But they do *not* include Atticus. The last surviving letter to him belongs to the middle of November 44, containing *inter alia* Cicero's decision to publish to the world his breach with Dolabella (who apart from his other many and grave shortcomings had persisted in refusing to pay back Tullia's considerable dowry) and a statement of his intention to come to Rome now since he

---

[58] *Phil.* 5.30; *ad famm.* XII.25.2.

[59] *ad famm.* X.28.2. Trebonius never read this letter. He had been murdered by Dolabella at Smyrna a week or so before Cicero wrote it. (Antony had a lower opinion of Trebonius' father than Cicero had; he called him 'a buffoon', '*scurra*': *Phil* .13.23.)

thinks it ought to be safe to do so.[60] The loss is irremediable. To these other correspondents Cicero never wrote with the frankness and freshness and carelessness which are the hall-mark of the Atticus letters; the reader can always sense that something is being held back, that we do not see the whole man.

Adsum igitur: with these words Cicero closed this last letter to Atticus, as if answering to his name as the Senate-roll was called.[61] And in the Senate on 20 December he outlined his programme for action. Antony still had eleven days of his consulship to run. Putting the programme into effect had to wait for the meeting of 1 January, when Hirtius and Pansa would be consuls. What Cicero wanted there is no doubt: a prompt and formal declaration that Antony was a *hostis populi Romani*, a rebel in arms against the lawful government without rights or standing or authority. He spelt this out plainly in his *Fourth Philippic*, delivered to the people later on 20 December to advise them of what was happening and instruct them how to understand it; by agreeing to his proposals about Decimus Brutus and Octavian and his legions the Senate had that day, by implication if not in so many words, adjudged Antony to be no consul but an outlaw, a *hostis*. We are back in the heady days of that other Decem-ber nineteen years earlier: the people are warned of the massacre and pillage which had threatened them, and Cicero draws a specific parallel between Antony and Catiline (he throws in Spartacus, too, for good measure). But they need have no fear; Cicero knows what to do, and will once again prove the saviour of his country from a bloodthirsty and treacherous brigand.[62]

The debate that opened on 1 January went on for four anxious days, Cicero's contribution being the *Fifth Philippic*. Fufius Calenus opened the debate—he was Pansa's father-in-law, which accounts for this honour—with advice to take no intemperate steps. He proposed sending a mission to Antony,

[60] *ad Att.* XVI.15.1.
[61] Ibid. 15.6.
[62] *Phil.* 4.1–5, 15.

telling him to withdraw from Cisalpine Gaul, to remain 200 miles from Rome, and to submit to the authority of consuls and Senate. Cicero was, of course, violently opposed to such a move; he launched another long attack on Antony's misdeeds, urging that it was ridiculous to send an embassy to such a man, and quite inconsistent with the decisions the Senate had reached on 20 December. He secured most of what he wanted. The armies of Decimus and Octavian were recognized as legitimate, with provision for bounties and in due course land-grants. Very important too, was the decision that all governors should continue to hold their provinces until the Senate should decide otherwise—which secured Decimus' position. As for Octavian, the Senate went further than Cicero proposed, and on the motion of Servilius Isauricus agreed that he should become a member of the Senate and be charged to co-operate with the consuls in the operations against Antony with the rank of propraetor; he was also to be allowed to stand for the consulship ten years earlier than the normal legal age (which meant, still thirteen years ahead). But Calenus' mission was approved and three consulars appointed to carry it out: Lucius Piso, Marcius Philippus, and Servius Sulpicius Rufus.[63]

Once again, we must be careful not to let Cicero's words deafen us to other arguments. Antony had been given his command in the Cisalpina by the vote of the Roman People; it could not properly be taken away from him by the Senate. Yet the Senate was ordering him to stay outside his province. Octavian had raised an army privately, without *imperium*, without public authority, and marched it to Rome. He was now uniquely made a member of the Senate without having ever submitted himself to the suffrage of the Roman People— a precondition which years earlier Cicero himself had held both desirable and necessary[64]—and his army and his command were legalized. This was what Cicero had been after; the plan which we first saw stirring in his mind six months earlier was now at full maturity. The 'Octavius' of

---

[63] *Phil.* 5, *passim*; Dio 46.29; Augustus *Res Gestae* 1; *ad famm.* XII.22.3.

[64] *pro Sest.* 137. Syme, *RR*, 167–8.

April has become the 'Caesar' of the *Third* and later *Philippics*, even *Caesar meus* in a letter to Decimus in January.[65] Octavian was to be the lever which would prise Antony away from Caesarian support and hence from power. The tool could then itself be discarded. Brutus was later insistent that this was a terribly dangerous game to play. But so long as Hirtius and Pansa were alive it was not so risky as it became once they were both dead. The crafty and experienced consular foresaw little difficulty in outwitting a callow nineteen-year-old. His tactics are pithily summarized in the famous jingle (he did not deny authorship) which was to cause him considerable embarrassment when someone repeated it to Octavian: *laudandum adulescentem, ornandum, tollendum*—the young man was to be lauded, applauded, and then discarded. Of course Cicero was taking a risk, but so too was Octavian; neither could afford *not* to. Antony could not be beaten by Cicero without Octavian's help, nor by Octavian without Cicero's.[66]

However, the voices of caution were for negotiation and compromise if it could be achieved. Men remembered the price paid six years earlier for intransigence and refusal even to try to negotiate. Winter compelled a delay in any serious fighting in North Italy. Perhaps the three consulars could secure that it would never begin at all. If not, enough had been done to provide for action should it prove necessary.

Having set his hand to the plough, Cicero showed amazing energy. He stood at the centre of a disparate and far-flung complex, which it was his self-imposed task to co-ordinate and direct. Pollio in Spain, Plancus in the Comata, Lepidus in Provence controlled armies of vital importance: all old Caesarians, none of them party to the assassination, they could easily come to make common cause with Antony (as in the end they did). Decimus Brutus must be heartened and informed about what was going on elsewhere; Quintus Cornificius with his legions in Africa must not be neglected;

---

[65] Above, p. 283, n. 12; *ad famm.* XI.8.2.

[66] The jingle: *ad famm.* XI.20.1. Cicero's acceptance of authorship: *ad famm.* XI.21.1.

and of course the 'liberators' in the East, Trebonius and Marcus Brutus and Cassius, were of central importance. All these men were separated by vast distances. Letters might take anything from ten days to two months or more to go to or from Rome, and were often in danger of being intercepted. Hence they were usually working in the dark, with out-of-date information about what was going on elsewhere; Rome too was sadly behind in its knowledge of what was happening even in North Italy, let alone in Spain and Gaul and Syria. But Cicero wrote to them all, tirelessly and doggedly demanding and vouchsafing news, rallying and heartening, cajoling and bullying. It was an astonishing display of energy and will. For a few months the Republic of Rome became a sixty-three year old consular, long withdrawn from public affairs, with a pen in his hand and a tongue in his head, sometimes elated, often discouraged, but always relentlessly concentrated on the task in hand: the destruction of Antony and the restoration of normal government. With his attention focused on that present task, it is no wonder that he seldom raised his eyes to look beyond it. This was both his strength and in the end his weakness. If asked, he would surely have replied that bridges needed to be crossed only when one came to them; the future would have to wait, for unless the present were secured there would be no future to worry about.

The Cicero we see in these last months is a Cicero we have always known, but fined down to the essentials and revealed to us with a greater clarity and economy of line than before. This was not a man who ever really thought long or deeply or constructively about the central political, economic, social, and administrative issues of his lifetime; it was not his style. The new man from a country town who had scaled the dizzy heights of the consulship by his own brilliance and application was the last man to be displeased with the view to be had from the summit. For him the Republic could never be 'an empty name, a mere word', as Caesar called it.[67]

---

[67] Suetonius *DJ* 77: *Nihil esse rem publicam, appellationem modo sine corpore et specie.*

What could be grander or more satisfying than to be an influential and respected consular, whose advice and counsel were sought by his equals, whose opinions were listened to by a thoughtful and appreciative Senate, whose eloquence was courted eagerly and applauded fervently in the courts, whose speeches swayed and instructed the assemblies, whose *gratia* and *auctoritas* spread to every corner of the world? These were the glittering prospects he had once rolled round his tongue with a loving and proprietorial anticipation: *locus, auctoritas, domi splendor, apud exteras nationes nomen et gratia, toga praetexta, sella curulis, insignia, fasces, exercitus, imperia, provinciae.*[68] These were the rewards of which he had been cheated and which now after the grey years of bitterness and humiliation seemed at last again to be within his grasp.

We must not be misled by treatises like the *de republica* and the *de legibus*.[69] 'Le vrai Amphitryon c'est l'Amphitryon où l'on dîne'; the true Cicero is the writer of the letters, or—if we must seek him in his treatises—the author of works like the *de Oratore*, the sincere admirer and hopeful successor of the great *principes civitatis* of his boyhood and young manhood. What interested him was not policy but politics. He was the archetypal conservative with a small 'c'. Politics fascinated and absorbed him: the day-to-day play of affairs, the gossip, the intrigue, the formal pageant, the clash and colour of personalities. Policies bored him; he could talk airy generalities as well as the next man and a good deal better than most, but that was as far as it went. His *moderator rei publicae* was an emperor without a suit of clothes, a sort of powerful and amiable watchdog whose task was to ensure that the politicians could carry on as usual without the disturbing threat of violence or revolutionary change. His *concordia ordinum* was not so much a policy as a practising politician's device for maintaining things broadly as they were. Cicero and Caesar were chalk and cheese. Caesar was a radical; his mind ranged easily and comprehensively over problems of ecumenical and historical proportions, his imagination supplied daring new solutions, his temperament spurred him to

[68] *pro Cluentio* 154. Above, p. 83.   [69] See Appendix C.

implement them; Caesar was a proud patrician who traced his ancestry back to the ancient kings of Rome, and beyond them to Aeneas and his goddess-mother Venus. Cicero's origins were humbler, his field of vision narrower. The Republic Caesar scorned was his ideal.

Unless we keep hold of this basic truth about Cicero, we shall never understand these tremendous last months, the power of the dream that drove him on, the final despair. 'In this correspondence, and nowhere else, do we find such a combination of noble sentiments, chastened eloquence, and perfect taste, qualities which are indicative of the Roman *gravitas* at its very best.' Thus Purser of the letters of this period, in admiration; but a little earlier he had correctly observed that 'questions of principle are substituted for questions of policy'.[70] The noble sentiments and chastened eloquence were an elegant but flimsy screen hiding a total nakedness of policy. Cicero had no policy to offer that could cement together men of such disparate interests and ambitions and character as Pollio and Plancus and Lepidus, Cassius and Decimus and Marcus Brutus, Hirtius and Pansa and above all Octavian. He had no policy to offer because no such policy was possible; the best that could be hoped for was a temporary and uneasy entente to cripple Antony. Even that was only partially realised, and quickly collapsed; but, granted it had succeeded (as it might well have done had Hirtius and Pansa not been killed), it would not have been the end of troubles but the beginning of new ones.

This is not to condemn Cicero, or question his sincerity. Nobody can doubt his sincerity, and it is neither a crime nor a sin to be a conservative with a small 'c' and to take a delight in politics. But for all his literary and oratorical genius, and despite his political craft and pragmatism, Cicero was no statesman in the sense that men like Gaius Gracchus and Julius Caesar and Augustus were statesmen. His Republic was dead, but the devoted lover refused to accept that the object of his love was cold and lifeless. The Republic had died old and sick and tired, but in his eyes it remained green and

[70] Tyrrell and Purser, VI.xxvii.

fair. New concepts were needed, new methods, new approaches, new assumptions; yet all he could offer were the old discredited ones, as he strove to hold back the advance of history with a palisade of words, desperately trying to inspire in a younger and disillusioned generation the reverence and affection which he had himself for the old outmoded ideals.[71] It is all noble and exciting and moving; but it was quite useless. Cicero's Republic had come to an end over forty years earlier, when Sulla first led a Roman army on Rome, and Cicero was eighteen years old. He was born too late. His spiritual home was the Rome of Cato the Elder or Scipio Aemilianus; in the Rome of Antony and Octavian he was an obstructive anachronism.

[71] Dolabella may be cited as an example of the more realistic approach of a younger man. He advised Cicero in June 48 (*ad famm.* IX.9.2–3): *Satis factum est iam a te vel officio vel familiaritati, satis factum etiam partibus et ei rei p. quam tu probabas; reliquum est, ubi nunc est res p., ibi simus potius quam, dum illam veterem sequamur, simus in nulla.* [Cf. p. 262, above.]

XIII

ARMS AND THE MAN

CICERO addressed the People in his *Sixth Philippic* on 4 January with words of instruction and encouragement. He deplored the mission to Antony as a criminal waste of precious time; the only good he saw in it was that Antony's intransigence would silence the voices that spoke timorously or treacherously for delay and compromise. The mission would achieve nothing.[1] Later in the month came the *Seventh Philippic* in which he came back to the same topic in the Senate, deploring the dampening effect the delay was having on public enthusiasm, the shoddy manoeuvres of Antony's friends, the talk of possible counter-proposals. There could be no peace with Antony, the nettle had to be grasped: 'If he refuses to obey the Senate, it will not be the Senate that has declared war on him, he will have declared war on Rome.'[2]

Cicero's confident prediction was justified. Antony refused to bow to the Senate's demands. Only two of the envoys returned at the beginning of February. (Sulpicius was dead, a victim of the rigours of his wintry journey: Cicero pronounced what was virtually his funeral oration in the *Ninth Philippic*.) They brought back not surrender but counter-proposals.[3] Antony asked for rewards for his soldiers and security of tenure for those veterans already allotted lands by himself and Dolabella; confirmation of his own and Caesar's dispositions; no enquiry into monies handled by himself as consul; an amnesty for his supporters. Cisalpine

[1] *Phil.* 6.5 and 16.
[2] *Phil.* 7.1–3, 9–12, 21, 26.
[3] *Phil.* 8. 25–8.

Gaul he was prepared to give up, but he must retain the Comata with six legions for the next five years.

Antony's proposals were not unreasonable, given his evident need to look to his own security. With good will and mutual confidence, something might have been worked out. But good will and mutual confidence were not to be had. Cicero described the conduct of Piso and Philippus as 'disgraceful and scandalous', and Antony's demands as 'intolerable'.[4] Another *Philippic* was duly delivered, the *Eighth*. Feeling ran high in the Senate, but Antony was not without supporters there, headed by Fufius Calenus. The word 'war' (*bellum*) was avoided, and instead, on the motion of Lucius Caesar, supported by Calenus and Pansa, it was agreed to declare a *tumultus*, which we may roughly gloss as 'a state of emergency'. Cicero poured scorn on such terminological niceties, and tore Antony's proposals to pieces, clause by clause. He finished by proposing that an amnesty be offered to all Antony's men who surrendered before 15 March; anyone hereafter joining Antonius should be held to have acted *contra rem publicam*.[5]

Just about now, startling news arrived from Marcus Brutus. In the autumn he had been at Athens; amongst those who joined him there were young Marcus Cicero and the obscure son of a freedman, Quintus Horatius Flaccus. Gathering money, arms, and troops, he proceeded to Macedonia, was recognized by the governor Quintus Hortensius as his legitimate successor, and added more troops to his forces. By the end of the year he had pocketed the legions of Publius Vatinius, governor of neighbouring Illyricum. When Antony's brother Gaius arrived early in January he was brusquely seen off and bottled up in Apollonia. Cicero was overjoyed, as he wrote to tell Cassius: though there was no certain news at Rome yet, it was rumoured that Cassius himself was in Syria with some considerable strength. 'If you hold what we think you hold, the Republic is shored up by powerful supports; from the western coast of Greece to

---

[4] *ad famm.* XII.4.1.   [5] *Phil.* 8.1 ff, 25–8, 33.

Egypt, we are fortified by the authority and armed forces of true patriots.'[6]

In fact, Cassius was moving with even greater speed and success than Brutus. On his arrival in Syria, the two Caesarian generals, Staius Murcus and Marcius Crispus, who were besieging Caecilius Bassus at Apamea, joined him with their six legions, as did Bassus with his legion; the total was brought up to eleven when Aulus Allienus, who was coming up from Egypt with four legions to join Dolabella, joined Cassius instead. Cassius gave the news to Cicero in a letter sent from Syria on 7 March.[7] About the same day, Cicero himself was writing to Cassius to tell him of his failure to get the Senate to recognize him as governor.[8] In January, en route to his province of Syria, Dolabella had passed through Asia and executed Trebonius at Smyrna. A thrill of horror greeted the news, and even Calenus proposed that Dolabella be judged a public enemy and his property confiscated. Cassius' successes were only rumoured at Rome—certainly the full strength of his position was not guessed at. The Senate decided that, once Antony had been beaten, Hirtius and Pansa should draw lots for Syria and Asia. Cicero then tried a direct appeal to the people in support of Cassius' claims, but was frustrated by Pansa's opposition and the caution of Cassius' family.[9]

However, as Cicero insisted in his earlier letter to Cassius in February, the issue of the war still hung on Decimus at Mutina.[10] Here, the attitude of Lepidus and Plancus was crucial. If they brought up their legions in support of Antony, or offered him a refuge if defeated, all would be lost. Cicero had no time for the shifty Lepidus. But Plancus was the son of an old friend, and as governor of Gallia Comata and consul-designate along with Decimus for 42 he had an obvious interest in safeguarding his prospects.[11] To Plancus, most

[6] ad famm. XII.5.1.
[7] Ibid. 11.1; cf. ad M. Brutum I.5.2.
[8] ad famm. XII.7.1; cf. Phil. 11.30.
[9] Phil. 11.15 and 32; ad famm. XII.7.1.
[10] ad famm. XII.5.2.
[11] Ibid. X.4.1. Before his death, Caesar had made certain dispositions in the

polished of all Cicero's correspondents, letters speed frequently. As far back as September 44 he had been assured of support, gently reminded of his consular prospects, and warned about Antony.[12] Again in December the same theme, the same delicate flattery, a friendly hint that Plancus has in the past enjoyed something of the reputation of a 'time server'—not that Cicero himself had shared this view.[13] Plancus promised Cicero that he could be relied on.[14] In December Decimus Brutus is assured of Cicero's efforts in his behalf; so too Cornificius in Africa.[15] We also have a letter written at this time by Quintus Cicero, expressing his profound distrust of Hirtius and Pansa; 'You would not credit the things I know those two did in Gaul; that ruffian Antony will seduce them to his side by companionship in their vices unless firm steps are taken to prevent it.'[16] Experience here turned out to be a poor guide, for the consuls proved loyal and reliable.

Towards the end of January, Cicero writes again to Decimus with encouraging news of the progress of the levy. (This is the letter in which Octavian has become *Caesar meus*.) And in a letter to Cornificius, he makes explicit his own claim to be 'the leader of the Senate and People of Rome'.[17] His main complaint is about the consulars (Calenus and Philippus and Piso chiefly): 'We have outstanding consuls, but disgraceful consulars; the Senate is courageous, but it is the men of most junior rank who are the most courageous.' The people, indeed the whole of Italy, are behaving splendidly, and Cicero has become a popular hero.[18] Tirelessly, his pen

---

light of his impending departure to fight the Parthians. These were, as we saw, confirmed after his assassination. Dolabella was to succeed him as consul for the remainder of 44; Hirtius and Pansa were designated consuls for 43, Decimus Brutus and Plancus for 42. Certain provincial governorships were also allocated in advance.

[12] Ibid. X.1.
[13] Ibid. X.3.3.
[14] Ibid. X.4.3.
[15] Ibid. XI.6.3, XII.22.3–4.
[16] Ibid. XVI.27.2.
[17] Ibid. XI.8.2, XII.24.2.
[18] Ibid. XII.4.1 (early Feb. 43, to Cassius).

flows on. Trebonius in Asia (dead now, but Cicero did not know it) is kept in the picture: 'the boy Caesar is outstanding, and I have great hopes of him.'[19]

In the first days of February, Cicero's high hopes seemed abundantly justified. The mission to Antony had collapsed; Plancus was loyal; Lepidus was lying low; Hirtius and Octavian were on their way to relieve Decimus; Marcus Brutus' successes in the Balkans were striking and complete; the rumours about Cassius were encouraging. Victory seemed only a matter of time. A measure of the discomfiture of the compromisers was the decision of the Senate about Macedonia on the receipt of Brutus' dispatches. Calenus as usual spoke first and argued against confirming Brutus' usurpation of the province. Cicero replied with his *Tenth Philippic*, ending with a grandiloquent motion that Brutus

as proconsul should protect, defend, guard, and keep safe the province of Macedonia, Illyricum, and the whole of Greece; that he should command the army which he himself has raised and organized; that for military purposes he should spend and levy any money which is the property of the state or can be levied; that he may borrow money for military purposes as he may see fit, and commandeer supplies; and that he should see to it that he and his army be held as near to Italy as possible.[20]

Brutus' illegal and violent usurpation of Macedonia was duly legitimized.

For the rest of the month winter still held up operations in North Italy. Early in March another attempt was made to break the deadlock: Piso and Calenus carried a motion to send a second mission to Antony. This time it was to consist of five consulars: Lucius Caesar, Piso, Servilius Isauricus, Calenus, and Cicero. It may come as a surprise that Cicero accepted nomination. The explanation is, as he admitted the next day, that he had been tricked into it.[21] Piso and Calenus had let it be assumed that Antony had now come to his senses; having got their mission accepted, however, they changed their tune about what was to be expected from, or

[19] Ibid. X.28.3.
[20] *Phil.* 10.25–6.
[21] *Phil.* 12.1.

offered to, Antony. Next day Servilius announced his un-readiness to serve; Antony's friends argued that the decision to send the mission was unalterable. Cicero would have none of this, delivered his *Twelfth Philippic*, joined Servilius in resigning—and the project collapsed.[22] A few days later, on 19 March, Pansa set out to join Hirtius and Octavian. During February their forces had lain in cantonments along the line of the Via Aemilia, south-east of Antony's major depot at Bononia (Bologna). They now moved forward, by-passing Bononia, which was abandoned. While they paused to await the arrival of Pansa with his four new legions, An-tony drew the noose tighter round Mutina. Everything hinged on Decimus' ability to hold out against superior numbers and resources until Antony could be brought to battle by the relieving armies.

But it took a long time for news of events in Rome and Italy to arrive in the provinces. Pollio in Spain felt particu-larly cut off; the normal delays were increased by the watch being kept by both Lepidus and Antony, whose agents examined all letters. Apart from any messages that arrived by sea, he was left in the dark. On 16 March he wrote to tell Cicero that he had received no instructions from the consuls until at last a letter had arrived the previous day in which Pansa exhorted him to place his army at the Senate's dis-posal—'But since Lepidus was coming out with public declarations and writing off to everybody that he was on Antony's side, this really put me in a very serious dilemma; for by what routes could I bring my legions through his province if he were hostile? Even supposing I got so far, am I expected to take wings and fly over the Alps, which are held by his troops?' He went on to express his surprise that Cicero had not written to tell him whether he could best serve the Republic by staying in Spain or bringing his army to Italy—striking proof of the ascendancy Cicero had ob-tained even over old Caesarians like Pollio.[23] Pollio's warning about Lepidus cannot have reached Cicero for several weeks, by which time events had moved well ahead; not that Cicero

[22] *Phil.* 12.3–6.   [23] *ad famm.* X.31.

ever had much hope of Lepidus. Plancus and Lepidus were apparently working for a peaceful settlement. On 20 March Cicero wrote to both of them. To Plancus he is courteous, once again reminding him how his own prospects are bound up with the restoration of normal government. But to Lepidus he is curt to the point of rudeness: 'So in my judgement', he concludes, 'you will be wise to abandon this peacemaking role, which finds no approval from the Senate or the people or any loyalist.'[24]

Behind these letters to Plancus and Lepidus lay dispatches which had arrived from them urging a settlement with Antony. Pansa had left Rome: the Senate was convened by Caecilius Cornutus, the Urban Praetor. Servilius Isauricus spoke out against further delay, and he was supported by Cicero in the *Thirteenth Philippic*. Peace with Antony and his satellites, with a bloodthirsty and treacherous gang of ruffians and degenerates—impossible and unthinkable and a confession that everything the Senate had so far done was wrong! He commends the loyalty of Plancus and Lepidus, with a word of admonishment to the latter to moderate the arrogance of his tone when addressing advice to the Senate.[25] Nothing new here. Much more interesting—and entertaining —is the second half of his speech.[26] Cicero produced a letter from Antony to Hirtius and Octavian—Hirtius had passed it on—and went through it, clause by clause, with his own comments and glosses. This was vintage Cicero: the trim figure with the noble head, broad brow, sensitive lips, and beautifully disciplined and modulated voice, weaving with his sure barrister's skill a net of gay and murderous wit, coarse raillery, pained incredulity, destructive logic, and moral fervour. It was a rich feast that he laid before the Senate in his last but one surviving public speech.

He needed to be at his best. Antony's letter, 'spirited, cogent, and menacing',[27] contained far too much truth for comfort. He bluntly told Caesar's old lieutenant and Caesar's adopted heir that they were playing into the hands of Brutus

[24] Ibid. X.6, X.27.   [25] *Phil.* 13.4 ff, 13 ff.
[26] *Phil.* 13.22–45.   [27] Syme, *RR*, 173.

and Cassius, working for the triumph of the Pompeian party, marching behind the Eagles of the old fox Cicero. He himself chose Dolabella, not murderers like Trebonius and Decimus Brutus. That he expected to win over Hirtius and Octavian we cannot believe; he was speaking over their heads to a wider audience: unhappy Caesarians in the Senate, Caesar's loyal veterans, everybody in Italy who dreaded the revival of the old Republic. For them he had a further warning. Plancus and Lepidus were on his side.[28]

Plancus like Pollio was on the fringe of things, with Lepidus and his legions between him and Italy. About the same time (20 March) as Cicero was writing to him, he penned another dispatch to the Senate to explain his dilatoriness. While recognizing the importance of an early declaration of loyalty, he had judged precipitate action unwise. He had had to make sure of the loyalty of his legions, who were being solicited by Antony with rich promises. He had had to sound out his neighbouring governors to try to concert action rather than spark off ruinous fighting. He had had to strengthen his army and recruit auxiliaries. But now all was ready, and he was at the disposal of the Republic, to hold firm or go where he was ordered, to hand over his province and army or turn the whole brunt of the war on himself.[29] The letter reached Rome on 7 April; but reports of Plancus' loyalty had arrived before it, and on 30 March Cicero had written to tell him how delighted everyone was.[30]

The moment of decision was approaching at Mutina, where Decimus was rumoured to be in grave difficulties.[31] Marcus Brutus wrote to Cicero on 1 April. Gaius Antonius was now his prisoner. He has heard of Cassius' success in Syria, but leaves it to Cicero to judge when the time is ripe to divulge the news. His own eyes were turned towards Dolabella in Asia, and he asked for money and reinforcements. He

[28] *Phil.* 13.22 ff.

[29] *ad famm.* X.8.

[30] Ibid. X.10. For the date of the receipt of Plancus' dispatch: X.12.2.

[31] Ibid. XII.6.2; *ad M. Brutum* II.1. On the authenticity of the collection of letters to Brutus, see Tyrrell & Purser, VI.cxxv–cxxviii.

ended by commenting on the conduct of Cicero's son, who was with him in Macedonia, in the warmest terms.[32] This letter reached Cicero on the eleventh, and he replied next day, advising that Gaius Antonius be held in custody until the fate of Decimus was known, and scotching any hopes of reinforcements or money. The news about Syria was already public knowledge, but despite Brutus' apprehensions that it might cause a turnabout in the attitude of the Caesarians Cicero was not too perturbed.[33]

Cicero was having to shuffle and deal his cards with enormous skill. Antony's letter to Hirtius and Octavian reveals how difficult the trick was. Certainly a large number of Caesarians were not prepared to acquiesce in Antony's assumption of the mantle of Caesar. Their reasons were various: simple distrust or distaste, fear for their own prospects, ambition for advancement. Victory for Antony must mean rich rewards for his adherents at the expense of other people's hopes. Octavian's interests, too, would not be served by a walkover for Antony. On the other hand they could all easily be alarmed if the threat of victory for the 'liberators' and the total eschewing of Caesarism became too apparent. Brutus realised this. He kept his army out of Italy; though its intervention at this point might have decided the issue, it might equally have solidified opposition. Hence his worry about the effect that might be produced if the news of Cassius' progress in the East were released too soon. And Cicero had to bear it in mind too, and shape his letters to his various correspondents accordingly. Thus Cassius can be told that if Decimus Brutus goes under he and Marcus Brutus are the only hope, the final redoubt.[34] Such sentiments were never for expression to Plancus or Lepidus. What Cicero was saying in his letters to Octavian we do not know. He was writing to him frequently at this time, but only a few fragments remain to tease us—the chance selection of a later

---

[32] *ad M. Brutum* II.3. For young Cicero's exploits, see also Plutarch *Brutus* 24.
[33] *ad M. Brutum* II.4.
[34] *ad famm.* XII.6.2.

grammarian interested in Ciceronian literary usage.[35] But here, too, had they survived, we should surely read nothing of the exploits and hopes of Cicero's Pompeian friends. Then, too, there were the legions themselves, not the new levies but the veterans. Throughout they showed a commendable reluctance to fight a civil war; they had even less taste for being led to fight and die against Caesar's friends and loyal supporters in behalf of Caesar's assassins.[36] Here lay the central importance of Octavian in Cicero's planning. Antony's charges sounded much less convincing when the commanders of the armies moving to fight him included, not only loyal lieutenants of Caesar like Hirtius and Pansa, but young Gaius Julius Caesar himself.

Antony, too, was an old lieutenant of Caesar's, and he had not served under him for so long and learned nothing. As the relieving armies neared their final concentration, he struck first. What followed we learn from a vivid account which Servius Sulpicius Galba wrote to Cicero the next day.[37] Early on 14 April,[38] Antony detached a compact striking force from his besieging army outside Mutina: two veteran legions, two praetorian cohorts, auxiliaries, and a strong force of cavalry. His aim: to intercept and destroy Pansa and his four raw legions on the last stage of their march to link up with Hirtius and Octavian. He meant to ambush them at the little town of Forum Gallorum, which stood astride the Via Aemilia some ten miles south-east of Mutina. Unluckily for Antony, Hirtius showed that the author of the eighth book of the *de Bello Gallico* could fight battles as well as write about them. The previous night, guarding against just such a move by Antony, he had detached the veteran Martian Legion and two praetorian

---

[35] Collected in Tyrrell and Purser, VI. pp. 352-7; and in vol. III of the Oxford Text of the *Epistulae* (W. S. Watt, 1958), pp. 157-61.

[36] Syme, *RR*, 180-1.

[37] *ad famm.* X.30. Galba, the regular commander of the Martian legion, had been temporarily seconded to Pansa. (He was the great-grandfather of the future Emperor Galba, the first to break the monopoly of the Julio-Claudians.)

[38] For the dates, see Tyrrell and Purser's commentary on *ad famm.* X.30, and Rice Holmes, *The Architect of the Roman Empire*, I.208-9.

cohorts (his own and Octavian's) to shepherd the Pansans in.

The Martians had no love for Antony—they remembered his summary execution of some of their comrades at Brindisi the previous year in an attempt to restore discipline. When Antony showed his cavalry, they went straight at them. Negotiating some marshland and woods, they and the praetorians formed into battle-line of twelve cohorts. Now Antony sprang his trap and launched his twenty-two cohorts from cover. The battlefield was bisected by the raised causeway of the Via Aemilia. On the government right, eight of the ten cohorts of the Martian Legion drove Antony's Thirty Fifth Legion back half a mile, but Antony sent his cavalry round their flank to take them from the rear. Galba spotted the danger and began to pull back, throwing out a screen of skirmishers. Meanwhile, on the causeway itself, Octavian's praetorian cohort was having a hard time of it against Antony's two. And the weak left wing—comprising only the other two Martian cohorts and Hirtius' praetorians— was pressed steadily back by Antony's Second Legion. But Antony's trap had been sprung on veterans, not raw levies. There was no rout, but a controlled retreat to the camp which Pansa had been busily fortifying. There the veterans, backed by the four green legions, stood their ground. Abandoning his attempt to carry the camp, Antony broke off the fight and began to withdraw. He had left it too late. Once again Hirtius showed what he was made of. Leaving Octavian to hold the base camp, he had marched to join the battle at the head of twenty veteran cohorts.[39] Towards evening they collided with Antony's victorious but tired twenty-two, and routed them. Antony got clear, but his losses were crippling. The government forces had been roughly handled, but the Eagles of both Antonian legions and all the ensigns of their constituent formations were captured—a measure of the completeness of their defeat. For all that, Galba closed his

[39] Viz., the Fourth and Seventh Legions (*Phil.* 14.27). Like the Martians, the Fourth was a former Macedonian legion which had deserted Antony for Octavian the previous year. Hirtius himself carried the Eagle of the Fourth into battle.

letter with an understatement worthy of a Wellington: *Res bene gesta est.*

A week later, on 21 April, Antony was forced to fight a second battle outside Mutina. Pansa lay dying of the wounds he had received in the earlier battle. Hirtius again led his troops to victory, but this time he did not live to exploit it. The siege was raised. Antony, beaten and bruised but not broken, rallied his survivors and headed doggedly west. Whether Lepidus or Plancus would give him refuge and new strength must now have seemed highly dubious.

News of Forum Gallorum did not reach Rome until the twentieth, six days after the battle. Indeed, there had earlier been rumours of an Antonian victory (presumably spread by stragglers from the first half of the engagement); Antony's sympathizers planned a seizure of power, and rumours were abroad that Cicero was going to seize the *fasces*, the symbols of supreme authority.[40] Meanwhile on 16 April Cicero was writing to Brutus justifying his policy of building up Octavian, and once again counter-attacking Brutus' criticism by pointing out that it would not have been necessary had Antony been got rid of along with Caesar. Five days later he could write again, with the victory known and his own policies vindicated not by argument but by events. The consuls had behaved excellently, as he had so often assured Brutus they would, and Octavian too—though Cicero does pause to wonder whether the young man will henceforth prove quite so docile as he has been. Once again the idol of the crowds, Cicero has been enthusiastically mobbed and escorted with shouts and cheers to the Capitol. The letter closes with a clear hint to Brutus to consider whether the time has not come to abate his over-clement attitude; of course Brutus must make up his own mind, but ought he not now to execute his prisoner Gaius Antonius?[41]

The same day, Cicero delivered the last of his surviving speeches, the *Fourteenth Philippic*. Servilius had moved that a

[40] *Phil.* 14.15 ff; *ad M. Brutum* I.3.2.
[41] *ad M. Brutum* II.5, I.3.1–3.

public thanksgiving be decreed, the *sagum* having first been formally abandoned.[42] Cicero however argued that the *sagum* must be retained until Mutina had been relieved. The proposal for a *supplicatio* he welcomed, as signalling the acceptance of what he had always argued—that Antony and his troops were *hostes;* for a public thanksgiving had never been, could never be, decreed for a victory over fellow-citizens. He moved that it should last for the enormous period of fifty days, since three men shared the victory, and that the three men be entitled *Imperatores*. In conclusion, he paid a sincere tribute to the men of the Martian Legion; urged the erection of a public monument; and moved that the Senate reaffirm its promises to reward its soldiers for their courage and loyalty.

News of the victory at Mutina, and of the deaths of Hirtius and Pansa, had reached Rome by 27 April, and was passed on that day by Cicero to Marcus Brutus, together with the information that Decimus and Octavian were in pursuit of Antony.[43] By now the final formal step had been taken of declaring Antony and his followers *hostes*. It was on the twenty-seventh, too, that the Senate settled down to tying up the loose ends of the war. Cassius and Marcus Brutus were commissioned to make war on Dolabella. Cicero's mind was turning to peaceful preoccupations, soliciting support for his son's election as a *pontifex*.[44] Already the process of putting into operation the third member of Cicero's trio of gerundives was afoot, and the young Caesar was to be quietly discarded. Decimus was voted a triumph, Octavian only an ovation. The legions of the dead consuls were put under the command of Decimus. Sextus Pompeius, whom Cicero had already publicly commended on 20 March, was about this time given the supreme command at sea. On top of this, Octavian was excluded from the commission appointed to distribute

---

[42] The *sagum* was a woollen cloak assumed by the Senate in times of *tumultus* in place of the toga, as a mark of the emergency. It had been assumed when the *tumultus* was decreed at the end of February after the failure of the mission to Antony: above p. 308.

[43] *ad M. Brutum* I.3.4. This is a separate letter from I.3.1–3.

[44] Ibid. I.5.1–3.

lands to the troops. All this, together with the commissions to Cassius and Marcus Brutus, underlined the truth of what Antony had written to Octavian: 'Whichever of us two falls, the Pompeians will profit.'[45]

But Octavian and Antony declined to resign themselves to what seemed to Cicero and many others the inevitable. Antony had too much courage and resilience, Octavian too much sense and persistence. When Cicero told Marcus Brutus on 27 April that 'the remnants of the enemy are being pursued by Decimus and Octavian', he was telling him what he *thought* was happening. The reality was otherwise. On 29 April Decimus wrote that he was hoping to prevent Antony's making another stand in Italy; but he was worried about Ventidius and that 'weathercock' (*ventosissimus*) Lepidus with his numerous first class legions.[46] So far Decimus' pursuit had scarcely been rapid, only twenty miles west of Mutina seven days after the battle, but his men were tired and weak after the long siege. On 5 May he writes again from Dertona, well over a hundred miles further west, complaining of delays and obstructions and sniping at Octavian's ambitions (he had his eye on one of the vacant consulships). Antony has been padding out his forces with freed slaves and anyone else he can lay his hands on; worse than that, Ventidius has joined Antony. Octavian is unco-operative: 'If only Caesar had listened to me and crossed the Apennines, I would have driven Antony to such straits that he would have collapsed through sheer lack of supplies without any fighting. But one can't give orders to Caesar, and Caesar can't give orders to his army.' Meanwhile, Decimus badly needs money to pay his seven legions; he has already run himself and all his friends into debt up to their ears.[47]

Ventidius Bassus was a colourful character. As a child, he had been captured by Pompeius Strabo at Asculum during the course of the Social War and led captive in his triumph.

[45] Ibid. I.15.9; *ad famm.* XI.14.2, 19.1; *Phil.* 13.50; Dio 46.40; *Phil.* 13.40. (Of course, as consul-designate Decimus was senior by far to Octavian.)
[46] *ad famm.* XI.9.1.
[47] Ibid. XI.10.

From obscurity he advanced to become Caesar's Quarter-master General. He had now raised the equivalent of three legions, mainly in Picenum. His experience in commissariat and transport work stood him in good stead as he boldly set off to march round the barrier of the government forces to join Antony, swinging wide across the Apennines. Had Octavian followed Decimus' advice, Ventidius could have been brought to bay before a junction was effected. As it was, his reinforcements were crucial for Antony; for Ventidius himself came the well-earned reward of a praetorship and a suffect-consulship before the year was out.[48]

On 6 May, Decimus wrote from north-east of Genoa. From captured papers he had found that Antony was writing to Lepidus, Pollio, and Plancus. He was now thirty miles behind Antony, too close for comfort. Antony feinted south to Pollentia (Pollenza) with his cavalry. Decimus took the bait and swung in the same direction, but Antony was not at Pollentia; he was heading across the border into Lepidus' province.[49]

These three letters from Decimus all reached Cicero on the same day in the third week of May. He was deeply disturbed: 'It seems that the war, so far from being stamped out, is blazing fiercely.' At Rome, people had imagined that Antony was a helpless fugitive, broken in spirit, his men a straggle of frightened and weaponless runaways. There was now a revulsion of feeling, and the air was full of criticism of Decimus' sluggishness.[50] This was very unfair to Decimus. He had been authorized to attach the veteran Fourth and Martians to his own command, but they refused to serve under one of Caesar's murderers. Cicero's *laudandum adulescentem, ornandum, tollendum* had been repeated to Octavian, increasing his unwillingness to help destroy Antony as a preliminary to his own discarding. The veterans were indignant at the exclusion of Octavian from the lands commission and hostile to Cicero as being responsible. And

---

[48] On Ventidius, see Syme, *RR*, Index *sub nomine.*
[49] *ad famm.* XI.13.1–4.
[50] Ibid. XI.12.

Octavian had refused to hand over to Decimus at least one (possibly all four) of Pansa's new legions.[51] Still, 25 May found Decimus surprisingly hopeful. He was uncharacteristically confident of Lepidus, adding that in any case the three armies of himself, Octavian, and Plancus ought to be enough. Cicero must not be alarmed: 'If you take the bit between your teeth, my life on it that the whole lot of them won't be able to stand up to you once you start speaking!'[52] This reached Cicero on 6 June, and cheered him enormously.[53] He was soon to be disabused. But we must now go back to follow what had been happening in Gaul.

Plancus wrote to Cicero at the end of April, with warm and almost filial gratitude. He had already crossed the Rhone en route for Mutina when he heard the news of the defeat of Antony and the relief of Decimus (about 27 or 28 April). Assuming that Antony would head for Gaul, he halted and stood ready to take him on. Meanwhile, he continued to work hard to keep Lepidus in line.[54] About 12 or 13 May, he wrote again, in high spirits. Lepidus had promised to work with him to bar Antony's route or fight; Plancus was to bring his own army to join Lepidus, who was weak in cavalry, Antony's strongest arm. Plancus concurred: he thought his own presence and that of his army would stiffen the uncertain loyalty of Lepidus' troops (who included Caesar's famous Tenth Legion). So he crossed the Isère on 9 May. Learning that Antony's vanguard had reached Forum Julii (Fréjus), he sent on his own brother Gaius with four thousand horse, himself following by forced marches with his four legions and the rest of the cavalry. Antony was boxed in: Plancus and Lepidus before, Decimus behind.[55]

The view that Lepidus must now realize the folly of linking himself with a defeated Antony was also held at Rome, as

---

[51] Ibid. XI.19 and 20. (It is not absolutely clear what is the implication of XI.20.4: *De exercitu quem Pansa habuit legionem mihi Caesar non remittit.*)

[52] Ibid. XI.23.

[53] Ibid. XI.24.

[54] Ibid. X.11.

[55] Ibid. X.15.

Cicero wrote to Decimus on 19 May.[56] On 15 May the situation was that Antony himself had reached Forum Julii, with Lepidus twenty miles to the west. Lepidus had further strengthened his promise to Plancus by sending him a hostage in the shape of his freedman Apella.[57] But by the end of the month Lepidus had shown his hand, and Plancus had pulled back.[58] Plancus set out what had happened in a letter dated 6 June. He was within forty miles of Antony and Lepidus when on 29 May Lepidus joined Antony, and the two advanced on Plancus. They were within twenty miles when Plancus was informed of their approach; he at once fell back across the Isère and destroyed the bridges, to give himself time to recover and rendezvous with Decimus. Cicero was to see that Octavian, or failing him some other commander, should be sent to help with strong reinforcements.[59] Ironically, Plancus was writing to tell Cicero about this dramatic turn of events on the very day that Cicero was sending off his own buoyant letter to Decimus, the point from which we started.

Plancus was not the only man on whom Lepidus practised his deception. About 18 May he promised Cicero his loyalty to Senate and Republic; on 22 May he wrote to thank him for refusing to credit the wicked rumours being spread by his enemies.[60] When on 30 May he wrote officially to magistrates and Senate to inform them of his *volte-face*, he put the responsibility on his troops and their reluctance to fight fellow-citizens.[61] This was no doubt partly true, but he need not have acquiesced so tamely; his legate, Juventius Laterensis, ashamed of this betrayal, fell on his sword.

Antony 'was himself again'. The prey had eluded Cicero's grasp, and lay secure on the borders of Italy recruiting his strength as his enemies began to fall into disarray. He had not yet won, but the odds had swung dramatically back in his favour.

---

[56] Ibid. XI.18.2.   [57] Ibid. X.17.
[58] Ibid. X.21.1–6.   [59] Ibid. X.23.
[60] Ibid. X.34.2, 34.3 (these are in fact two separate letters).
[61] Ibid. X.35.

Decimus had heard the worst when he wrote for the last time to Cicero on 3 June, a brief and anxious letter.[62] He needed money; legions must be brought from Africa and Sardinia, Marcus Brutus recalled to Italy. The latter had replied to Cicero's letter of 21 April with a forthright re-affirmation of his constitutionalist principles; Gaius Antonius was not going to be executed until he had been formally tried and sentenced by the Senate or the People. And Cicero should not be so ready to grant to himself that licence which he condemned in his opponents.[63] Brutus was still far from happy about Octavian and his ambition for one of the vacant consulships:

I fear that your 'Caesar' will think that he has been raised so high by your decrees that if he is made consul he will never come down again. If Antony could use the apparatus of monarchy which another man had left behind to try to make himself king, what do you suppose will be in the mind of a man who thinks that he can covet any positions of power he chooses, on the authority not of a dead tyrant but of the Senate itself? That is why I shall withhold my praise for your success and foresight until I begin to be convinced that 'Caesar' will be content with the extraordinary honours he has so far received. 'So,' you will say, 'you mean to put me in the dock for another man's crime?' Most certainly I do, if you could have prevented it.[64]

This was written on 15 May. Four days later, Brutus transmitted to Cicero the news that Dolabella had been beaten by Tillius Cimber and King Deiotarus, and was now in flight. Cassius, too, had set off for Cilicia to deal with him on 7 May. On 2 June, young Lentulus Spinther (son of the consul of 57) reported from Pamphylia that Dolabella had been refused admittance to Antioch and had made off in the direction of Laodicea; his troops were deserting in droves, and Cassius was only four days' march away.[65] The hopes Cicero had expressed to Cassius in February had come true,

[62] Ibid. XI.26.

[63] *ad M. Brutum* I.4.1–3.

[64] Ibid. 3–6. (Again, this and the preceding are two separate letters.) Brutus in his letters would not give Octavian his name of 'Caesar' even by the implication of calling him 'Octavianus'. He calls him 'Octavius', and only uses 'Caesar' when he is ironically mimicking Cicero.

[65] *ad famm.* XII.15.7 (an official dispatch).

and the eastern half of the empire was in the hands of Pompeians 'from the western coast of Greece to Egypt'. Meanwhile, a day later but over 1,500 miles away, Decimus was appealing for reinforcements and the recall of Marcus Brutus to Italy. But Brutus was marching, not westward to deal with an Antony he supposed was finished, but eastward to join Cassius and deal with a Dolabella he thought might still be dangerous. And Cicero sat helpless at Rome, at the nerve centre of communications which travelled always too slowly and arrived always too late.

Since the battles of Forum Gallorum and Mutina, Octavian and the Senate had steadily drifted apart. The deaths of the consuls worked in his favour. Veterans who had followed Hirtius and Pansa against Antony were not so ready to follow Decimus. They looked in preference to the young Caesar, who had avoided any embarrassing links with his adoptive father's murderers, and had been lavish in his distributions and promises to Caesar's old soldiers from the very first.[66] Had Hirtius survived Mutina, and pursued Antony with Decimus' army added to his own legions, Antony would almost certainly have been finished off, and Octavian's freedom of manoeuvre dramatically curtailed. But now Octavian could turn his eyes towards a consulship— as Marcus Brutus guessed that he would. Indeed, Appian recorded (on what evidence we do not know) that Octavian privately suggested to Cicero that the two of them should hold the consulship together for the rest of the year. It could be that there was something in it; Cicero was a natural possibility for a second consulship, and his age and experience would make admirable partners for Octavian's extreme youth. There had been rumours of Cicero's wanting the *fasces* after Forum Gallorum. And when Brutus wrote from Macedonia on 15 May, he added in a postscript that he had just been told that Cicero had become consul—though his tone suggests that he was not prepared to accept the report as reliable.[67] The silence of the contemporary letters of

[66] *ad Att.* XVI.8.1 (Nov. 44).
[67] Appian *BC* 3.82; *Phil.* 14.15; *ad M. Brutum* I.3.2, 4.6. (The names of

Cicero is far from decisive, for so delicate a matter would have been reserved for Atticus' ear, and no letters to him survive. On the other hand, it is easy to see how the story could later have been invented. The verdict on it must remain 'non-proven'.

Octavian bided his time, and remained with his troops near Bononia while Decimus set off after Antony. During June he was being encouraged to count on the consulship by certain individuals (who are not named); Cicero wrote to warn him to abandon such extravagant hopes, and reproved Octavian's relatives (clearly, Marcius Philippus and Gaius Marcellus), and openly denounced these intrigues in the Senate.[68] Brutus had always been deeply distrustful of Octavian's ambitions and potential, and a stern critic of Cicero's policy in this respect. The fullest expression of this criticism is found in two letters which he wrote, one to Cicero and the other to Atticus. The first is usually dated July 43, but an earlier date in December or January suits better: regardless of date, however, Brutus makes his position plain. He has read part of a letter from Cicero to Octavian:[69]

Your expressions of loyalty towards me and your concern for my safety [he tells Cicero] in no way surprised or moved me. Such expressions I am well used to, they are even trite. But I was distressed, as distressed as I could possibly be, by what you had to say about me and my friends in that section of your letter to Octavius. The way in which you thank him for his services to the Republic, so ingratiatingly and deferentially commending our safety to him, you make it perfectly obvious that the tyranny has not been got rid of, all we have is a new tyrant in place of

Caesar and Cicero were finally linked in the consular *fasti* in 30, when young Marcus as suffect-consul for the last third of the year was the colleague of Octavian. Coincidentally, he was in office as consul when the news of Antony's death was announced at Rome: Dio 51.19.)

[68] *ad M. Brutum* I.10.3.

[69] Ibid. I.16. Tyrrell and Purser (VI. no. 864, note) date this letter to mid-July 43. Watt (Oxford Text, vol. III) ventures '? July'. But the whole tenor of the letter seems to fit far better a date around January when Antony was *in armis* in the North and still a potent and undefeated threat. The objection that after receiving such a letter Cicero could never again have written to Brutus in such friendly terms as he did between January and July I find quite unconvincing; he had to put up with a lot of brusque rudeness from Brutus (as years earlier from App. Claudius and Cato), yet he still came back for more.

the old. Read your own words, and dare to deny that these appeals of yours are not the appeals of a subject to a king! . . . Seek no favours for me from your Caesar, nor for yourself either, if you will take my advice.

This is only a sample from a very long letter; but the flavour is the same in the letter Brutus wrote to Atticus in June:[70]

I know that everything Cicero has done was done with the best of intentions. But he seems to me to have done some things—how shall I put it?—'clumsily', though the most sensible of men, or 'from interested motives', though he did not hesitate for his country's sake to incur the enmity of Antony at the height of his strength. I do not know what to write to you, save this one thing: Cicero has stimulated rather than repressed the boy's greed and lust for unbridled power. . . . Let Octavius address Cicero as his 'father', let him seek his advice in everything, let him praise him and thank him; Cicero will none the less discover that words are quite the opposite of deeds. . . . Long life to Cicero by all means, if he can secure it, cap in hand and subservient—if he feels no shame for his years and his honours and his past glories! For my part, I shall wage war on the reality itself, that is to say on autocracy and extraordinary commands and tyranny and naked power which wishes to place itself above the laws; nothing will deter me.

Cicero answered these criticisms in a long letter to Brutus in July. He pointed out that he had moved decrees in favour of Decimus and Plancus, even Lepidus, as well as Octavian. He quoted Solon:

Solon said that a country was held together by two things, rewards and punishments. No doubt there is a proper limit to both, as to everything else, a golden mean. However, this is not the place to debate so large a question. But I do not think it out of place to explain what I have been aiming at during this war in the motions which I have moved in the Senate. After Caesar's death and the memorable Ides of March, you have not forgotten, Brutus, what I said about the omissions of you and your friends, about the size of the storm which loomed over the Republic. Through you, a great scourge had been destroyed, a great sore removed from Rome, you had won heroic fame: but the apparatus of monarchy was transferred into the hands of Lepidus and Antony. . . . I was perhaps headstrong, you others perhaps more prudently left the city you had liberated and ignored the enthusiastic support which Italy was offering you . . . This much I do say: this young lad Caesar, to whom we owe it that we still survive, is like a river that flows from the spring of my counsels,

[70] *ad M. Brutum* I.17. For the date, see Tyrrell and Purser, ad loc.

if I am to be frank. I secured him honours—none of them, Brutus, undeserved, none of them unnecessary. When first we began to reclaim our freedom, when as yet the heroic courage of Decimus or Marcus Brutus had not bestirred itself for us to recognize it, when our whole protection lay in that boy who had torn Antony from our throats, what honour ought not to have been decreed to him?[71]

Cicero had had to try to be all things to all men. He had to hold on to the army commanders, Plancus, Pollio, Lepidus (if it could be managed), and Octavian, and the consuls Hirtius and Pansa; that is to say, to loyal Caesarians and to Caesar's heir himself. Otherwise, Antony could not have been resisted. He was therefore forced to advance their interests, secure them honours, encourage their hopes, while soft-pedalling his own support for and approval of the acts and plans of Caesar's assassins—even put in pleas and excuses for them. It was all very well for Brutus to complain; he had quitted Italy, done nothing to oppose Antony directly or succour Decimus at Mutina. The original fault had lain with him and the other 'liberators'; they had sown the wind, and now they were reaping the whirlwind; they had destroyed the tyrant, but not the tyranny—as Brutus himself confessed. Cicero had not murdered Caesar and spared Mark Antony; it was not his fault that Hirtius and Pansa had died, and so upset his calculations. Of course, his policy had been risky, but no policy could have been anything but risky short of quiet and submissive acquiescence in Antony's usurpation of power. Secure in Macedonia, Brutus could afford to cavil. Decimus and Plancus saw Cicero's activities in quite another light. But even they were not identical in their views. Decimus asked for legions from Africa to come, and Marcus Brutus. Plancus asked for legions from Africa, and Octavian. There was no pleasing everybody.

The sands were fast running out for Cicero. In his last surviving letter to Marcus Brutus (27 July), he repeated his

[71] Ibid. I.15.4–7. Cicero did not make the point, but we should not let it pass, that Brutus' own command in Macedonia and that of Cassius in Syria were both 'extraordinary' and had both been won by force. But he does get in one nasty dig at Brutus, which shows how annoyed he was by Brutus' sniping: *cedebas enim, Brute, cedebas, quoniam Stoici nostri negant fugere sapientis.*

appeal that he return to Italy with his army. Money, urgently needed to keep the troops loyal, was desperately short; a special property tax had been imposed, but the fraudulent returns of their resources made by the rich meant that it realized scarcely enough to satisfy two legions. Cicero reiterated his hope that he would be able to control Octavian, but his words are flaccid and carry no conviction.[72] Next day, Plancus sent from Gaul the last datable letter in the whole correspondence.[73] From Pollentia, Decimus had edged warily northwards to join Plancus by about the end of June. Between them, the two consuls-designate mustered fourteen legions, but only four were veterans. The vast difference between seasoned troops and raw recruits was a commonplace: 'Just how little reliance can be put on green troops in battle', writes Plancus, 'we know from all too frequent experience.' He and Decimus needed reinforcements, the veteran legions of the African army and more immediately those of Octavian, before they could venture a decisive battle. (Significantly, *he* does not suggest sending for Marcus Brutus.) He himself was bombarding Octavian with appeals, and Octavian kept promising that he would join him without delay. But Plancus could see that his gaze was fixed elsewhere. Plancus shared Cicero's feelings towards Octavian and had approved his policy;

But the fact that Antony is alive today, that Lepidus has joined him, that they have formidable armies, that they have hopes, that they are ready to dare—all this they can put down to Caesar's account. I will not go over well-trodden ground again; but from the moment he gave me his personal promise that he was on his way, if only he had been as good as his word the war would have been finished by now . . . What calculations of his own, what advice from others have lured him away from such certain glory, vital to his own security as well, and set him dreaming of a couple of months of a consulship, frightening everybody to death and making the most fatuous demands, I simply cannot fathom.[74]

Octavian had no change of heart; he wanted the consulship, even a truncated consulship of a few months' duration.

[72] Ibid. I.18.1, 4–5.   [73] *ad famm.* X.24.   [74] Ibid. 24.3–7.

And Pollio now showed his hand. Wary as ever, he had written to Cicero on 8 June that his three legions were reliable, that he was resisting the overtures of Lepidus and Antony, and that he himself was still loyal: he awaited orders from Rome.[75] Much has been made of the integrity of Pollio;[76] like that of Marcus Brutus, it was not always and everywhere in evidence. Pollio had been sitting on the fence, screening his devious ambivalence behind convenient pleas that nobody was telling him what to do. But once he saw who was winning, he needed no telling; he left his province and with two of his legions joined Antony and Lepidus.

No reinforcements had arrived from Africa; the enemy's army was now stronger by two veteran legions. Octavian became consul; Decimus was stripped of his command. Plancus saw the hopelessness of it all, and Pollio won him over to Antony. Decimus set off to join his friends in the East by a roundabout route, but he was betrayed to Antony, who demanded, and received, his head. He paid for it with his own brother's life. Gaius Antonius was executed in reprisal on the orders of Marcus Brutus; even for him, the game had now become too rough to insist any longer on scrupulous observance of the rules, and he began to allow himself 'that licence which he had condemned in others'.

For the last few months of Cicero's life, we have to do without the help of letters or speeches. It matters very little. He had lost all influence over events, and was swept helplessly along. In July, four hundred of Octavian's legionaries had appeared in Rome to demand the consulship for their commander. The Senate refused: Octavian was too young. The army demanded that Octavian lead them on Rome: he fell in with their demand. Early in August, a second Caesar crossed the Rubicon, this time with eight legions. Two veteran legions had at last landed from Africa, and together with a legion of recruits they were posted to defend the capital. Predictably, they all went over to Octavian. Cornutus, Urban Praetor and acting head of state, com-

---

75 Ibid. 32.4–5.   76 Syme, *RR*, 5, etc.

mitted suicide. A last rumour flickered in this time of many rumours: the Martian and Fourth Legions had mutinied against Octavian. It was false.

On 19 August, the future Augustus, himself nineteen, became consul along with his cousin Quintus Pedius.[77] The sentence of outlawry on Dolabella was revoked—small good it did him, for he committed suicide when Laodicea fell to Cassius. A special court was established to try Caesar's murderers. Octavian left for the north, and in his absence (but with his approval) the sentences of outlawry on Antony and Lepidus were also rescinded. These two now entered Italy, with superior forces, but forces they could not use to fight Caesar's heir and avenger; in any case, the three had other people to fight than each other—that could wait.

At the end of October, the three generals met near Bononia, and two days of conferring and bargaining resulted in agreement to divide the western provinces between themselves and jointly to prosecute the war against Brutus and Cassius in the East. Money and land were needed to satisfy their soldiers, and old scores were waiting to be settled; both objects were to be realized by widespread proscriptions and confiscations. These were at first kept secret, but an initial list of seventeen names was immediately sent to Pedius in Rome. Cicero's name was on it; Antony had seen to that.

Cicero had left Rome for his villa at Tusculum. His last surviving words, a fragment of a letter to Octavian, had been written to thank the young consul for allowing him to go: 'Your grant of leave of absence to myself and Philippus gives me a twofold pleasure, for it implies forgiveness for what is past and indulgence for the future.'[78] Brutus was right, it seemed, after all: Cicero did 'fear death and exile and poverty too much'.[79] His brother Quintus and young Quintus were with him; they rashly ventured back to Rome to get money to help them get away to join Brutus in Macedonia,

[77] The month's name was still, of course, *Sextilis*.
[78] Tyrrell and Purser, VI.354, no. 15. Watt (Oxford Text, vol. III) 160, no. 23B.
[79] *ad M. Brutum* I.17.4.

but were betrayed and executed. Cicero himself could still have escaped, and he did actually take ship, but then put back to land again and repaired to his villa between Formiae and Caieta, whence he had sailed to join Pompey six years before. Why he did not take his chance again now, we cannot say. Perhaps he remembered all the misery which that earlier voyage had led to; perhaps he was too upset by the deaths of his brother and his nephew; he surely shrank from the prospect of hearing Brutus say 'I told you so'. He was a broken man, once more dashed abruptly from the golden pinnacle of success to the black pit of failure. Above all, he was tired and old, 'too old to go again to his travels'. Exile he still feared, but death no longer held any terrors. When his pursuers came up with him, he quietly gazed at them with his left hand grasping his chin in a characteristic gesture, and then bent his head for the sword-stroke. The hands that had written the *Second Philippic* were cut off too, and sent to Rome. There, after they had been treated with indignity by Fulvia (widow of Clodius and now wife of Antony and soon to be mother-in-law of Octavian), head and hands were displayed on the Rostra—'at sight of which', wrote Plutarch, 'the Romans shuddered, for they seemed to see there not the face of Cicero, but the image of Antony's soul.'

Cicero died on 7 December 43, one month short of his sixty-fourth birthday. We can read accounts of his death by Plutarch, Livy, and Appian. Livy judged that he bore none of his misfortunes as a man should have, except his death; yet, for Livy, he was still 'a great and memorable man, and it would need a Cicero to praise him fitly'. 'We all have our faults,' wrote the Elder Seneca; 'Cato lacked moderation, Cicero constancy.' Quintilian noted the same defect, but tempered it: 'Some think him lacking in fortitude, but this charge he himself answered very well when he said that he was timid, not in facing dangers, but in anticipating them; which he proved by his death, which he confronted with the most steadfast spirit possible.' Pollio, too, observed that he could wish that Cicero 'might have borne success with greater moderation and adversity with more constancy.'[80]

That Cicero only too often failed to exemplify in his own person that discipline and firmness which the Romans professed to recognize and admire in their great national heroes, it would be foolish to deny (although it ill became Pollio to point it out).[81] *Constantia* is not a perfect virtue, however, complete in itself. It could not have co-existed with Cicero's mercurial effervescence, his nervous brilliance, his quick sympathy, his gaiety and wit, and above all his inventive imagination and sensitive insight. The letters of Cato and Brutus would be a poor exchange for those of Cicero.

It is difficult to state baldly that Cicero's public career was a failure, for it was a failure only if judged at the very highest level. In many ways it was both brilliant and successful. From relatively obscure origins he rose to the heights of dignity and authority. For most of his life he was the unchallengeable master of public and forensic oratory. His consulship brought him fame and unprecedented honours. Throughout his political life he was a powerful factor to be reckoned with by friends and opponents alike. His prestige and influence with the settled classes of Italy were always important. He was unsurpassed as a moulder of public opinion. And his performance in the last twelve months of his life, when he established his remarkable dominance and led the forces which were opposed to Antony, was truly remarkable. His energy **and**, at the conscious level, his genuine love of country cannot fail to arouse admiration even in those who feel no sympathy for his objectives.

Yet, in the final analysis, he *was* a failure. After the year 63,

---

[80] Plutarch *Cicero* 47–8; Livy *frag.* 120; Appian *BC* 4.19–20; Seneca *Controv.* 2.4.4; Quintilian *Inst. Or.* 12.1.17; Pollio cited by Seneca *Suas.* 6.14–15. The whole of Seneca *Suas.* 6 and 7 contain much interesting material in assessment of Cicero.

[81] The Elder Pliny (*NH Praef.* 31) tells a story of how Pollio was composing declamations against Plancus which were to be published only after Plancus was dead and unable to reply. On hearing of this, Plancus simply remarked that 'only ghouls fight against the dead': *cum mortuis non nisi larvas luctari*. It was, I suspect, by confining his fighting to the dead that Pollio won his reputation for frankness.

nothing went right for him. Standing back and taking a broad view, it is easy to see how this happened. His own view was a blinkered one; he never penetrated to an understanding of the basic economic and social issues that cried out for remedy, and which were bound to continue to be a source of political instability until something was done about them. His estimation of himself was too high; his mastery of the spoken word was such as to bewitch not only his audiences but himself as well. *Facta verbis potiora*; but there was in Cicero too much of the scholar's weakness for solving problems in the study, too much of the advocate's preoccupation with argument. For all his moods of despair and disillusion, he was a natural optimist; and this optimism, fed by his quickness and versatility of intellect, encouraged him from time to time to acts of almost incredible rashness. Above all, for a man who purposed to be a controlling force in Roman politics, he lacked that *clientela* which was indispensable to such a role. He neither inherited one, nor acquired one; and he was never admitted into the inner circle of those who possessed them.

For Cicero, the year 63 was critical and decisive. Had his consulship fallen in a less exciting year, he might never have been lured into his later mistakes. He would probably have continued in his public career with less extravagant ambitions, and more easily have accommodated himself to compromise and a counselling role, an influential *consularis* without ambitions to be a *princeps civitatis*. But his immense success as consul seduced him into entertaining ideas above his real station, leaving him with the appetite for a controlling position without the basic means to satisfy it, either in the shape of widely based political support and connections or— to be honest—the intellectual and moral equipment for such a role. For the next twenty years, 'the glory of the Nones' was to hang around his neck like a millstone dragging him further and further down.

We may condemn Cicero or not, as we are inclined. We may be irritated by him, or charmed. We may be tolerantly contemptuous, or we may feel affection and even admiration

without shutting our eyes to his many and grave shortcomings. The verdicts will tell us more about the judges than
about the judged. We know far too much about Cicero to
have to rely on the judgement of others, even if those others
be his contemporaries; and about *them* we know quite enough
to be sure that they did not possess all the virtues he had
while sharing none of his faults. *Te totum in litteris vidi.*[82] If
something of 'the whole man' has been caught in this book,
the reader will need no outside assistance to make up his own
mind about a man whom we know more intimately than any
other man in ancient history.

[82] Quintus to Marcus: *ad famm.* XVI.16.2.

APPENDIX A

Some points in the chronology of the year 63

1. The Date of the Consular Elections

The usual date for the consular elections was July. There is no evidence that this was not the date originally fixed in 63. The *onus probandi* lies on those who would deny that the elections in 63 were fixed for July.

On Cicero's initiative, the elections were postponed after he had received information of Catiline's inflammatory talk about *miseri* and *calamitosi*: *Tum igitur his rebus auditis meministis fieri senatus consultum referente me ne postero die comitia haberentur ut de his rebus in senatu agere possemus.* The next day, Catiline made a spirited reply which elicited sounds of distress from his audience but no stern action: *congemuit senatus frequens neque tamen satis severe pro rei indignitate decrevit.* Catiline stalked out of the Senate in high spirits. Disturbed by all this, and knowing that already (*iam tum*) sworn supporters armed with swords were being introduced into the election place by Catiline, Cicero went down to preside at the elections with his bodyguard and breastplate: *his rebus commotus . . . descendi in campum.*

This is the account given by Cicero in public in late November and it is clearly authoritative (*pro Murena* 50–3). Obviously only a brief space of time elapsed between the date originally fixed and the actual holding of the postponed elections, a few days at most. Cicero talks of his proceeding to preside over the elections as following on the debate in the Senate on the day originally fixed, and following almost at once.

Against the view that all this took place in July, it has been argued:

(a) Plutarch (*Cicero* 15) in referring to the meeting at which the Senate passed the Ultimate Decree—a meeting which can be dated to 21 October (see below)—says that it was 'not long after' (οὐ πολλῷ δ'ὕστερον) the elections at which Silanus and Murena were returned as consuls in 62. It is argued that 21

October could not be described as 'not long after' a date in July, hence the elections must have been held later than July.

(b) The future emperor Augustus was born in 63. Suetonius (*Divus Augustus* 5) tells us that he was born in late September, 'on the ninth day before the kalends of October'. In a later chapter (94) he adds that on the day Augustus was born the Senate was debating 'the conspiracy of Catiline'. Rice Holmes argued (*The Roman Republic*, I.458–61) that since the date cannot be that of the meeting of 21 October when the Ultimate Decree was passed it must relate to an earlier discussion of Catiline's revolutionary plans or activities and must therefore relate to the discussion in the Senate about Catiline's *miseri* and *calamitosi* speech. That discussion took place on the day originally fixed for the consular elections. Hence the elections were originally fixed for a date late in September, and the postponed elections were held later than that.

It is theoretically possible that for some unknown reason the elections in 63 had been fixed for September and not (as was usual) July, but this evidence is nowhere near enough to establish it. There is no suggestion that the elections were fixed unusually late in any of our ancient sources, let alone any explanation why. Plutarch's 'not long afterwards' is too vague and fragile to build on; it might mean anything. As to Suetonius, there is not the slightest reason why the Senate should not have been discussing what he could loosely call 'the conspiracy of Catiline' on a number of occasions between July and October. The passage in question does not inspire confidence. Suetonius is telling stories about portents alleged to have preceded or attended or followed Augustus' birth. Augustus' father Octavius was kept away from the Senate because his wife was in labour. The absence was noticed, and a certain Publius Nigidius calculated from the hour of the child's birth that a world-ruler had been born. The whole thing reeks of *ex post facto* construction and no doubt Suetonius (who had a weak spot for this sort of nonsense) was merely repeating a well-embellished tale which added piquancy to the alleged prediction by a pregnant synchronism of a grave threat to the fabric of Roman government and society and the birth of the future architect of stability and social justice and order. For the inventors of such fairy-tales it would have been enough that in September 63 the Catilinarian business was very much in the air.

This being so, we may hold to a July date both for the originally scheduled and for the postponed consular elections.

23—c.

2. *The Ultimate Decree*

The *senatus consultum ultimum* authorizing the consuls to take
special measures for the public security is referred to by Cicero
in his First Catilinarian (4) when he says that 'this is now the
twentieth day since the decree was passed'. Asconius (5C) refers
to Cicero's pardonable habit of rounding off figures and says
that to be precise it was the eighteenth day and not the twentieth.
The First Catilinarian was delivered on 8 November. This fixes
the date of the Ultimate Decree to 21 October.[1]

3. *The Insurrection of Manlius*

Manlius openly raised the standard of revolt at Faesulae on 27
October. Fact and date were reported to the Senate by Lucius
Saenius who had had a letter from Faesulae. We should expect
Saenius' announcement to the Senate to have been made three
or four days after the event (Sallust *Catiline* 30).

4. *The Meeting in Laeca's House*

Cicero dates this in *pro Sulla* 52. It took place 'on the night which
followed the day after the nones of November' (the nones was
the fifth): that is to say, during the evening and night of 6/7
November.

5. *The Catilinarian Orations*

The *First* was delivered in the Senate on 8 November. This
follows from the fact that Cicero in referring to the meeting in
Laeca's house (evening 6 November) says it took place 'the night
before last'—*noctem illam superiorem* (*in Cat.* I.9).

The *Second* was addressed to the people the following day (*in
Cat.* II.12).

The dates of the *Third* and *Fourth* and of the affair at the Mulvian Bridge are not controversial.

6. *The Trial of Murena*

The internal evidence of the speech (cf. especially sections 79 and
84) shows that it was delivered (a) before the apprehension of
the conspirators at Rome and the debate on their punishment,
(b) after Catiline and Manlius had openly taken the field and
been declared public enemies. Catiline left Rome on the evening
of 8 November and after staying a few days near Arretium set off

[1] Or possibly 22 October, depending on whether the reckoning is inclusive
or exclusive.

for Manlius' camp with *fasces* and other consular insignia. News of this led to his being outlawed (Sallust *Catiline* 36). This should give a date for his outlawry just after the middle of the month. So Murena's trial falls between then and early December.

7. *Timetable of Events*

The main dates can be conveniently set out as follows:

July. Elections due but postponed. Senate discusses Catiline's inflammatory pre-election speech. No action taken. Elections completed.

21 October. Ultimate Decree passed urging consuls to take special measures.

27 October. Manlius in open insurrection.

1 November (approx). Senate informed of Manlius' move.

6 November (evening). Meeting in Laeca's house.

7 November (morning). Abortive attempt on Cicero's life.

8 November. First Catilinarian. Catiline leaves Rome (evening).

9 November. Second Catilinarian.

17 November (approx.) Catiline and Manlius outlawed.

Late November. Trial of Murena.

2/3 December (night). Arrests at Mulvian Bridge.

3 December. Examination of arrested conspirators in Senate. *Third Catilinarian.*

5 December. Fourth Catilinarian. Decision on conspirators.

These notes are deliberately brief, and avoid over-detailed scrutiny—which is often misdirected. For fuller discussions, see Rice Holmes *The Roman Republic*, I.458–70; Hardy, *The Catilinarian Conspiracy*, chapters V–VIII. I have merely set down the arguments I have myself followed.

APPENDIX B

The Debate in the Senate on 5 December 63

IN THE TEXT I have mainly followed Sallust's presentation of the debate. For all that one recognizes that he has heightened the effect and compressed or ignored many of the contributions, it is far and away the fullest, most informative, and most convincing account.

Apart from Sallust, and Cicero's own *Fourth Catilinarian* and his letter to Atticus of March 45 (*ad Att.* XII.21), we have reports of the debate from the following: Appian (*Civil Wars* II.5–6); Dio Cassius (XXXVII.35–6); Plutarch (*Cicero* 20); and Suetonius (*Divus Julius* 14). They are all in general harmony, but of varying texture and with some differences of detail.

Cicero wrote a lost work *On His Consulship* (*de consulatu suo*). This was certainly known to Plutarch, who refers to it specifically for information in connection with the story of the letters so mysteriously delivered to Crassus (*Crassus* 13). Some or all of the other authorities may have used it too. We know also of another now lost work by Cicero, a secret account of recent political history which he began in 59. He writes to Atticus in the spring of that year announcing his intention to compose it, and to reserve it for Atticus' ears alone; it is to be in the caustic vein of the Greek historian Theopompus, or even more savage (*ad Att* II.6.2). It is pretty certainly to this same work that Dio Cassius refers (XXIX. 10) in dealing with the year 57 when he speaks of a 'secret' work of Cicero's *de consiliis suis* (*On His Policies*) which contained 'terrible' things about Caesar and Crassus and others. Dio says it was so explosive that Cicero put it under seal and gave it to his son with instructions that it was not to be opened or published in Cicero's lifetime. The *de consiliis suis* was certainly used at first or second hand by the commentator Asconius (83C), who makes it clear that it contained damaging attacks on the behaviour and activities of Caesar and Crassus in 63 and earlier.

This being noted, we do not know how much (if anything)

either the *de consulatu suo* or the *de consiliis suis* had to tell later authors about the detailed course of the debate in the Senate on 5 December, nor whether any or all of them made use of it for this purpose.

Plutarch says that all who spoke after Silanus supported his proposal for the death penalty until Caesar's turn came. Cicero implies as much in his letter of March 45, though referring specifically only to Murena and the fourteen ex-consuls who followed Silanus. But Hardy (*Conspiracy*, p. 90) holds this disproved by Sallust and Appian 'who assert that, before Caesar's turn came, Tiberius Nero proposed that the question should be postponed'. Leaving aside the question why in any case these last two authors should be preferred, the statement simply is not true. All that Sallust 'asserts' (it is not in fact an assertion but an aside) is that later in the debate Silanus was perturbed by Caesar's speech and announced that he would vote for Nero's motion. He neither says nor implies that Silanus sprang to his feet as soon as Caesar sat down; his account is perfectly consonant with his having waited a while after Caesar spoke until Nero's compromise motion gave him the chance to slide out of his earlier tough position. As for Appian, a glance at his account shows that he is not necessarily dealing with the course of the debate in strict chronological order. Quite sensibly, he mentions the earlier consensus in favour of death, and notes that later many fell in with Nero's motion. Then, having got this out of the way, he moves to the opposed proposals of Caesar and Cato. Although his account is far sketchier than Sallust's, he adopts basically the same approach, which is artistically and historically satisfying and neat.

We should in any case expect Nero to have followed Caesar in the debate. After the consuls-designate the ex-consuls were called on for their opinions. Next in precedence should have come the men of praetorian standing: the praetors-designate and the praetors followed by the ex-praetors. (Like the consuls-designate, the praetors-designate would in a few weeks be actually holding executive office with chief responsibility for the administration.) Caesar was a praetor-designate, Nero an ex-praetor. This fits in with Cicero's letter of March 45 with its clear implication that the only senators who spoke before Caesar were the men of consular standing.

Dio also says that all who spoke before Caesar voted for death, but it is doubtful what this is worth. Dio's account is careless and scrappy; he also says (wrongly) that all who spoke after Caesar and before Cato supported Caesar. This sort of casual over-simplification does not inspire confidence in Dio in matters of detail. Suetonius' notice is too brief to add anything.

There has been argument about just what it was that Caesar proposed. Was it really life imprisonment and confiscation of property, or was it indefinite detention until the crisis was past and the prisoners' case could be looked at again? Both Plutarch and Appian present us with the latter. But Cicero in the *Fourth Catilinarian* is clear that the former was the proposal made by Caesar (section 10). Sallust is in agreement with Cicero. I find it hard to believe that Cicero could have got away with such gross distortion even four years after the event (the date of the publication of the *Catilinarians*), and the proposal for public confiscation of the prisoners' property (Cicero, Sallust, Plutarch) ill accords with a temporizing motion. It makes better sense of Nero's proposal and Cicero's speech to accept that Cicero's version is correct. Plutarch and Appian (or their sources) must then be supposed to have taken it that *in fact* the result of Caesar's motion would have been to postpone a decision on the conspirators, since it was unlikely that any prohibition against ever raising their cases again would long have availed against ambitious or calculating tribunes. Thus, while in theory proposing imprisonment for life and no appeal, Caesar must have been aware that this would in practice amount to postponement of the final decision.

Lastly, when did Cicero deliver his set speech? Sallust ignores it. Dio says that Cicero 'summoned the Senate and having disturbed and frightened the senators persuaded them to sentence the prisoners to death'. This is vague enough in all conscience, certainly no help, especially since Dio appears to place Cicero's contribution before Caesar's, which is clearly disproved by the speech itself as we have it. Appian refers first to Caesar's speech, then to Cato's, and finally to Cicero's. It is true that the *Fourth Catilinarian* as we have it makes no mention of Cato's speech. But (as argued in the text) Cato was strictly reviving Silanus' original proposal in more ample terminology.[1] Cicero when presenting the *Fourth Catilinarian* to the world in 59 may have chosen to play down Cato's intervention. Cicero's speech certainly reads like a speech delivered in summation, and the last word before the vote was taken we should expect the consul to have reserved to himself.

[1] Above, p. 138.

APPENDIX C

The de re publica *and the* de legibus

THESE TWO treatises are essentially literary exercises in imitation of Plato's *Republic* and *Laws*. The first takes the form of a discussion between Scipio Aemilianus and his friends in 129, the year of Scipio's death, with the object of eliciting his view about what is the *optimus status reipublicae* (*de rp.* 1.33). The second consists in a conversation between Cicero himself, his brother Quintus, and Atticus, in which Cicero is invited to draft laws for this ideal state: *Atqui si quaeris ego quid exspectem*, says Atticus, *quoniam scriptum est a te de optimo rei publicae statu, consequens esse videtur ut scribas tu idem de legibus: sic enim fecisse video Platonem illum tuum* (*de legg* 1.15).

In the *de re publica,* Scipio begins by passing in review the three basic systems of government, monarchy, aristocracy, and democracy, and rehearsing their potential weaknesses. For him the ideal state is a mixture of all three elements, which he finds in the Roman state as it has in fact historically developed. He follows this (*Book 2*) with a brief survey of the history of Rome in support of his thesis, and touches on the question of the ideal statesman, though the work is very fragmentary at this point (2.64–70). In the third book the place of justice in the state is vindicated, and in the fourth questions of social classification, the maintenance of public order, and education are discussed. Little remains of the fifth book, though here mention was explicitly made of the need for a *rector* or *moderator* (5.8 ff.). In the fragmentary sixth and last book, the great worth and fine rewards of the true statesman are set out in rather emotional terms, and the whole is rounded off with the famous *Somnium Scipionis* with its vision of the eternal world to come after death.

The *de legibus* opens with a general discussion of law and justice; the second book states and justifies specific laws governing the religious life of the state; and the third sets out and defends laws governing the functions and powers of the officers and organs of state. The remaining books, probably three in number, have not survived; indeed, Cicero may well not have lived to complete them.

Both works have great charm and literary merit, and contain useful historical information. Both made Greek thinking and Roman history available and intelligible to a wide new audience. But both are essentially backward looking, and Cicero makes no secret of this: 'An censes, quom in illis de re publica libris persuadere videatur Africanus omnium rerum publicarum nostram illam veterem fuisse optumam, non necesse esse optumae rei publicae leges dare consentaneas? ... Ergo adeo exspectate leges quae genus illud optumum rei publicae contineant, et si quae forte a me hodie rogabuntur quae non sint in nostra re publica nec fuerint, tamen fuerunt fere in more maiorum qui tum ut lex valebat' (de legg. 2.23).

What we find in these treatises is, then, not a practical blueprint for the Roman state but a nostalgic and idealized picture of that state as it had been before the disruptive tribunate of Tiberius Gracchus (de rp. 1.31; 3.41). The magistrates have wide powers, which they are to use with discretion and restraint, aided in this by limitation of tenure and the encumbrance of colleagues with equal and blocking powers; the Senate is a body of wise and experienced and unselfish men, offering sage advice to magistrates and people; the people are sovereign, but docile and undemanding.

That Cicero would have liked to have been born in 206 and not in 106, we need not doubt. That for a few years after his consulship he was occasionally tempted in his more optimistic moods to believe that his *concordia ordinum*, guaranteed by Pompey and inspired and directed by himself, might put the clock back is also true—though here we must note that the practical politician takes over and there is less concern with abstract justice and high morality and much more with such crude realities as the need to pay a realistic and immoral price for the political support of the knights (*ad Att.* II.1.8; above, p. 165). But the *de re publica* was written between 54 and 51, the *de legibus* begun probably about 52, then broken off and resumed in 46–44. Both are the work of a man who has retired from an active role in politics, disappointed and disillusioned, and who finds refuge in a more congenial and idealized past (above p. 223). No attempt is made in either to analyse what went wrong with that ideal Republic except at a trivially moralizing level, or to suggest practical solutions for present problems. Nowhere is there any recognition of the central truth that Rome has long outgrown her *polis* origins and constitution (above, p. 28). Thus the two treatises do no more than confirm what the letters reveal, that Cicero failed to face up to the fact that fundamental changes were needed if stability was to be restored and maintained.[1] But what the treatises do *not* reveal, and what the letters *do*, is that in practice Cicero, given the chance to play a directing and influential role, was only too ready to abandon philosophizing in favour of the pragmatic work of political horse-trading—that he was not as ingenuous as these two dialogues might lead one to believe. Cicero was ready to write about Utopia as a literary and intellectual exercise to occupy his retirement from politics and in wistful tribute to an admired past. But he knew that Utopian ideals and ideas have no place in real life. *Nam Catonem nostrum non tu amas plus quam ego ; sed tamen ille optimo animo utens et summa fide nocet interdum rei publicae; dicit enim tamquam in Platonis* πολιτείᾳ, *non tamquam in Romuli faece sententiam* (*ad Att.* II.1.8). The man who made that criticism of Cato never himself fell into the same trap.

---

[1] Cf. above pp. 303–6. Warde Fowler (*Rome*[3], 81) also observed of Cicero that he was 'never tired of writing and talking, little used to profound thinking'.

BIBLIOGRAPHY

I. *Ancient Sources*

In addition to the surviving speeches and letters and treatises of Cicero himself, we have Asconius' commentary, written in the mid-first century A.D., on five of the speeches (ed. Clark, Oxford, 1907); this work, together with other ancient commentaries on the speeches, comprises the collection *Ciceronis Orationum Scholiastae* (ed. Stangl, Vienna, 1912).

As well as a *Life* of Cicero, Plutarch (late first century A.D.) also composed *Lives* of a number of other leading Romans of this period: Marius, Sulla, Lucullus, Crassus, Sertorius, Pompey, Caesar, Cato, Antony, and Brutus. And we have a *Life* of Atticus by Atticus' friend and contemporary, Cornelius Nepos.

Sallust's *Catilinae Coniuratio* is immediately relevant, and his *Bellum Jugurthinum* is interesting for the background of politics in the age of Marius and as an analysis of what Sallust took to be some of the root causes of the troubles of the late Republic. Of his *Histories*, which took their start from the year 78, only meagre fragments remain (ed. Maurenbrecher, Teubner, 1891).

Livy's *History* for this period survives only in scattered fragments or in a form so drastically abbreviated (the *Epitome* or *Periochae*) as to be of little use. Appian covers the Ciceronian period in the second and third books of his *Civil Wars*; so too does Cassius Dio in Books 36–47 of his *Roman History*; and Velleius Paterculus has an outline sketch in the second book of his *Histories*. Velleius wrote in the early first century A.D., Appian about a hundred years later, Dio some seventy years later still; but all of them were able to draw on a wealth of sources from Cicero's own time.

Suetonius in the early second century A.D. wrote biographies of Julius Caesar and Augustus (*Divus Julius* and *Divus Augustus*). Caesar's own *Bellum Gallicum* is predominantly a military history of his Gallic campaigns, his *Bellum Civile* of those of the Civil War, but both contain matter of political importance. The *Bellum Alexandrinum* and *Bellum Africum* are of uncertain but contemporary authorship.

These are the main, continuous sources available to us. Much valuable information can also be gleaned from a large number of other ancient works: most notably Quintilian's *Institutio Oratoria*, the *Auctor de viris illustribus*, Valerius Maximus, Strabo's *Geography*, the *Natural History* of the Elder Pliny, and the *Attic Nights* of Aulus Gellius. The fragments of orators contemporary with Cicero are collected in *Oratorum Romanorum Fragmenta* (ed. Malcovati, Pavia 1955).

II. *Modern Works*

In the notes to each chapter, I have deliberately kept references to modern works to a minimum; and often, when the subject-matter is well-worn, I have eschewed them altogether. The ancient evidence is readily available in a number of modern books, and for the fullest narrative history of the period, with meticulous documentation of the sources, the reader is referred to the works of Rice Holmes (below).

The list that follows includes, in addition to books or articles cited in the notes, a selection of other works to which the reader may turn for more detailed discussion of particular issues and topics (some of them only peripheral to the subject of this book) or for full bibliographies of them. The inclusion of a book or an article in this list does not mean that I accept its arguments or conclusions or approach either in whole or in part, only that I judge it a serious and worthwhile contribution to the under-standing of the Ciceronian period.

(a) *General Histories*

The Cambridge Ancient History, Vol. IX (Cambridge, 1932)

CARCOPINO, J. *Histoire Romaine*, Vol. II (Paris, 1929–36)

MARSH, F. B. *A History of the Roman World 146–130 B.C.* (2nd edit., revised by Scullard, Methuen, 1959)

MOMMSEN, T. *The History of Rome* (English Trans., London, 1880)

RICE HOLMES, T. *The Roman Republic*, 3 vols. (Oxford, 1923)
    The Architect of the Roman Empire, Vol. I (Oxford, 1928)

SCULLARD, H. H. *From the Gracchi to Nero* (Methuen, 1959)

SYME, R. *The Roman Revolution* (Oxford, 1939)

(b) *Biographies of Cicero*

BOISSIER, G. *Cicéron et ses amis* (11th edit., Paris, 1899)

CARCOPINO, J. *Les Secrets de la Correspondence de Cicéron* (Paris, 1947); English Trans. by E. O. Lorimer, London, 1951.

COWELL, F. R. *Cicero and the Roman Republic* (London, 1948)

Frisch, H. *Cicero's Fight for the Republic* (Copenhagen, 1946)
Gelzer, M. *Cicero: ein biographischer Versuch* (Wiesbaden, 1969)
Haskell, H. J. *This Was Cicero* (London, 1942)
Peterson, T. *Cicero: a Biography* (Berkeley, 1920)
Smith, R. E. *Cicero the Statesman* (Cambridge, 1966)
Strachan-Davidson, J. L. *Cicero and the Fall of the Roman Republic* (London, 1898)

(c) *Editions of the Letters*
How, W. W. *Cicero: Select Letters* (Oxford, 1925)
Shackleton-Bailey, D. R. *Cicero's Letters to Atticus* (Cambridge, 1965–8)
Stockton, D. L. *Thirty Five Letters of Cicero* (Oxford, 1969)
Tyrrell, R. Y. and Purser, L. C. *The Correspondence of Cicero* (Dublin, 1904–33)
Oxford Classical Texts *ad familiares* (Purser, 1901); *ad Atticum* I–VIII (Watt, 1965); *ad Atticum* IX–XVI (Shackleton-Bailey, 1961); *ad Quintum fratrem, ad M. Brutum, fragmenta* (Watt, 1958)

(d) *General*
Adcock, F. E. *Roman Political Ideas and Practice* (Ann Arbor, 1959)
Astin, A. E. '*Leges Aelia et Fufia*' (*Latomus* 23 (1964), 421 ff)
Austin, R. G. (ed.). *Cicero: pro Caelio* (2nd edit., Oxford, 1952)
Badian, E. *Foreign Clientelae* (Oxford, 1958),
    Roman Imperialism in the Late Republic (Pretoria, 1967 and Oxford 1968)
    'Marius and the Nobles' (*Durham Univ. Journ.* 56 (1964), 141 ff)
    'Waiting for Sulla' (*JRS* 52 (1962), 47 ff)
Balsdon, J. P. V. D. 'The History of the Extortion Court at Rome' (*BSR* 14 (1938), 98 ff)
    'Roman History, 58–56 B.C.' (*JRS* 47 (1957), 15 ff)
    'The Ides of March' (*Historia*, 7 (1958), 60 ff)
    '*Auctoritas, Dignitas ,Otium*' (*CQ* 54 (1960), 43 ff)
    'Roman History, 65–50 B.C' (*JRS* 52 (1962) ,134 ff)
    'The *Commentariolum Petitionis*' (*CQ* 57 (1963), 242 ff)
    '*Fabula Clodiana*' (*Historia* 15 (1966), 65 ff);
    Life and Leisure in Ancient Rome (London, 1969)
    Roman Women (London, 1962)
Boak, A. E. R. 'The Extraordinary Commands from 80 to 48 B.C.' (*AHR* 63 (1958), 890 ff)

BROUGHTON, T. R. S. *The Magistrates of the Roman Republic* (New York, 1951–2)

BRUNT, P. A. 'The Army and the Land in the Roman Revolution' (*JRS* 52 (1962), 69 ff)

'*Amicitia* in the Late Roman Republic' (*Proc. Camb. Phil. Soc.* 191 (1965), 1 ff)

'The *Equites* in the Late Republic' (2nd Internat. Conf. of Econ. Hist., 1962 (Paris, 1965) I.117 ff)

'The Roman Mob' (*Past and Present* (December 1966, 65 ff)

CARCOPINO, J. 'Sylla, ou la monarchie manquée' (4th edit., Paris, 1947)

CARY, M. '*Asinus Germanus*' (*CQ* 17 (1923) 103 ff)

COLLINS, J. H. 'Caesar and the Corruption of Power' (*Historia* 4 (1955), 445 ff)

DOREY, T. A. (ed.). *Cicero* (London, 1965)

DOUGLAS, A. E. (ed.). *M. Tulli Ciceronis Brutus* (Oxford, 1966)

FRANK, T. *An Economic History of Rome* (Baltimore, 1927);
An Economic Survey of Ancient Rome, Vol. I (Baltimore, 1933)

FREDERIKSEN, M. W. 'Cicero, Caesar, and the Problem of Debt' (*JRS* 56 (1966), 128 ff).

FRISCH, H. 'The First Catilinarian Conspiracy' (*Class. et Med.* 9 (1947), 10 ff)

GELZER, M. *Die Nobilität der römischen Republik* (Leipzig, 1912). English Trans. by R. Seager, *The Roman Nobility* (Oxford, 1969)

Pompeius (Munich, 1949)

Caesar, Politician and Statesman (Oxford, 1968)

GREENIDGE, A. H. J. *The Legal Procedure of Cicero's Time* (Oxford, 1901)

GRUEN, E. S. 'P. Clodius Pulcher' (*Phoenix* 20 (1966), 120 ff)

'Pompey and the Roman Aristocracy' (*Historia*, 18 (1969), 71 ff)

HARDY, E. G. *The Catilinarian Conspiracy* (Oxford, 1924)

Some Problems in Roman History (Oxford, 1924)

HEITLAND, W. E. (ed.). *pro. C. Rabirio* (Cambridge, 1882)

HENDERSON, M. I. '*de Commentariolo Petitionis*' (*JRS* 40 (1950), 8 ff)

'The process *de repetundis*' (*JRS* 41 (1951), 71 ff)

'The Establishment of the *Equester Ordo*' (*JRS* 53 (1963), 61 ff)

HEUSS, A. 'Cicero und Matius' (*Historia* 5 (1956), 53 ff)

HILL, H. *The Roman Middle Class* (Oxford, 1952)

JONES, A. H. M. *Studies in Roman Government and Law* (Oxford, 1960)

KYTZLER, B. 'Matius und Cicero' (*Historia* 9 (1960), 96 ff)

LACEY, W. K. 'The Tribunate of Curio' (*Historia* 10 (1961), 318 ff)

LAST, H. M. Review of H. J. Haskell, *This Was Cicero* (*JRS* 33 (1943), 93 ff)
  Review of L. R. Taylor, '*Party Politics*' (*Gnomon* 22 (1950), 360 ff)

LINTOTT, A. W. *Violence in Republican Rome* (Oxford, 1968)

McDONALD, W. 'The Tribunate of Cornelius' (*CQ* 23 (1929), 196 ff)
  '*Clodius and the Lex Aelia Fufia*' (*JRS* 19 (1929), 164 ff)

MARSH, F. B. 'The Policy of Clodius' (*CQ* 21 (1923), 30 ff)

MEYER, E. *Caesars Monarchie und das Prinzipat des Pompeius* (Stuttgart, 1922).

MOMMSEN, T. *Römisches Staatsrecht* (Leipzig, 1887–8)
  Römisches Strafrecht (Leipzig, 1899)

MUNZER, F. *Römische Adelsparteien und Adelsfamilien* (Stuttgart, 1920)

NICOLET, C. *L'Ordre Equestre à l'Epoque Républicaine* (Paris, 1966)

NISBET, R. G. (ed.). *de Domo Sua* (Oxford, 1939)

NISBET, R. G. M. (ed.). *in L. Calpurnium Pisonem* (Oxford, 1961)
  'The *Commentariolum Petitionis*' (*JRS* 51 (1961), 84 ff)

POCOCK, L. G. 'A Note on the Policy of Clodius' (*CQ* 19 (1925), 182 ff)

REID, J. S. (ed.). *pro P. Cornelio Sulla* (Cambridge, 1882)

SHACKLETON-BAILEY, D. R. 'Sex. Clodius—Sex. Cloelius' (*CQ* 54 (1960), 41 ff)

SEAGER, R. 'The First Catilinarian Conspiracy' (*Historia* 13 (1964), 338 ff)

SHERWIN-WHITE, A. N.: '*Poena Legis Repetundarum*' (*BSR* 17 (1949), 5 ff)
  'The Extortion Procedure Again' (*JRS* 42 (1952), 43 ff)
  'Violence in Roman Politics' (*JRS* 46 (1956), 1 ff)

SMITH, R. E. *Service in the Post-Marian Roman Army* (Manchester, 1958)
  'Caesar's Consulship in 59 B.C.' (*Phoenix* 18 (1964), 303 ff)

STEVENS, C. E. 'The "Plotting" of 66/65 B.C.' (*Latomus* 22 (1963), 397 ff)

STOCKTON, D. L. 'Cicero and the *Ager Campanus*' (*TAPA*, 93 (1962), 471 ff)

STRACHAN-DAVIDSON, J. L. *Problems of the Roman Criminal Law* (Oxford, 1912)

STRASBURGER, H. *Caesars Eintritt in die Geschichte* (Munich, 1938)

SUMNER, G. V. '*Lex Aelia, Lex Fufia*' (*AJP* 84 (1963), 337 ff)

SYME, R. *Sallust* (Berkeley and Cambridge, 1964)

'Caesar, the Senate, and Italy' (*BSR* 14 (1938), 1 ff)

Review of Gelzer, *Caesar* (*JRS* 34 (1944), 92 ff)

TAYLOR, L. R. *Party Politics in the Age of Caesar* (Berkeley, 1949)

The Voting Districts of the Roman Republic (Rome, 1960)

Roman Voting Assemblies (Ann Arbor, 1966)

'Cicero's Aedileship' (*AJP* 60 (1939), 194 ff)

'Caesar's Early Career' (*CP* 36 (1941), 113 ff)

'The Rise of Julius Caesar' (*Greece and Rome* 26 (1957), 10 ff)

TREGGIARI, S. *Roman Freedmen during the Late Republic* (Oxford, 1969)

WARDE FOWLER, W. *Social Life at Rome in the Age of Cicero* (London, 1908)

WEINSTOCK, S. 'Clodius and the *Lex Aelia Fufia*' (*JRS* 27 (1937), 215 ff)

WISEMAN, T. P. 'The Ambitions of Quintus Cicero' (*JRS* 56 (1966), 108 ff)

'Two Friends of Clodius' (*CQ* 60 (1968), 297 ff)

WIRSZUBSKI, CH. *Libertas as a Political Ideal at Rome* (Cambridge, 1950)

'Cicero's *Cum dignitate otium*: A Reconsideration' (*JRS* 44 (1954), 1 ff)

YAVETZ, Z. 'The Failure of Catiline's Conspiracy' (*Historia* 12 (1963), 485 ff)

Note: For detailed discussions of the long controversy which has raged over the terminal date of Caesar's command in Gaul, and the manoeuvres to recall him to Rome, see: Adcock (*CQ* 26 (1932), 14 ff); Stevens (*AJP*, 1938, 169 ff); Balsdon (*JRS* 29 (1939), 57 ff, 167 ff); Elton (*JRS* 36 (1946), 18 ff); Cuff (*Historia* 7 (1958), 445 ff)

INDEX

M'. Acilius Glabrio (cos 67), 44, 46, 59

Acton (Lord), 240

C. Aculeio, 5

L. Aelius Lamia (pr 42), 188

Aelius Ligur (tr 58), 191–2

Q. Aelius Tubero, 275

M. Aemilius Lepidus (cos 78), 15, 104, 185

M. Aemilius Lepidus (cos 46), 111, 219, 281–2, 288, 291, 296, 299, 302, 305, 309, 311–15, 320–3, 327–331

L. Aemilius Paullus (cos 50), 116, 184–5

M. Aemilius Scaurus (cos 115), 3

L. Afranius (cos 60), 162, 181, 199, 254–5

ager Campanus, 86, 178–9, 206–10

M. Agrippa (Vipsanius), 13

Ahenobarbus, see Domitius

Alexandria, 199, 264, 266–7

A. Allienus, 309

Allobroges, 126–9, 156, 231

Ameria, 9

amicitia, 66

Q. Annius, 111

Annius Chilo, 130, 133

T. Annius Milo, 37, 191–3, 202, 205, 207, 209–11, 218–20, 224–5, 229, 254, 262

C. Antonius Hybrida (cos 63), 36, 63, 71, 79, 81, 89, 96, 101, 117, 121, 125, 140, 148, 168–9, 228, 279, 282

C. Antonius (pr 44), 297, 308, 314–315, 330

L. Antonius (tr 44), 291

M. Antonius (cos 99), 5, 6, 8, 18

M. Antonius (cos 44), 13, 49, 221, 247, 249, 252–3, 259, 265, 280–306, 307–31

Apamea, 291

Apella, 323

L. Appuleius Saturninus (tr 100), 21, 87, 92

C. Aquilius Gallus (pr 66), 64

Archias, 4, 153–4

Ariobarzanes, 239

Arpinum, 1f, 119

Arretium (the lady from), 12, 31, 51

Q. Arrius (pr 64), 114

C. Asinius Pollio (cos 40), 291, 299, 302, 305, 312, 314, 321, 328, 330, 332–3

assemblies, 39f

Sex. Atilius Serranus (tr 57), 192

Atticus, see Pomponius

Attius, 17

Attius Tullus, 3

T. Aufidius, 64

augurate, 221–2

Augustus, see Julius

Aurelia, 19

C. Aurelius Cotta (cos 75), 12, 16, 19

L. Aurelius Cotta (cos 65), 16, 19, 41–2, 44, 46, 74, 192, 282

P. Autronius Paetus (cos des 65), 74f, 83, 112–13, 124, 132, 155–7

Balbus, see Cornelius

Bibulus, see Calpurnius

Bona Dea, 159–61, 177

Brutus, see Junius

Q. Caecilius (uncle of Atticus), 65

Q. Caecilius Bassus, 291, 294, 309

M. Caecilius Cornutus (pr 43), 313, 330–1

L. Caecilius Metellus (cos 68), 45